REDEFINING LIBERAL ARTS EDUCATION IN THE TWENTY-FIRST CENTURY

REDEFINING LIBERAL ARTS EDUCATION IN THE TWENTY-FIRST CENTURY

EDITED BY ROBERT E. LUCKETT JR.

University Press of Mississippi / Jackson

The University Press of Mississippi is the scholarly publishing agency of
the Mississippi Institutions of Higher Learning: Alcorn State University,
Delta State University, Jackson State University, Mississippi State University,
Mississippi University for Women, Mississippi Valley State University,
University of Mississippi, and University of Southern Mississippi.

www.upress.state.ms.us

Frontispiece by Pete Halverson

The University Press of Mississippi is a member
of the Association of University Presses.

Copyright © 2021 by University Press of Mississippi

All rights reserved

First printing 2021

∞

Library of Congress Cataloging-in-Publication Data

Names: Luckett, Robert E., Jr., editor.
Title: Redefining liberal arts education in the twenty-first century /
Robert E. Luckett Jr..
Description: Jackson: University Press of Mississippi, 2021. | Includes
bibliographical references and index.
Identifiers: LCCN 2020053615 (print) | LCCN 2020053616 (ebook) | ISBN
978-1-4968-3316-7 (hardback) | ISBN 978-1-4968-3317-4 (trade paperback) | ISBN
978-1-4968-3318-1 (epub) | ISBN 978-1-4968-3319-8 (epub) | ISBN 978-1-4968-3320-4
(pdf) | ISBN 978-1-4968-3360-0 (pdf)
Subjects: LCSH: Education, Humanistic—United States. | Education,
Higher—United States. | Education, Higher—Curricula—United States.
Classification: LCC LC1023 .R33 2021 (print) | LCC LC1023 (ebook) | DDC
370.11/2—dc23
LC record available at https://lccn.loc.gov/2020053615
LC ebook record available at https://lccn.loc.gov/2020053616

British Library Cataloging-in-Publication Data available

CONTENTS

Foreword. A Robust Liberal Arts Education:
Opportunities and Concerns in the Twenty-First Century
WILLIAM D. ADAMS
ix

Introduction. Collaboration and Interdisciplinarity in the Knowledge Economy
CANDIS PIZZETTA
3

PART 1: DIGITAL HUMANITIES, TECHNOLOGY, AND THE LIBERAL ARTS

Chapter 1. Digital Humanities as a LEAP High-Impact Practice
SERETHA D. WILLIAMS
13

Chapter 2. Technology in the Liberal Arts Classroom: Updating the Classroom Toolkit
MONICA FLIPPIN WYNN
24

Chapter 3. Teaching Art History to STEM
YUMI PARK HUNTINGTON
36

PART 2: THE ARTS AND THE LIBERAL ARTS

Chapter 4. An Interdisciplinary Approach to Cultivating Visual Literacy
SARAH ARCHINO
57

Chapter 5. Revisiting Erwin Panofsky's "The History of Art as a Humanistic Discipline"
FLOYD W. MARTIN
71

Chapter 6. Dancing the Humanities: Engaging with Liberal Arts Education
LAUREN ASHLEE MESSINA
81

PART 3: PEDAGOGY AND THE LIBERAL ARTS

Chapter 7. Test-Oriented Pedagogy in the Teaching of Communication Skills
HELEN O. CHUKWUMA
95

Chapter 8. Flexible Thought for the Test-Focused Student
KATHY ROOT PITTS
104

Chapter 9. Developing a More Student-Sensitive Approach in the Liberal Arts
LAWRENCE SLEDGE
118

PART 4: WRITING AND THE LIBERAL ARTS

Chapter 10. Conversation in the Writing Center:
Developing Student Rhetorical Awareness, Critical Thinking, and Translingual Dispositions
TATIANA GLUSHKO AND KATHI R. GRIFFIN
133

Chapter 11. Translingualism, Transhistoricism, and Shakespeare in a Freshman Seminar
ERIC J. GRIFFIN
152

Chapter 12. The Liberal Arts Faculty Writing Boot Camp
PRESELFANNIE W. MCDANIELS, BYRON D'ANDRA OREY,
RICO D. CHAPMAN, AND MONICA FLIPPIN WYNN
169

PART 5: SOCIAL ISSUES AND THE LIBERAL ARTS

Chapter 13. You Can't Say That: Warnings, Political Correctness, and Academic Freedom
RASHELL R. SMITH-SPEARS
183

Chapter 14. Not All Apples Are Red
KATRINA BYRD
196

Chapter 15. Liberal Arts and Humanities as "Molders of Consensus" in the Public Arena
THOMAS M. KERSEN
208

PART 6: THE AFRICAN AMERICAN EXPERIENCE AND THE LIBERAL ARTS

Chapter 16. Historical Memory and the Meredith Monument at Ole Miss
ROBERT E. LUCKETT JR.
225

Chapter 17. [Re]Engineering a New Liberal Arts Experience: Future Studies and HBCUs
JOSEPH MARTIN STEVENSON, DAWN BISHOP MCLIN, AND KAREN C. WILSON-STEVENSON
243

Conclusion. Redefining Liberal Arts Education: Challenges and Opportunities
MARIO J. AZEVEDO
258

ABOUT THE CONTRIBUTORS
275

INDEX
279

FOREWORD

A Robust Liberal Arts Education

Opportunities and Concerns in the Twenty-First Century

On Friday, October 7, 2016, I had the pleasure to keynote the Conference on the Liberal Arts: (Re)Defining Liberal Arts Education in the 21st Century at Jackson State University. I was grateful to be there and congratulated the conference organizers on the choice of topic for the gathering. There's no more important question in higher education in the United States right now than the future of the liberal arts. So this conference is on the leading edge of something that everyone who cares about higher education should be thinking about.

As I thought about how I might contribute to this moment, it seemed to me that given my job and the role of NEH, and in light of the fact that I see the humanities across the entire country, it might be helpful—I hope it's helpful—if I try to provide some framing for the very particular discussions that have been going on here today and that that will go on the rest of the day and into the weekend.

I'll establish this framework by making an argument, a very simple argument, and maybe one that is somewhat surprising, but here it is: I think the liberal arts—I should say already and quickly the liberal arts and sciences—are more important now in the United States than they have ever been in our history.

That's a long time. The general idea of liberal learning goes all the way back to the beginning of the Republic, when you consider what our founders were actually talking about and how they thought about education. They were talking about the concept and values of liberal learning, though of course liberal learning had some different dimensions at the time.

But now I think the notion and the practices of liberal learning count more than ever. And I want to suggest they count more than ever—this might be the slightly surprising part—precisely because of how practical and useful they are.

Utility is not something that we typically talk much about when we talk about the liberal arts, but I want to make the argument that they are profoundly practical. And I particularly want the students in the audience—and I'm so glad you're here to hear me when I say this—to know that there is vast utility in the liberal arts and sciences. I want to talk about what those forms of utility are.

William James had a wonderful phrase when he talked about the importance of philosophy to what he called the "conduct of life." I want to borrow James' wonderful phrase and expand it a little in saying that the liberal arts matter precisely in the sense of how and how much they contribute to the conduct of life.

But I also want to suggest that we need to change some of the ways in which we talk about and think about the liberal arts if we want to extract all of their practical and pragmatic value for us in this time and in this place: the United States in this relatively new century.

Specifically, I want to explore the meanings that I am giving to this idea of utility or the pragmatic applicability of the liberal arts, and then I want to talk about some of the changes that I think we need to make in the ways we think about the liberal arts and sciences and about how we talk about this form of education.

Let me say right from the outset that I am aware of how against the grain my argument runs with respect to how we typically think about the liberal arts. For the most part, we think about them, and we have historically thought about them, as being distinctly non-utilitarian, non-pragmatic, maybe anti-pragmatic. We've tended to think about them as existing in a place beyond the realm of necessity: they are beautiful, meaningful, but also inessential.

John Adams famously said once, "I must study politics and war that my sons may have the liberty to study mathematics and philosophy," as if the liberal arts await the accomplishment of all those other more fundamental things. That's a very common idea, and it goes all the way back to the first thoughts about liberal learning in the West, at least to Aristotle, who talked about the life of the mind as being something that comes after the economy, after the family, after the realm of necessity has been satisfied and we have the leisure to think about all the other things that aren't as immediately important as these first things.

But, as I'm saying, I want to make the argument that the liberal arts matter to us now precisely because of their utility. I want to mention four principal areas of their usefulness: the world of work and the economy (this is aimed particularly at the students in the audience); the world of citizenship and civic life; the world of culture (I don't mean museums and libraries, but culture in the sense of our lived culture); and the world of moral life or what might also be called the existential sphere.

Let me begin with the world of work and the economy, since this is the place where the liberal arts are least often talked about. What I want to say is this: I think we tend regularly to underestimate, to undervalue, to undersell the relevance of the liberal arts and sciences to the topics of work and work readiness.

Most of what is required in organizational life, for instance—where I've spent my entire career—is not, as it turns out, technical skills, though in certain kinds of organizations technical skills are very important. What's really most important in this organizational sphere, where most of us end up most of the time, are a number of fundamental intellectual capacities, beginning most especially and importantly with the capacity to communicate.

I've been an organizational leader for a reasonably long time now. I've led some large and complex organizations. I can't tell you the number of times that I've observed careers getting stuck or set back because people could not communicate powerfully in speaking or in writing or in both. The surest way to freeze a career is to fail to communicate effectively, to demonstrate incapacity with that skill and that resource, which is fundamental in every phase of organizational life. So writing and speaking are enormously important. And, as we all know, those skills are exercised very powerfully in the liberal arts and sciences.

Second, I have in mind certain conceptual capacities, by which I mean the capacity first and foremost to analyze the world into fundamental components and, quickly following that, the ability to reintegrate those component parts into meaningful wholes. These analytical and integrative skills are also hugely important in the day-to-day work of organizations in every kind of business in this country and around the world.

The third capacity I'm thinking of lies in the creative and imaginative sphere—the capacity to create, to exercise the imagination in meaningful ways in relationship to the work that is at hand in any organization, in any economic setting.

Fourth is a sense of intellectual depth and breadth. I don't know any organization where a wide-ranging grasp of the world, a wide-ranging grasp of human experience, isn't a huge advantage. Whether you're selling things or designing things or making things, the richness of your understanding of human life and experience is always a benefit to your progress through organizations, to your ability to make sense of the work and to make sense to and of other people.

And, speaking of other people, and last but not least, we all know how important interpersonal and social capacities are in organizations of all kinds. If you don't have those interpersonal and social capacities, you're going to get stuck. You're not going to advance. You're not going to be able to contribute meaningfully to the work of the organization.

We all know, I think, how powerfully liberal learning speaks to all of these capacities through very disciplined encounters with demanding and wide-ranging subjects, everything from the life sciences to the physical sciences to philosophy to the study of religion and literature and art. All of those encounters build these capacities, and to stop with any one thing, to stop with any one discipline, with any one focus, is to limit necessarily the breadth of these fundamental intellectual capacities and, of course, the power of those capacities, as well.

So, in these ways, I think we need to rearticulate the ways in which liberal learning, the liberal arts and sciences, cultivate and enhance the basic intellectual capacities that one uses at work, that one uses in the economy, that one uses in all phases of economic life.

Sphere two, in this wonderful sense of William James' "the conduct of life," is the world of civic life and citizenship. I can't imagine that anyone in this room would suggest now in our current circumstances that we have perfected the notion of citizenship and that we are confident that we have a civic culture adequate to our aspirations and to the challenges of democracy.

Danielle Allen, the philosopher at Harvard, speaks about participation readiness. There's work readiness, and there's participation readiness, and we have to understand how critical participation readiness is to the health of our democratic political culture and how dangerous it is for us as a country not to focus on this.

And that means a couple of important things. First, we must have citizens who are acquainted in some reasonably significant degree with the history of this country and all of the complex conflicts that we as a people have experienced over time and that put continuing pressures on our collective life. We have to be literate in the history of the country.

We also have to be literate in what I will call the principles of liberal democracy. There was a very interesting show the other day on NPR. Some people might have heard it. A faculty member at a well-known institution of higher learning was talking about how skeptical some of his students were with the entire concept of democracy.

Now I can understand why this current time in our history and in the nation's life might make some people skeptical, but there can't be a fundamental skepticism about the principles of democracy. And there can't be ignorance with respect to the fundamental principles of liberal democracy, the philosophical foundations of this way of living together, and the formations that undergird our aspirations to live as a democratic people.

Third, in this realm of civic life and culture, is something that was very powerfully communicated today by Dean Thomas Calhoun in an interesting talk that he gave. We must have a citizenry that is culturally literate, and I mean culturally literate in two forms or two dimensions.

First, cultural literacy in terms of the cultural complexity of our country. Dean Calhoun did a great job of showing how multifaceted our diversity is becoming and how much more complex it will become over time. We must have a citizenry that is educated in the cultural diversity of the nation, and we also have to have a citizenry that is educated in the cultural diversity of the world.

We are watching every day the misery that unfolds in parts of the Middle East. Who knew in 2002 that fifteen years later we would be watching the implosion of the Middle East around the differences among Sunni and Shia forms of Islam? How many Americans would be able to parse those differences, at least in a way that would permit us to judge the actions of our leaders or the proposals of our leaders? Now we understand, I think, just how little we understand about this important part of the world when it matters most.

It's a terrible deficit in our own culture if we are not able to look around the global community and make sense, to some degree, of what is happening there. I am so pleased to learn that Jackson State has a world history requirement for all students. That's a great thing, and that's exactly the kind of thing I mean. And, at Jackson State, it's not just for some students—it's not for liberal arts students as opposed to engineers, as I understand it. It's for every student, and that's exactly the right way to be thinking about the problem and challenge of cultural literacy.

Last but not least in these dimensions of utility and pragmatism, I want to mention one that's maybe the hardest of all to talk about but in some ways the most important, which is what I call the utility of the liberal arts in terms of our moral lives, our moral imaginations, and the whole topic of moral wisdom.

What I'm talking about is meaning and purpose in our individual lives. Everybody in this room understands how challenging life can be in almost every dimension that we inhabit, and which together constitute what I am trying to call the moral sphere or the sphere of moral life and wisdom.

Education in the liberal arts doesn't immediately erase the challenges we face as individuals trying to sort out our lives, because those challenges are part of being human. But they do give us resources to reflect on the meaning of our lives and the challenges that we face as individuals going through the world, in some of the same ways that religious life speaks to some of these same topics. And, by the way, one of the great topics for liberal arts and sciences is religion, the importance of religion and religious life in almost every culture in the world.

So, this whole domain of moral life, of moral imagination and moral wisdom, should be one of the things we're thinking about when we're thinking about why we educate students and for what we are trying to educate them.

To summarize briefly so far, I am saying that we need to reclaim the ground of utility, of pragmatism, of the usefulness of the liberal arts and sciences in helping us negotiate these various dimensions of our lives ways that no other educational practice possibly can.

But—and here's the second part—I think that to do this effectively, to be persuasive about the pragmatic power of the liberal arts and sciences, we need to change the way we talk and think about the liberal arts in some specific ways.

First, I think that we need to have a more democratic language and description of the liberal arts and sciences. Second, we need to put greater emphasis as educators on curricular innovation, and, as we do that, we need to make sure, and Dean Calhoun talked about this as well, that the liberal arts and sciences that we're practicing have greater relevance to the civic lives our students will actually live.

Let me talk just briefly about both of these things. It is true I think that the liberal arts historically have had an elitist resonance, and I think that's still true in the culture today. If you listen to what people say about the liberal arts out there in the culture, you hear this complaint, a reasonable and justified complaint, that all of this is very well and good for leaders and cultural elites, but we're talking about real life here and the lives of normal people. I think there is some truth to the complaint that this has been a form of education, a philosophy of education, that has had an elitist sensibility about it for a very long time.

So, we need to make something of a course correction here. We need to find ways of demonstrating that this is a truly democratic form of education, that it speaks to all people and all lives—that it speaks to everyone as they enter the spheres of work, of citizenship, of culture, and the moral life.

The pragmatic framework that I have been talking about is a start, but it's only a start. I think we have to make clearer and more decisive connections between the liberal arts and sciences and our democratic aspirations as a people. We really need to begin to think and talk about it as education for membership in contemporary society that's relevant to all lives as they are lived in this time and in this place.

Secondly, we need to be very bold and experimental in shaping the future curriculum of the liberal arts and sciences, and one way in which we need to do that is being modeled here at Jackson State. I think we need to move away from what has been the model of the curriculum in most institutions that I know about, that is, the distributive model of the liberal arts where you take a little bit of this and you take a little bit of this and you take a little bit of this. To do this we need to get back to discussions with the faculty about the core competencies and subjects of a truly liberal education. This is not an easy discussion, as faculty here know, but it is essential to the well-being of our students.

Second, and this I find irritates a lot of people when I say it, we need to move away from disciplinary specialization across the entire curriculum—in the sciences, the social sciences, the humanities, and the arts—toward a more integrated, cross-disciplinary practice of the liberal arts.

Let me explain what I mean by both this new core and this interdisciplinary approach to the liberal arts.

First of all, I think we need to experiment with what I like to call interdisciplinary mashups. That's not a technical term, but I find that it's a useful term. And here's an example drawn from the great category, the broad category, of the liberal arts and sciences. We ought to be trying, I think, much more deliberately to integrate the sciences and the humanities and the social sciences in ways that are relevant to our students and that require cross-disciplinary conversations between faculty. We need to pursue that integration for a couple of reasons.

In addition to an absence of cultural literacy in this country, I would say there's an acute problem of scientific and technical literacy. We can approach that by developing a set of common problems that scientists, philosophers, historians, literary critics—you name it—can engage together.

One of the most productive and, I think, obvious ways to do this is to develop perspective for our students on the thing that is driving so much of our contemporary world, and that is the progress of science and technology. We have a country, an economy, a world economy now being driven largely by technological change. What a remarkable opportunity we have as humanists and social scientists and scientists to think critically and cooperatively about the evolution of science and technology, as it's shaping our lives, and to give our students some perspective on that development in ways that they can carry with them once they graduate.

There are many, many other examples of these kinds of disciplinary mashups, and one of the most important has to do with the category of relevance. The great irony of our time is this: as we experience deep public skepticism about the humanities, about the arts, about anything that is not fundamentally vocational—it's at that very moment that we need more than ever the insights that come from that entire array of disciplines practiced in the university. We need all of the fundamental forms of knowledge represented in our colleges and universities to come to terms with the grand challenges that confront us as members of the global community.

Think about it. I've already mentioned the advance of technology and science. Think about another problem that I know is very much on the minds of people here and has been throughout the entire history of the institution, and that is the question of race relations in the history of the United States.

We're not going to solve or even approach that problem in a meaningful way without understanding a great deal more about our history, without understanding a great deal more about our cultural differences, and a great deal more about the common humanity that underlies all of these differences. That's the topic of conversation that we need to be engaged in, and those are the skills that we need to be promoting among our students and in our curricula across all kinds of institutions.

Take another topic that is now hugely important in this political season, the topic of immigration. We're seeing major migrations all around the world, which of course have specific effects in individual countries, including our own. We can't understand these effects and the migrations causing them without having a feel for culture and without having a feel for language—without an understanding of where people are coming from and how they live their lives.

That is the opposite of a scenario of exclusion. It is a scenario of intellectual curiosity and openness and inclusion, and those forms of thinking—curiosity, openness, inclusion—come from acquaintance with the humanities, with the liberal arts, and with the concrete realities of those people that we need to understand.

Another thing that we could think about as a grand challenge that is very significant is the challenge of democracy itself. What does it mean to be a citizen in this country now? What does it mean to participate? What do you need to be a participating citizen? What are the skills you need? These again are things that range across many disciplines and that require what I am calling interdisciplinary mashups in the service of the civic engagement of our students.

Let me conclude in the following way. This is a time of extraordinary pressure on the practice of the liberal arts and sciences and the humanities specifically, but it's also a time of extraordinary opportunity. We have to take advantage of that opportunity, as I've been saying, by an organized embrace, if you will, of the notion of the utility and the pragmatic consequences of the liberal arts and sciences.

In the professional sphere, we need to talk about how the forms of knowledge and intellectual capacities, nurtured by the humanities, by the social sciences and the sciences, contribute to professional life and the world of work.

We need to demonstrate and talk about how the forms of knowledge and habits of mind and thinking, advanced by the liberal arts, contribute to cultural competency and literacy both locally and globally.

In the political sphere, we need to demonstrate how the forms of knowledge and habits of mind, cultivated by the liberal arts and liberal learning, contribute to citizenship and, in that wonderful phrase of Danielle Allen's, to "participation readiness."

And we need to show our students, finally, how and why the liberal arts are essential to the search for meaning in life and to the establishment of a meaningful life. This means that we have to restore our aspiration to educate the whole person. We can't be thinking about education and the aspirations we have for education in very narrow technical and vocational ways. If we do, we're letting down our students and we are also, in the end, letting down our country.

> William D. Adams, Chairman
> National Endowment for the Humanities

REDEFINING LIBERAL ARTS EDUCATION IN THE TWENTY-FIRST CENTURY

INTRODUCTION

Collaboration and Interdisciplinarity in the Knowledge Economy

CANDIS PIZZETTA

In 2015 Simon During's essay "Precariousness, Literature, and the Humanities" appeared in the *Australian Humanities Review*, arguing that the rise of neoliberalism signaled the end of the humanities as we have known them under social capitalism.[1] Neoliberalism and its emphasis on free trade, deregulation, privatization, and reduced government spending have meant that the social functions of the liberal arts that were "important enough to be supported by the state and unified civil society" are rather less valued by private individuals, governments, and corporate entities.[2] This shift can be measured in the declining numbers of PhDs awarded in the humanities and the ever-shrinking number of undergraduates earning degrees in the liberal arts.

For a period during the beginning of the mid-twentieth century boom in growth of colleges and universities, the liberal arts were the ideal of a practical and flexible college degree. In 1945, after World War II and with the shadow of communism appearing to threaten democratic ideals, a committee of Harvard professors came together to define how general education contributed to the development of the ideal citizen, who was described as a "gregarious, worldly, curious, widely competent, intellectually unconstrained, and full-blooded participant in worldly affairs, and, explicitly, an exemplary citizen of the kind of modern democratic society exemplified by the triumphant US."[3] This effort, which was titled *General Education in a Free Society* but more commonly referred to as The Redbook, defined the purpose of liberal arts education for more than half a century and assured that general education had a humanistic bent, which, over the course of the next seventy years, would delineate a clear difference between the liberal arts and the sciences, the primary characteristic of that difference residing in an "openness to the extraneous, which renders all identities provisional."[4] The value of that openness has never been easily measured and has come to be viewed as impractical and even undesirable in recent decades. As the sciences appear dedicated to the production of knowledge that can be commercialized, the liberal arts seem to have become fixated on the study of culture and society in a way that cannot easily be translated into commercial success. This perceived lack of economic value has been paired with declining state support for universities and an even sharper reduction in universities' support for the liberal arts.

Despite the supposed decline in the value of the liberal arts, most faculty members believe in the transformative power of these disciplines. As Melissa Mowry notes in her essay "The State of the Profession: Work, the Humanities, and Transformation," students who find that a liberal arts discipline awakens them to some human truth often become majors or, heaven help them, liberal arts professors.[5] Although all liberal arts faculty have had a somewhat similar transformative experience, the liberal arts need not to be defended but scrutinized in an effort to define ways to make their value more apparent to a variety of stakeholders.

Behind Mowry's comment lies the argument that the liberal arts are, by their very nature, elitist and exclusionary, more devoted to creating other academics than to defining a living presence outside the academy.[6] As if to emphasize this point, in response to a call for a more utilitarian approach to the liberal arts, Mark Bauerlein's *New York Times* article "Where Dickinson Fits In" argues that we need not prove the value of the liberal arts but simply "proclaim it with fervor and students will come—and administrators will notice."[7] Bauerlein is correct that some students are drawn to the liberal arts by passion for a discipline, but he is incorrect in thinking that that alone will save the liberal arts from obscurity.

As an English professor, and a voracious reader of fiction, I understand the transformative power of literature and value the study of literary trends and countertrends as offering insight into the deepest regions of both the individual and collective human psyche. Yet I recognize that the study of literature and history and philosophy can be viewed as effete, as disconnected from the gritty reality of commerce and the daily lives of our students. In fact, that negative conception of the liberal arts began to appear almost immediately after the publication of the Harvard group's Redbook, as the number of college students expanded and included more and more middle-class and working-class students. For the study of the liberal arts, the general education as defined by The Redbook's "whole man" is by its nature elitist and exclusionary—it simply did not leave room for a non-elite identity.

As Chris Buczinsky and Ginger Rodriguez note in their essay on the challenges of teaching working-class students about literature, their students attend college to earn a degree in order to improve their economic situation.[8] The vast majority of students at colleges and universities across the country take on student debt and struggle to overcome a host of other difficulties for exactly the same reason. Faculty in the liberal arts know the challenge of engaging students in disciplines when students and their parents do not see those courses as connected to their future employment opportunities. As frustrating as conversations with students about the usefulness of a course can be, they simply mirror the attitudes that politicians, the general public, and even university administrators often have toward the liberal arts. This chasm between the ideal of the liberal arts and the expectations of students, administrators, employers and other stakeholders has created what Ronan McDonald terms "precarity," the institutionalized uncertainty that liberal arts units face and the professional insecurity that many academics confront, becoming part of a new "precariat class" that encounters increasing ambiguity about the future of liberal arts institutions and the place of the liberal arts professor.[9]

Of course, merely reviewing the problems in the liberal arts does not help to identify ways to more fully engage liberal arts units, faculty, and students in the changing structure of higher education. One obvious connection between the liberal arts and the future of education is the potential of the liberal arts to take part in the knowledge economy. The liberal arts serve as a bridge between the world of raw fact and the application of those facts to decision making, planning, and public discourse that humanizes and de-objectifies, so that facts become meaningful. By embracing the collaborative and interdisciplinary opportunities so obviously part of the study of the liberal arts, we can begin to create connections between liberal arts disciplines and other areas of higher education. By emphasizing the social aspects of our work, we can debunk the myth of the isolated professor churning out unreadable and unread esoteric journal articles and create an image of the liberal arts that embraces public life.

As Todd Presner notes in his essay "The Humanities—Bigger and Bolder," collaboration is a long-standing part of humanities-based learning.[10] The rise of science-technology-engineering-arts-math (STEAM) curricula that include arts and humanities courses suggests that some of the most fertile areas of research in the liberal arts involve crossovers with science and technology. In fact, Presner offers one innovative solution that uses the "big challenge" model from the sciences as a way to reorganize study in the liberal arts using "big questions" to drive the creation of centers of learning that largely do away with divisions according to discipline. Presner imagines a series of "humanities research labs" to tackle large, collaborative projects that cross departments and even institutions.[11]

In these labs graduate students would be admitted to projects rather than departments. One aspect of this idea that helps solve the image problem of the liberal arts is that these big questions would involve partnerships with communities and would encourage a wider dissemination of the knowledge produced. For Presner, "new multidisciplinary fields such as environmental humanities, digital humanities, medical humanities, and urban humanities . . . are not based on, limited to, or derived from departments."[12] The key element in Presner's "big humanities" idea is the dissolution of disciplinary organization to liberal arts colleges. Of course, many liberal arts faculty object to this approach, claiming that we cannot confer degrees in "big ideas" and that we cannot merge our different views of research and jargon to create stand-alone interdisciplinary research units. Collaboration and sharing information, they agree, are valuable parts of the plan to save the liberal arts, but that plan must exist within the current university structure.

Yet the current organization of the university, indeed of academe, often limits the sharing of information and ideas. The organization of the university is at odds with how the liberal arts could be most productive. Even in the evaluation of faculty, the university narrowly measures output of knowledge by discipline, but grand challenges, partnerships with a university press, and the publication of results digitally and outside traditional academic outlets could lead to a "broad public resonance" that encourages public discourse and sustains enthusiasm for liberal arts study as relative to discourse on issues that involve individuals outside the academy.[13] Achieving that collaborative synthesis will require a more flexible approach to university structure and openness to experimentation in creating new extradisciplinary units. Presner's suggestion is not as revolutionary as it may sound. Universities have for decades been creating centers and institutes that pull in faculty from a variety of liberal arts disciplines. However, those high-profile units require additional funding, something that most colleges and universities do not have or are not willing to expend on vanity projects for the liberal arts. Our challenge is to make the restructuring of our units both productive and cost-effective.

Two examples of interdisciplinarity that have expanded interest in liberal arts disciplines incorporate two key elements that offer solutions for the rest of us: technology and cultural engagement. Both digital humanities and multimedia studies combine the best of social and cultural critique found in the liberal arts with emerging technologies, allowing a study of the relationship of culture and technology even as those new areas of knowledge develop. In an article on a sociological study using gaming literacy theory at the University of Chicago, Patrick Jagoda argues that the liberal arts can prepare students for gaming literacy, because liberal arts study requires that "people make sense of processes that constitute complex systems, emergent forms of play that both recognize and transcend rules, and play processes that create dynamic social contexts."[14] In other words, shared ideas and the ability to address complex issues and to develop solutions is the kind of thinking required in both academic and professional contexts. I doubt that early digital humanities and media studies pioneers were thinking explicitly about the job skills that their students would gain through these new fields, but we can tackle the reorganization of the liberal arts and the creation of new approaches to knowledge with career preparedness as one of our objectives.

Within our current knowledge economy, cognitive labor, including social skills like communication, collaboration, and creativity, has increased the free circulation of knowledge and information. Being able to recognize and harness the power of this new capitalist formation can mean for the liberal arts the difference between a slow fading into obscurity and an expanding profile in the changing landscape of higher education. In his article on the failed potential of MOOCs, Lawrence Hanley notes that despite the disappointing economics of MOOCs, the experiment multiplied the variety of approaches available for both teaching and educational collaboration. Hanley argues that knowledge collaboration is self-propagating and that each attempt we make in higher education to collaborate with nonacademic entities moves us closer to long-term viability in this era of declining state support.[15]

Collaboration with nonacademic entities also means that in addition to configuring liberal arts units according to "big ideas," we need to build into our curriculum a focus on career planning. As academics we often avoid this aspect of mentoring unless students evince an interest in becoming academics themselves. Part of our reticence is due to the fact that most of us have spent the vast majority of our working lives in traditional academic posts. We do not have the backgrounds to serve as career counselors, but we are excellent researchers and regularly innovate in our approaches to teaching. Career counseling cannot be such a stretch.

The view of the liberal arts as being separate from commerce and as having no direct connection to job preparation is not confined to faculty. As Mowry points out in her essay on the relationship between the humanities and employment, "We are, to paraphrase one administrator, the 'book people,' not the jobs people."[16] We often prefer to think of ourselves as being above economic ends, especially with regard to our study of human culture. Still, the cultural insights, the creativity, and the communication skills required for liberal arts studies have a measurable value in the business world. Almost 70 percent of economic activity is propelled by consumption, much of which involves cultural products or products with a cultural component. In exemplary economies, those with low unemployment and high wages and worker satisfaction, the distribution of occupations includes roughly 25 percent of jobs in knowledge services such as education, government, health, and business services. By contrast, science-related jobs make up only 15 percent of these economies. Not only is the knowledge economy vital to a robust economy, but, even in more technical fields, the skills of the culturally trained knowledge worker are critical. As Hearn and May note, project failures in areas from IT to supply chain management to environmental disasters can be traced to a breakdown in human cultural factors and "social governance and deliberation."[17]

If we are honest with ourselves, we know that the liberal arts are not separate from economic ends. Universities in Western democracies have long benefited from the capitalistic value of the knowledge they produce. Academics and students in liberal arts disciplines regularly engage in the act of knowledge creation. The processes of social and artistic innovation that are so valuable in our economy are embedded in the processes of analysis and critique innate to liberal arts disciplines. Instead of distancing ourselves and our students from production, we need to acknowledge that we are in the business of meaning making. To engage with the knowledge economy, the liberal arts must have relevant curricula that recognize "the world as a place of meanings and values, as opposed to a place of bare physical processes."[18] Cooperation, collaboration, communication, and creativity are all fundamental academic values.

There is not a single solution to reversing the apparent decline in support for the liberal arts. There are multiple answers, approaches, models, and systems that can precipitate change. Increasing the perceived value of liberal arts education will require sophisticated and flexible solutions that cross disciplinary boundaries and create new philosophies of education. It will be difficult, so it is a good thing that we all have been trained as innovative, critical thinkers who can find solutions to complex problems.

Notes

1. Simon During, "Precariousness, Literature and the Humanities Today," *Australian Humanities Review*, no. 58 (May 2015): 51–56.

2. During, "Precariousness, Literature and the Humanities Today," 52.

3. Geoffrey Galt Harpham, "Finding Ourselves: The Humanities as a Discipline," *American Literary History* 25, no. 3 (Fall 2013): 516.

4. Harpham, "Finding Ourselves," 512.

5. Melissa Mowry, "The State of the Profession: Work, the Humanities, and Transformation," *English Language Notes* 47, no .1 (2009): 49–57.

6. Mowry, "State of the Profession," 52.

7. Mark Bauerlein, "Where Dickinson Fits In," *New York Times*, October 17, 2010, accessed May 15, 2016, http://nytimes.com/roomfordebate/2010/10/17/do-colleges-need-french departments/where-dickinson-fits-in.

8. Chris Buczinsky and Ginger Rodriguez, "In the Shadows of BP: Teaching Humanities to Underprepared Students," *International Journal of the Humanities* 9, no. 5 (August 2011): 69–76.

9. Ronan McDonald, "'Did the Humanities Have It Coming?' A Response to Simon During," *Australian Humanities Review*, no. 58 (May 2015): 59.

10. Todd Presner, "The Humanities—Bigger and Bolder," *Seminar—A Journal of Germanic Studies* 50, no. 2 (2014): 154–60.

11. Presner, "Humanities—Bigger and Bolder," 157.

12. Presner, "Humanities—Bigger and Bolder," 155.

13. Presner, "Humanities—Bigger and Bolder," 158.

14. Patrick Jagoda, "Gaming the Humanities," *Differences: A Journal of Feminist Cultural Studies* 25, no. 1 (Spring 2014): 196–97.

15. Lawrence Hanley, "After the Massive Open Online Courses: Re/Making Humanities in the Era of Cognitive Capitalism," *International Journal of the Humanities: Annual Review* 12 (June 2014): 23–28.

16. Mowry, "State of the Profession," 49.

17. Greg Hearn and Harvey May, "The Role of the Humanities in the Knowledge Economy: Critique or Cornerstone?," *International Journal of the Humanities* 5, no. 10 (January 2008): 88, 89, 98.

18. "Worth of the Humanities," *AmeriQuests* 9, no. 1/2 (January 2012): 4.

Bibliography

Bauerlein, Mark. "Where Dickinson Fits In." *New York Times*, Oct. 17, 2010. http://nytimes.com/roomfordebate/2010/10/17/do-colleges-need-frenchdepartments/wheredickinson-fits-in.

Buczinsky, Chris, and Ginger Rodriguez. "In the Shadows of BP: Teaching Humanities to Underprepared Students." *International Journal of the Humanities* 9, no. 5 (August 2011): 69–76. Humanities International Complete, EBSCOhost. Accessed July 25, 2016.

During, Simon. "Precariousness, Literature and the Humanities Today." *Australian Humanities Review*, no. 58 (May 2015): 51–56. Humanities International Complete, EBSCOhost. Accessed May 15, 2016.

Hanley, Lawrence. "After the Massive Open Online Courses: Re/Making Humanities in the Era of Cognitive Capitalism." *International Journal of the Humanities: Annual Review* 12 (June 2014): 23–28. Humanities International Complete, EBSCOhost. Accessed May 15, 2016.

Harpham, Geoffrey Galt. "Finding Ourselves: The Humanities as a Discipline." *American Literary History* 25, no. 3 (Fall 2013): 509–34. Humanities International Complete, EBSCOhost. Accessed May 15, 2016.

Hearn, Greg, and Harvey May. "The Role of the Humanities in the Knowledge Economy: Critique or Cornerstone?" *International Journal of the Humanities* 5, no. 10 (January 2008): 87–93. Humanities International Complete, EBSCOhost. Accessed August 10, 2016.

Jagoda, Patrick. "Gaming the Humanities." *Differences: A Journal of Feminist Cultural Studies* 25, no. 1 (Spring 2014): 189–215. Humanities International Complete, EBSCOhost. Accessed May 20, 2016.

McDonald, Ronan. "'Did the Humanities Have It Coming?' A Response to Simon During." *Australian Humanities Review*, no. 58 (May 2015): 57–61. Humanities International Complete, EBSCOhost. Accessed July 25, 2016.

Mowry, Melissa. "The State of the Profession: Work, the Humanities, and Transformation." *English Language Notes* 47, no. 1 (Spring 2009): 49–57. Humanities International Complete, EBSCOhost. Accessed July 25, 2016.

Presner, Todd. "The Humanities—Bigger and Bolder." *Seminar—A Journal of Germanic Studies* 50, no. 2 (May 2014): 154–60. Humanities International Complete, EBSCOhost. Accessed July 25, 2016.

"The Worth of the Humanities." *AmeriQuests* 9, no. 1/2 (January 2012): 1–7. Humanities International Complete, EBSCOhost. Accessed July 25, 2016.

DIGITAL HUMANITIES, TECHNOLOGY, AND THE LIBERAL ARTS

CHAPTER 1

Digital Humanities as a LEAP High-Impact Practice

SERETHA D. WILLIAMS

As a professor of English in a department whose primary mission is to improve undergraduate writing, my pedagogy has focused on the recursive process and strategies for teaching persuasive and expository writing. Even in a non-composition-based course, I am mindful that I am expected to make students good writers. In a study on student writing improvement, cognitive psychologist Daniel Oppenheimer and his research team observe, "[The] field of Writing Studies [in the United States] has largely focused on process and context to understand college writing and often focused on ethnographic methods." The study found that student writing in college improved over time. However, Oppenheimer argues, the results "should be considered in the context of broader growth—writing proficiency is just one domain in which college students are expected to improve."[1] Critical thinking, knowledge application, and information literacy skills are equally important to student development, and these skills, like writing, develop as students progress toward graduation.

Thus, singularly equating student success with writing proficiency is a narrow-sighted strategy; instead, English and other humanities disciplines must incorporate multimodal approaches to course design and assessment. Twenty-first-century learners must be trained in written, oral, visual, and audio literacies. Most of our students will enter a digitized workplace in which employers will expect them to generate multimedia or interactive documents, not eight-page source-based essays.

The Liberal Education and America's Promise (LEAP) initiative crafted by the Association of American Colleges and Universities (AAC&U) is one method higher education is embracing to bridge the gap between the academy's desire to educate the whole person and the job market's push for skills-based education. One of the goals of LEAP is to facilitate outcomes that promote broad-based learning and foster skills employers find desirable in employees. The two do not have to be mutually exclusive. LEAP learning outcomes promote "knowledge of human cultures and the physical and natural world, intellectual and practical skills, personal and social responsibility, and integrative and applied learning" as part of a liberal education model. The LEAP learning outcomes map to prescribed, high-impact teaching and learning practices that include "first-year experiences, common intellectual experiences, learning communities, writing-intensive courses, collaborative assignments and projects, undergraduate research, diversity/global learning, service learning, community-based learning, internships and capstone courses and projects."[2] High-impact practices (HIPS) are designed to promote student engagement and to improve learning outcomes in undergraduate education.

Shari McMahan's case study of high-impact practices at California State University-Fullerton suggests that HIPS positively affect retention, grade point average, and graduation rates. The LEAP initiative proposes that writing skills are only one measure of student growth. However, many composition and literature classrooms continue to foreground essay writing despite evidence that assignments such as the research paper may not be the best instrument for teaching critical or analytical skills. Jennie Nelson's research on the undergraduate research paper found that "if most students view the research paper assignment as an exercise in reproducing information for the teacher-as-examiner, then it cannot promote independent thinking, critical analysis, or responsible writing."[3] Nelson and other rhetoric and composition scholars have suggested revamping the research paper assignment and evaluating student success by examining student achievement in other ways.

Borrowing the language of Stephen Witte, Neil Nakadate, and Roger Cherry, Nelson proposes a "'rhetoric of doing' [that requires] active inquiry, thoughtful analysis and evaluation, and the presentation of new knowledge to an interested community of readers."[4] The "rhetoric of doing" aligns with the essential learning outcomes and high-impact practices LEAP supports. Writing for students is the primary method composition instructors remedy the teacher-as-examiner model, but the audience is an imagined audience. Using digital humanities methods and tools, students can write for real audiences and produce research that other student-scholars would view and use.

Digital humanities (DH) is both a burgeoning academic discipline and a methodology. At its most basic level, DH applies new media and information technologies to understand, preserve, and communicate past and evolving ideas about the humanities. Although scholars inside and outside the field disagree about the definition of the term *digital humanities* and debate its distinction as a field separate from other humanities disciplines, DH exists and is a viable and distinguishable field of study.

In the "Brave Side of Digital Humanities," Fiona Barnet describes a DH conference panel in which the disconnect between the audience practitioners and the scholar panelists was palpable. The panel liberally employed the term *digital* and included projects that were digital but did not follow any specific DH methodology. The audience objected to the panelists' loose interpretation of DH projects. Matthew Kirschenbaum's article "What Is Digital Humanities and What's It Doing in English Departments?" frames the debates surrounding the amorphous nature of DH.[5]

Many academics do not agree on what DH is or what it involves. Some doubt computing's or technology's role in the humanities classroom. For the purposes of this article, those debates about what constitutes DH or whether DH methods are good for humanities scholarship are not central. Instead, DH is a burgeoning transdisciplinary field in which intersectionality and multimodal discourse are essential. As such, DH methods and tools are appropriate for a humanities classroom modeled on the "rhetoric of doing" and are informed by LEAP essential learning outcomes. DH is a high-impact practice that helps students achieve liberal education outcomes with many methods and tools.

DH researchers ask questions about patterns, frequencies, and meanings. Their questions develop out of the types of analysis they need for a project. The may need to analyze a word for frequency; word trends; comparisons; and the identification of names, places, periods, and sentiment. They may want to look at the data after it has been collected and then develop a search question or a grounded theory question. Digital humanities assignments focus on the process of conducting research, emphasize the importance of publication, and serve as a foundation for future student collaborations and scholarship. Digital projects do not replace research papers in undergraduate curriculum. Instead, digital humanities projects are equally valuable assessments of students' mastery of proposed learning outcomes. Furthermore, DH projects provide students with an opportunity to write and publish for an audience and to receive feedback from peers and other scholars. DH methodologies and project-based assignments are ways professors can involve undergraduates in discovery and publication with a wide array of tools.

LEAP identifies critical thinking skills as a priority for liberal education in the twenty-first century. Caroline Crawford's work on humanities instruction in this century suggests that in our shift from the "Industrial Age" to the "Information or Digital Age," students' ability to navigate and apply technology is a vital component of demonstrating critical or higher-order thinking skills. As evidence of this shift, Crawford discusses the revision of Bloom's taxonomy to reflect digital age thinking skills. Creating is now the pinnacle of Bloom's classification of thinking behaviors and involves "putting elements together to form a coherent or functional whole [or] reorganizing elements into a new pattern or structure through generating, planning or producing."[6] In experiential discovery learning, and project-based classrooms, creating is the aspirational learning outcome, but many undergraduate tasks begin and end with lower-level thinking skills.

As Nelson observes, for example, the undergraduate research paper in practice facilitates students' remembering, understanding, applying, and analyzing information. How, then, do we move undergraduates from lower-order skills to the higher-order skills they need to achieve the LEAP essential learning outcomes? Psychologists Kristie Campana and Jamie Peterson suggest using the classroom to model authentic or real-world experiences.[7] But the parameters of the classroom can extend to incorporate media and technology literacy into the humanities classroom. DH projects have the potential to facilitate higher-order thinking, and text mining and exhibit building can give undergraduates research outlets for a public demonstration of competency.

My work with digital humanities began with a summer project I led for our campus's Center for Undergraduate Research. I served as a faculty mentor for three students interested in learning to use the platform Voyant to conduct quantitative research on African American poetry. Students researched whether quantitative analysis could be used to support qualitative assertions of black poetry as a distinct genre of American poetry. The students first had to digitize the collected works of Langston Hughes, Margaret Walker, Maya Angelou, Gwendolyn Brooks, and Alice Walker. Once the texts were scanned, the students had to create a "clean" text stripped of styles, line breaks, and punctuation that might inhibit Voyant from reading the document accurately. Voyant allows users to upload multiple texts and compare word occurrences. The students assessed the frequency of words and phrases related to three main categories that, through qualitative research, they determined recur in the scholarship of black poetry: memory, identity, and music.

The students did not produce a research paper but designed a formal poster and a website that documented their results.[8] They presented their research to faculty and students on campus and at two statewide student research conferences. Only one of the students was an English major; the other two were computer science and psychology majors. Therefore, we had numerous conversations about the nature and purpose of humanities research and considered ways their current research might inform their future research in other disciplines. These conversations are a part of a metacognitive discourse that composition scholars suggest is integral to both knowledge production and writing processes.

During the 2016 summer session, I taught the Introduction to Women's and Gender Studies (WGST 1101) course online for the first time. Online courses lend themselves readily to DH projects and defend against "silo-building," as Caroline Crawford refers to it, "within which learners feel a sense of aloneness and disconnect from the larger learning community."[9] In WGST 1101, one of the primary learning objectives is to build competency in recognizing and applying terms used in the field. Intro is the only course all potential minors are required to take; thus, teaching the key concepts students need to navigate upper-division coursework is imperative, but assessing students' understanding of and ability to apply terms has been difficult, because of the sheer number of concepts and the limitations of working in a traditional class environment.

In the online course, I designed an assignment in which the students created content and shared knowledge on a professional format. I asked students to contribute to a media analysis project in which they researched digital media to find examples that illustrated or challenged concepts we studied in the course. Each student was required to document bibliographic information and to write a 100- to 200-word analysis of the source. I assessed the students' understanding of the terms by looking at the quality of the textual, visual, or audio source they selected and by evaluating the paragraphs they wrote to explain how the text illustrated or challenged the concept. I soon discovered that many students at the end of the term were not able to apply those terms effectively. The next time I run the course, I will assign this project as a midterm and a final task, giving the students an opportunity to revise their projects over the course of the semester.

Admittedly, the transition from a traditional composition-based learning environment to a twenty-first-century experience-centered and object-based classroom has its challenges. First, I have had to retool my approach to teaching, my course design, and my expectations of student-learners. Second, deciding which platforms to use in my courses has been as difficult as teaching myself to use the DH tools. Nevertheless, I intend to include DH activities in all my courses. Because I teach more English composition classes than upper-division English or Women's and Gender Studies courses, incorporating DH into freshman English makes sense for research purposes, but I am unsure how effective DH projects will work with first-year students. To date, little quantitative research has been done on DH and college writing; most research is anecdotal.

In fall 2016, I taught three sections of English (ENGL) 1101, College Composition I. The primary text for the course was Margaret Walker's novel *Jubilee*. Writing assignments are scaffolded around the novel, moving from descriptive to expository to rhetorical analysis and, finally, to argument. Instead of a long research paper, the culminating assignment was a review of original source documents. Students learned the basics of archival research by reviewing Walker's personal journals digitized and made accessible by the Margaret Walker Center at Jackson State University. They searched for key terms in the journals and correspondence, including *cooking, religion, civil rights, family,* and *writing*. They then transcribed the portion of the document relevant to their term, summarized the content of the document, and evaluated the document by considering the ways the document gives them insight into *Jubilee* and Walker's life.

With this assignment, students developed an understanding of rhetorical awareness and participated in metacognitive discussions regarding the role of research in society. In addition, the students learned to use Omeka as a tool for publishing their research; each original source review was collected and exhibited on the site. Omeka is an open source content management system where users store digital artifacts and publish multimedia exhibits. Once the students uploaded their original source artifacts, transcriptions, and short essays, they created and published an exhibit they named *Margaret Walker Transcribed*. Digital media specialist Olin Bjork suggests that the "research orientation of humanities computing" aligns well with research-based learning outcomes embedded in most first-year composition programs. Bjork argues most composition courses focus heavily on secondary research, while "many of these students will major in highly quantitative, primary research fields."[10] Introducing first-year students to primary source research and digital publishing platforms may prepare students for writing situations they are more likely to encounter in third- and fourth-year courses.

In spring 2017 students from fall 2016 ENGL 1101 had the opportunity to continue their research on Walker in ENGL 1102, this time in a DH environment. The classes met in a computer lab three times a week, and the assignments involved archival and secondary research, close reading of literary texts, digitizing and basic coding of texts, collaboration, and multimodal presentations of research. The primary collaborative DH assignment for ENGL 1102 was a hypertext assignment. The students were required to conduct a close reading of Margaret Walker's iconic poem "For My People" and find internet sources to link to the poem to explicate terms or ideas other students might not understand. Hypertexting expands upon the skills students learned in ENGL 1101, and ENGL 1102 is designed to teach the source-based paper. By the end of the course, students should be able to find and evaluate sources, integrate them into their writing, and demonstrate contextual awareness.

I scaffolded assignments to support student success in meeting the learning outcomes for the hypertexting assignment.[11] The prerequisite skills for the assignment included an ability to find and evaluate sources and to analyze a poem. Leading up to the assignment, I provided instruction on navigating databases and search engines, using Boolean search techniques. In addition, the students were assigned a series of close readings and mini-research projects to work on individually and as a group. Along with the close reading of "For My People," the hypertexting project required students to research unfamiliar terms, and background on Margaret Walker.

My attempt to implement this project took longer than I planned in the course syllabus. I allotted two weeks, but the project took closer to four weeks. The students had minimal computer skills, and almost none had coding skills. Although I created templates for their pages, groups were not able to manipulate the pages as I had hoped. The students spent more time working on the coding for the pages than they did on the close reading of the poem. The content of the close reading for some groups was more summary than analysis or explanation, but the hyperlinks they researched and created added value to the project. They did meet the outcome of contextual awareness, because they had to research a culture, a period, and a poem with which they were not familiar. In the end, eight students represented the groups during the Women's and Gender Studies Symposium at Augusta University, and I moderated a panel. The students' screenshots of their websites, which were not live, were shared via a PowerPoint presentation.

The students, again, were supposed to use Omeka to collect and publish their research, but during the project we could no longer access the Omeka website from our campus computers. The Omeka site blocked all traffic from our servers, and our IT specialists were unable to resolve the problem until the end of the semester. The students managed to begin the Omeka *Writing Margaret Walker* exhibit, but they were not able to connect their digital assignments to the Omeka site.

In another course, ENGL 4360 Studies in World Literature, I used MyHistro, a digital timeline platform, and Omeka to teach information literacy. Studies in World Literature is cross-listed as an English and humanities class. By topic, the course is global in its perspective. By design, I wanted to make the course multidisciplinary, incorporating DH to trace the steps of Langston Hughes over continents and through time. Initially, I intended to use Google Earth to create a map of Hughes's travels and encounters with renowned writers, performers, artists, and political figures, but teaching the students to use the software was a daunting task in addition to all the work they would have to do for the course. Instead, we used MyHistro, a click-and-paste platform. Students created a geographic timeline of Hughes's autobiographies. Each entry on the timeline explained the significance of a place or a year for Hughes. The assignment was collaborative. Half of the class worked on *The Big Sea*, and the other half worked on *I Wonder as I Wander*. For the Omeka project, students worked individually to create a collection of items related to a theme of their own design. Some collections included documents related to Hughes's interest in blues and jazz music, his literary influences, and his involvement in theater.

The digital projects enhanced the learning experience by requiring the students to conduct research, evaluate sources, and digitally publish their findings. Moreover, the course design allowed students to discover Hughes and global writers whom they have never read. As a result, the students conducted high-level research valuable not only to other students but to instructors and scholars studying Hughes. As Alison King in "From Sage on the Stage to Guide on the Side" suggests, experiential learning "move[s] [students] away from the reproduction of knowledge toward the production of knowledge."[12]

Finally, my ENGL 4310 Studies in Feminism course was cross-listed as English, Women's and Gender Studies, and Humanities. The theme for the course was "Mad Women in the Attic." I organized the course around this theme because madness is a motif in women's literature that intersects with gender studies' concerns with women's health. We watched films and read texts of literary madness. Because the course included students with varying knowledge levels of feminist theory ranging from novice to advanced, I differentiated assignments giving students the choice of developing traditional English literature assignments such as annotated bibliographies and essays or creating original work that related to the idea of literary madness or mental health issues.

Most students chose the traditional options. In "Devil in the Digital: Ambivalent Results in an Object-Based Teaching Course," Mark Turin admits his surprise at his students' resistance to nontraditional methodologies.[13] My students were no different. Of the four students who submitted original creations, only one met the criteria of the assignment. Students could submit poetry, visual art, or character blogs accompanied by a seven-page reflective written response about the project. The reflection required the student to situate the project within creative and/or medical discourse about madness and insanity and to take a position on the trope of madness in creative productions. The goal was for students to determine whether "madness" is subversive.

The visual art project of one student was superb. The images she created were high quality, and her reflection statement integrated specific evidence from the texts into her analysis of her art and discussion of madness. She earned the Outstanding WGST Student Award for this project. Working in an alternative genre served her well and encouraged her to operate at the highest level of Bloom's taxonomy. For those three students whose projects were superficial and did not demonstrate higher-order thinking, the option was a disaster. I gave them the opportunity to revise the project, but they did not have the skills necessary to create work and to apply theory to their work. When I assessed the project at the end of the semester, I had no opportunity to revisit the assignment or reteach the skills.

DH is a means to teach students to write with a purpose, to consider audience, and to behave as scholars, but I do not propose an abandonment of traditional composition genres and practices. Instead, I argue that by focusing primarily on the production of traditional writing as evidence of learning, we miss opportunities to engender in students a rhetorical awareness that prepares them to think and write in a multitude of situations and genres for diverse purposes. The humanities-based classroom should generate learning environments in which students act as cocreators of knowledge. DH assignments are high-impact educational opportunities that involve undergraduates in discovery and publication and prepare them for the digital environments they will encounter in the workforce.

Notes

1. Daniel Oppenheimer, Franklin Zaromb, James R. Pomerantz, Jean C. Williams, and Yoon Soo Park, "Improvement of Writing Skills during College: A Multi-Year Cross-Sectional and Longitudinal Study of Undergraduate Writing Performance," *Assessing Writing* 32 (2017): 15, 21, 23. accessed April 4, 2017, doi: 10.1016/j.asw.2016.11.001.

2. American Association of Colleges & Universities, LEAP Essential Outcomes, https://www.aacu.org/leap/essential-learning-outcomes; Association of American Colleges & Universities, LEAP High Impact Practices, https://www.aacu.org/resources/high-impact-practices.

3. Shari McMahan, "Creating a Model for High Impact Practices at a Large, Regional, Comprehensive University: A Case Study," *Contemporary Issues in Education Research* 8, no. 2 (2015): 111–15; Jennie Nelson, "The Research Paper: A 'Rhetoric of Doing' or a 'Rhetoric of the Finished Word'?," *Composition Studies/Freshman English News* 22, no. 2 (1994): 65–75.

4. Stephen Witte, Neil Nakadate, and Roger Cherry, *A Rhetoric of Doing: Essays on Written Discourse in Honor of James L. Kinneavy* (Carbondale: Southern Illinois University Press, 1992; Nelson, "Research Paper," 66.

5. Matthew Kirschenbaum, "What Is Digital Humanities and What's It Doing in English Departments?," in *Debates in the Digital Humanities*, ed. Matthew K. Gold,. (Minneapolis: University of Minnesota Press, 2012).

6. Liberal education and liberal arts education are not synonymous. AAC&U uses the phrase *liberal education* and describes it as broad-based learning with opportunities for in-depth learning. The curriculum includes the arts but is not limited to the traditional curriculum of liberal arts education. Association of American Colleges & Universities, "What Is a 21st Century Liberal Education?," https://www.aacu.org/leap/what-is-a-liberal-education; Caroline M. Crawford, "Instruction in the Humanities: Shifting Teaching and Learning Expectations and Tools with the Digital Age," *International Journal of the Humanities* 8, no. 2 (2010), 230; Lorin W. Anderson and David R. Krathwol, eds., *A Taxonomy for Learning, Teaching, and Assessment: A Revision of Bloom's Taxonomy of Educational Objectives* (New York: Longman, 2001): 67–68.

7. Kristie Campana and Jamie Peterson, "Do Bosses Give Extra Credit? Using the Classroom to Model Real-World Work Experiences," *College Teaching* 61, no. 2 (2013): 60–66.

8. Taylohr Brown, Diamond Jenkins, and Walter Quiller, "Text Mining and Digital Humanities: Quantitative Analysis of African American Poetry," Scholarly Commons Augusta University, http://hdl.handle.net/10675.2/565703; Taylohr Brown, Diamond Jenkins, and Walter Quiller, Mining Black Culture: A Digital Humanities Project, https://miningblackculture.wordpress.com/.

9. Crawford, "Instruction in the Humanities," 230.

10. Olin Bjork, "Digital Humanities and the First-Year Writing Course," in *Digital Humanities Pedagogy: Practices, Principles and Politics*, ed. Bret D. Hirsch, 102–3 (Cambridge, UK: Open Book, 2014).

11. Kathleen Hogan and Michael Pressley, eds., *Scaffolding Student Learning: Instructional Approaches and Issues* (Louiseville, Quebec: Brookline Books, 1997).

12. Alison King, "From Sage on the Stage to Guide on the Side," *College Teaching* 41, no. 1 (1993), 35.

13. Mark Turin, "Devil in the Digital: Ambivalent Results in an Object-Based Teaching Course," *Museum Anthropology* 38, no. 2 (2015), 127.

Bibliography

Anderson, Lorin W., and David R. Krathwol, eds. *A Taxonomy for Learning, Teaching, and Assessment: A Revision of Bloom's Taxonomy of Educational Objectives*. New York: Longman, 2001.

Association of American Colleges & Universities. LEAP Essential Outcomes. https://www.aacu.org/leap/essential-learning-outcomes.

Barnet, Fiona M. "The Brave Side of Digital Humanities." *Differences: A Journal of Feminist Cultural Studies* 25, no. 1 (2014). doi: 10.1215/10407391-24200003.

Bjork, Olin. "Digital Humanities and the First-Year Writing Course." In *Digital Humanities Pedagogy: Practices, Principles and Politics*, edited by Bret D. Hirsch, 97–119. Cambridge, UK: Open Book, 2014.

Brown, Taylohr, Diamond Jenkins, and Walter Quiller. Mining Black Culture: A Digital Humanities Project. https://miningblackculture.wordpress.com/.

Brown, Taylohr, Diamond Jenkins, and Walter Quiller. "Text Mining and Digital Humanities: Quantitative Analysis of African American Poetry." Scholarly Commons Augusta University. http://hdl.handle.net/10675.2/565703.

Campana, Kristie, and Jamie Peterson. "Do Bosses Give Extra Credit? Using the Classroom to Model Real-World Work Experiences." *College Teaching* 61, no. 2 (2013): 60–66.

Crawford, Caroline M. "Instruction in the Humanities: Shifting Teaching and Learning Expectations and Tools with the Digital Age." *International Journal of the Humanities* 8, no. 2 (2010): 229–44.

Hogan, Kathleen, and Michael Pressley, eds. *Scaffolding Student Learning: Instructional Approaches and Issues*. Louisville, Quebec: Brookline Books, 1997.

King, Alison. "From Sage on the Stage to Guide on the Side." *College Teaching* 41, no. 1 (1993): 30–35.

Kirschenbaum, Matthew. "What Is Digital Humanities and What's It Doing in English Departments?" In *Debates in the Digital Humanities*, edited by Matthew K. Gold, 3–11. Minneapolis: University of Minnesota Press, 2012.

McMahan, Shari. "Creating a Model for High Impact Practices at a Large, Regional, Comprehensive University: A Case Study." *Contemporary Issues in Education Research* 8, no. 2 (2015): 111–15.

Nelson, Jennie. "The Research Paper: A 'Rhetoric of Doing' or a 'Rhetoric of the Finished Word'?" *Composition Studies/Freshman English News* 22, no. 2 (1994): 65–75.

Oppenheimer, Daniel, Franklin Zaromb, James R. Pomerantz, Jean C. Williams, and Yoon Soo Park. "Improvement of Writing Skills during College: A Multi-Year Cross-Sectional and Longitudinal Study of Undergraduate Writing Performance." *Assessing Writing* 32 (2017): 12–27. Accessed April 4, 2017. doi: 10.1016/j.asw.2016.11.001.

Turin, Mark. "Devil in the Digital: Ambivalent Results in an Object-Based Teaching Course." *Museum Anthropology* 38, no. 2 (2015): 123–32.

Witte, Stephen, Neil Nakadate, and Roger Cherry. *A Rhetoric of Doing: Essays on Written Discourse in Honor of James L. Kinneavy*. Carbondale: Southern Illinois University Press, 1992.

CHAPTER 2

Technology in the Liberal Arts Classroom

Updating the Classroom Toolkit

MONICA FLIPPIN WYNN

The technological explosion has landed in higher education. In "Technology Doesn't Teach, Teachers Teach," Bill Goodwyn acknowledges that we have witnessed a seismic change in classroom instruction, student engagement, and teacher innovation, and these integrated platforms, without a doubt, have influenced the institutional systems and caused both disruption and delight in our academic disciplines.[1] Nowhere is this sentiment more debated than in the liberal arts classroom.

Technology utilization in the classroom has increased steadily over the last few years, and liberal arts educators are not really opposed to this technological burst of activity. However, John Ottenhoff argues that "educators are concerned with whether increasing use of technology in the curriculum has any discernable impact upon the ways in which we envision and practice liberal arts education."[2]

Edward Finn, a college liaison for technology and faculty, is concerned that when there are a variety of ways in which classrooms can be transformed, where learning outcomes and student engagement are improved and faculty are invigorated and motivated, then those mediums should be explored.[3]

For Katherine McKnight, technology has, in effect, "changed the classroom configuration and the methods of instruction. Liberal arts educators must work to review the pedagogical components of their curriculum and find ways to utilize some of these tools" in their classrooms because liberal arts students in the twenty-first century "need curricular opportunities to move from passive receivers of information, to engaged producers and creators."[4]

The options for technological implementation of these digital tools for faculty are so numerous that if a teacher were looking to include digital tools into his or her curriculum, the sheer number of possibilities would be enough to induce apprehension on starting the task. So, how can teachers get started? Where do you look for these digital tools? Is there a guidebook to navigate how to incorporate them into the classroom? The remainder of this chapter will review how teachers can develop a digital toolkit to integrate technology into their liberal arts curricula and classrooms. In addition, we will review several items from my digital toolkit and examine how they might be integrated into other liberal arts classrooms.

One approach to beginning the process of identifying a diverse set of digital possibilities is to create a digital toolkit. What is a digital toolkit? If you contemplate what a toolkit is, you often think of a hodgepodge of objects or items that somehow are organized and located in a similar place and, when manipulated, help you complete or finish a task. That is exactly how one can think of a digital toolkit. It can be a grouping of software tools, applications, examples, and instructions that individuals can utilize to investigate, shape, revise, and organize courses and curriculum.[5]

Teachers can then determine what digital tools work with specific curricula and disciplines. Devising your own toolkit with digital resources can assist with removing fear or trepidation of integrating these digital tools in the classroom. The digital toolkit is constructed with user-friendly tools and resources that incorporate the 2.0 web platform. The 2.0 platform generated and shaped the participatory and collective practices that include blogs, wikis, Facebook (remember Myspace), YouTube, Twitter, and Instagram. Some institutions provide digital toolkits to assist faculty with implementing technology into their courses. For example, Pace University's website includes a toolkit with links to different features and resources, including open education resources, which usually are provided at no cost, and instructions on how to get started in your classroom.[6] Check whether your institution's academic technology department provides a similar option as you begin to look for resources.

Many academic disciplines are working to make it easier for teachers to bridge the pedagogical and technological platforms. "The Pedagogy Toolkit," a humanities project led by Alex Christie at Brock University, established a website to provide information on digital tools. This website goes beyond providing resources. Information seekers can find suggestions on how to construct these digital tools into various humanities curricula by providing examples, templates, and support.[7]

After determining to build a digital toolkit, how do you select the digital tools? This seems to be the $100,000 question. Nonetheless, there are some excellent places to begin. For instance, most major academic conferences have workshops or panels on teaching and new innovations. I have found great resources and confirmed some of my ideas just by conversing and networking with colleagues. Although there is never enough time, if you can spare thirty minutes once a week, there are new journals and books focusing on technology and teaching available at your institution's library. The great thing about the university library, if there is a book, video, or article that you need and it is not available at your location, you can use interlibrary loan. With it I have found several helpful readings and videos on graphics and creating media that I have incorporated into my classes.

However, it is just as easy to begin within your own classroom or office. I did, and I was surprised at the tools that I had been integrating into my courses without realizing they were digital tools with wide-ranging digital capacity. Most teachers are currently utilizing quite a few digital resources, but they rarely know all the benefits or options of those digital tools. For instance, many of us use Google and even Google Drive in our classrooms, but we might not know that the entire digital platform can be integrated as combined tools in our curricula or provide collaborative options for group projects, including Google Hangouts, which is quite similar to Skype.[8] If you include polls or surveys in your traditional or online courses, you may be using poling options available in your university's learning management system. If not, there are other tools such as Survey Monkey and Poll Everywhere, which, if added to your toolkit, can be integrated to ask students about class content or other matters.

I have been accumulating resources for my digital toolkit since 2009. Some of the tools have worked and were appropriate for my discipline, while others were not compatible. Though it may be difficult to know whether certain tools will work for you, as you build your toolkit and select various tools and resources, the toolkit will grow and be indispensable. A noteworthy addition to any digital toolkit is a new strategy believed to increase student engagement and learning outcomes: flipping the classroom. The term "flipped" was introduced during the mid-2000s, although several of the components of the flipped classroom have been practiced in curricula for years. Flipping a classroom involves switching the order of how student learning occurs, particularly outside scheduled class time. Course content is provided through online teaching options delivered in a variety of ways, such as videos, podcasts, readings, and websites and homework must be completed before class.[9] The underlying strategy is to bring the active components, like writing, asking questions, developing presentations, and problem solving, into the real-time classroom, and transferring lectures and other content as assigned homework tasks.

This flipped method continues to trend and has positive support, but critics suggest there are several issues with the flipped-classroom platform. Often there are problems with dated technology and materials, as well as frustrated students. In addition, critics contend that students should not be responsible for their own teaching and learning. According to Mike Kaspar, "Teachers must be provided with rigorous professional development to learn how to make strategies such as flipped classrooms work in the classroom. This has to be about more than students watching YouTube lectures at home. Bad pedagogy is bad pedagogy whether it's flipped or not."[10]

Teachers who integrate technology into their curricula should be digitally and computer literate in order to create content that links to the course curriculum and is academically essential for the student. In addition, teachers must confirm that all students are connected on and off campus. Teachers should make sure to ask on the first day of classes whether students are connected to the internet at home or have a smart phone or other device that they can utilize to review the content. Teachers should make sure that all content is available for all types of screens and devices. Implementing this strategy within my curriculum increased student engagement, collective participation, and insightful conversations and discussions Students became passionate problem solvers as well as curious thinkers and sought out more opportunities to collaborate with classmates.

In my flipped communication classes, I have had some success, but it is not a perfect science. Because students came to class unprepared and had not reviewed the lectures and other materials provided, we fell behind and needed to utilize actual class time to make sure all students were prepared and at the same place. I began including quizzes for students to take with every lesson to check whether they were reading and viewing assigned materials. In addition, specific concepts required a class lecture and clarity beyond watching a video on the topic. Some tools to use for collaboration and assessing student learning in the flipped classroom include:

a. Creating word maps or infographics
b. Organizing group projects and presentations
c. Assigning in-class writing activities and peer reviews
d. Building Wikipedia pages, a class favorite.

"Flipping the classroom" is an excellent tool to add to your toolkit, but you should take time to review it before deciding to make the switch.

Digital storytelling is another excellent option that can be incorporated in the toolkit. Digital storytelling "combines the art of telling stories with a mixture of digital media, including text, pictures, recorded audio narration, music and video." Teachers don't have to be experienced in the various options, but you should know your way around the computer. And there are excellent resources available that can help with editing, music, graphics, and photos. Integrating digital storytelling into the classroom invites participation, engagement, and critical thinking and proposes a diverse method to discuss and review material and allow students to demonstrate their comprehension through the stories they weave and create.[11] Digital storytelling offers a unique mode of presentation to visualize and fuse the course content; however, some teachers may be hesitant to attempt integrating these tools because they do not have experience with the digital process or creating videos, graphics, and audio. In addition, they are perplexed as to how they can create content to correlate with their curriculum.

Originally, these media classroom tools were rarely implemented outside communication or media departments, but today many of the tools involved in the digital storytelling process are commonplace and can be found on your cellular device. Digital storytelling, according to Charlotte Hamilton, director of College Educational Technology Services at Houston Community College, "can help students learn and become more engaged." Beyond the student impact, "for faculty to work in a collaborative group environment using 21st century teaching techniques and learning new technology" provides the opportunity to think outside the box for instructional projects.[12]

There can be a downside in adding this digital tool to your toolkit. If teachers do not understand the storytelling process and are not familiar with the concepts or the tools needed, they take a chance of disengaging students in the class and not adequately preparing them to tackle course assignments. However, most universities offer some form of training to incorporate this platform into your classes.

In my graduate and undergraduate classes, I implement digital storytelling in the final projects. In one of my graduate theory courses, the students researched gentrification. Their project included interviews with neighborhood activists, newcomers to the neighborhood, and urban policy researchers. They took photos of the communities and conducted research at the public library to find old photographs of the neighborhood throughout the various periods. They developed graphs and images with supporting evidence and statistics, and they collaborated to scour the network for free music without any copyright infringements. Students then worked to edit and upload their projects to a website, which they designed.

In my undergraduate research methods course, students did a research project through digital storytelling. They interviewed professors discussing research and theory, and the digital projects included photos and interviews with research librarians and the Office of Research discussing the Institutional Review Board process. The students led focus groups that were tracked and incorporated in the project, and they had writing components to complete, including an introduction for the website and a literature review in APA format. In these assignments, the students compiled and produced stories that informed course learning objectives and were excellent visual assessments of the program. Digital Storytelling projects can be generated in all academic departments from English, art, history, sociology, biology, and medicine to political science, religion, and leadership and entrepreneurial studies. All the needed resources are available for students either online or in public libraries. Digital storytelling is an excellent collaborative and interdisciplinary option for students to learn to use archival and real-time videos with a cellular device and to edit and transfer those media to a computer. Students can have the opportunity to incorporate twenty-first-century skills in their analysis, writing, and diverse perspectives.

One of the first items added to my toolkit was blogging. A blog can include text or video (vlog) and create opportunities to communicate with audiences via authentic and original content. Priya Sharma at Penn State believes blogs are a wonderful opportunity for students to be collaborative. In addition, blogging assignments allow students to "reflect on current events and issues have been found to increase student engagement and curiosity and facilitate a deeper understanding."[13] Blogs are easy to set up and navigate and can be made private or public, depending on the course goals and objectives. Teachers can create individual blogs or a class blog and allow students to post with an assigned code or hashtag if the blog is public and viewable on the internet.

Blogs do not incur many technical issues. Most glitches arise with unclear criteria and guidelines, which can cause assignment nightmares and student content to be misdirected and fail to accomplish learning goals. Educators should ensure they have provided enough information, so students know what and why they are blogging for the assignment. In my classes, I discuss expectations for the blog assignments and include examples to assist students with understanding the process and the expectations, especially if they are new to blogging platforms. It is crucial to include a blogging rubric and guidelines, which mention word requirements. When blogs are integrated properly, the student content can be profound.

In my classes, I have utilized blogs throughout the curriculum. In media law and ethics courses, the students are required to review case law and comment utilizing evidence and current societal examples. In my communication history and theory courses, students correlate theoretical foundations with everyday insights. In these classes, peer critiques are helpful in providing diverse perspectives to the subject matter. You can find many available sites that have blogging platforms, and most are free at first. In addition, learning management systems include blogging options. To make it easier for my students, I purchased a domain and website, which allows me to generate blogs for my students.

I include several social media platforms in my digital toolkit and have implemented Instagram as one of my digital tools. Social media offers so many options for the classroom, but, as always, it should not be integrated without a strict adherence to pedagogy and consideration of the climate and culture of your environment. It is good to remember that your classroom digital natives use these same tools in other settings. Recently, a student indicated how excited he was to use Instagram in his class and was surprised a teacher assigned it. Fitri Handayani believes teachers should be "jumping" at the opportunity to use this social medium in the classroom.[14]

Michael Kirst, excited about the available options and the low cost, agrees that there are many options for bringing Instagram into the classroom.[15] It can be a remarkable tool for an online or hybrid course, and I integrate it in my public speaking classes. Students are required to complete several presentations, including introductions, impromptu remarks, and elevator speeches. As an alternative to uploading these speech videos to the learning management site, I ask the students to upload these videos to the class Instagram page. It creates a sense of community, as most students begin talking about their public speaking issues. With the other two small speeches, students are asked to provide constructive critiques to other students.

Because there was little research on Instagram or curricular examples to review on its usability in the classroom, I was hesitant to try it. One of the biggest drawbacks of incorporating change in the curriculum is the time it takes to research and revise courses, yet Instagram had good potential to motivate and engage my students, so the time and effort was worth it. In my media and society class, students can upload video or photos that correlate with what we are discussing to validate their understanding of concepts and terms. They associate the photo or graphic to a chapter and incorporate the term, idea, and concept in the comments section. Students also can review what other students have written and selected for their assignments, so diverse perspectives are discussed and debated with this exercise. This tool allows me to provide substantive tasks that work for all students, and the assessments are comparable to other tasks.

When integrating Instagram, I do not ask the students to utilize their own social media, but I create a course Instagram with a password and login that every student receives in the first assignment. Students are not allowed to download photos or other content uploaded by another student. We discuss privacy components, and I explain the rationale for the course Instagram so that students do not have issues participating. When I incorporated Twitter in my courses, there were concerns about free speech and what students post. Initially, I followed my students; however, legal liability and my responsibility to report issues changed the way I incorporate any social media, and the implementation of a class site that does not connect with students' own social media has been a better alternative, although it does add more time to the process.

When integrating Instagram assignments, you need to include thorough guidelines, screen shots, and rubrics. In my photojournalism course, this was an excellent way to share photos and create student portfolios. There have been few student complaints; most issues center around forgetting the password to the site. While many may find this tool incompatible with the curriculum, my initial use was for an administrative task. I scheduled attendance in a freshman seminar course using Instagram. The students enjoyed being able to upload a different photo each week with a comment. While it worked well only with my freshman students, it saved time and got rid of paper forms.

Teachers in all academic areas are recognizing that they can incorporate technology today, and not just those who profess to be technological gurus. All of us will need to adapt and commit to finding ways to incorporate these tools into our curricula and to develop toolkits for our classes. Edward Finn contends, "If the purpose of education is to expand individual minds and allow students to explore and create knowledge, technology is yet another tool for faculty to utilize and to enhance the learning environment. However, doing so requires faculty, administration, library and IT staff to communicate and to collaborate with the common goal of enhancing the educational experience of every student." For Finn, "First and foremost, technology can only be effective in the classroom if guided by pedagogical concerns, respect for students' needs, and continual dialogue and feedback."[16] The challenge is to merge them all and successfully to prepare our students to live and work in the twenty-first-century environment. The liberal arts are recognized for teaching such transformation and acceptance. It is our tradition.

Notes

1. Bill Goodwyn, "Technology Doesn't Teach, Teachers Teach," *Huffington Post* (blog), November 6, 2012, http://www.huffingtonpost.com/bill-goodwyn/technology-in-the-classroom_b_1857369.html; John Ottenhoff and Charles Blaich, "Technology and Liberal Arts

Education," Center of Inquiry, Wabash University, http://www.liberalarts.wabash.edu/technology-and-the-liberal-art/.

2. "'Reclaiming the Value of the Liberal Arts for the 21st Century': Strategies for Integrating Career Development with Traditional Arts and Sciences Curricula," *EAB* (2016), https://www.cwu.edu/trustees/sites/cts.cwu.edu.trustees/files/Reclaiming%20the%20Value%20of%20the%20Liberal%20Arts%20for%20the%2021st%20Century_EAB_2016.pdf; John Ottenhoff, "Center of Inquiry Technology Consultations," *Center of Inquiry,* Wabash University, http://www.liberalarts.wabash.edu/technology_liberal_arts/.

3. Edward W. Finn III, "Technology and the Liberal Arts: Expanding the Dialogue," *The Evolllution* , August 9, 2016, https://evolllution.com/programming/teaching-and-learning/technology-and-the-liberal-arts-expanding-the-dialogue.

4. Katherine McKnight, "Top 12 Ways Technology Changed Learning," Teaching Hub, http://www.teachhub.com/how-technology-changed-learning; Finn, "Technology and the Liberal Arts."

5. Leah Anne Levy, "Why Digital Literacy Is Important for Teachers," USC Rossier Online, July 25, 201, https://rossieronline.usc.edu/blog/teacher-digital-literacy/.

6. Pace University, "Digital Toolkit," https://www.pace.edu/its/teaching-and-learning/digital-toolkit.

7. Alex Christie, "Pedagogy Toolkit," http://pedagogy-toolkit.org/documentation/documentation.html.

8. Pamela Vaughn, "17 Google Marketing Tools You Should Be Utilizing," Blog Hub Spot, https://blog.hubspot.com/marketing/google-business-tools-for-marketers.

9. Colin Lankshear and Michele Knobel, "New Literacies: Everyday Practices and Classroom Learning," *Open, New Literacies: Everyday Practices and Classroom Learning,* 2nd ed. (Maidenhead, UK: Open University Press, 2006).

10. Edward Graham and Tim Walker, "What Flipped Classrooms Can (and Can't) Do for Education," *NEA Today,* March 29, 2013, http://neatoday.org/2013/03/29/what-flipped-classrooms-can-and-cant-do-for-education/.

11. Bernard R. Robin, "The Power of Digital Storytelling to Support Teaching and Learning," *Digital Education Review,* December 2016, https://files.eric.ed.gov/fulltext/EJ1125504.pdf; Daniel Trudeau, Katie Pratt, and Brad Belbas, "Digital Storytelling and the Liberal Arts," Associated Colleges of the Midwest (2016, February), http://www.acm.edu/professional_development/project/27/digital-storytelling-and-the-liberal-arts; Charlotte Hamilton, "Houston Community College: Embedding Digital Storytelling across the Higher Education Curriculum," https://www.storycenter.org/case-studies/hcc.10.1016/j.compedu.2004.10.013.

12. Eugene Lang, "Distinctively American: The Liberal Arts College," Academy of Arts and Sciences, http://www.projectpericles.org/projectpericles/about/history/attachment.pdf; Hamilton, "Houston Community College."

13. Kendra Oliver, "Teaching with Blogs," Vanderbilt University Center for Teaching, 2016, https://cft.vanderbilt.edu/wp-content/uploads/sites/59/Oliver_Blog-Guide_2016.pdf; Katie Bohn, "Blogging in the Classroom Can Help Both Students and Educators," *Penn State News,* September 16, 2016, https://news.psu.edu/story/426340/2016/09/16/research/blogging-classroom-can-help-both-students-and-educators; Nancy Malcolm, "Analyzing

the News: Teaching Critical Thinking Skills in a Writing Intensive Social Problems Course," *Teaching Sociology* 34, no. 2 (April 2006): 143–49.

14. Fitri Handayani, "Instagram as a Teaching Tool? Really," *Proceedings of the Fourth International Seminar on English Language*, 2016, file:///C:/Users/mflippinwynn/Downloads/6942-13821-1SM.pdf.

15. Michael Kirst, "Instagram as an Educational Tool for College Students," March 12, 2016, http://collegepuzzle.stanford.edu/?p=5057.

16. Finn, "Technology and the Liberal Arts."

Bibliography

Abe, Paige, and Nickolas Jordan. "Integrating Social Media into the Classroom Curriculum." *About Campus* 18 (2013): 16–20. doi:10.1002/abc.21107.

Abdulkafi Albirini. "Teachers' Attitudes toward Information and Communication Technologies: The Case of Syrian EFL Teachers." *Computers & Education* 47 (2006): 372–98. doi: 10.1016/j.compedu.2004.10.013.

Allen, William H. "Improving Instruction through Audio-Visual Media; Techniques in Teaching Science, Mathematics, and Modern Foreign Languages." In *California State Department of Education, Los Angeles*, Report NDEA-3B, 1963.

Anders, George. "That Useless Liberal Arts Degree Has Become Tech's Hottest Ticket," *Forbes* July 29, 2015.

Berk, Ronald A. "Teaching Strategies for the Net Generation: Transformative Dialogues." *Teaching & Learning Journal* 3 (2009). http://www.ronberk.com/articles/2009_strategies.pdf.

Bohn, Katie. "Blogging in the Classroom Can Help Both Students and Educators." *Penn State News*, September 16, 2016. https://news.psu.edu/story/426340/2016/09/16/research/blogging-classroom-can-help-both-students-and-educators.

Brooks, Christopher. "2015 Study of Faculty and Information Technology Report." Educause Center for Analysis and Research. February 16, 2016. https://library.educause.edu/resources/2015/11/2015-study-of-faculty-and-information-technology-report.

Christie, Alex. "Pedagogy Toolkit." http://pedagogy-toolkit.org/documentation/documentation.html.

Cuban, Larry. *Teachers and Machines: The Classroom Use of Technology since 1920*. New York: Teachers College Press, 1986.

"Definition Massive Open Online Courses." https://www.openuped.eu/images/docs/Definition_Massive_Open_Online_Courses.pdf.

Dunn, Joseph. "Reviving Liberal Education: A New Age Needs the Old Traditions." *America: The Jesuit Review*. (Blog) October 3, 2016. https://www.americamagazine.org/issue/reviving-liberal-education.

Finn, Edward W. III. "Technology and the Liberal Arts: Expanding the Dialogue." Teaching and Learning. August 9, 2016. https://evolllution.com/programming/teaching-and-learning/technology-and-the-liberal-arts-expanding-the-dialogue.

Firmin, Michael W., and Deanna J. Genesi. "History and Implementation of Classroom Technology." *Procedia–Social and Behavioral Sciences* 93 (October 2013): 1603–17. https://doi.org/10.1016/j.sbspro.2013.10.089.

Fitzpatrick, Michael. "Classroom Lectures Go Digital." *New York Times*, June 24, 2012.
Giuliano, Christopher A., C. A. Moser, and Lynette R. Moser. "Evaluation of a Flipped Drug Literature Evaluation Course." *American Journal of Pharmaceutical Education* 80 (May 25, 2016).
Goodwyn, Bill. "Technology Doesn't Teach, Teachers Teach." *Huffington Post*. (Blog) November 6, 2012. http://www.huffingtonpost.com/bill-goodwyn/technology-in-the-classroom_b_1857369.html.
Graham, Edward, and Tim Walker. "What Flipped Classrooms Can (and Can't) Do for Education." *NEA Today*. March 29, 2013. http://neatoday.org/2013/03/29/what-flipped-classrooms-can-and-cant-do-for-education/.
Hamilton, Charlotte. "Houston Community College: Embedding Digital Storytelling across the Higher Education Curriculum." https://www.storycenter.org/case-studies/hcc.
Handayani, Fitri. "Instagram as a Teaching Tool? Really." *Proceedings of the Fourth International Seminar on English Language* (2016).
Jones, Del. "Offbeat Majors Help CEOs Think outside the Box." *USA Today* July 24, 2001.
Jones, Marshall G. "A Brief and Sketchy History of Technology in the Classroom." *Online Learning Tools* (Blog), (2013), http://oertools.weebly.com/blog/a-brief-and-sketchy-history-of-technology-in-the-classroom.
Judge, Sharon, Kathleen Puckett, and Burcu Cabuk. "Digital Equity: New Findings from the Early Childhood Longitudinal Study." *Journal of Research on Technology in Education* 36 (2007): 383–96, doi: 10.1080/15391523.2004.10782421.
Kanter, Martha J. "The Relevance of Liberal Arts to a Prosperous Democracy." Remarks at the Annapolis Group Conference. Department of Education. June 22, 2010. https://www.ed.gov/news/speeches/relevance-liberal-arts-prosperous-democracy-under-secretary-martha-j-kanter%E2%80%99s-remarks-annapolis-group-conference.
Kirst, Michael. "Instagram as an Educational Tool for College Students" March 12, 2016. http://collegepuzzle.stanford.edu/?p=5057.
Lang, Eugene. "Distinctively American: The Liberal Arts College." Academy of Arts and Sciences. http://www.projectpericles.org/projectpericles/about/history/attachment.pdf.
Lankshear, Colin, and Michele Knobel. "New Literacies: Everyday Practices and Classroom Learning." *Open, New Literacies: Everyday Practices and Classroom Learning*, 2nd ed. Maidenhead, UK: Open University Press, 2006.
Levy, Leah Anne. "Why Digital Literacy Is Important for Teachers." USC Rossier Online. July 25, 2018. https://rossieronline.usc.edu/blog/teacher-digital-literacy/.
Ludy, T. Benjamin Jr. "Psychology and the New Education: A History of Teaching Machines." *American Psychologist* 42 (1988): 703–12. http://aubreydaniels.com/institute/sites/aubreydaniels.com.institute/files/History%20of%20teaching%20machines.pdf.
Malcolm, Nancy. "Analyzing the News: Teaching Critical Thinking Skills in a Writing Intensive Social Problems Course." *Teaching Sociology* 34, no. 2 (April 2006): 143–49.
McConaughy, James L. "Is the Liberal-Arts College Doomed?" *Journal of Higher Education* 9 (1938): 59–67, http://www.jstor.org/stable/1974088?seq=1#page_scan_tab_contents.
McKnight, Katherine. "Top 12 Ways Technology Changed Learning." Teaching Hub. http://www.teachhub.com/how-technology-changed-learning.
Oliver, Kendra. "Teaching with Blogs." Vanderbilt University Center for Teaching. 2016. https://cft.vanderbilt.edu/wp-content/uploads/sites/59/Oliver_Blog-Guide_2016.pdf.

Osika, Elizabeth Reed, Rochelle Y. Johnson, and Rosemary Buteau. "Factors Influencing Faculty Use of Technology in Online Instruction." *Online Journal of Distance Learning Administration* 12 (2009).

Ottenhoff, John. "Center of Inquiry Technology Consultations." Center of Inquiry, Wabash University. http://www.liberalarts.wabash.edu/technology_liberal_arts/.

Ottenhoff, John, and Charles Blaich. "Technology and Liberal Arts Education/" Center of Inquiry, Wabash University. http://www.liberalarts.wabash.edu/technology-and-the-liberal-art/.

Pace University. "Digital Toolkit." https://www.pace.edu/its/teaching-and-learning/digital-toolkit.

"'Reclaiming the Value of the Liberal Arts for the 21st Century': Strategies for Integrating Career Development with Traditional Arts and Sciences Curricula." *EAB* (2016), https://www.cwu.edu/trustees/sites/cts.cwu.edu.trustees/files/Reclaiming%20the%20Value%20of%20the%20Liberal%20Arts%20for%20the%2021st%20Century_EAB_2016.pdf.

Reid, Pat. "Categories for Barriers to Adoption of Instructional Technologies." *Education and Information Technologies* 2 (June 2014): 383–407. https://link.springer.com/article/10.1007%2Fs10639-012-9222-z.

Robin, Bernard R. "The Power of Digital Storytelling to Support Teaching and Learning." *Digital Education Review*, December 2016. https://files.eric.ed.gov/fulltext/EJ1125504.pdf.

Rockmore, Dan. "The Case for Banning Laptops in the Classroom." *New Yorker*, June 6, 2014. http://www.newyorker.com/tech/elements/the-case-for-banning-laptops-in-the-classroom.

Scholz, Claudia W. "MOOCs and the Liberal Arts College." *MERLOT: Journal of Online Learning and Teaching* 9, no. 2 (2013). http://jolt.merlot.org/vol9no2/scholz_0613.htm.

Shelton, Kaye, and Karen Pederson. *Handbook of Research on Building, Growing, and Sustaining Quality E-Learning*. Hershey, PA: Information Science Reference, 2017.

Smith, Frederick James. "The Evolution of the Motion Picture: VI—Looking into the Future with Thomas A. Edison: An Exclusive Interview with the Master Inventor, the Sixth of a Series of Articles on the Motion Picture." *New York Dramatic Mirror*, July 9, 1913, pp. 24, 42. Thomas A. Edison Papers, Rutgers School of Arts and Sciences (1913). http://edison.rutgers.edu/NamesSearch/GlocDocuments.php?glocNum=SC13&glocOrder=6333&GlocFileName=sn13&start_offset=0&.

Speed, Edward. "A CEO's Advice to a Millennial: A Liberal Arts Degree Matters." *Rivard Report*, February 8, 2016. https://therivardreport.com/a-CEO-responds-to-a-millennial/.

Stolzfus, Matthew, and Caroline Miller. "Setting Up Students for Success in the Flipped Classroom," *Pearson Higher Education*, August 24, 2016.

Straumsheim, Carl. "Still in Favor of the Flip." *Inside Higher Education*, September 9, 2013. https://www.insidehighered.com/news/2013/10/30/despite-new-studies-flipping-classroom-still-enjoys-widespread-support.

Trudeau, Daniel, Katie Pratt, and Brad Belbas. "Digital Storytelling and the Liberal Arts." Associated Colleges of the Midwest. February 6, 2016. http://www.acm.edu/professional_development/project/27/digital-storytelling-and-the-liberal-arts.

Vaughn, Pamela. "17 Google Marketing Tools You Should Be Utilizing." Blog Hub Spot. https://blog.hubspot.com/marketing/google-business-tools-for-marketers.

CHAPTER 3

Teaching Art History to STEM

YUMI PARK HUNTINGTON

A decade ago, using Blackboard and PowerPoint in the classroom was considered innovative. Since then educational technology has grown to include graphic software, social media, blogs, and other tools designed for the classroom, such as interactive word clouds and real-time question-and-answer. It has even become possible to talk to an artificial intelligence machine in one's living room and order household items. In only a decade, the technology in human society has developed beyond our imagination, moving forward faster than educators can adapt.

To accommodate to these dramatic technical developments in society, educators must conceive what society needs from them and adjust their teaching methods to support students who are engaging new technologies. At the same time, the traditional approaches that art historians have employed since the sixteenth-century work of Giorgio Vasari cannot be neglected.[1] These are the bedrock of art historical pedagogy and theoretical engagement, providing a foundation for different ways of thinking that can complement contemporary technological approaches. Given the possibility of revolutionizing existing curriculum while balancing with traditional pedagogy, art historians confront a variety of opportunities to enhance their teaching with technology, even as questions arise concerning how best to do so.

Even in the face of these exciting new opportunities, contemporary society has challenged scholars of the humanities to justify the need for any education in the liberal arts at all. Graduates in humanities fields do not earn the highest salaries, and humanities departments typically bring less revenue to universities than programs in science, technology, engineering, and mathematics (STEM). As a result, the enrollment of students in the humanities is shrinking compared to engineering, science, and technology departments.[2] Recent educational agendas and administrative policies have promoted training in STEM fields more than ever.

Despite such implicit claims to the contrary, scholars of the liberal arts have a great deal to offer students of STEM fields. Babette Alina, director of policy for the Rhode Island School of Design, once commented, "How do you solve these problems we are going to have in the future like clean water and climate change? It requires a lot of imagination and creative thinking to deal with these global challenges."[3] Because educators have recognized the importance of visual literacy for STEM, a new slogan, "STEM to STEAM" (the "A" standing for "Arts"), has been popularly adopted into various university curricula.

This movement includes both art historians and art educators across the country who have organized various affiliated groups and initiatives. One, a group called Art Historians Interested in Pedagogy and Technology, has offered many conference sessions at the College Art Association (CAA) conference and the Southeastern College Art Conference (SECAC). In February 2017, CAA offered a special session called "STEM to STEAM with Art History," which shared information about various pilot programs in universities and university museums to show how art history pedagogy can be integrated with STEM methods and goals.[4]

These attempts are proactive and stimulating but mainly focus on the important role of art history to STEM fields. It is crucial to emphasize that art history and other humanities disciplines increase empathy and teach ethical and moral issues, but if the humanities, including art history, focus only on emotional intelligence and empathy, that limitation reveals a vulnerable tipping point. In fact, such efforts are not just an attempt to expand interest and emphasize empathy beyond traditional STEM fields but offer a fundamental reshaping of the way scientists and engineers are trained. This chapter introduces the technical teaching skills for STEM students who can learn about acute analytical thinking through art history classes. Additional curriculum pilot programs aimed at stimulating creativity and emphasizing ethical issues associated with traditional scientific research are possible. Through innovations in pedagogy and new approaches to the liberal arts in the modern educational environment, educators in the humanities can not only maintain but increase their importance across a board range of fields. By introducing a new teaching method for art history suitable for STEM students, I am also answering the critical question of why art history, as a discipline, needs to be taught to STEM students. The visual literacy and analytical skills obtained through art history pedagogy can greatly enhance STEM research in the future.

Many scholars have acknowledged the relationship between science and art. Scientists Robert and Michèle Root-Bernstein believe scientists need intuitive insight. Some scientists have discussed that feelings and mental images are required and crucial. Albert Einstein suggested "a certain connection" between "the physical entities, which seem to serve as elements in thought" and "relevant logical concepts."[5] In other words, mental images related to intuitive insights also connect to logical thinking. The proper combination of logic and feeling can stimulate better scientific theory.

Like scientists, art historians prove their theories through both intuition and logical argument, especially emphasizing formal visual analyses and the contextualization of objects into religious, social, and political systems. The art historian Anne D'Alleva describes the similarities and differences of STEM and art history in terms of academic discipline. "Theory in art history works ... like true experimental science. Scientists have working hypotheses, or theorems, and they engage in experiments to see if those hypotheses are true. Often, that process of experimentation leads to a revision of the hypotheses and further experimentation." According to D'Alleva, "In art history, theory helps you frame better questions about the artworks or cultural practices you're studying, and then the process of exploring the answers to those questions helps you develop a more productive theoretical framework, one that generates further questions."[6] Of course, such a comparison by an art historian could be biased in favor of art history without acknowledging the full complexity of scientific inquiry.

Still, D'Alleva's analysis reveals an important underlying difference between science and art history. While scientists are trained to test the facts of theorem, art historians must observe broad-ranging aspects of society, religion, and culture to develop a complex theoretical framework, reflecting the logic of multiplicities.[7] While D'Alleva argues that the goal of both disciplines is the same, namely, to prove theories, their approaches to theory are quite different. If these two approaches could be synthesized and students trained in them simultaneously, it might be possible to have innovative theories in both fields, perhaps even helping to solve some of the major issues confronting our society.

Visual literacy and analysis, paramount to both art history and science, are among the core elements that can help us synthesize these disparate disciplines. Indeed, when scientists observe specific phenomena, the skills of an art historian can lead to important discoveries. Albert Szent-Györgyi discovered ascorbic acid vitamin C by analyzing the colors of fruit. Szent-Györgyi later received the Nobel Prize and said, "I suppose I was led by my fascination by colors. I still like color." By questioning changes of color in fruit over time, Szent-Györgyi realized that the fruit was becoming damaged due to polyphenol compounds interacting with oxygen to create a brown or black color. By observing a group of fruit that did not change color even after becoming damaged in this way, he discovered vitamin C, a sugar-like compound.[8] As we all know today, vitamin C enhances many aspects of human health, and many people in the contemporary era are taking it as a part of their supplementary support in order to fight against nutrient deficiencies and inflammation as well as strengthen the immune system. Szent-Györgyi's interest in visual analysis led from observation to theory, helping him discover a new chemical component in nature. This is not just an example of finding facts about the natural world but of how to think in terms of visual analysis and experimental design.

Indeed, other scientists have lauded artistic training for providing skills essential to all aspects of scientific life. Robert Root-Bernstein, a MacArthur Fellowship recipient and professor of physiology, observed, "Many Nobel Prize winners... and members of the [Royal Society] and [National Academy of Sciences] have explicitly commented on how avocations develop useful skills: hand-eye coordination; knowledge of tools and processes; better visual imagination; improved ability to communicate using words, image, and models; the stage presence of the practiced performer; and a refined scientific aesthetic sensibility."[9] In other words, scientists who have learned about visual language and culture are better able to work creatively and productively through scientific and professional processes. It is therefore vital to expose STEM students to art history and the humanistic perspective, to teach them theoretical aspects of the logic of multiplicity and practical aspects of visual and analytical skills.

The movement to provide STEM students with such an education has grown substantially and even been included in commercial programs, such as the Art and Medicine program at the University of Texas at Dallas and the Arts in Medicine project by Columbia University Medical Center. Amy Herman, the developer of the program called The Art of Perception, has organized programs of study that allow people from various occupations to reconsider the performance of their own professional duties through the analysis of various art objects. Herman developed the program for medical students to improve their observation skills by examining artifacts at the Frick Collection. Later, she applied similar methods to enhance the visual analysis skills of law enforcement professionals across a wide range of agencies, including the New York Police Department, the Federal Bureau of Investigation, the Department of Justice, and the Secret Service. Her program succeeded and led to a partnership with the *New York Times*.[10] Herman's Art of Perception program shows the unlimited possibilities for adapting the teaching methods of art history to other academic and professional disciplines.

One way in which art historians can support the transition from STEM to STEAM is by targeting material to students of different backgrounds in need of varying skills of visual analysis and creativity. In executing these methods, it is always important to ask oneself practical questions geared to one's specific audience, such as: (1) How can we incorporate new technology into the classroom in an efficient way? (2) How can we keep up with rapidly changing educational technologies? (3) What is the role of these new tools in enhancing critical thinking and writing skills for STEM students? (4) What guidelines should the teacher place on the syllabus governing the use of technology in the classroom? (5) How can art historians assess whether these new pilot programs are actually working for STEM students? By answering these questions, art historians and art educators can create new courses and develop effective ways to teach analytical skills and enhance creative thinking for STEM students using the discipline of art history.

The new approach to art history pedagogy for STEM students proposed here emphasizes the students' ability to generate and pursue their own interests in the subject. This method allows teachers to target curricula to varied audiences, from general education students to specialists in STEM fields, opening up audiences beyond the typical liberal arts student. The method also provides a key way to engage STEM students with an interdisciplinary approach to visual analysis that can be important to their future careers. Other art educators can adapt these programs to teach STEM students in relevant and effective ways.

In many institutions of higher education, an art appreciation class forms part of the general education requirements for graduation. For this reason, STEM students often fill these courses designed for nonspecialists. The instructors, however, generally have backgrounds in fine arts or art history, creating an immediate disparity between the skills and expectations of the students and the instructor. Art appreciation teachers most often rely on the standard pedagogy for students of the fine arts or art history, because it is within that model that they themselves were trained. Faced with an audience of broader background and interest, some instructors may struggle to approach and teach STEM students, who in turn struggle to learn the skills of reading visual images based on complex culture, social, and religious contexts.

I argue, though, that art appreciation is the perfect way for STEM students to become engaged with a broad range of humanities subjects, including art history and much more, because of their relationships to STEM fields and broader humanistic inquiry. One main reason is that art appreciation focuses on visual language and design, which are as relevant when plotting a statistics chart or building a robot as when visiting an art museum. Furthermore, studying visual language can involve dealing with fashion, trends, and popular culture, compelling issues for young students. By redesigning the art appreciation curriculum, educators can enhance their ability to teach STEM students while impressing upon them the importance of developing visual literacy in contemporary society. Instead of teaching paintings, sculptures, and architectural buildings based on a textbook, an instructor can select specific artifacts that engage STEM disciplines and the broader humanities.

When I teach art appreciation, the first step is to do a student survey. Through this questionnaire, I inquire about each student's background, major, interests, expectations for the class lectures, and learning style, and even the ways they want to be assessed through exams. The options for assessment and teaching styles relate to the auditory, visual, and tactile learning styles. Of STEM major students, 90 percent prefer to have a visual format for their assessment and teaching methods.[11] As for many people, visual engagement is a primary way of thinking for STEM students because it relates to their own field. STEM textbooks use visual diagrams, charts, and models to help students understand complicated concepts and generate analysis. One can think of various images and charts used in the three core STEM majors of math, chemistry, and biology, including graphs of integral calculus and proofs of the Pythagorean theorem in math, molecular models and diagrams in chemistry, and the "tree of life," a visual genealogy diagram, in biology.

Obviously, visual literacy is relevant in STEM disciplines and well beyond the humanities. This means that students are required to interpret images within a particular context, recognize what they are seeing, and be able to articulate both context and content in oral and written explanations. For many, visual literacy requires the ability to produce visual diagrams and explanations of their own to communicate their research to others.

Based on these facts, I have developed a pilot project for teaching three specific majors within STEM: mathematics, chemistry, and biology. In teaching students from these fields, I emphasize how they can apply the visual literacy of their own subjects to learning about art and material culture. In particular, I match specific concepts of math, chemistry, and biology with artworks that express similar ideas either visually or conceptually. Because of their own discipline, they can more easily develop their visual skills by combining their own knowledge with art appreciation.

For mathematics, I use the concepts of integral calculus and the Pythagorean theorem. Both concepts are well explained through visual diagrams. Calculus is often used to calculate the area under a curve using integrals. Because it can be used to calculate the negative space in an area, it can be

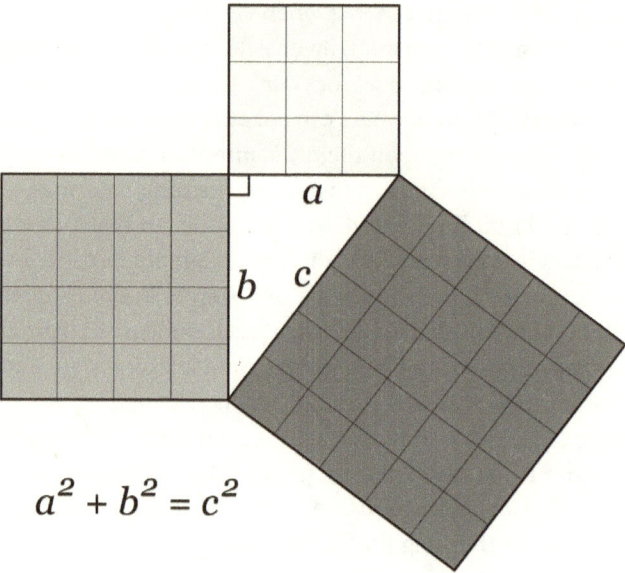

Figure 3.1. Pythagorean theorem.

applied to many other STEM fields, like engineering. Although explanation through words and equations is clear enough, the concept is even better understood through visual diagrams using lines, shapes, and colors. Pythagoras discovered the Pythagorean theorem, which explains the relationship among the three sides of a right triangle as an equation relating the length of sides a, b, and c.[12] In order to explain this concept more easily, most textbooks use diagrammatic images that correlate the lengths of sides a, b, and c, often in vivid primary colors (Figure 3.1). Furthermore, mathematical proofs of this theorem can be performed visually through the manipulation of such diagrams without reference to equations at all. The concept of the Pythagorean theorem is well conveyed through visual explanations.

These basic mathematical concepts are also expressed in various artworks, both functional and abstract. The Pythagorean theorem is seen in *The Red and Blue Chair* (Figure 3.2), a piece of furniture created by Gerrit Rietveld. I engage STEM students in discussions of the relationship between the Pythagorean theorem and *The Red and Blue Chair* through a several-stage process. First, I show the image of the Pythagorean theorem and illustrate how the concept is explained through visual language. Second, I show the picture of *The Red and Blue Chair* next to the previous image. With both images on the screen, I explain the background of this whimsical and vibrant furniture, emphasizing the role of Rietveld in the Bauhaus style. In

Figure 3.2. Gerrit Rietveld, *The Red and Blue Chair*, 1923, 85.1x 66 x 66 cm, Painted Beechwood, © 2019 Artists Rights Society (ARS), New York / c/o Pictoright Amsterdam.

particular, this furniture presents rectilinear volumes interacting as vertical and horizontal lines. For example, the volumes in the chair image appear in the primary colors of red, blue, and yellow, matching the visualization of the Pythagorean theorem.

Finally, I expand upon my explanation of the Bauhaus and emphasize how the movement attempted to unify the creative arts and practical concerns of manufacturing, bringing to the fore essential geometric issues like form, volume, and color. After some discussion, students are able to decode the visual language of this Bauhaus furniture in terms of creative expression and its relationship to mathematical and practical concepts. The relationship between the Bauhaus approach and the elegant mathematics of the Pythagorean theorem is an excellent way for students to understand not only this particular chair but the motivations of artistic movements more generally.

Once this basis in art history is established, we can make connections to other artists and movements with related ideas. For example, I connect Rietveld's use of primary colors on his furniture in 1923 with the De Stiji

Figure 3.3. Piet Mondrian, *Composition with Red, Blue, and Yellow*, 1930, Frame: 66 x 66 x 10 cm, Image: 45 x 45 cm, Oil on canvas, Kunsthaus Zürich, Donated by Alfred Roth, 1987 Kunsthaus Zürich.

movement led by the painter Piet Mondrian. Mondrian created rigid and simple structures colored with primary pigments. By creating the ideal structure and space on the two-dimensional canvases, he thought this perfect place that he created would replace the nature destroyed by humans and their technology.[13] His ideas of structuring and organizing nature are visualized in his painting *Composition with Red, Blue, and Yellow* (1930), which bears similarities to the structured visualizations of the Pythagorean theorem. It is possible to understand Mondrian's painting as an expression of dialectical relationships.

Mondrian's aim was to express the world through opposites, such as black and white pigments or vertical and horizontal lines. In the beginning of his painting career, Mondrian employed a naturalistic style to depict the ideal natural world that he visualized, but his later works consisted of lines, shapes, and colors that symbolized the ideal space, expressed in a geometric and simplistic way. The simple way of understanding the relationship among the three sides of a right triangle explained by Pythagoras correlates with Mondrian's later paintings. Through comparison between Mondrian's *Composition with Red, Blue, and Yellow* (1930) (Figure 3.3) and the Pythagorean

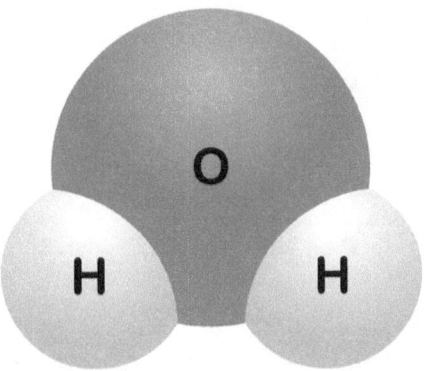

Figure 3.4. Water molecules.

theorem, STEM students are able to understand the visual image and the sophisticated language of geometry. The class discussion provides an opportunity to enhance visual analytical skills, especially for mathematically inclined students.

In an example from chemistry, I show artwork in relation to molecular models and equations. Chemical reactions convert reactants to products whose properties differ from those of the reactants. Scientists use equations and diagrams to represent the chemical parts and the process of reaction in a compact and easy-to-understand way. "A combination reaction," for example, "is one in which two or more substances (the reactants) are combined directly to form a single product." Sodium and chlorine combine to form sodium chloride (table salt), while water is the combination of hydrogen and oxygen (Figure 3.4). Many instructors in chemistry departments utilize the visualization of chemistry when they teach the concept of molecules and how an individual molecule moves and reacts in a specific environment. They use video or pictures to show movements of water molecules in three different environments: solid, fluid, and gas. By showing these pictures, instructors teach a different concept of kinetic and potential energy possessed in a water molecule.[14]

Such scientific visualizations are reflected in the shapes and composition of *Contact Lens* (2011) (Figure 3.5) by Haruka Kojin, a Japanese architect who uses geometric and organic elements simultaneously in his own artwork. In *Contact Lens* he employed multisized, flat, acrylic discs in a three-dimensional space, which changes our normal perception of the space. By integrating different types of flat and curved lenses of various sizes, the space is filled with reflected images through lights arranged around the space. A portion of the space is viewed through the acrylic discs, and the display is

Figure 3.5. Haruka Kojin, *Contact Lens*, 2011, Installation Art, the MOT Museum of Contemporary Art Tokyo © designboom.

flipped or distorted. Each portion of the images in the space become one large picture to represent the entire space, and these reflected images from a small individual flat disc eventually become a part of the space.

These ideas can be related to the processes of chemical reactions, such as the relationships of a part to the whole and the direction of the process from source to result. The main visual and theoretical points of Haruka Kojin's *Contact Lens* are easy for chemistry students to understand and allow them to decode the visual language of artwork. The visual connection between chemical reactions and *Contact Lens* is explored in the classroom following the same pedagogical sequence used in the math examples.

In the discipline of biology, the tree of life (Figure 3.6) is a visual diagram that shows the lineage of species and visually explains the relationships between natural living organisms, past and present. Charles Darwin's 1837 notebook (Figure 3.7) contains a version of the tree of life as part of his argument for the origin of species. The visual diagram is used among many biologists to understand topics like genealogy and paleontology, especially the relationships between seemingly disparate species. Many instructors in biology ask students to draw what they see in animal anatomies from microscopes. By training them to draw what they are seeing, students can better find and detail a change occurring in the natural world.[15]

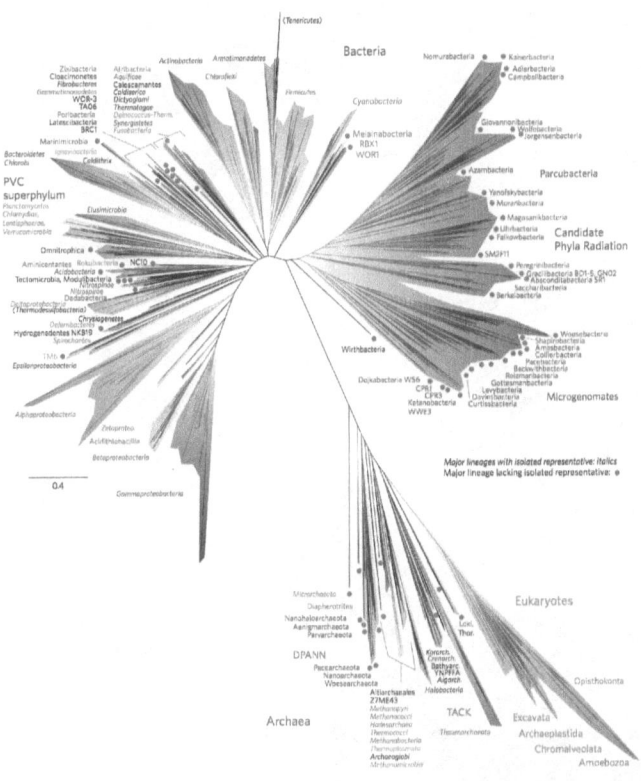

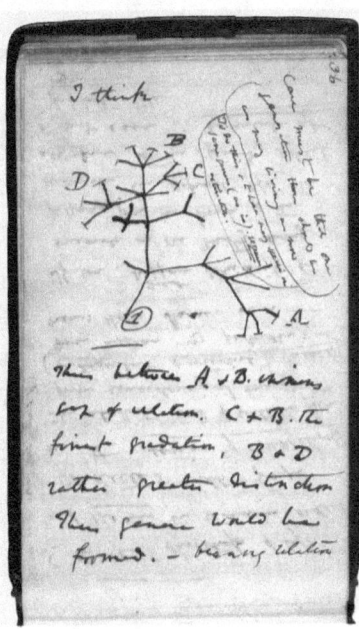

Top: **Figure 3.6.** *Tree of life*, 2016. From Hug Baker, Anantharaman, et al. "A new view of the tree of life," Nature Microbiology 1, 16048 (2016).

Bottom: **Figure 3.7.** Charles Darwin, *Tree of Life*, 1837, MS DAR, 121, p. 35 Reproduced by kind permission of the Syndics of Cambridge University Library.

Figure 3.8. Kate MacDowell, *The God of Change*, 2011, 30.48 x 26.67 x 5.08 cm hand-built porcelain
© Kate MacDowell.

This same concept of the relationship between species is well illustrated in porcelain sculptures called *The God of Change* (2011) and *Invasive Flora* (2009) by Kate MacDowell (Figures 3.8 and 3.9). In these sculptures MacDowell combines animal and human characteristics in detailed white porcelain. MacDowell sees the connection between human anatomy and the natural environment in both romantic and dynamic ways. In *The God of Changes* (2011), an eight-legged frog containing an open uterus and fetus connected with an umbilical cord might seem odd, but the idea of connections between nature and humanity is clear. This connection is also recognizable in the tree of life.

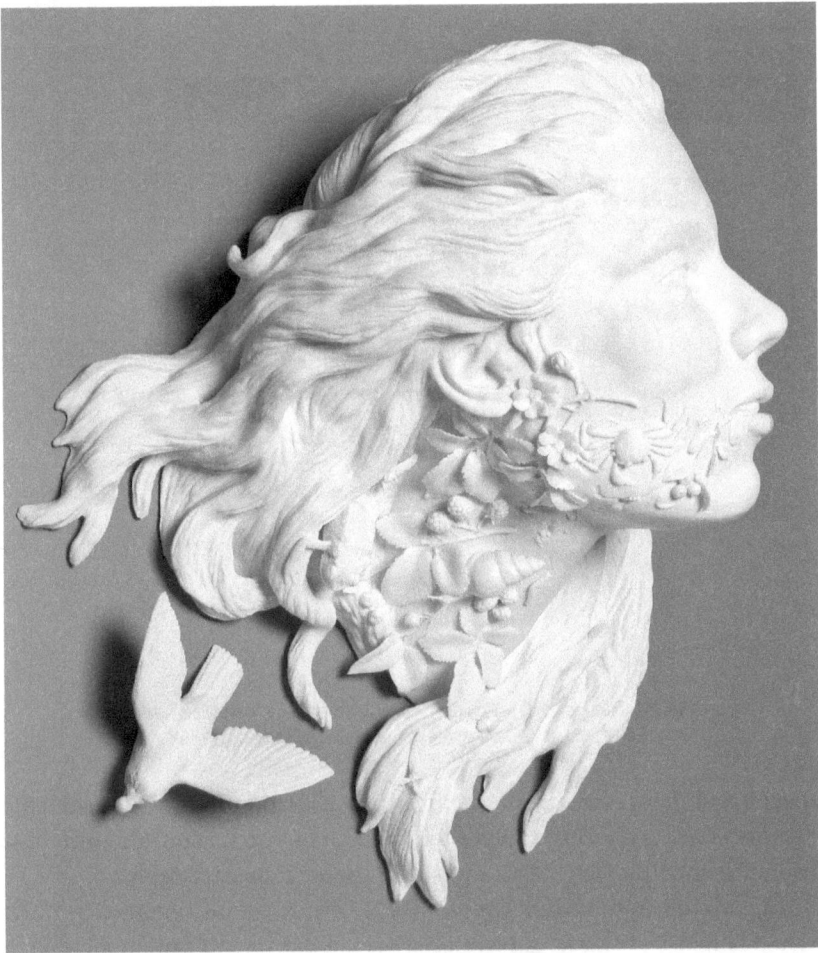

Figure 3.9. Kate MacDwell, *Invasive Flora*, 2009, 40.64 x 43.18 x 20.32 cm hand-built porcelain © Kate MacDowell.

In another figure, *Invasive Flora* (2009), the profile of a beautiful woman is gradually dominated by the natural world, again expressing a connection between nature and humanity. The gradual disappearance of the female face under a dominating, natural growth could be interpreted in various ways: one, that the human species is a part of the natural world, and another, that nature and humanity can be considered as one. MacDowell's ceramics are finely created and show the details of both nature and the human worlds; they display the relationships between organisms, living and extinct, like the tree of life. These interpretations relate to the dynamics of the tree of life diagram, which in a visual format articulates the relationships between

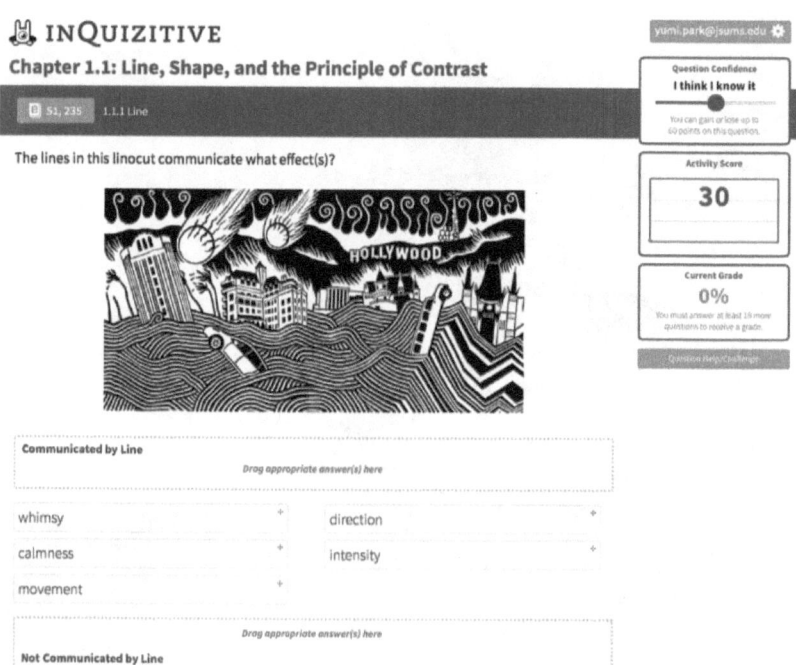

Figure 3.10. *InQuizitive Exercise*, image courtesy Stanley Donwood/ TAG Fine Arts, from *Gateways to Art: Understanding the Visual Arts*, 2nd ed., Thames and Hudson Inc., New York.

species and changes over time. Exploring such relationships, STEM students identify similar concepts conveyed through these two images and learn how two different visual languages can speak about similar concepts.

In addition to the connection of STEM fields with art history through visual language, the use of technology is a great way to bridge the divide between the humanities and the sciences. Art appreciation, especially, is often taught as an online class, providing an immediate and, indeed, required venue for technology use in pedagogy. For example, the publisher Thames & Hudson developed a program called "InQuizitive Exercise" (Figure 3.10), which provides several interactive ways to understand a single image, including textual explanations, listings of art historical vocabulary, and descriptions of related artistic movements.

These types of exercises correspond to typical STEM pedagogy. The practice of analyzing artifacts and understanding visual cognition leads to greater awareness of multiple dimensions of scientific phenomena and to quicker, more creative analysis. In addition, activities like the "InQuizitive Exercise" force students to develop curiosity about subjects and search for answers to their own questions. Through these exercises, as well as in-class discussion and evaluation, students learn better how to express their own ideas, arguments, and critical thinking.

Using technology in the classroom creates additional links between STEM and art history. Art history, in particular, as the study of visual and material objects in relation to history and culture, has had to adapt to new techniques of art production and dissemination, including technologies of pedagogy. Notable recent innovations include projects such as ARTstor, Neatline, and Omeka, as well as pedagogical tools such as the flipped classroom and social media.[16] Although art historians have been on the forefront of integrating the changing digital society into both their scholarship and teaching, STEM students and faculty sometimes overlook these connections and remain unaware of points of contact between their disciplines and others. In fact, art history offers intensive training for students to increase their analytical skills and critical thinking in our modern, image-driven world.

Various major institutes continue to build digital platforms for image-based classes. The University of Virginia launched Neatline, an add-on for the George Mason University project Omeka. Neatline is a tool not only for exploring artwork but for creating timelines and other visualizations used to analyze numerical data and visual materials. Since these resources are provided as open source, other institutions are welcome to participate. Through Omeka, George Mason University has collaborated with Fordham and New York universities to create digital art history and history classes. Because these platforms are designed to work with image-focused assignments, many art history instructors have developed digitally formatted art history classes. Within these, students can create their own blog-style assignments and receive piggyback comments from instructors and peers. Such digital class formats will strengthen connections between the STEM and art history disciplines.

The exercises in this chapter are only a few among many possibilities. Regardless of the particular methods, we must initiate the movement from STEM to STEAM, putting the arts and visual culture in dialogue with the sciences. Since various STEM disciplines have acknowledged the importance of visual proficiency through art historical analysis, and since many scientists have employed visual skills with distinguished results, it should not be difficult to find more ways to promote the arts within the sciences. Much of science is based on the skills of observing, recognizing patterns, imagining, and synthesizing, all of which are key educational components in art history classes.

To evaluate the results of my proposed program of study, it will be important in the future to track learning outcomes and provide statistical analyses.

With only one semester of experience, I cannot yet provide wide-ranging evaluations of whether these techniques help STEM students enhance their performance in their own fields after they have been trained under these specific pilot programs. Herman, the developer of the "Art of Perception," has not provided any statistical results from participants who attended her programs. Results from other groups, such as medical students, FBI agents, and police officers, will also be crucial. After collecting and analyzing data on learning outcomes from a broad range of students engaging in art history, teachers can improve their techniques for changing STEM to STEAM in a more productive way. Furthermore, the questionnaires evaluated by STEM students will be helpful for enhancing the structure of these pilot programs. With these more effective systems, STEM students will develop strong creative thinking and find new ways to see the world in multidimensional thought processes. Art history pedagogy could be made much more effective by utilizing newly developed online programs and social media activities. The field of art history does not simply teach empathy or appreciation of arts and the humanities but improves specific analytic skills to help STEM students find solutions to the problems of the world.

Notes

1. Vasari's *The Lives of the Most Excellent Painters, Sculptors, and Architects*, written in 1550, introduces well-known Renaissance period artists in a historical aspect. This publication is often considered the first work of true art history.

2. This result has become a serious issue in the humanities, as Colleen Flaherty examines in "Liberal Arts College Students Are Getting Less Artsy," *Inside Higher Ed*, February 2, 2017.

3. Jackson Slotkin, "A Hero for the Arts and Sciences: Upcoming Marvel Covers Promote STEAM Fields," *NPR*, August 28, 2016.

4. The information was gained by attending the Southeastern College Art Conference at Roanoke in 2016 and the College Art Association Conference at New York City in 2017.

5. Robert and Michèle Root-Bernstein mentioned many different examples of successful scientists who utilized analytical skills to find the new theories and discoveries, in *Sparks of Genius: The Thirteen Thinking Tools of the World's Most Creative People* (New York: Houghton Mifflin, 1999); Kiley, John F. *Einstein and Aquinas: A Rapprochement* (The Hague: Martinus Nijhoff, 1969), 22.

6. Anne D'Alleva, *Methods and Theories of Art History* (Laurence King, 2005), 12.

7. D'Alleva, *Methods and Theories of Art History*, 11.

8. This particular knowledge has been provided in Root-Bernstein and Root-Bernstein, *Sparks of Genius*, 41.

9. Robert Root-Bernstein et al., "Arts Foster Scientific Success: Avocations of Nobel, National Academy, Royal Society, and Sigma Xi Members," *Journal of Psychology of Science and Technology* 1, no. 2 (2008): 57–58.

10. "Art and Medicine." Edith O'Donnell Institute of Art History, University of Texas, https://www.utdallas.edu/arthistory/medicine/; Arts in Medicine Studio, Columbia University, Department of Medical Humanities and Ethics, https://www.mhe.cuimc.columbia.edu/our-divisions/division-narrative-medicine/clinical-mission/arts-medicine-studio. Herman's various projects are documented in her most recent publication, Amy E. Herman, *Visual Intelligence: Sharpen Your Perception, Change Your Life* (Boston: Eamon Dolan/Houghton Mifflin Harcourt, 2016).

11. These statistical data have been obtained throughout the three years of surveys in art appreciation classes at Jackson State University, from spring 2015 to spring 2017. Fifty-six out of seventy-eight enrolled students participated in the survey. Out of these, fifty-one expressed a desire to study the subject based on a visual approach rather than textual or tactile approaches. They preferred to watch videos and see images rather than read a text.

12. The basic concept of integral calculus is based on John R. Fanchi, *Math Refresher for Scientists and Engineers* (Hoboken: Wiley-IEEE Press, 2006), 107; and Khan Academy, https://www.khanacademy.org/math/calculus-home/integration-calc. The basic concept of the Pythagorean theorem is based on Allen R. Angel and Stuart R. Porter, *A Survey of Mathematics: With Applications* (Reading: Addison-Wesley, 1985), 177.

13. Debora J. Dewitte, Ralph M. Larmann, and M. Kathryn Shields, *Gateways to Art: Understanding the Visual Arts* (New York: Thames and Hudson, 2015), 537.

14. "Chemical Equations," Chemistry Explained, http://www.chemistryexplained.com/Di-Fa/Equations-Chemical.html. In a telephone conversation with the author on February 23, 2017, Ken S. Lee, professor of chemistry at Jackson State University, mentioned how instructors in the Chemistry Department generally utilize the visual image to provide the basic concept of molecules and their movements in elements.

15. Basic knowledge about the tree of life here is based on Laura A. Hug et al., "A New View of the Tree of Life," *Nature Microbiology* 11 (May 2016), 1. In a personal conversation with the author on October 6, 2017, Gloria Miller, visiting assistant professor of biology at Jackson State University, shared the methodologies of teaching her students in order to increase analytical skills.

16. These websites and associated information can be found at http://artstor.org, http://neatline.org, and http://omeka.org.

Bibliography

Angel, Allen R., and Stuart R. Porter. *A Survey of Mathematics: With Applications*. Reading: Addison-Wesley, 1985.

"Art and Medicine." Edith O'Donnell Institute of Art History, University of Texas, https://www.utdallas.edu/arthistory/medicine/; Arts in Medicine Studio, Columbia University, Department of Medical Humanities and Ethics, https://www.mhe.cuimc.columbia.edu/our-divisions/division-narrative-medicine/clinical-mission/arts-medicine-studio.

"Chemical Equations." Chemistry Explained. http://www.chemistryexplained.com/Di-Fa/Equations-Chemical.html.

D'Alleva, Anne. *Methods and Theories of Art History*. London: Laurence King, 2005.

Dewitte, Debora J., Ralph M. Larmann, and M. Kathryn Shields. *Gateways to Art: Understanding the Visual Arts*. New York: Thames and Hudson, 2015.

Ede, Siân. *Art & Science*. London: L. B. Tauris, 2005.

Fanchi, John R. *Math Refresher for Scientists and Engineers*. Hoboken: Wiley-IEEE Press, 2006.

Flaherty, Colleen. "Liberal Arts College Students Are Getting Less Artsy." *Inside Higher Ed*, February 2, 2017.

Herman, Amy. *Visual Intelligence: Sharpen Your Perception, Change Your Life*. New York: Eamon Dolan/Houghton Mifflin Harcourt, 2016.

Hug, Laura A., Brett J. Baker, Karthik Anantharaman, Christopher T. Brown, Alexander J. Probst, Cindy J. Castelle, Cristina N. Butterfield, Alex W. Hernsdorf, Yuki Amano, Kotaro Ise, Yohey Suzuki, Natasha Dudek, David A. Relman, Kari M. Finstad, Ronald Amundson, Brian C. Thomas, and Jillian F. Banfield. "A New View of the Tree of Life." *Nature Microbiology* 1 (May 2016): 1–6.

Khan Academy. https://www.khanacademy.org/math/calculus-home/integration-calc.

Kiley, John F. *Einstein and Aquinas: A Rapprochement*. The Hague: Martinus Nijhoff, 1969.

Root-Bernstein, Robert, Lindsay Allen, Leighanna Beach, Ragini Bhadula, Justin Fast, Chelsea Hosey, Benjamin Kremkow, Jacqueline Lapp, Kaitlin Lonc, Kendell Pawelec, Abigail Podufaly, Caitlin Russ, Laurie Tennant, Eric Vrtis, and Stacey Weinlander. "Arts Foster Scientific Success: Avocations of Nobel, National Academy, Royal Society, and Sigma Xi Members." *Journal of Psychology of Science and Technology* 1, no. 2 (2008): 51–63.

Root-Bernstein, Robert, and Michèle Root-Bernstein. *Sparks of Genius: The 13 Thinking Tools of the World's Most Creative People*. New York: Houghton Mifflin, 1999.

Slotkin, Jackson. "A Hero for the Arts and Sciences: Upcoming Marvel Covers Promote STEAM Fields." *NPR*, August 28, 2016.

Vasari, Giorgio. *The Lives of the Most Excellent Painters, Sculptors, and Architects*. Translated by Caston du C. de Vere. Edited with an introduction and notes by Philip Jacks. New York: Modern Library Paperback Edition, 2006.

THE ARTS
AND THE
LIBERAL ARTS

CHAPTER 4

An Interdisciplinary Approach to Cultivating Visual Literacy

SARAH ARCHINO

Seeing appears to be a transparent and automatic process. Unlike the prerequisite steps of learning an alphabet or grammar, necessary for textual literacy, the physical and unconscious nature of sight leads many to assume a natural level of visual literacy exists and that we and our students are capable, efficient, and critical observers and analysts. Although research has demonstrated that "looking is a practice much like speaking, writing, or signing, it requires guided, intentional, and repeated practice," for many university students, and their faculty, the assumptions of visual literacy as a natural or innate skill persist.[1] Art history is in a unique position to challenge this erroneous reasoning and contribute this necessary training to our liberal arts curricula.

As outlined in a 2004 conference white paper, the term "visual literacy" encompasses "understanding how people perceive objects, interpret what they see, and what they learn from them."[2] To this I would add that the demonstration of visual literacy introduces another metric, that of efficient and effective communication. The nature of this skill set is interdisciplinary, but visual literacy has been confined to humanities and arts departments and largely sequestered in graduate-level programs despite the potential benefits to an undergraduate audience across disciplines. Our current omission of visual literacy from the core requirements of the standard liberal arts degree can be addressed through the closer integration of art history into the campus-wide or general education curriculum.

Beyond the discipline's emphasis on the structure and conveyance of meaning through observation and inference, art history offers a prolonged and rigorous training in close looking. An image can serve as a nexus for the development of critical thinking: exposure to visual skills training increases the ability to differentiate between objective and subjective conclusions and to communicate through oral and written language. Abigail Housen, researcher on aesthetic education and cofounder of Visual Thinking Strategies, has explained, "Art affords an ideal environment for such teaching and learning. It provides an object of collective attention—something concrete for a classroom to observe and experience, provoking thoughts and feelings while at the same time generating simultaneous and distinctive meanings."[3]

The following essay builds a rationale for creating art history courses focused on skill sets of visual literacy and proposes some models for how such courses could move beyond discipline-specific instruction to impact learning across departments. Trained practice in close looking and visual literacy offers multiple benefits, including the focused development of critical thinking, interpretive, communicative, and creative skills most central to the liberal arts ideal. With this in mind, I piloted an undergraduate course during Furman University's May 2017 term. "Art and the Science of Observation" took ten students to New York City, where we spent three weeks in a range of museum settings, conducting exercises targeting these precise skill sets. Most had no background in art or art history.

This interdisciplinary collaboration is based on a trend in medical school curricula; since the first program of this type debuted in 1998–1999, over seventy clinical programs have partnered with art institutions to provide visual analysis training with the aim of improving diagnostic skills.[4] This has been the subject of scholarship and discussion in the medical school community, culminating in a June 2016 symposium at the Museum of Modern Art and the publication of a resource database for medical school programs.[5] Yet, despite the centrality of the widely documented outcomes among these models to our professed educational goals, undergraduate institutions have not adopted any similarly focused protocol for promoting visual literacy.

Part of the resistance to this proposed curriculum model is that, unlike other forms, visual literacy is often marginalized as an intuitive skill set. This assumption comes at a cost to our students, who are unprepared to read visual sources with sophistication and fluency. Despite a continual bombardment with images, our students lack the interrogative skills to approach these sources. They might be able to glean some content, but the untrained viewer is often unable to articulate the reasons for their "gut" reaction or to explain their interpretation. We would not accept this level of fluency with a text source, and it should be unacceptable to allow students to rest at this low level of proficiency with visual sources.

We live in an image-centric culture, a shift away from text, which W. J. T. Mitchell has categorized as the "pictorial turn"; scholarship has reinforced this theory, noting that, as the means of communication change, particularly in moving to the digital, "so much of our media and everyday space is increasingly dominated by visual images."[6] Still, there remain certain biases against the image. We assume serious texts are those without accompanying pictures, or we infer that images and other data visualizations explain complicated arguments because they bridge a gap between the reader and difficult information through a more intuitive mode of nonverbal communication. As one study lamented, "The prevailing assumption is that language is paradigmatic for meaning and that images simply entertain or illustrate, proving a respite from serious academic work. Further, the picture bears the stigma of being an easy read, useful only in scaffolding early literacy development, but not valuable as a tool for adolescent and adult learning."[7] Indeed, once children use pictures as a stage of preliterary development, they are no longer encouraged to consider pictorial representation as a component of literacy.

In 1994 Mitchell predicted that "the problem of the twenty-first century is the problem of the image."[8] We have an imperative to teach our students how to best navigate this visual space and debunk their assumptions that an intuitive understanding of an image is sufficient. If we are going to do justice to this changing terrain, it is important to acknowledge the need to provide opportunities and guidance for students in this mode of literacy. The cognitive gaps between the visual and the textual make this translation between types of literacy a challenge for students—precisely the reason that they should be expected to cultivate this as a specific skill. We must also recognize that visual images are not merely pictures but documents with relational meanings dependent on the circumstances of their viewer. By training students to build flexibility and fluency in responding to art, we can prepare them for the contemporary task of navigating their changing visual world.

Indeed, the costs of ignoring visual literacy are greater than the inability to read an image for information; in dealing with art, students learn more than how to decode images. They are faced with a primary source document that forces them to grapple with uncertain, polysemic layers of meaning. They are required to analyze and draw conclusions from a source providing multiple channels of information. The work of art contains both factual data that can be gathered for analysis and artistic or interpretive interventions that build to a statement or inferred conclusion. As students practice the differentiation between what can be found within the work of art and what is a result of their interpretation or bias, they rehearse the distinction between observation and inference, or the objective and subjective.[9]

Given the importance of teaching medical students to be mindful observers of their patients and to differentiate between observation and what may be a premature or unconsciously inferred diagnosis, the use of art has become common in clinical training. Despite the pressures of discipline-specific instruction during medical school training, the demonstrable and significant benefits of visual analysis training through art have earned a place in the curriculum. Take, for example, the results from a program where third-year medical students from Robert Wood Johnson Medical School in New Brunswick, New Jersey, participated in one three-hour exercise, centered on large-group discussion of eight artworks. As is common among many medical school programs, the sessions were conducted according to the Visual Thinking Strategies (VTS) method.[10] This approach guides group discussion through a series of three simple questions: "What is going on in this picture? What do you see that makes you say that? What more can we find?" A trained facilitator is charged with neutrally paraphrasing student comments, drawing attention to the visual components they address, and linking student comments to move toward consensus or to highlight contradictions. Critical to this model is the neutrality of the facilitator, who does not seek to correct misinterpretations or to provide additional information. In placing the students in control of the conversation, the group is motivated to participate, resulting in a higher level of engagement with the image and with other student comments.

After this workshop, the medical students were evaluated, and their written responses to a series of patient photographs were compared to a pretest of similar images.[11] In the posttests, their use of subjective language, including vague terms such as "normal" or "healthy" decreased by 65 percent, replaced by more concrete language based in factual or objective terminology. Students were also more reliant on visual analogies to help explain their observations, an increase of 80 percent over pretest responses.

At the same time, students demonstrated greater gains in observational skills and concrete, objective language. Their posttest responses allowed for more analysis and interpretation, avoiding common flaws of premature diagnosis or error. For example, the use of speculative language, wording that frames an observation as one possibility among many and allows for multiple interpretations of visual data, increased by 62 percent in posttest responses. Instead of focusing on what details students believed to be most relevant to the perceived pressing medical issue, which was common in the pretest responses, students framed their posttest evaluations on a broad scope of observations (a 40 percent increase), including notes about "the patient's surroundings, the patient's perspective, or emotional state." In terms of teaching methods of inquiry, research, analysis, and flexibility to undergraduates, these results suggest significant improvements in sophisticated reflection and critical thinking could be achieved.

It is necessary to overcome a certain amount of skepticism, from both students and faculty, about the relevance of art history to their own fields. We are all under pressure to cover a critical mass of discipline-specific material and to address critical thinking and writing skills. Yet the statistics demonstrate that art historical training and its outcomes of visual literacy and analysis offer concrete benefits that contribute to student success in fields of study. Furthermore, once experienced, these gains did not go unnoticed or unappreciated by the students; a "substantial proportion" of the students themselves reported that the single workshop had increased their mindfulness about the processes of observation and interpretation.[12] Other programs have noted similar positive feedback about their museum experiences, which students rate as significant to their training and beneficial to their clinical rounds. What might initially appear as a distraction from their medical studies turns out to be a significant element of their training.

The short duration of most medical school visits to the museum suggests that students can improve their observational skills in a short period of exposure to these protocols. Yale University School of Nursing students visited university art museums during the first semester of their coursework for a single ninety-minute program.[13] A posttest asked students to analyze a series of six patient photographs, with a time limit of ten minutes for each image. When the results were compared with a control group of students who participated in a classroom lecture, participants in the museum program made significantly more observations on the timed writing sample, with a median number ranging from fifty-one to sixty-eight; the control group ranged from thirty-six to fifty-five.

It is not enough to train our students to observe and interpret, but they must practice translating this visual information into language, so that their work can be transmitted to others. There is a significant gap between the visual and the verbal, and repeated practice provides students the opportunity to experiment with different modes of communication and to learn from their omissions and failures. A seemingly simple exercise, such as having one student describe a sculpture to a partner who cannot see the object but must draw a rendering based solely on verbal information, allows both students to experience the frustrations of this translation process, to see what information was most necessary, and to learn for themselves how better to prioritize and communicate their observations. Experiencing that process once allows them to understand the difficulties and challenges of the assignment, prompting them to be more mindful of their language; but repeated practice allows students to refine and reshape the way they communicate with their peers.

Student volunteers at the University of Texas Health Science Center San Antonio were brought to the McNay Art Museum for three 90-minute, programs.[14] They worked in small groups with museum educators, based on VTS protocols, to study three works during each visit. Based on a comparison of pre- and post-tests, students dramatically increased the time they spent writing responses to a set of six images, moving from an average of 32.69 minutes (pretest) to an average of 57.25 minutes (posttest). This reflects a change in both their observational habits and their ability to communicate information, as the length of student responses for each artwork doubled, from an average of 122.27 words on the pretest to an average of 247.31 words on the posttest. Within that increase, they became more efficient at communicating their observations, nearly tripling the number of discrete pieces of objective information included in their responses from an average of 13.66 to 34.28.

The participants in this program attributed these improvements to their experiences in the museum. Their program evaluations credited the program with improved "listening skills" as well as "learning more about collaboration and group processes" and "learning to appreciate multiple perspectives on the same image." Students also remarked that they had learned the value in not immediately trying to find a conclusion or solution, but rather taking time for observation and reflection.

One of the most intriguing measurements by this group was a significant increase in student tolerance for ambiguity after their participation in the training. Using Budner's Tolerance of Ambiguity Scale, student responses showed they were more likely to consider uncertain situations as promising rather than threatening, demonstrating a mental flexibility that allows for more-efficient and successful navigation of unknown situations where complete information might not be possible.[15] Given the multivalent and coexisting layers of meaning made possible in art with increased visual literacy, students demonstrated a measurable increase in their tolerance for ambiguity and uncertainty. In my recent course, students increased their tolerance by an average of 10 percent.

Indeed, while the primary benefits of improved observational skills and communicative precision are demonstrable and relevant to a wide range of disciplines, the secondary benefits are no less compelling. The cultivation of mindfulness, an awareness of personal biases, and an increased ability to navigate ambiguous situations are skills central to the conception of a liberal arts education. Through the process of small-group work and class discussions in the museum or gallery, students become more mindful of their personal biases and the impact of those biases on their observations and conclusions.

We may assume that looking is universal, but seeing is not an objective experience; it is one mediated by a range of factors and biases.[16] The structure of working in both large- and small-group discussion is central to the success of this model, particularly in helping students to self-diagnose the difference between observation and analysis. At the beginning they are often much more capable at detecting one another's cognitive leaps to conclusions than they are at finding their own blurred boundaries. They begin by thinking that what they find in the work is obvious, or a simple matter of seeing rather than a subjective interpretation of a discrete set of facts. As students work together, they learn that initial impressions or conclusions differ widely within the group, allowing them to explore the existence of their biases and to witness how they impact the subjective interpretation of objective observations. Working in small groups and sharing their observations teaches close listening and the consideration of alternative interpretations, which students must then choose to reject based on counterevidence, or to further refine through the addition of information gathered from their observations. Students are forced to weigh multiple possibilities, even allowing contradictions to coexist rather than to be resolved, in ways that happen but can be difficult to replicate in the real world. Additionally, because the students are uncertain about what information is most important in their search for meaning or interpretation, they are less biased than they would be if presented with strictly discipline-specific images. Training their eyes through artworks allows them to decenter their observations and focus on working from the object. Sharing their observations teaches them to listen to the interpretations of others, which again they must choose to reject or further refine.

Teaching practices of close looking, sometimes referred to as "slow looking," provides a counterbalance to our students' natural inclination toward speed and multitasking. A 2001 study estimated the average viewer spent 27.2 seconds looking at an image, and now much of that time is consumed by taking photos with their phones.[17] By asking our students to consider an artwork more fully, we allow them to experience for themselves the benefits of mindful observation.

Jennifer Roberts, the Elizabeth Cary Agassiz Professor of the Humanities at Harvard, requires her students to decelerate and spend three hours observing the single painting that will form the basis for a research paper. She considers this a deliberate attempt to structure, or restructure, the timing of her students' work, with the time frame "explicitly designed to seem excessive."[18] In relocating students into the museum for this assignment, she finds value in breaking from their usual environment and its attendant distractions. Students keep a log of their observations, noting how they change in the duration of their focused study, along with questions that arise during the process. Although students initially resist the parameters of the assignment, Roberts reports that her students are routinely "astonished" by what observations emerge. Our students need such opportunities for thought and reflection, even more so because so many are governed by their task-oriented, high-achieving schedules.

Mindful, slow observation challenges student assumptions about the ease of looking at pictures, as students find themselves working through primary sources. Instead of prioritizing their abilities to research and document the work of others, which has a place in the educational process, looking carefully at a work of art brings them in contact with an original document that needs to be analyzed and interpreted. This process becomes easier with repeated practice and allows students to understand through their experience that they are becoming independent thinkers who are equipped to read and interpret the visual world.

If we list the pedagogical benefits of this model, including the ability to interrogate primary sources, the critical distinction between objective and subjective information, the construction of team-built and independent interpretation, the ability to convey more information through more-concrete language, and the understanding of different points of view and the importance of our own biases to our conclusions, we have a list of skills integral to the liberal arts education.

Pushing students to move beyond their gut feelings about an object, giving them not just a more descriptive vocabulary but a methodology for looking, has relevancy far beyond art history. By framing the skills of art history through the lens of visual literacy, we create a new relevancy for widespread exposure to the discipline. As students are required to take a series of composition courses, it is possible to imagine a general education sequence that required some training with images. Regardless, an emphasis on the skill set developed through the mindful and guided study of art counters the common assumption of art history as a self-indulgent, enjoyable course of study with little relevancy to the job market. With the field positioned as a means of developing critical skills with visual materials, and by combatting the assumption that these skills are naturally conferred upon sighted individuals, a better awareness of visual literacy and its development can highlight the importance of art history to the liberal arts curriculum and the benefits it can offer to students.

This training must follow a pedagogical course of development that targets and cultivates a discrete skill set. The VTS method is the most common model, attractive for its flexible and basic structure and its track record with measurable results across various student populations. By asking three questions and paraphrasing student responses, the VTS-trained facilitator leads students through a process of looking carefully, noting observations, providing relevant evidence, listening to the opinions of classmates, and reconciling disparate points of view. There is no emphasis on conveying "correct" or historical information about the objects studied; this encourages students to take risks that are often discouraged in an academic environment. With art as a prompt, something that requires analysis and allows for multiple perspectives, students cultivate a more flexible and mindful approach to seeing. In my course students work from a range of materials, including representational, narrative art, portraits, modernist abstractions, photography, and contemporary art. Each genre encourages students to work with different visual cues and to vary their approaches to seeing. The observation of a photograph such as *Waterbearer* by Lorna Simpson is different from reading Jacques-Louis David's portrait of Antoine-Laurent Lavoisier or one of Willem de Kooning's *Women*, yet all three require students to take in and organize a great deal of visual information, all layered and coded by the artist.

The course I developed is based on the VTS protocol, featuring a series of constructivist exercises where I must surrender some of my authority to teach students that their conclusions are valuable, not necessarily because they are true or complete but because they are derived from their observations and their ability to thoughtfully move from objective statements to subjective, team-built consensus. Indeed, as this course is designed to develop visual literacy rather than to impart art-historical knowledge, there is a necessary shift in emphasis from content to skill. Embracing this process, I allow the conversation to veer away from what a more informed, scholarly opinion might posit. This is not always easy, and, while imperfect for a traditional art history class, the trade-off allows students to focus explicitly on improving visual literacy.

There are divided opinions as to whether a follow-up should include more factual and contextual information about the works studied, or whether external facts are irrelevant to the pedagogical goals of this approach. In some programs, students are not allowed to contribute comments informed by any past aesthetic or art-historical training. In other models, each session concludes with a professor or museum educator presenting an informational unit. My preference is to introduce relevant contextual information throughout the process, which allows students to respond to changing conditions and incorporate facts with their observations and analysis. I do this with the belief that this contributes to flexible thinking and responsive reinterpretations, rather than with the intention of arriving at art-historically sound conclusions.

The benefits of any interdisciplinary exchange must be weighed against the sacrifices of moving away from the core content and methodologies of a field. In considering the pragmatics of offering new types of courses within an art history department, it is important to separate the discipline-specific goals of traditional coursework from the skills-based goals of this interdisciplinary model. By no means should art history courses universally reject traditional content in favor of visual literacy. Equally important is the continued campaign to show the independent merits of studying art as a field, not just a service component or competency for other majors on campus. Yet, by demonstrating the relevancy of studying art and providing access to one element of art-historical scholarship to a broader academic audience, we legitimize the dedicated study of artwork and the importance of teaching and learning about the power of images. Skills do not need to come at the cost of course material, although separate curricular designations might help to keep that distinction visible.

There is a reciprocal benefit for art history as a discipline in this investment beyond our department. If liberal arts schools embrace visual literacy as an important component of general literacy and a tool for critical thinking and analysis, art history is positioned to become a central component of general education criteria. Putting art-historical content aside for the moment, we teach a specific skill set that benefits the larger student population and combats the silo effect within individual departments. A deeper appreciation for the need for visual literacy and a more precise understanding of the skills demanded in the acquisition of such literacy also legitimizes art history as a critical area of study, not just relevant to an understanding of past images but a tool for understanding our contemporary world. Furthermore, enhancing our visibility on campus could boost the number of majors and minors, as many students are unacquainted with the field.

While some risks exist to this interdisciplinary collaboration, particularly in the pragmatics of offering service courses for other departments, the following strategies might help manage these potential dangers and serve as models for adoption in the liberal arts curriculum. Given the successful results from short-term immersive experiences among medical schools, it appears that the development of short-term courses on visual literacy provides an opportunity for specialized training without creating excessive demand. This is a pressing issue for smaller departments with issues of coverage or staffing. Shorter summer or winter terms allow for courses to create an integrated cohort and potentially to travel to urban centers with multiple collections for study; the course I led in New York capitalizes on this opportunity for experiential learning.

Another way to integrate visual literacy courses into existing curricula could be to work within the structure of Writing-Across-the-Curriculum or writing-intensive courses. These classes are often departures from traditional disciplinary offerings and allow for a focus on writing and textual literacy, so it is possible to incorporate visual literacy into the syllabus. This would work best for colleges with on-campus access to a permanent collection but could be adapted for galleries with a strong schedule of exhibitions.

The workshop model is inspired from current medical school models, where the curricular demands of training leave little time for additional enrichment. Studies have shown that even single-session workshops of a few hours have demonstrable impact on observation and communication skills. In the interest of raising the visibility of art history programs across campus, workshops in partnership with a targeted class provide some of the benefits discussed in this essay without the necessary commitment of a full course.

The goals of this visual literacy practice must be clearly communicated to faculty and potential students. While a record of wide-ranging success has been established at the medical school level, this is new terrain for undergraduate education. It thus becomes necessary to focus on the relevant skills of the medical school model, namely, the improvement of observational acuity and communication, along with the secondary benefits of flexibility, mindfulness, and self-awareness. Without fail, these keywords appear within the justifications of a liberal arts degree. Now we need to connect them to the undergraduate opportunities provided by the study of art.

Assessment can be based on practices adopted by the existing medical programs to promote sharing and comparative analysis. Although our student populations and desired content-specific outcomes are different, they share a common core of observation, communication, and critical thinking. Assessment of student progress is made through a comparison of pre- and post-course writing samples. In my course students have a timed period to study a series of images and write objective descriptions. These essays are evaluated according to the number of observations made, the level of language used in their description, and the ability to differentiate objective and subjective observations.

To gauge secondary benefits, including the increased tolerance for ambiguity and student self-perceptions of mindfulness and capability, my students completed quantitative measures, including Budner's Tolerance of Ambiguity Scale, the Mindful Attention Awareness Scale (MAAS), and Five Facet Mindfulness Questionnaire (FFMQ).

While the course will never approach the discipline-specific content or training found in a traditional art history course, I believe this adds a new value to our offerings that would serve a larger community of students and our majors by reinforcing the importance and validity of seeing, interpreting, and communicating. We have the potential to make students aware of the need for visual literacy and to build their skill set from an amateur level to one of fluency. Furthermore, I believe this model bridges a significant divide between the arts and the sciences and contributes to the overarching mission of a liberal arts education.

Notes

1. Deandra Little, Peter Felten, and Chad Berg, "Liberal Education in a Visual World," *Liberal Education* 96 (Spring 2010), 46.

2. Quoted in James Elkins, "Introduction: The Concept of Visual Literacy, and Its Limitations," in *Visual Literacy*, ed. James Elkins (New York: Routledge, 2008), 2. In the introduction to his text, Elkins laments the continued marginalization of visual literacy despite the evidence of its relevance to undergraduate learning.

3. Abigail Housen, "Art Viewing and Aesthetic Development: Designing for the Viewer," in *From Periphery to Center: Art Museum Education in the 21st Century*, ed. Pat Villeneuve (Reston, VA: National Art Education Association, 2008), 7.

4. My thanks go to Ann Grimaldi, curator of education at the Weatherspoon Art Museum, University of North Carolina Greensboro, for so generously sharing her expertise and insights from her "Art of Observation" program.

5. This model largely originated with an experimental program between the Yale University Medical School and the Yale Center for British Art in 1998–1999. Results from this pilot program were reported in a 2001 letter to the editor; see Jacqueline C. Dolev, Linda Krohner Friedlaender, and Irwin M. Braverman, "Use of Fine Art to Enhance Visual Diagnostic Skills," *Journal of the American Medical Association* 286 (September 2001): 1020–21. In June 2016 many of these programs shared their experiences at the Museum of Modern Art's conference The Art of Examination: Art Museums and Medical School Partnerships. Documents from this conference can be found at https://www.utdallas.edu/arthistory/medicine/.

6. Mitchell first introduced the term in his 1994 text *Picture Theory*; however, in his essay "Visual Literacy or Literary Visualcy?," in *Visual Literacy* (James Elkins, ed.), he complicates this phrase by pointing to other significant historical turns and refuting the concept of purely visual media. It is not the uniqueness of this moment that is most critical, but simply the terms of shifting priorities from text to image; see also Marita Sturken and Lisa Cartwright, *Practices of Looking: An Introduction to Visual Culture* (Oxford: Oxford University Press, 2001), 370.

7. Elizabeth Thomas, Nancy Place, and Cinnamon Hillyard, "Students and Teachers Learning to See, Part 1: Using Visual Images in the College Classroom to Promote Students' Capacities and Skills," *College Teaching* 56, no. 1 (2008): 23–27.

8. W. J. T. Mitchell, *Picture Theory: Essays on Verbal and Visual Representation* (Chicago: University of Chicago Press, 1994), 2.

9. Alexa Miller, Michelle Grohe, Shahram Khoshbin, and Joel T. Katz, "From the Galleries to the Clinic: Applying Art Museum Lessons to Patient Care," *Journal of Medical Humanities* 34 (2013): 433–38. In Harvard Medical School's first-year elective course, discussion centered on artworks allows students to learn the difference between observation and inference—an important leap in differentiating the objective from the subjective.

10. Sona K. Jasani and Norma S. Saks, "Utilizing Visual Art to Enhance the Clinical Observation Skills of Medical Students," *Medical Teacher* 35 (2013): 1327–31. For a complete analysis of the VTS methodology, see Philip Yenawine, *Visual Thinking Strategies: Using Art to Deepen Learning across School Disciplines* (Cambridge: Harvard Education Press, 2013).

11. Jasani and Saks, "Utilizing Visual Art," 1327–31.

12. Jasani and Saks, "Utilizing Visual Art," 1329.

13. Linda Honan Pellico, Linda Friedlaender, and Kristopher P. Fennie, "Looking Is Not Seeing: Using Art to Improve Observational Skills," *Journal of Nursing Education* 48 (2009): 648–53.

14. Craig Klugman, "Art Rounds: Teaching Interprofessional Students Visual Thinking Strategies at One School," *Academic Medicine: Journal of the Association of American Medical Colleges* 86 (2011): 1266–71.

15. Klugman, "Art Rounds," 1267.

16. Johanna Shapiro, Lloyd Rucker, and Jill Beck, "Training the Clinical Eye and Mind: Using the Arts to Develop Medical Students' Observational and Pattern Recognition Skills," *Medical Education* 40 (2006), 264.

17. Jeffrey K. Smith and Lisa F. Smith, "Spending Time on Art," *Empirical Studies of the Arts* 19 (July 2001): 229–36.

18. Jennifer Roberts, "The Power of Patience," *Harvard Magazine* (November 2013).

Bibliography

Dolev, Jacqueline C., Linda Krohner Friedlaender, and Irwin M. Braverman. "Use of Fine Art to Enhance Visual Diagnostic Skills." *Journal of the American Medical Association* 286 (Sept. 2001): 1020–21.

Elkins, James. "Introduction: The Concept of Visual Literacy, and Its Limitations." In *Visual Literacy*, edited by James Elkins, 1–10. New York: Routledge, 2008.

Housen, Abigail. "Art Viewing and Aesthetic Development: Designing for the Viewer." In *From Periphery to Center: Art Museum Education in the 21st Century*, edited by Pat Villeneuve, 172–79. Reston, VA: National Art Education Association, 2008.

Jasani, Sona K., and Norma S. Saks. "Utilizing Visual Art to Enhance the Clinical Observation Skills of Medical Students." *Medical Teacher* 35, no. 7 (2013): 1327–31.

Klugman, Craig. "Art Rounds: Teaching Interprofessional Students Visual Thinking Strategies at One School." *Academic Medicine: Journal of the Association of American Medical Colleges* 86, no. 30 (October 2011): 1266–71.

Little, Deandra, Peter Felten, and Chad Berg. "Liberal Education in a Visual World." *Liberal Education* 96, no. 2 (Spring 2010): 44–49.

Miller, Alexa, Michelle Grohe, Shahram Khoshbin, and Joel T. Katz. "From the Galleries to the Clinic: Applying Art Museum Lessons to Patient Care." *Journal of Medical Humanities* 34, no. 4 (2013): 433–38.

Mitchell, W. J. T. *Picture Theory: Essays on Verbal and Visual Representation*. Chicago: University of Chicago Press, 1994.

Mitchell, W. J. T. "Visual Literacy or Literary Visualcy?" In *Visual Literacy*, edited by James Elkins, 11–13. New York: Routledge, 2007.

Pellico, Linda Honan, Linda Friedlaender, and Kristopher P. Fennie. "Looking Is Not Seeing: Using Art to Improve Observational Skills." *Journal of Nursing Education* 48 (November 2009): 648–53.

Roberts, Jennifer. "The Power of Patience." *Harvard Magazine* (November 2013). https://harvardmagazine.com/2013/11/the-power-of-patience.

Schaff, Pamela, Suzanne Isken, and Robert M. Tager. "From Contemporary Art to Core Clinical Skills: Observation, Interpretation, and Meaning-Making in a Complex Environment." *Academic Medicine* 86, no. 10 (October 2011): 1272–76.

Shapiro, Johanna, Lloyd Rucker, and Jill Beck. "Training the Clinical Eye and Mind: Using the Arts to Develop Medical Students' Observational and Pattern Recognition Skills." *Medical Education* 40, no. 3 (March 2006), 263–68.

Smith, Jeffrey K., and Lisa F. Smith. "Spending Time on Art." *Empirical Studies of the Arts* 19 (July 2001): 229–36.

Sturken, Marita, and Lisa Cartwright. *Practices of Looking: An Introduction to Visual Culture*. Oxford: Oxford University Press, 2001.

Thomas, Elizabeth, Nancy Place, and Cinnamon Hillyard. "Students and Teachers Learning to See, Part 1: Using Visual Images in the College Classroom to Promote Students' Capacities and Skills." *College Teaching* 56, no. 1 (2008): 23–27.

Yenawine, Philip. *Visual Thinking Strategies: Using Art to Deepen Learning across School Disciplines*. Cambridge: Harvard Education Press, 2013.

CHAPTER 5

Revisiting Erwin Panofsky's "The History of Art as a Humanistic Discipline"

FLOYD W. MARTIN

Using a definition of liberal arts found in medieval universities, the seven liberal arts are grammar, rhetoric, logic, geometry, arithmetic, music, and astronomy. In considering universities today, the definition is broader and includes humanities subjects in fine arts areas. Furthermore, in current usage, it implies a broad general education that equips one for solving problems and encountering specialized areas of knowledge. The discipline of art history today is considered a humanities subject within the liberal arts, though it is a relatively recent arrival to the academy.[1]

In this context Erwin Panofsky's essay "The History of Art as a Humanistic Discipline" appeared in 1938. When written, art history was a newer discipline in the universities in the United States, and one reason for the essay was to argue for its place alongside more traditional humanities subjects. The essay is also a succinct statement about the tasks and thinking required of an art historian specifically, and a humanities scholar more generally, contrasted with the approaches of a scientist.[2]

"The History of Art as a Humanistic Discipline" remains a useful document for students learning about methodology and history of the discipline, and it contributes to the discussion about the role of liberal arts education in the twenty-first century.[3] I will point out some of the important points Panofsky makes about the study of humanities, matters he considered important at the time he wrote and ones still important today. Then I will consider some subjects and topics addressed in recent news articles that, though seemingly distant from the subject of art history or humanities, are ones where an approach grounded in the liberal arts discipline of art history contributes to new ways of thinking and solving problems. The liberal arts foundation articulated by Panofsky can lead to new ways of thinking about reading, the practice of medicine, criminal justice, and political matters.

Erwin Panofsky (1892–1968) was a brilliant art historian, most celebrated for his methodology of iconography and iconology. This system was presented in *Studies in Iconology: Humanist Themes in the Art of the Renaissance* (1939), and its most famous example was the article published five years earlier examining Jan van Eyck's *Arnolfini Portrait* in the National Gallery in London.[4] To put his essay concerning art history as a humanistic discipline in a wider context, it is helpful to keep in mind Panofsky's biography.

Starting his academic career at the University of Hamburg in 1920, he thrived as teacher and writer. He was a visiting scholar at New York University during the 1931–1932 academic year. It was in 1933 that the Nazi government enforced policies that purged German universities of Jewish, radical, and "decadent" scholars and artists. Panofsky permanently immigrated to the United States in 1934, spending most of his career at the Institute for Advanced Studies at Princeton University. He was among many teachers and scholars who came to the United States, and the discipline of art history gained importance within the country's educational system because of this. Walter W. S. Cook, chair of the Institute of Fine Arts of New York University, said that he believed Hitler was his friend because the Führer shook the tree and Cook gathered the apples.[5]

Other famous publications were on iconology; Abbot Suger, the founder of the Gothic style; Early Netherlandish painting; and the idea of the Renaissance. Panofsky was a man of wide interests, and his writings include an important 1936 essay about the art of motion pictures, and a clever 1963 article about the Rolls-Royce hood ornament. His emphasis on the humanities must be seen not only as a reflection of the learning he had and the subjects he liked but his observations as a young scholar and teacher in Germany on rising militarism and his forced exile by a government that saw him as less than human.[6]

"Art History as a Humanistic Discipline" was published by Princeton University in a book entitled *The Meaning of the Humanities*, and the content can be viewed in the context of the social and political situation of the 1930s. The ideas were first presented in a series of lectures at Princeton in the 1937–1938 academic year, and, since Panofsky was then at the Institute of Advanced Studies, his inclusion was a logical choice. Editor Theodore Greene in his introduction makes reference to forces the humanist must work against, such as dictators, mob hysteria, and propaganda.[7]

Panofsky's coauthor Robert Lowry Calhoun, in his essay "Theology and Humanities," is most emphatic about the need for humanistic studies in the shadow of fascism and war: "In the prisons, the concentration camps, and the graves of the newest autocracies, and in exile from their borders, are thousands of journalists and men of letters, artists and musicians, historians, philosophers, preachers and theologians. Dictators," as Calhoun sees them, "treat them as active men and women whose professional activities must be whipped into line.... In the eyes of hard-headed dictators, the humanities are not irrelevant."[8] Although Panofsky's discussion of art history and humanities does not note the world situation, he was one of two scholars in the project who were immigrants, and the desire to have a focus on humanities and what they represent in terms of respect for ideas and other people at this point in history is not surprising.

The essay begins with an account of the aged Immanuel Kant, nine days before death, standing up for a visit by his physician and refusing to sit down until his guest had first. He then said (in German of course), "The sense of humanity has not yet left me." Panofsky, lover of words, uses this episode to discuss *humanitas* ... on one level, simply a kind of politeness, but on a more important level, expressing a twofold difference. First is the difference between what is human and what is less than human; second is the difference between what is human and what is more than human. There is the classical sense of cultured human versus barbarian or between human and less-than-human. Medieval history brought the sense of humankind versus divinity, or between humanity and God. From this discussion comes the idea that humanities in the academy are based on Renaissance humanistic ideals. A humanist, according to Panofsky, rejects authority but respects tradition.

Panofsky then contrasts the humanist with the scientist. For the former, records never age, but, for the latter, more recent scholarship is better than something older. For example, if a contemporary scientist read Newton or Leonardo, he would do so as a person interested in history and the history of science. Art historians, trying to figure out the meaning and context of works of art, are part of the humanities. There are steps. First is observation, either of natural phenomena by the scientist or of human records by the humanist. Then there is analysis, decoding, and interpretation. Finally results are classified or coordinated into a coherent system.

Michael Ann Holly, in *Panofsky and the Foundations of Art History*, highlights Panofsky's declaration that the humanist must bring the past to life. In his "History of Art" essay, Panofsky, contrasting the humanist's work with that of the scientist, notes, "The humanist, dealing as he does with human actions and creations, has to engage in a mental process of a synthetic and subjective character: he has mentally to *re-enact the actions* and to *re-create the creations*. It is in fact by this process that the real objects of the humanities come into being." Holly shows how Panofsky was influenced by historian and philosopher Wilhelm Dilthey (1833–1911), whose writings wrestled with how humanist methods on the one hand offered sweeping generalizations about history and on the other verified facts in ways established by science.[9] Using as an example the discovery of an artist's contract, which seems to relate to a particular altarpiece, Panofsky goes on to show how what is superficially obvious may not be true. For example, is the document authentic, a forgery, or a copy? Might the altarpiece itself be authentic, a forgery, or a copy? A valid conclusion requires "checking," but knowing how and what to check requires experience and education.

Panofsky further discusses the active versus the contemplative life and how the humanities represent the latter. Humanities give life to static records and to events long past. He makes a subtle distinction: knowledge is something that can be possessed and is often identified with the sciences, whereas learning is a process and is often associated with the humanities. The idea of mastering how to learn is a key goal of humanistic studies.

Panofsky's own studies made him interested in the world of the humanists of the late Medieval and early Renaissance periods in Europe, and he built his art historical methodology on this understanding. We can see Panofsky himself as a historical, humanistic figure, which then allows us to use ideas and concepts that interested him and to apply them to current problems and events. Like Panofsky and the historical figures he admired, the person educated in the humanities within the liberal arts understands the importance of careful reading, observation, and thinking about contemporary issues.

The importance of care in reading and spending time to think is made clear in a recent *New York Times* article comparing speed reading with traditional methods. In "Sorry, You Can't Speed Read," Jeffrey M. Zacks and Rebecca Treiman, professors of psychological and brain sciences at Washington University in St. Louis, examine the history of speed reading over the last fifty years or so.[10] The article begins with a Woody Allen joke: "I read *War and Peace* in twenty minutes. It's about Russia." More seriously, the authors' studies show that faster reading speeds result in loss of meaning, and they make a distinction between speed reading and skimming a text.

The ability to skim a text is a good skill to have, particularly in the academic environment, but that is not the focus of this article. The authors go on to emphasize that reading is more than perception of words; it requires getting meaning from groupings of words. They explain that "the big bottleneck in reading isn't perception (seeing the words) but language processing (assembling strings of words into meanings). Have you ever tried listening to an audio recording with the speaking rate dialed way up? Doubling the speed, in our experience, leaves individual words perfectly identifiable—but makes it just about impossible to follow the meaning. The same phenomenon occurs with written text."

As educators interested in the liberal arts, learning from reading is a basic skill our students need and that we need. The article concludes, "If you want to improve your reading speed, your best bet—as old-fashioned as it sounds—is to read a wide variety of written material and to expand your vocabulary." A liberal arts education emphasizes reading and variety of study. Old-fashioned, perhaps, in our world of sound bites and YouTube videos, but our students need to learn to take the time to read different types of things and to find meanings that shed light on larger issues to be faced in one's future.

Looking and analyzing are basic activities for the discipline of art history, and in other liberal arts disciplines, we hope our students will learn reading, or hearing, followed by analysis. Another recent article in the *New York Times* examines the work of Amy Herman, author of *Visual Intelligence: Sharpen Your Perception, Change Your Life*.[11] Herman worked as a lawyer, did not like it, worked in development at an art museum, got an advanced degree in art history, and now has a business where she works with medical students, business executives, and law enforcement personnel in the context of art museums. Her goal is to teach individuals how to look carefully at details and context in order to determine meaning.

At an earlier point in her career, when she was on the staff at New York's Frick Collection, Herman had a program with the medical college of Cornell University, where medical students looked at works in the museum to increase their powers of observation and perception.[12] Thanks to this program, and similar ones at Yale University and the University of Texas, many medical schools now include similar sorts of humanities studies and use theater and acting experiences within their curricula.

The recent *Times* article about Herman focused on a session she conducted at the Metropolitan Museum of Art with New York City policemen. Herman said this about a typical painting of any type: "It's extremely evocative and perfect for critical inquiry. . . . What am I seeing here? How do I attach a narrative to it?" She further clarified that her goal is not what we might categorize as art appreciation but using visual arts as something that can increase perception and give meaning to situations that are far from the context of museums and art. "I've had people say, 'I hate art,' and I say, 'That's not relevant.' This is not a class about Pollock versus Picasso. I'm not teaching you about art today; I'm using art as a new set of data, to help you clear the slate and use the skills you use on the job. My goal when you walk out the door is that you're thinking differently about the job." Herman likes to encourage engagement with two different works of art. Vermeer's *Mistress and Maid* (1666–1667) in the Frick Collection shows a lady seated at a table, handing over or being handed a mysterious piece of paper. "There are so many different narratives," she said. "The analysts come away asking more questions than answers—'Who's asking the question? Who's doing the talking? Who's listening?' The cops will say, 'It's a servant asking for the day off.'"[13] In this case, an artist, known for using light and color to create enormous visual clarity, has made a work that has much ambiguity.

Similarly, a more recent example Herman likes to use, James Rosenquist's *House of Fire* (1981), at the Met, shows three seemingly random sections: an upside-down bag of groceries, a bucket under a window shade, and a group of aggressively thrusting lipsticks. "It's really conducive to good dialogue," she said. "How many times do officers have to make order out of chaos? So many times in our work we come across things that don't have a coherent narrative."[14]

Connecting the discipline of art history and the professions of medicine, business, and law enforcement reminds us that one of the points of a liberal arts education is to prepare the student to face all kinds of adjustments and change, regardless of one's career path. The skills of observation and analysis learned in the context of art history are valuable far beyond that one limited discipline. Looking at art and discussing it may seem irrelevant to one's work as a policeman on a superficial level, but, when we think about the skills learned, we can see how relevant many academic pursuits are to individuals who end up in a variety of different careers.

Yet another recent article speaks of the importance of a liberal education in the medical profession. In this case the authors asked whether medical schools belong in the context of a liberal arts institution or if they should be classified as trade schools. Not surprisingly, since they are from Dartmouth, the authors argued that the liberal arts setting is appropriate, noting the need for doctors to understand micro and macro systems, communications, and social constructs such as class, gender, and race, and ethics.[15]

In the fall of 2016, art history was almost eliminated as a field of study for secondary and university students in Great Britain. Not surprisingly, many in the nation's art community who commented on the eventual "saving" of the art history qualification emphasized many of the points noted by Panofsky and others defining liberal arts education. For example, Charles Saumarez Smith, of the Royal Academy, noted, "Art history teaches rigorous analytical skills and requires students to engage not only with art but with history, literature, politics, languages and the sciences."[16]

Observing this discussion and resolution and noting how some politicians in the United States were urging cutting liberal arts funding in preference for science, technology, engineering, and mathematics (STEM) education, Noah Charney compared STEM studies and approaches with those found in the humanities. He pointed out that humanities subjects teach a person "how to do whatever you need to do in the future" and instill confidence in using other disciplines of study. In his conclusion, he noted that the study of humanities "teaches students how to learn."[17] Those with this type of learning can be creative, can see the dangers of restricted viewpoints, will avoid intolerance of new ideas, and engage in a wider way of seeing.

Another reference in a recent *New York Times* article underscores the importance of humanism and a liberal arts background. The paper has a public editor. A typical weekly column might address the amount of space given to particular political candidates, or how the wording of a headline might suggest some sort of bias. In April 2016 Margaret Sullivan, public editor since 2012, wrote her final column, as she left the position to become a columnist for another paper.[18]

First, she summarized the great changes she observed at the newspaper between 2012 and 2016. What was run as a traditional print operation, with some digital aspects on the side, changed to a digital media company. Digital advertising and partnerships with other companies replaced the old model of revenue from print advertising. This is a perfect example of the type of change that someone with a strong liberal arts background can navigate better than someone whose only background might be training in the old way of doing things.

At the end of her column, Sullivan made recommendations for the *Times* staff to keep in mind in the midst of these big changes in how a newspaper operates. Some of those points are relevant to us today in thinking about the value of liberal arts. First is her plea to have editorial control superior to business control. She believes that the newspaper's values, expressed in what to publish and how to present topics, should guide business decisions about what digital media to use or what will sell quickly. Another of her pleas is basic: "Don't underestimate the importance of line editing and copy editing. ... It may seem invisible, but it matters enormously." This, like the earlier discussion about speed reading versus reading for comprehension, emphasizes clarity and precision in expressing ideas, so basic in humanities and liberal arts studies. Though old-fashioned, good basic writing skills—words spelled correctly, proper grammar, and persuasive writing—continue to be necessary in the world of digital media and fast communication.

These threads come back together in thinking about Panofsky's explanation of why his subject of art history is a humanistic discipline within the larger universe of the liberal arts. Such education has at its center a desire to have each student find his or her own sense of worth and profession, and to give each student the skills to work in any calling that is followed. Liberal arts education has a focus on each person recognizing the full humanity of others, past and present, and honoring that. Those with this experience know why the aged Kant said, "The sense of humanity has not yet left me."

Notes

1. In 1874, Charles Eliot Norton became professor of fine arts at Harvard and was one of the earliest appointments in art history. The discipline became more prominent with the German-trained figures like Panofsky who fled Germany in the 1930s and contributed to universities in the United States. See Vernon Hyde Minor, *Art History's History* (Upper Saddle River, NJ: Prentice-Hall, 2001), 20–23.
2. Erwin Panofsky, "The History of Art as a Humanistic Discipline," in *The Meaning of the Humanities*, ed. Theodore Meyer Greene (Princeton: Princeton University Press, 1938), 89–118. The essay is reprinted in Erwin Panofsky, *Meaning in the Visual Arts* (Chicago: University of Chicago Press, 1955), 1–25, where the publication date is given as 1940. Panofsky in 1953 wrote a related piece comparing the European and US educational systems: "Three Decades of Art History in the United States: Impressions of a Transplanted European," *Meaning in the Visual Arts* (Chicago: University of Chicago Press, 1955), 321–46. This was originally published as "The History of Art," in *The Cultural Migration: The European Scholar in America*, ed. W. Rex Crawford (Philadelphia: University of Pennsylvania Press, 1953).
3. A version of this paper was given at the [Re]Defining Liberal Arts Education symposium at Jackson State University in October 2016. At the symposium, William Adams, Chair of the National Endowment for the Humanities, was the keynote speaker. Only a few months after the symposium, the new administration of President Donald Trump floated the idea of abolishing it, as well as the National Endowment for the Arts and the Corporation for Public Broadcasting, a situation that emphasizes clearly why considering the importance of liberal arts in the twenty-first century is essential to national life.
4. Lee Sorensen, "Panofsky, Erwin," *Dictionary of Art Historians* (website). www.dictionaryofarthistorians.org/panofskye.htm; Erwin Panofsky, *Studies in Iconology: Humanistic Themes in the Art of the Renaissance* (New York: Oxford University Press, 1939); "Jan van Eyck's 'Arnolfini' Portrait," *Burlington Magazine* 64, no. 472 (1934): 117–27.
5. Minor, *Art History's History*, 22. Panofsky recounts Cook's comment in his "Three Decades of Art History in the United States," *Meaning in the Visual Arts*, 332.
6. Bibliographies of Panofsky's writings are found on *the Dictionary of Art Historians* website (note 4 above) and in Michael Ann Holly, *Panofsky and the Foundations of Art History* (Ithaca: Cornell University Press, 1984), 241–43; Holly, *Panofsky and the Foundations of Art History*, 106.

7. The lectures were called the Spencer Trask Lectures, Meaning of the Humanities. Other scholars were Ralph Barton Perry, "A Definition of the Humanities"; August Charles Key, "History and the Humanities"; Robert Lowry Calhoun, "Theology and the Humanities"; and Gilbert Chinard, "Literature and the Humanities." Perry was Professor of Philosophy at Princeton; Key was Professor of History at the University of Minnesota; Calhoun was Professor of Historical Theology at Yale; and Chinard was Professor of French Literature at Princeton. The editor of the book, Theodore M. Greene, was Professor of Philosophy at Princeton. See preface to *Meaning of the Humanities*, vii; Greene, *Meaning of the Humanities*, xvi.
8. Robert Lowry Calhoun, "Theology and Humanities," *Meaning of the Humanities*, 121–22.
9. Holly, *Panofsky and the Foundations of Art History*, 34–39; Panofsky, "History of Art," 105. The italics are Panofsky's.
10. Jeffrey M. Zacks and Rebecca Treiman, "Sorry, You Can't Speed Read," *New York Times*, April 17, 2016, SR9.
11. Sarah Lyall, "Is There a Perp in the Painting?," *New York Times*, April 27, 2016, C1; Amy E. Herman, *Visual Intelligence* (New York: Houghton Mifflin Harcourt, 2016).
12. Leslie Berger, "By Observing Art, Med Students Learn Art of Observation," *New York Times*, January 2, 200.
13. Illustrated at http://collections.frick.org/view/objects/asitem/items$0040:274.
14. Illustrated at http://www.metmuseum.org/art/collection/search/482613.
15. Leslie Henderson, Glenda Shoop, and Lisa V. Adams, "Why Get a Liberal Education? It Is the Life and Breath of Medicine," *The Conversation* (Dartmouth University), August 15, 2016.
16. Sally Weale, "Art History A-Level Saved after High-Profile Campaign," *The Guardian*, December 1, 2016. https://www.theguardian.com/education/2016/dec/01/art-history-a-level-saved-from-being-axed-after-high-profile-campaign.
17. Noah Charney, "The Art of Learning: Why Art History Might Be the Most Important Subject You Could Study Today," *Salon*, January 15, 2017, http://www.salon.com/2017/01/15/the-art-of-learning-why-art-history-might-be-the-most-important-subject-you-could-study-today/. See also Patricia Cohen, "A Rising Call to Foster STEM Fields, and Decrease Liberal Arts Funding," *New York Times*, February 22, 2016, Business Day, B1. Typically STEM refers to science, technology, engineering, and math, with an added "A" for arts.
18. Margaret Sullivan, "Public Editor No. 5 Is Yesterday's News," *New York Times*, April 17, 2016, SR9.

Bibliography

Berger, Leslie. "By Observing Art, Med Students Learn Art of Observation." *New York Times*, January 2, 2001.

Calhoun, Robert Lowry. "Theology and Humanities." In *The Meaning of the Humanities*, edited by Theodore Meyer Greene, 119–50. Princeton: Princeton University Press, 1938.

Charney, Noah. "The Art of Learning: Why Art History Might Be the Most Important Subject You Could Study Today." *Salon*, January 15, 2017. http://www.salon.com/2017/01/15/the-art-of-learning-why-art-history-might-be-the-most-important-subject-you-could-study-today/.

Cohen, Patricia. "A Rising Call to Foster STEM Fields, and Decrease Liberal Arts Funding." *New York Times*, February 22, 2016, Business Day, B1.

Henderson, Leslie, Glenda Shoop, and Lisa V. Adams. "Why Get a Liberal Education? It Is the Life and Breath of Medicine." *The Conversation* (Dartmouth University), August 15, 2016.

Herman, Amy E. *Visual Intelligence: Sharpen Your Perception, Change Your Life*. New York: Houghton Mifflin Harcourt, 2016.

Holly, Michael Ann. *Panofsky and the Foundations of Art History*. Ithaca: Cornell University Press, 1984.

Lyall, Sarah. "Is There a Perp in the Painting?" *New York Times*, April 27, 2016, C1.

Minor, Vernon Hyde. *Art History's History*. Upper Saddle River, NJ: Prentice-Hall, 2001.

Panofsky, Erwin. "The History of Art." In *The Cultural Migration: The European Scholar in America*, edited by W. Rex Crawford, 82–111. Philadelphia: University of Pennsylvania Press, 1953.

Panofsky, Erwin. "The History of Art as a Humanistic Discipline." In *The Meaning of the Humanities*, edited by Theodore Meyer Greene, 89–118. Princeton: Princeton University Press, 1938.

Panofsky, Erwin. "Jan van Eyck's 'Arnolfini' Portrait." *Burlington Magazine* 64, no. 372 (1934).

Panofsky, Erwin. *Meaning in the Visual Arts*. Chicago: University of Chicago Press, 1955.

Panofsky, Erwin. *Studies in Iconology: Humanistic Themes in the Art of the Renaissance*. New York: Oxford University Press, 1939.

Panofsky, Erwin. "Three Decades of Art History in the United States: Impressions of a Transplanted European." In *Meaning in the Visual Arts*, 321–46. Chicago: University of Chicago Press, 1955.

Sorensen, Lee. "Panofsky, Erwin." In *Dictionary of Art Historians*. www.dictionaryofarthistorians.org/panofskye.htm.

Sullivan, Margaret. "Public Editor No. 5 Is Yesterday's News." *New York Times*, April 17, 2016, SR9.

Weale, Sally. "Art History A-Level Saved after High-Profile Campaign." *The Guardian*, December 1, 2016. https://www.theguardian.com/education/2016/dec/01/art-history-a-level-saved-from-being-axed-after-high-profile-campaign.

Zacks, Jeffrey M., and Rebecca Treiman. "Sorry, You Can't Speed Read." *New York Times*, April 17, 2016, SR9.

CHAPTER 6

Dancing the Humanities

Engaging with Liberal Arts Education

LAUREN ASHLEE MESSINA

As a concept studied in a master of fine arts thesis, Dancing the Humanities is an approach to liberal arts education explored in great detail as part of a movement-based performance process study. This performance, *#MakingofaMovement*, provides an example of activist dance performance as a means to facilitate a learning experience rich in transformation and empathy on behalf of participating performers and audience members. Through an emancipatory research paradigm, complete with exploration of textual and embodied knowledge, problems of disunity and ethnic identity unawareness or disengagement are addressed through the creative process. Inspired by choreographies of protest, black performance theory, and culturally relevant teaching, research and creative processes merge into one purposeful effort. These efforts contribute to unique experiences of difference, belonging, and connection discovered by participants in the performance event. *#MakingofaMovement* represents just one significant path to engage student performers and observers in a moving journey of reflection and revelation. Dancing the Humanities is one of many original ideas that sparked this performative journey.

Imagine standing in the center of a dimly lit room. Mirrors face you on one side, a blank wall on the other. Large, floor-to-ceiling windows connect the shadows of the night to the laboratory that is your studio space. Surrounded by other performers in the cast, you have been asked to come up with eight to ten gestures to represent various aspects of resistance. After reading the choreographer's notes on twelve different books and films about dance and social activism, you pinpoint several action words from the texts that stand out to you as indicative of resistance. You close your eyes and begin to move your body in response to a question—how to protest on behalf of someone else? Protest, meaning, active objection to an issue that you or another do not condone. In this instance, the issue has been undefined. What do you do? How do you take what you know in theory and (re)present it with practiced action, movement?

According to religion and philosophy scholar Kimerer LaMothe, "Words succeed when they move.... Words communicate, if and when they do, kinetically and viscerally." For LaMothe, "Words can guide a person in making moves that sensitize her to the dawning of particular sensations—of ideas—but those ideas will not and cannot be hers unless she can make the moves that make them hers—unless she can recreate them in herself as expressions of her own capacity to move."[1]

This chapter explores the ways in which activist dance performance provides a framework for educators concerned with constructing classrooms that inform and involve students in matters of social justice. Thus, activist dance performance is used as a tool to imagine the possibilities available within practice-led research models to facilitate a variety of learning outcomes. Here, I discuss Dancing the Humanities as an active learning approach to liberal arts education that uses movement to tackle contemporary social issues. Dancing the Humanities prioritizes movement and participation as essential classroom goals in a progressive educational framework. In this way, movement and participation hold power to fuse deeper connections between the philosophical, theoretical, and worldview-oriented undertakings of a liberal arts education and the action-oriented practice of everyday life.

Liberal arts education holds the potential to play a significant role in responding to social problems by helping students to develop a range of intellectual and practical skills, social responsibility, and a general understanding of the world at large. Liberal arts education encourages students to respond to complex and changing issues. For this reason, an engaged relationship between theory and practice is necessary in liberal arts learning models. A Dancing the Humanities approach catalyzes this engaged relationship by encouraging individual agency and cultivating students' sense of social responsibility beyond the classroom.

Agency and involvement galvanize students to engage with social justice issues by empowering them to take learning, advocacy, and progressive action into their own hands. This empowers students and transforms their perspectives about their own abilities. This mind-set reinforces positive feedback loops that cultivate unity in a classroom of students working together toward common goals. Unity enables an atmosphere conducive to the kind of transformative-empathetic learning introduced in other sections of this research.

In this chapter I explore challenges related to unity and individuality that occurred within the choreographic process, and I discuss how these challenges were addressed through the performance project. Then I provide examples of #MakingofaMovement's key features and strategies that represent the resulting Dancing the Humanities educational approach.

Dance is vital to humanity. I define "dancing" as individual or collective movements that shift the positions or physical locations of bodies in relationship to self, other, and environment. This definition of dancing enables me to explore diverse ways in which shared social, political, and artistic ideas can be expressed physically by groups of people working toward a particular cause. As a unique expression of human cultures and histories, dance transfers activist knowledge from body to body.

In an example of this kind of knowledge transfer, bell hooks describes the university learning environment in a way that suggests the powerful potential of collaboration and agency. hooks advocates for a transformed classroom that emphasizes student empowerment, communal learning, support, and an engaged pedagogy that responds to ever-changing classroom dynamics. In the case of dance classrooms, this kind of "spacious" teaching enables every student voice to be heard.[2] The spacious dance classroom looks diverse, in terms of movement style, student population, incorporated learning-practices, and independent choices.

As both a graduate student and an instructor in a dance department at a private, liberal arts university, movement is my central subject of study. Every class requires some degree of activity. This combination of mental and physical activity keeps the classroom lively and participants engaged. In many modern dance classes, the instructor performs the role of guide, dancing alongside students in the warm-up, walking throughout the studio classroom to deliver tactile feedback during exercises, and encouraging a consistent state of mindfulness by posing relevant questions about the body and the dance. In these classes students are often given the opportunity to collaborate in the creative process by contributing movement to shared group choreography, partnered duets, and individual evaluative solos. Similar to hooks's classroom, this atmosphere of collaboration allows each participant to experience a sense of responsibility to contribute to the group with discussion and invested energy. The whole student, body and mind, is invited into the learning process.

Kimerer LaMothe articulates a paradigm for human movement that dismantles the ideological structures of Western scientific materialism in favor of a philosophy birthed in bodily movement and the natural world.[3] She argues for movement-oriented ways of knowing and sensory re-education in which the body and mind share a more holistic relationship than traditionally experienced in Western context(s). LaMothe extends the idea that we are always in a state of becoming, that humanness is not fixed. Her work also creates space for the idea that bodily, movement-oriented modes of knowledge are of particular value. LaMothe repositions movement as effective and substantial. For LaMothe, bodily movement, as opposed to matter or mind, is central. Movement is the thing that makes us who we are and, as a result, makes what is. LaMothe argues that dance is vital to humanity: humans evolved to participate in the activity of dance in order that we might become, connect, heal, and cultivate relationships with the natural world around and in us.

Transformative-empathetic learning opportunities rank high on the list of important features necessary to incorporate liberating practices in the Christian university dance classroom. Although many American university cultures contain dynamic experiences of political activism in campus and course content, on the contrary, my experience at Belhaven University felt, in many ways, socially and politically insulated. I attribute this to the university's emphasis on traditional Christian values, dedicated Christian worldview course content, and a main campus location in the conservative state of Mississippi, a state often deemed less progressive than the majority of the United States. I am not opposed to emphasizing Christian worldview perspectives in the learning process. In fact, a significant factor of my decision to relocate to the South for this program was due to this facet of the university's agenda. However, since this approach emphasizes an in-depth exploration of Christian perspectives on curricula, it tends to discourage other cultural philosophies and political perspectives that diverge from those advocated by the university. This context challenges progressive dance teaching practices that incorporate alternative paradigms regarding the body and movement. In contrast, these progressive approaches, like the ones I am advocating for, tend to be favored by secular liberalism, often at odds with conservative Christianity.

This tension creates unique challenges particular to the Christian university dance department setting. The Christian worldview curricula is often less welcoming to progressive practices typically incorporated into contemporary modern dance classrooms (e.g., yoga, body-mind centering, meditation, ritual, and breathing practices), because these practices are perceived to have originated from philosophies that are at odds with American Christianity. Secondly, because these dance teaching frameworks, like democratic, egalitarian, and independent learning hierarchies, have not been explicitly prescribed or exemplified in biblical examples of knowledge instruction, many dance practitioners in Christian university settings might be disinclined to engage with them.

In an effort to reconcile this fraught relationship between the Christian university concert dance experience and the heated political circumstances of the US racial and economic climate (influenced by 2016 US presidential campaigns), *#MakingofaMovement* facilitates a path toward more transformative and empathetic responses on the behalf of participants and viewers alike. In keeping my desire to investigate my personal role in social change, I sought to offer *#MakingofaMovement* as an outlet for student dancers and audience members to explore their contributions, intentional or otherwise, to situations of resistance and protest.

Inspired by Susan Foster's research on choreographies of protest, physical interventions in which people's bodies enact symbolic action, I embarked on a journey to create *#MakingofaMovement*, an evening-length choreographic work performed by a cast of ten university dance students and one creative writing student.[4] *#MakingofaMovement* incorporates elements of story told through movement, spoken word, and song. The choreography and musical selections contain groovy, humorous, and reflective features that support the narrative journey. In this production, I utilize solo, duet, and group dances to display significant moves of resistance in a Christian, concert dance setting. Over the course of the performance, a narrator character emerges to express ideas that are foundational to a clear understanding of the work. She speaks about real and imagined experiences related to the ebb and flow of community, the troubled waters of race, and the challenge of participating in protest.

Furthermore, *#MakingofaMovement* engages students in a form of social justice activism, deliberate action(s) performed to influence any level of change in society. This "change in society" benefits not only the observing audience but the student performers themselves. These students are asked to contribute to the creative learning process through improvisation, looking at the world from another's point of view, and discovering their role in influencing change. Within this environment of Dancing the Humanities, engaging movement in the reconciliation of theory and practiced action necessary to deal with issues of social conflict, the cast finds new ways to bring encouragement, healing, and comfort to one another, in response to negative events taking place in the world around them.

As a means of generating movement material and involving the student performers in the subject of the work, I used the rehearsal process to investigate the struggle to overcome oppression from systemic injustices. I guided the students to become more aware of current discourses regarding intersectional equality by sharing notes and ideas that I gathered during protest movement research. I facilitated group discussions on the topic of unity as a common goal and further influenced student awareness and engagement by posting (private group Facebook page) links to some of the film and media resources that I surveyed during the summer. In our time together, students were empowered to express their own diverse thoughts and beliefs about current sociopolitical issues through movement and speech. To explore current events of difference-related unrest in the studio, I encouraged students to recognize and embody the moments in *#MakingofaMovement* in which the group dynamic shifted from one of division to one of acceptance and support. Students experienced this support physically by collaborating with one another to create group lifts, share one another's weight in partnering moments, and express through movement an overall idea of longing for a better world for everyone involved.

Dancing the Humanities developed a route to more fully understand the function of *#MakingofaMovement* as a performance-based educational framework. The work and approach corresponded to my growing desire to participate more actively in the communities around me through the ways in which I engage with space and power relationships in bodily movement and has influenced the research trajectory of my entire graduate journey. Several key features of the creative processes utilized within *#MakingofaMovement* dovetail with the Dancing the Humanities approach to liberal arts education.

One key feature related to the creative process involved in *#MakingofaMovement* had to do with ethnic identity and its influence on student engagement with the production and its themes. The ethnic frame I assumed would be necessary to accomplish the work is one I describe as "dancing while Black," although the boundaries of this framework have less to do with dance and more to do with experiencing the Black ethnic identity. I imagined this frame would enable both performer and audience to experience the rich history of the African American struggle within the United States. However, I also immediately recognized challenges related to representing black bodies and/or themes with a majority-white cast. Simple situations that I believed had little to do with ethnicity became unexpected opportunities to discuss the apparent advantages and limitations of the cast's identity as a whole. In these moments, I sympathized with Rebecca Rossen's attention to representation and embodiment of personal ideas, while choreographing on other bodies.[5]

In *Dancing Jewish*, Rossen describes the kind of dance that can be created on the basis of inserting oneself into a particular ethnic frame. In both her movement solo and excerpts from her book, Rossen considers what inserting oneself into a Jewish frame enables, and questions how that frame can be moved with and against, exploring what it means to "dance Jewishly." In doing so she argues that dancing like or as a Jew is put on, in a sense. This kind of dancing is socially constructed and can be choreographed or formulated and performed/embodied afresh.

Rossen's work advances a mutually inclusive relationship between identity politics and ethnic dance. Her writing illustrates how identity, Jewish identity in this case, is performed and choreographed. Her dance offers a resonant picture of how transference from body to body, different bodies, in choreography, enables particular kinds of experiences from both performer and audience. Although I differentiate between Rossen's work (Jewish female choreographer re-creating her work on a professional male dancer/choreographer who is also Jewish) and my own (African American choreographer setting new work on a cast of student dancers who are mostly white), I relate her struggle with different choreographic frames of reference, gendered or racial, to the challenges I experienced in the project.

An example of one such ethnic-identity-related struggle: one dancer commented during one of our first rehearsals, "Maybe we're all just too white," after noticing her fellow cast members struggle to learn movement generated by my body and a *Soul Train* video clip. My heart immediately fell out of my chest. Having never been one to blame difficult issues on a person's color, I did not want this student to feel inferior in any way, due to a stereotypical understanding of whiteness as it relates to rhythm, style, and a sense of cool.[6]

To gauge the cast's thoughts about the work and their role in it, I took some time during a mid-project rehearsal to ask them several questions. First, I asked what the dance was about. In response, performers described the dance as being about Black history, black/white, race, gender, prejudice, equality, unity, social justice, protest, and advocating for African American people. I add "human connection" to this list. Second, I asked how the performers viewed themselves within the work. In response, some said *rebel, passive, child in poverty, mother* or *woman tired in older years*, and *a human*. Others imagined themselves representing equality, as a narrator, a "human buoy" (anchored while everyone else floats by), and a white man judging and enjoying dancing.

These conversations pointed me in the direction of the second feature of the performance that correlates to the Dancing the Humanities approach. Although the cast did not contribute movement vocabulary, they were asked to contribute to the creative process by naming their role within the work, labeling their thoughts and feelings regarding various themes related to the work, and collaborating in a shared meaning-making experience. As previously stated, the issue of protest, although having an implied connection to

Black lives, had not been defined. Some might ask, "What's the main point or reason for doing what we are doing if we have not selected an issue to protest?" At the point when these questions arose, the choreographic strategy of *#MakingofaMovement* became clear. After these discussions, the dance began to flourish within an open system framework. This framework was one in which the open system of meaning related to the dance frequently exchanged feedback with the surrounding environment, influenced by each performer's experience, information, and energy. This open system framework allowed performing participants to find their own space and voice within the work. The system also enabled the audience to create their own stories and conclusions about what took place onstage. All participants shared the responsibility to produce meaning through movement, song, and empathetic connections that led to transformation of the body-mind being.

This idea of shared responsibility and creating knowledge together contributed to the development of unity among cast members. Unity is a desired outcome of the transformative-empathetic learning experience integral to Dancing the Humanities. Unity allows us to face issues of social conflict head-on and actively respond as a community. The search for unity presents both the research problem and solution. Demonstrated by the performers' spoken words and bodily postures, the struggle with unity, being *we* and *one*, lay beneath the surface of every aspect of the scholarly and creative process involved in choreographing and organizing *#MakingofaMovement*.

One example of a particularly inspiring unity-building activity engaged students in a simultaneous experience of both critical reflection and physical activity. One Friday afternoon I stood in front of the university's entire body of dance students and faculty in a weekly department meeting to share some information about my individual MFA thesis project in preparation for the weekend performances. I used this time to ask the following questions as a survey of student experiences: How do we participate? In forwarding a cause or movement, what do we do and how do we move? Have you ever been part of, experienced, a rally, walk, and/or speech? What did you do physically? Answers included *run*, *walk*, *clap*, and *sit and listen*. I would add to this list: *stand*, *nod* or *shake head*, *link hands* or *arms*, *march*, *sing*, *speak*, and *lie prostrate on the ground*.

Next, I asked everyone present to stand and close their eyes, saying, "Imagine a movement your body performs in protest. What does protest look like for you in movement?" Then I directed everyone to open their eyes and look around the room while maintaining the position or movement decided upon. The response was astounding. Almost everyone was standing in the same position, with one arm raised, fisted or open hand.

This inspiring moment provided students with a direct point of shared gestural connection to the many other bodies surrounding them in the space, contributing to the concept of engaging student bodies in purposeful movement that correlates to the theoretical ideas being explored in liberal arts classrooms at a given time.

Extending this unity-building activity concept further, I incorporated a bonding ritual created specifically for the cast group. This ritual is one I like to refer to as the "Hooding Ceremony." To provide additional context for this ritual ceremony, "Hands-up-Hoodies-up Fed Up!" (a point of climax within the dance performance) begins with a single speaker standing, bathed in light, in a black hooded sweatshirt and jeans near the audience seated before her. She speaks to them confidently, later confessing her uncertainty "not that we will overcome, but that we will overcome as we." She ends her speech with the desperate statement that, "We are FED UP with being not just one." As the music starts loudly, the audience sees this figure disappear into the shadows behind the curtain. Ten dancers, dressed in the same attire, converge upon the stage space in military-like fashion. The dancers file into rows, standing and kneeling with their backs to the audience and their heads bowed, hoods up.

After purchasing ten black, zip-front hoodies for the dancers in the cast (the speaker wore her own) during tech week, I wanted to incorporate some special way to distribute these hoodies before a dress rehearsal. For this reason, I requested that all eleven cast members meet me in the graduate office before the evening's performance, informing them that I wanted to give them their hoodies. In the graduate office, I proceeded to hand each dancer a hoodie, one by one, and ask that they put it on but leave the hood down until everyone was wearing theirs. Then, after a brief pause, I asked them to pull their hoods up together. Standing in a circle with them, I proceeded to describe the hood as a symbol. To me, the hood stood for many things. The hood represented unity through similarity. As an article to pull on and take off, the hood also provided an element of choice and individuality: dancers were permitted to pull their hoods on or off at any time, in a particular section of the dance. Foremost, the hood represented a form of shelter.... Given the topic of this last dance section, indicative of Black Lives Matter protest themes, this concept created the most memorable image for me. I instinctually told the cast, "The hood will protect you."

In the contemporary US, the hood is often a symbol that marks one as seemingly more dangerous. Rather than protection, this symbol invites danger. After a few initial chuckles, a reflective moment of pause fell over everyone in the room. Although nothing was said, this was a moment of silence in memory of those who experienced the pulling on of the hood, walking with heads down, not as protection, but as a foreshadow of impending doom.

As an educator, I firmly believe that movement and participation hold tremendous potential to enliven the learning experience for students in a variety of disciplines. By incorporating an engaged pedagogy that requires students to take ownership of their own learning journey in a fresh and active way, we have the power to influence the direction of social activism as a part of everyday life. Dancing the Humanities represents just one of many inspired paths to do just that. To summarize ideas explored in this chapter, let us recall attention to the significance of transformative-empathetic learning practices for university dance classrooms. The original strategies involved in the creative process of *#MakingofaMovement*, ethnic identity exploration and unity building activities, encourage an atmosphere of acceptance, that of self and others. Diverse experiences of this kind promote an open-mindedness that is particularly beneficial to the Christian university liberal arts setting described at the beginning of the chapter. Transforming experiences of empathy in the creative process also set the stage for similar interactions to take place between performers and audience members. This engaging audience interaction is discussed in greater detail in additional research sections.

Although *#MakingofaMovement* accomplished much within the limits of the project's setting and requirements, there is still work to be done to create and/or emphasize more experiences of this kind in dance and other educational fields. I suggest that we begin to facilitate more and deeper conversations about the pedagogy of dance activism to give our students an understanding of dance that highlights movement's power to influence change on behalf of participants and observers. This kind of active communication might act as a catalyst to empower new generations of dancers who are already interested in exploring what dance does for them and for others. Although I advocate the importance of this research for the dance classroom, I strongly encourage dance practitioners to mobilize this mission and put the "act" in activism by taking it to the streets, so to speak. Community interactions with dance performances of this kind hold power to unite disparate populations and entities.

Notes

1. LaMothe, Kimerer L., *Why We Dance: A Philosophy of Bodily Becoming* (New York: Columbia University Press, 2015).

2. bell hooks, *Teaching to Transgress: Education as the Practice of Freedom* (New York: Routledge, 1994); Tone Pernille Ostern, "Teaching Dance Spaciously," *Nordic Journal of Dance* 1 (2010): 47–57.

3. LaMothe, *Why We Dance.*

4. Susan Foster, "Choreographies of Protest," *Theatre Journal* 55, no. 3 (2003): 395–412.

5. Rebecca Rossen, *Dancing Jewish: Jewish Identity in American Modern and Postmodern Dance* (Oxford: Oxford University Press, 2014).

6. For this reason, I sought the guidance of scholar-artist Mila Thigpen, whose work looks at the civil rights era and Black Lives Matter movements. Thigpen helped me to decipher possible ways in which the cast could evocatively and truly embody someone's experience. She encouraged me to paint an image for the cast, to sit down with them and watch some videos of protest and arrest. She recommended asking them, "When was the last time you actually feared for your life?" and to openly share experiences.

Bibliography

Brooks, Daphne A. *Bodies in Dissent: Spectacular Performances of Race and Freedom, 1850–1910.* Durham. NC: Duke University Press, 2006.

Brown, Jayna. *Babylon Girls: Black Women Performers and the Shaping of the Modern.* Durham, NC: Duke University Press, 2008.

DeFrantz, Thomas F. *Black Performance Theory.* Durham, NC: Duke University Press, 2014.

Foster, Susan Leigh. "Choreographies of Protest." *Theatre Journal* 55, no. 3 (2003): 395–412.

Foster, Susan Leigh. *Reading Dancing: Bodies and Subjects in Contemporary American Dance.* Berkeley: University of California Press, 1986.

hooks, bell. *Teaching to Transgress: Education as the Practice of Freedom.* New York: Routledge, 1994.

Jackson, Naomi, and Toni Shapiro-Phim, eds. *Dance, Human Rights, and Social Justice: Dignity in Motion.* Lanham, MD: Scarecrow Press, 2008.

LaMothe, Kimerer. *Why We Dance: A Philosophy of Bodily Becoming.* New York: Columbia University Press, 2015.

Manning, Susan. *Modern Dance, Negro Dance: Race in Motion.* Minneapolis: University of Minnesota Press, 2006.

Ostern, Tone Pernille. "Teaching Dance Spaciously." *Nordic Journal of Dance* 1 (2010): 47–57.

Rossen, Rebecca. *Dancing Jewish: Jewish Identity in American Modern and Postmodern Dance.* Oxford: Oxford University Press, 2014.

PEDAGOGY
AND THE
LIBERAL ARTS

CHAPTER 7

Test-Oriented Pedagogy in the Teaching of Communication Skills

HELEN O. CHUKWUMA

The twentieth and twenty-first centuries have propelled scientific study and research to such a degree that the arts and humanities are almost effaced. This has its background in humanity's quest for mastering the world and the environment through technology and science. Tremendous progress was made in health, space exploration, transportation, agriculture, war technology, and other fields. Jobs followed the discoveries and inventions, and science became king and displaced the arts. Yet technology without humanities is barren and reductive of the human essence and being. There is need therefore to return to the basics of our humanity and revisit our basic human art, which is communication or the art of beating machines. This is an essential part of the program of education in our higher institutions. For indeed man's social nature is built on communication, the sustainable aspect of our humanity.

In this regard, the mission of the College of Liberal Arts at Jackson State University "is to nurture the minds and spirits of its students and *to develop and refine students' spoken, written and analytical skills*, their artistic and creative talents, their knowledge of the humanities and the social and behavioral sciences and the ways *in which technology can be used to advance their capacity to understand world events and* contribute to improvements in the human condition [my emphasis]."[1] Without equivocation, the liberal arts and humanities are the bedrock of the Academy; it is the beginning of the journey to knowledge acquisition and the end objective of university education. That is why universities designate courses from the humanities as core courses required for every university entrant. Communication, the imparting or sharing of ideas and information, is the core of all academic endeavors. Thus, communication is dialogic with the known or assumed presence of a listener, reader, audience, or referent. In its very nature, communication is a skill, a learned and acquired means of transmitting, socializing, learning, and disseminating knowledge.

Communication as a skill is learned at an early age and is graded to adulthood where the final stage is attained in the university and prepares the whole person for life, professions, interrelationships, and jobs. The three components of communication are reading and comprehension, speaking, and writing. Thus, Sir Francis Bacon's famous quotation resounds even today: "Reading maketh a full man, conference a ready man and writing an exact man."[2] The earliest schools of Europe and Western civilization, called grammar schools, were places that specialized in the three "Rs": reading, writing, and arithmetic. These are the prongs of liberal arts education and exposure for all students in the Academy to date. Students who enroll in the university are required to build on their knowledge of the three communication skills for effective learning outcomes. They are taught to discard the rote method of memorization and regurgitation and to build up their own parameters of embedding knowledge and building up their own style and repertoire of communication to legitimize it as their own.

This paper, then, has two aspects: one, to show the effectiveness of test-oriented pedagogy in teaching communication skills in the liberal arts and, two, to show the continued relevance of the liberal arts in the millennium age. In addition, communication is an ephemeral entity, which needs anchoring. The pedagogy for students to achieve mastery, confidence, and competence in communication at this level is based on three prongs: a) student centrism, b) immediacy and inclusiveness, and c) test rigor and regularity. These three prongs form the basis of my analysis in this paper.

Pedagogy in communication is student centered. As such, communication classes should have fewer than twenty students enrolled, but enrollment for classes like communication and composition is usually twenty-five to thirty and sometimes more. These problems are, however, surmountable with the provision of learning tools like iPads and laptops in the classroom and language laboratories. These resources break down the barrier of the classroom encounter for the instructor and students. The classroom is no longer a stage, with the stiff demarcation of the students sitting far away from the teacher in wonderment and trepidation. Technology has lifted students to a position of being contributors to the learning process where they are mandated to prepare for class, ask questions, and state their opinions and concerns.

In a way students tend to dictate the pace of the class, though the instructor supervises and directs. Each student remains an individual with his or her own intellect and pace of understanding, and the instructor adjusts class activity, especially in the area of testing. This form of teaching, empowering students with aid and responsibility, forms individual mastery and propels self-improvement. Topics and ideas given out for discussion challenge students to research and inquire, and they require student input in class. In this setting the teacher is a director of activities, with students working under supervision, and in testing, teamwork, partnership, collaboration, and group-assigned tasks are used to great effect.

Testing is the end game of teaching. Every class has some provision for testing, as in reading and comprehension, oral presentation in the form of group work, and writing. Continuous assessment drives student attendance, and, in its immediacy and inclusiveness, testing subjects students to in-class assignments designed to build on their speed of response in comprehension and articulation. Students are called upon to respond to colleagues, ask questions, answer questions, and open vistas for argument and persuasion. Inclusive testing creates an environment where every student is heard. The students address class, analyze a work, air their views, and give their opinions. Students must take their turns in addressing class on a given topic and be able to sustain their own parts of the argument. This develops critical thinking and analytical reasoning.

I will give a practical example with my honors class in world literature. There was a three-person group presentation on Catullus's lyrics. Catullus was a Roman poet in ancient times who wrote love poems to his mistress Lesbia, a married woman. Since the theme was love, the questions and discussion that followed were robust. The question that polarized class was whether the group thought that the mistress was sincere and reciprocated Catullus's professed love. A member of the group then proceeded to lecture his classmates on love and women's infidelity and how Lesbia would remain uncaring. The topic of women's infidelity proved a heated argument in class, with some blaming Catullus for falling in love with an adulterous woman. I had to direct class with an explanation of the Greek concept of love as Agape and love as Eros, and I added a moral element of restraint and integrity. Class adjourned with a better understanding of "true love" and "erotic love." The looks on their faces were revealing. They questioned whether Catullus's emotion was love or just sealed in the realm of lust. With inclusiveness, every member of class has the freedom to express an opinion and is taught how to defend it.

Test rigor and regularity prepare students for tests on short notice. Depending on the size of class, students write essays regularly. Communication exercises at all levels prepare students for mental capacity building and develop quick responses to tasks and exercises. Take-home essays have their pitfalls; the better option is to give written assignments in class that prepare students to think and respond under the pressure of time. These assignments confirm original thought and execution, and they increase confidence in the students' ability to perform. Regular tests may be a burden to instructors but have their own advantage in learning outcomes for students. Writing topics are drawn from everyday news and social concerns such as immigration, legalization of marijuana, bilingualism in America, capital punishment, guns on campus, and many others, and students are encouraged to make suggestions for topics.

In her book *Teaching to Transgress*, bell hooks believes teaching students to transgress racial, sexual, and class boundaries to achieve the gift of freedom is a most important goal. When students transgress, they not only state their opinion and take a position; they must argue to convince their audience. Important too is guiding students to think for themselves, have an opinion, and be able to defend it.[3] Teachers must continue to look for ways of improving how to teach; how you impart knowledge is as important as what you teach.

There are some pedagogical strategies to consider for testing. First, the element of surprise is important in capacity building for instantaneous response in communication, both in writing and speaking. In-class writing is challenging for students, but they adjust mentally and physically. This prepares them for interviews and communication in the workplace. Second, teachers can ask for students' input into topics. When students are invited to suggest topics for essays, they are elated, and the argument over which topic to accept increases class participation and interest even if some guidance from the instructor may be needed for topic relatedness and currency. Frequent tests lead to students' acquisition of communication skills and give instructors data to assess the students' rates of development and learning, and inclusive class discussions and brainstorming topics promote interest and self-confidence.

Written communication challenges millennials. This is the result of the influence of computer language and lack of written training at school. This situates Bacon's phrase "writing maketh an exact man" in bold perspective. Students know what they want to say, but they lack the skill to communicate it in form and meaning. There is a sense of urgency that attends college writing, which corrodes skills such as grammar, spelling, and vocabulary. Students can acquire proficiency in writing only through practice in frequent tests. Nowhere is such practice as needed as in written communication, because students have to unlearn the colloquialisms and cryptic computer dialogue to acquire the skills of communicating in a universal formal language. In-class testing presents an environment of immersion in teaching communication skills, where the student is exposed to reading or listening, speaking, or writing skills. The classroom is thus a training ground with its challenges, and later a familiar environment for self-assertion and intellectualism. Students shed the inhibitions and challenges of public speaking, dialogic responses, and effective writing practices.

The "stress" technique in testing for communication skills is a result-oriented pedagogy. Kathleen Smith bears this out in chapter 15 of the "Instructor's Manual" to Jean Wyrick's *Steps to Writing Well*. Here she outlines steps to writing well under pressure and how to plan, organize, and respond to such tests. Pressure develops in students the mechanism of quick response to any communication challenge at any time. This prepares students for the workplace and job interviews. Oral communication as part of in-class testing also comes with its own pressure. This in-class activity trains and exposes students to critical thinking skills and quick communication in a question-and-answer format. It also gives students audience awareness, courtesy, and the ability to surmount public nervousness. It trains students in clarity of thought and direct, concise execution. In oral communication, students improve their elocution, vocabulary, and stylistic rendition.

Smith suggests six "Guidelines for Effective Delivery" and suggests that students "think of the talk as a conversation with peers. For a pleasing delivery, do the following:

1) Monitor your voice. Avoid a monotone and make sure the back row can hear you.
2) Make eye contact. Look at everyone in the room and don't read from your notes.
3) Avoid distractions. Don't interrupt yourself with "ummm" and "you know."
4) Consider instructional aids. These include handouts, samples, posters...
5) Adjust and adapt. Look at the audience to see if you need to slow down or restate a point.
6) End well. Consider making a humorous comment or having a question and answer period.[4]

She did not add courtesies from the speaker such as salutations and greetings, and sometimes students may want to include introductions and a statement about the topic or title. Together, these can make the speaker seem spontaneous as well as articulate.

With regard to the acquisition of writing skills, tests are challenging to students because of several factors, including weak exposure to grammar and the mechanics of English usage, limited vocabulary, and incomplete analytical skills. Students are taught the basic sound patterns of English from the word, the sentence structure, and sentence formation to paragraphs, summaries, essays, long essays, and research papers. Long stretches of activities spanning two or more semesters ground the students' formation. Each of these processes is structured through testing, and the number of times students practice and the manner of execution form the backbone of students' proficiency in communication skills. The importance of writing is underscored because it remains the lasting medium of formal communication. Students' problems with effective communication in writing stem from how to effect a transition from colloquial or conversational English, or what John Edgar Wideman calls the "the language of talk," to formal English.[5]

Thus, paradigmatic interferences carry over from the "language of talk" to their formal English, especially in writing. These come under four headings: phonetic, syntactic, basic grammar, and nonce formations. Phonetics, or pronunciation of speech sounds in the general mode of conversational English, is marked by ellipsis, nasalization, homophones, and other meaningful grunts. Ellipsis in speech, or the omission of some sounds, and the tendency to shorten the articulation of words are understood because of habit and the contexts of use. Students tend to carry these over into writing, and when they do they send the wrong signal and meaning. Phonetically induced errors are corrected by the habit of consulting a good dictionary, which furnishes the phonetic symbols and the meanings of the words. Such an explanation written on the board and explained in a classroom impacts students.

In the realm of sounds, homophones are problematic in students' writing, especially in spelling. Homophones are words with similar sounds but with different meanings and functions within a written sentence. With these sentence constructions and errors in mind, O'Neal and Trabasso state that "there appears to be a correspondence between the written symbols we use as letters and spoken forms of the words."[6] In other words, the relationship between phonology and orthography can be empirically proven.

O'Neal and Trabasso offer an explanation by establishing the patterns of reading and writing "from the print (the orthographic representation) to sound (the phonological representation) to meaning (semantic representation). When we write we do the reverse, namely, we go from meaning to sound to spelling (as semantics to phonology to orthography)."[7] With practice, students acquire the proficiency of such automatic transitions of the use of words in whatever medium.

Part of the interference with student writing from the "language of talk" is the syntax of speech elements in sentences and paragraphs. These syntactic errors are found in sentence fragments and run-ons with no subject or linkages. This shows a lack of sequencing that, though understood in talk, is confusing in formal writing. Some class time needs to be devoted to basic grammar, sentence structure, parts of speech, their functions, and their interrelationship within the sentence. Experience shows that, while most students have strong grammar backgrounds, they are careless or forget them. Other students need proper and rigorous grounding in basic grammar.

Grammar is the cornerstone of correct writing. The most common areas of weakness are in verbs, tenses, pluralization, and word comparisons. Plurals and apostrophes are often confused, but verbs, their tenses, and subject-verb agreement pose a far greater problem in students' writing and underscore the need for continuous, rigorous instruction and testing and for instructors of English communication to pay more attention to grammar.

Comparisons may be odious, but students must be exposed to the correct usage of comparative modifiers. Students jumble the order of the three degrees of comparison and sometimes form new ones and attempt to give the words a superlative and repetitive meaning. Although we can recognize our students' creative energy in their effort to communicate in writing, we need to channel this energy along the lines of correct and universal English while maintaining our peculiar American English.

As for lexicon and nonce formations, students are encouraged to build on their vocabulary through reading and the use of a thesaurus, and they should practice using these new words in their writing and oral communication. When students introduce creative words to the English lexicon, they lack recognition and currency. Albeit unlikely, one day some of these nonce formations may gain currency in English usage and be included in dictionaries. In the meantime, practice makes perfect in acquiring communication skills. Written papers must bear marks for mistakes and corrections, and instructors must confer with students about their communication skills, especially in writing.

As we have seen, the liberal arts remain relevant in the millennial age, especially as students prepare for the communication challenges of the global sphere. With the drive for technology, industrialization, economics, business, and banking, enrollment has diminished in some liberal arts courses in the university, and this is understandable. Yet the study of the liberal arts in a STEM age adds the missing "A" for the "arts" to that acronym. The liberal arts humanize us and can rescue humanity from the robotic world of machines. Communication skills are the bedrock of literacy and professional excellence.

It is analytical and critical thinking that prepares one for job opportunities and for the ability to control one's world and engender positive outcomes in job positions.

Most liberal arts courses are expansive and offer gateways to the world's peoples and cultures. This is knowledge across borders. The liberal arts offer a foundation of knowledge that can be transmitted to other disciplines such as law, banking, management, public health, and social work. And liberal arts teaching includes civic engagement and cultural outreach. The liberal arts prepare students to inquire, explore, analyze, and absorb. This system of inquiry teaches students to cultivate the value of informed judgments on political, social, religious, and cultural issues. This solid foundation gets students ready for the challenges of the outer world.

The liberal arts will compete in the Academy with this complex world of science, technology, and business. Not only will the foundational liberal arts courses continue to be required, interdisciplinary courses will grow as more departmental majors and minors are offered. The Academy can establish units of interdisciplinary studies whose main function is to offer viable options for majors and minors to students to suit their interests and aspirations. Every discipline needs liberal arts input in the conventions of researching, writing reports, and findings; presenting data to colleagues at conferences and round tables; and preparing to publish data. Interdisciplinary learning is a viable option in today's world.

Communication skills are the bedrock of literacy and professionalism in all fields of endeavor and prepare students for the tasks of brainstorming, analytical reasoning, argument, judgment, and taking a position. We humans create machines that have to do our bidding, and our language has to continue to be human and edifying.

Notes

1. "Mission Statement, College of Liberal Arts," Jackson State University, *Founders Day Brochure*, 2017.

2. Francis Bacon, "Quotes," Brainy Quotes, https://www.brainyquote.com/quotes/quotes/f/francisbac399408.html.

3. bell hooks, *Teaching to Transgress: Education as the Practice of Freedom* (New York: Routledge, 1994).

4. Kathleen Smith, *Instructor's Manual to Steps to Writing Well* (Boston: Wadsworth Cengage Learning, 2014).

5. John Edgar Wideman, "Foreword," in Zora Neale Hurston, *Every Tongue Got to Confess: Negro Folk-Tales from the Gulf States* (New York: Perennial, 2002), xx.

6. Deborah Sears Harrison and Tom Trabasso, eds., *Black English: A Seminar* (Hillsdale, NJ: Lawrence Erlbaum Associates, 1976), 171.

7. Harrison and Trabasso, *Black English*, 172.

Bibliography

Bacon, Francis. "Quotes." Brainy Quote. https://www.brainyquote.com/quotes/quotes/f/francisbac399408.html.

Harrison, Deborah Sears, and Tom Trabasso, eds. *Black English: A Seminar*. Hillsdale, NJ: Lawrence Erlbaum Associates, 1976.

hooks, bell. *Teaching to Transgress: Education as the Practice of Freedom*. New York: Routledge, 1994.

Hurston, Zora Neale. *Every Tongue Got to Confess: Negro Folk-Tales from the Gulf States*. New York: Perennial, 2002.

"Mission Statement, College of Liberal Arts." Jackson State University. *Founders Day Brochure*, 2017.

Smith, Kathleen. *Instructor's Manual to Steps to Writing Well*. Boston: Wadsworth Cengage Learning, 2014.

Wideman, John Edgar. "Foreword." In Zora Neale Hurston, *Every Tongue Got to Confess: Negro Folk-Tales from the Gulf States*. New York: Perennial, 2002.

Wyrick, Jean. *Steps to Writing Well*. Boston: Wadsworth Cengage Learning, 2014.

CHAPTER 8

Flexible Thought for the Test-Focused Student

KATHY ROOT PITTS

It is a common complaint that students taught in today's traditional classrooms are so targeted on mastering standardized tests that they do not practice critical thinking skills. They have been rewarded primarily for achievements at the memory, understanding, and application stages of Bloom's taxonomy, and little time and energy has been devoted to complex thought processes.[1]

Remembering facts is essential, but to string all of those loose facts together in a meaningful way, students need to exercise their higher cognitive skills. A taxonomy of learning levels must recognize a nonconstructive phase at some midpoint beyond the application level of knowledge, past the analysis/evaluation levels, but just before the fully creative stage, a "precreative moment," where the mind takes the many pieces that it has collected, all those piles of facts and formulas, and prepares to assemble them into unique thoughts.

Bloom's 2001 taxonomy was revised to reflect dynamics between the knowledge levels, especially the higher functions of creative thought's "putting elements together to form a coherent or functional whole; reorganizing elements into a new pattern or structure through generating, planning, or producing."[2] My concern, though, is that there be a strong focus in our schools on studying the creative works of great minds *while* exploring and encouraging creativity in students. Granted, analysis and synthesis are deconstructive and reconstructive mental activities, but "precreative" here refers to analysis and synthesis that is further triggered by the unique workings of each individual mind—inspiration, one might say, that creative impetus that helps to make you and me two totally different people.

Studying should be fun. When we were children, we made play out of creative imagination, and through that imagination we developed our identities. Visualize two children dumping on the floor their Tinkertoy canisters. I like this analogy because I can use it to treat studies as a game. Now, Tinkertoys were developed around the Pythagorean theorem. According to toy historian Todd Coopee from the site Toy Tales: "The set's spools each had eight holes drilled every 45 degrees around the perimeter and one hole in the middle. They could be connected using wooden sticks of different sizes. Regardless of their size, each stick in the set was cut to a correct length to form 90-degree triangles—a practical application of the Pythagorean theorem that served to fortify the structures that kids built."[3] Geometry does make the building set standard and scientific, but no matter that two Tinkertoy sets just off the assembly line will be identical and both designed using the Pythagorean theorem—a constant for everyone—when two creative children begin constructing with those identical sets, their constructions will be completely different from each other's. This is how lessons should work. Begin with facts and patterns, but finish with creative individuality.

Building blocks trigger an unpredictable creative process that is much like the freedom of applied liberal arts. In contrast, focusing on standardized testing and rigid curricula is not allowing our students the highest creative level of learning. To continue with toy analogies, what we have in our schools now is like reconstructing a jigsaw puzzle rather than creating with building blocks. With a jigsaw puzzle, we might approach completion many different ways. I might look for the corner pieces. Someone else might start from a single patch of green grass in the middle and move out, but if we are patient, we both will arrive at the same finished picture of a garden. We want our students to be able to move beyond a square frame, though.

Education should work at that level of creativity illustrated by the Tinkertoy analogy. Before deep perception and creation can evolve out of the hierarchy represented by Bloom's categories, each individual's mind must effect a disassembly of facts in order to move on to a constructive and uniquely creative process. We must spill our blocks on the floor and try for something new. Still, even on the creative "fun" level, facts are essential. They are a student's separate building blocks. Creativity, in contrast, cannot be taught to a student as a cold fact. The instructor cannot "teach" creativity simply because creativity is a highly personal and organic mental process. It is the difference between following a blueprint and painting a masterpiece. The masterpiece is significant because it is both unusual and inspirational. It touches us, but, being as we are not the artist, we could not have painted that exact picture ourselves. It is the brainchild of the artist.

Granted, creativity is an individual and seemingly solitary process, but here lies an enigma. Creativity does not isolate the artist, the scientist, or the student. Instead, a keen relationship exists where someone can create something that I would never have conceived, a painting, for instance, yet now that it is done, I can attempt to understand and appreciate it. Only Salvador Dali would have painted *The Persistence of Memory*, but I am able to relate even though I would never have produced the same painting. Creativity is a marvelous mystery; it draws on the deep thought processes of the individual, yet the product of that individual's creativity pulls us together as a group. It is the special role of the audience to understand the efforts of the creator and thereby share in the creative process. Thoughtful and studied creativity, both producing *and* sharing, in the arts or the sciences, is humankind at our most noble. It is the pinnacle of Bloom's taxonomy, and it is where we want our students to go.

Like the artist, creative students must devote themselves to study and practice their creative skills. I emphasize "practice," because practice is essential to mastery. It might seem contrary to common lore to insist that creativity must be practiced. We tend to think of creativity as a kind of divine inspiration, but any truly accomplished artist or writer will admit that the gift of talent is not enough, for with talent comes the obligation of hard work. The most talented people build on their natural abilities with practice. This holds for scholars as well. Scholars in all fields must exercise their critical muscles. A brain is not merely a receptacle for storing facts; it is an idea processor. A critically practiced brain absorbs facts, combines them, and produces ideas that are unique. Ideas lead to art, inventions, advancements, spirituality, empathy, and social change.

The arts, with symbols, emotions, connections, and instinctive "gut" knowledge, are the mind at its most active. In contrast, memorization is one of the least complex levels of knowledge, and it is much of the stuff of standardized tests. Now standardized tests do measure the sort of basic understanding that follows rigid formulas. Still, what concerns me is that by primarily teaching students to succeed at standardized tests while we neglect the creative impulse, we are depriving our students of the opportunities to exercise and appreciate their higher mental functions that make for a rich life of the mind. This sort of creativity is the backbone of the liberal arts. In fact, Sandra Ruppert of the Arts Education Partnership points to independent studies that indicate that a liberal arts education even improves SAT scores in non-liberal-arts areas.[4]

Profound creativity is an internal process of each individual mind, and there the teacher cannot go. We can set facts and theories before our students and tell them what we know or guess, but then we really should make the space to let creativity happen. Teachers who limit student creativity might be stunting their students' future ability to think creatively. Lisa Tsui, author and researcher for the Urban Institute, warns that "beyond the immediate instruction delivered, educators are affecting students' long-term outlook on intellectual pursuits and their habits of mind via exposure to a certain intellectual ethos that is fostered within classrooms."[5]

Tsui, in treating several case studies, describes a school she refers to as "School D," the school in the study that exhibited the highest critical-thinking development and where students were encouraged "to approach topics in ways that they may not have experienced before: to grapple with complex issues, consider multiple perspectives, question authoritative sources, and develop one's own nuanced interpretation." These students were debating theories in education classes, interpreting cultural influences on literature, and examining multiple viewpoints in history courses. Through interviews with students, teachers, and administrators, it was determined that students were able to make interdisciplinary connections, advance their own independent ideas, and question conventional wisdom intelligently.[6] Students whose minds are unfettered are capable of doing much on their own, and teachers might do best by simply presenting the information and then encouraging the students' creative processes to engage.

Liberal arts courses are, by definition, grounded in the "practice" of creativity. According to Vicki Baker, Roger Baldwin, and Sumedha Makker in their return to a 1990 study by economics professor D. W. Breneman, this runs opposite from the professional training direction that even many liberal arts colleges have chosen to take. Baker, Baldwin, and Makker find that college-level interest in the liberal arts is on a rapid decline, a trend that has these professors calling for a return to the truly "liberal arts" college. What is fascinating is that, at the time of their publication in the *Association of American Colleges and Universities*, Baker was an economics professor, Baldwin was in educational administration, and Makker was a certified public accountant, yet they had the foresight to appreciate the cultivation of the mind and the character development that liberal arts provide.[7]

Since the creative process cannot be prescribed to students, the present educational community has taken the unfortunate tack of stopping short after Bloom's "understanding" phase of knowledge.[8] This is about as far as teachers can go before students must take over their own thinking. It is hard for teachers to trust that students can take the facts and methods that they have been taught up through the understanding stage and move beyond to creative ability.

In another toy analogy, my father taught me to ride a bike by running alongside and holding the seat until some instinct told him when the moment was right to let go. This experience is common to most kids. I knew how the bike worked, had practiced with training wheels, had suffered a few bruises, had gotten up my nerve until finally I could pedal on my own. My father's patience and our hard work led up to this first ride, but the accomplishment itself my father could not do for me. From the moment he let go, the mastery and the path I would follow were my own. Nonetheless, he was afraid to let go, and I was afraid to be released. In our classrooms, creativity begins the moment the bike's seat is let free.

As with the fear of falling off the bike, fear is the reason our schools are so test focused. Teachers fear allowing students to practice their creative reasoning processes gradually. Rather, they leap into simplified and cautious reiteration of facts, so that creative learning is seldom reached. So much accountability is now demanded of teachers that they risk their jobs if student ability cannot be measured and proven on standardized tests. Students, in turn, expect to be handed facts. They too are afraid of failure, and they now demand detailed study guides before tests and dread essay exams. We do not trust in practice that leads to mastery and creativity. We are afraid to let go of rote memorization and simple, replicable formulas.

In the forms of fill-in-the-blank, multiple choice, and matching, testing does not take students past Bloom's "understanding" level and cannot evaluate the higher functions of creativity. Part of this problem is due to teacher anxiety in an educational system that has judged its students and teachers based on standardized testing since the start of the 1900s, when there was a scarcity of teachers, and underqualified individuals had to stand in for them. At that time standardized testing might have made sense, but now we depend on standardized testing so much that it has become a crutch and a hindrance to learning.

This is not the case in the schools of Finland. According to Duke University research, "they [Finnish schools] have come out on top in the OECD [Organization for Economic Cooperation and Development] rankings even though, as a nation, they have abolished standardized testing. They view it as antiquated as a method, inefficient as way of actually measuring the most important learning, and a dis-incentive to great, inspiring teaching."[9]

In the freshman year for all college majors, whether liberal arts or STEM, a philosophy of liberal arts course should be offered. This course could give students interpretive tools linked over students' academic careers to a significant number of liberal arts courses. Students would apply and practice the interpretive skills they learn in this philosophy course to those subsequent liberal arts courses. These classes would help them practice and build their creative and critical thinking skills, emphasize hard work, and be writing and discussion rich.

The philosophy of liberal arts course would be based on a "philosophical" approach to the liberal arts, examining music, paintings, literature, and history, and if well-applied will cause students to understand, analyze, and evaluate course materials with "subjective" logic that sets the groundwork for deep thinking in the sense that creative thought is always personal but guided with flexible logic. With flexible logic come problem-solving skills. Students would learn to work problems and formulate meaningful opinions rather than just follow recipes. Flexible and creative thinking would help in pursuits of advanced scholarship and professional careers.

The aim of the philosophy of liberal arts course, combined with standard liberal arts courses, is to give students in college prolonged practice in applied critical thinking that will improve their abilities to think deeply in any areas of their lives. Students will become adept at achieving profound knowledge *on their own* by examining the arts using the techniques of philosophers who wrote on art and literature. Eventually, students will be better able to think critically without reservation, as they will become, in a sense, philosophers themselves.

To give students the tools that promote informed creative processes and help them determine deep meaning, the philosophical aspects of this class would teach the fundamentals of logic, empirical burden of proof, logical fallacies, and perspective, including the values and beliefs born of diverse culture and upbringing, relative and absolute truth, the play of emotions in logical conclusions, and recognition that perceptions are fluid and changing. Tools for a philosophy of liberal arts class would be argument maps, Socratic question-and-answer dialogue, debate, diagramming, brainstorming, and, on the high end, evaluating others' critical studies of aesthetics in the arts and literature.

Teachers would introduce students to the well-considered observations of critics. This would not be a class where students learn everything that there is to know about logic or philosophy; they would simply be encouraged to explore and exercise their own abilities to think while they use examples from the liberal arts as the media for that exploration. Students would discover and value their own ideas as well as the creativity of others, create for themselves, and use logic in these several processes.

This philosophy of liberal arts course and the subsequent traditional liberal arts courses would give students materials that they could use as patterns for guided critical thinking. Students would develop their interpretive skills (hermeneutics) by distinguishing among areas of interpretation. For instance, Plato's reality or imitative theory held true knowledge and form in the greatest esteem, yet in narrative we find the artist's voice combined with imitation. In drama we find pure imitation. The student might explore the "mirror idea," suggesting that the best art most accurately depicts all views of reality as meaningful. It is empiricist reality; the mind is passive with all people viewing reality the same. Students might explore Plato's worldview of the true reality of form and idea compared to daily reality of appearances and the further diluted imitations of art. If art copies appearances, is it inferior to reality? If imitation threatens to appeal to the irrational emotions, might it therefore celebrate the coarser aspects of humankind?[10] A teacher might, based on the ideas of Plato, lead the class in a discussion as to whether students value realistic art over personally expressive art.

In another example, author-based, expressive theory treats the individual mind as creative. Such creation may amount to the simple outpouring of feelings, or maybe it can be likened to the creative power of godly inspiration. Students might be drawn into a biographical determination as to whether a work is highly personal. They might debate whether those expressed feelings, personal to the artist, are shared universally, and whether the artist creates a useful bond between the artist and the audience. Is the sharing of these emotions worthwhile? William Wordsworth felt that this natural empathy of humankind, dignified through art, is noble. Longinus in the first century saw poetry as the product of sublime creation that connects the artist to the audience in a highly elevated relationship with a significant bond beyond the ordinary.[11]

From another philosophical perspective, audience-oriented theories, like the affective/pragmatic theories, attempt to describe how the audience *participates* in art. Horace's *Art of Poetry* determines, "The aim of the poet is either to benefit, or to amuse, or to make his words at once please and give lessons of life." These aims can be justified through various philosophers, like Sir Philip Sidney, who sees the goal of poetry's being to teach, entertain, and lead the reader toward virtue and perfection. Students would explore Aristotle's concept of art as "therapeutic," with art's effecting a cathartic purge by exhausting the emotions.[12] Students might consider art and literature as entertaining, inspiring, or even utilitarian, as these works purge harmful emotions, elicit desired reactions, or simply teach.

Finally, with the idea of "art for art's sake," structuralists' objective theory concentrates on form and coherence while considering the artistic work to be a "structure" for examination in and of itself. Oscar Wilde, in his *The Decay of Lying*, suggests that art never expresses anything but itself, and bad art comes from imitating nature and life: "Art is our spirited protest, our gallant attempt to teach nature her proper place." W. K. Wimsatt and Monroe C. Beardsley in their "The Intentional Fallacy" would say that we cannot know the author's intention; we have only the work itself to examine, and must limit our interpretation with the work itself.[13]

These approaches to literature and art are a small assortment of the many ways that the arts can be interpreted and suggest the initial philosophical guidances that a philosophy of liberal arts course could take. Students should start the course with a simplified handbook that supplies basic theories of art and literary interpretation in order to make this vast subject manageable. The handbook would direct students to supplemental reading selections for further perusal, and teachers and students would practice multiple interpretive responses to creative works.

As the course progresses, more interpretive tools will emerge. There are psychoanalytical, feminist, Marxist, deconstructionist, historical, and cultural criticisms that can be applied to the arts and are meaningful formats for the deep exercise of the critical mind. One important aspect of this course would be the vast choice of perspectives that force students to think rather than mimic. Making critical depth-of-knowledge judgments requires that students observe problems through varied perspectives. Students will be exposed to how analytical interpretation can offer dynamic answers from many angles. Recognizing these perspectives and *thinking about them* will lead students to become problem "solvers" rather than just automatons reciting the simple answers. The liberal arts is a fertile medium for developing critical skills because the arts are not locked into black-and-white interpretations. They can be argued from many sides with validity.

Literature, music, and visual arts are perfect platforms for critical and creative thinking because they invite interpretation and personal response. Students would be graded in a nonthreatening way for process and participation (how they arrive at conclusions) over prescribed outcomes (parroting a "right" answer). Grading would be fluid and focused primarily on whether there is any pattern of logic to their essay-style answers. The arts are less intimidating when offered as subjective personal-response courses, because they validate students' own views.

One significant misconception in liberal arts education is that the arts are without structure, and anything goes, and that the process of creation is so individual and subconscious that teaching and testing methods defy regulation. Twenty-one and nineteen must always equal forty in a math class, but in the liberal arts, we question how the arts can be used to prepare students for life skills that will demand uniformity and specific knowledge. Students of the arts would learn facts, but they would learn interpretive strategies as well. Students would not just spill their emotions on paper. They would be offered factual knowledge, and they would be graded on the attainment of those facts, but then their course of study would evolve toward the *interpretation* of facts through the practice of critical thinking.

The philosophy of liberal arts class would present students with philosophical tools to talk about the liberal arts, thereby laying a "critical thinking" foundation. Students are given a twofold task: (1) become acquainted with philosophical theories about the arts, and (2) apply those theories to some art object. Barry Oreck, consultant in arts education, research, and professional development, recognizes the technique of bringing art into the classroom to help students find their creativity. Still, he understands that these teachers would not necessarily be art experts but rather would use the arts, in some cases, to "promote creative teaching techniques."[14] Similarly, teachers would be expected to be experts in neither the liberal arts nor philosophy in this philosophy of liberal arts classroom; they would simply use a combination of the liberal arts and philosophy to exercise students' critical thinking abilities. Students would learn to contemplate and articulate opinions while developing high reasoning skills through the exercises of logic and argument about select art, music, and literature pieces. This classroom would be rich in discussion and debate.

Psychology, sociology, history, fine arts, and music recognize the need for learning facts, but they call for analysis and strategies as well and can be treated to individual interpretation once students are given facts and allowed to exercise their minds, while teachers are trusted to do their jobs. The National Education Association, according to Stephanie Overman, addresses how teachers are constrained by the public with rules and standardized, statistical demands for results.[15] Unlike, for instance, the Finnish school system that promotes the arts, the United States has undervalued the arts.

In her thesis Lauren Knight compares attitudes of the Finnish educational community to that of the United States and finds that "in Finland, the arts are interwoven through their entire education system and hold the same value as other subjects. In the United States the ... NCLB [No Child Left Behind] has all but killed art education throughout the country, because it only focuses on standardized test scores and not on the enhancement of the whole child. On the contrary," Knight continues, "it has not been recognized in America that art education helps to improve other subject areas. In addition, NCLB also has put pressure on teachers to produce high test scores from their students with little to no additional financial support."[16]

Jeffrey Scheuer, media and political writer, expounds on the "plasticity" of a liberal arts education and how that education leads to inventive thought. He recognizes the "stable but impermanent fields of inquiry" that give the mind free range to speculate and invent. The use of art projects to exercise critical thinking was used successfully for grading student comprehension of literature. According to artist Tara Shoemaker Holdren, students were asked to create art that connected with the literature, showed comprehension of themes, offered personal interpretation, and communicated well: "When the researcher used art projects to assess reading comprehension in this study, students enjoyed higher levels of engagement with the text, collaborative problem solving, and increased thinking stamina." Through the artistic creation process itself, students were able to interpret their readings more profoundly and enjoy a depth of experience that delved beyond the standard classroom examination.[17]

Although liberal arts teach well-rounded thinking, a quality that employers want, standardized tests do have their place. We should continue with standardized testing, but we should recognize its limits. Standardized tests can only monitor fundamental knowledge. Education should not stop at this level. We need to help students' interest grow, not by stifling them but by opening them up to critical thinking in the arts. The President's Committee on Arts and the Humanities recognizes the higher levels of reasoning that we lose when we diminish the role of the liberal arts in education: "Arts integration is the practice of using arts strategies to build skills and teach classroom subjects across different disciplines. When implemented effectively and with rigor, students receive both high quality arts instruction and subject matter instruction reading, math, science and other subjects within an integrated lesson plan."[18]

When we give students the tools to think for themselves, then we have promoted the highest form of knowledge: creativity. To create means to produce something new. People are afraid of what they do not understand, but if we only impart the knowledge that we can harness, then what happens to our inventions, our mysteries, and our discoveries?

We can have structure, but in such a way that students and teachers are not slamming into obstacles. We can provide direction, like how a tree grows toward the sun, not limitations. For students to achieve critical thinking, teachers must be trusted to teach and students trusted to self-motivate. Teachers should be allowed to do their jobs without excessive regulation, because regulation defeats the learning process, and students want to learn. Children can drive you crazy with questions, and teenagers challenge everything. Their minds are not lazy, but their minds can be made dull with too many limitations and rote memorization.

There is a false assumption among some of the educational community that the ability to earn a salary is the only thing that students and their parents want, and that they should be satisfied with that. Based on this notion, students are sent to college to prepare only to join a prosperous middle class, but money and possessions do not nourish the mind and the soul.

As Aristotle considers in his *Nicomachean Ethics*, there is a rational principle motivating both humans and lower life forms that aims simply to preserve lives while satisfying physical appetites. Then there is that specifically human, irrational principle that makes us virtuous and strong in the face of troubles, is linked with the activities of the soul, and is naturally connected to what we perceive as human excellence: "The life of money-making is one undertaken under compulsion, and wealth is evidently not the good we are seeking; for it is merely useful and for the sake of something else. And so one might rather take the forenamed objects to be ends; for they are loved for themselves. But it is evident that not even these are ends; yet many arguments have been thrown away in support of them."[19]

Help our students join the "Great Conversation" that Robert M. Hutchins envisioned in 1952, when he insisted that industry and the sciences create an environment of specialization, and though specialization is not bad in and of itself, it does not tend to support a sense of community. We must have a common language of culture, tradition, and thought that the liberal arts provide. We would do well to continue studying and creating from the "cultural" thoughts of those who went before, and share in that "Great Conversation."[20] We should want our students to have cultivated, aristocratic minds—minds that are ennobled and inspired to see beyond a salary. After all, clinging with all you have to a paycheck seems a type of desperation. Financial security is a necessary goal, but our students' worth will not plateau with their highest paychecks. The liberal arts help make our lives' journeys meaningful because the arts deal with the intellectual refinements of human culture.

We shortchange our students' very humanity when we imagine that all they want to show at the end of their lives are money and possessions. Ask them: "Fine, so you've got a pile of money, but what exactly are you alive for? What are your deepest thoughts and philosophies? What has history taught you? What novel can you relate to and why? What paintings move you emotionally?" Ask them what it means to be human, or help them, to paraphrase Robert Frost, find their places "among the infinities."[21]

Notes

1. Patricia Armstrong, "Bloom's Taxonomy," Vanderbilt University: Center for Teaching, accessed June 7, 2016, https://cft.vanderbilt.Edu/guides-sub-pages/blooms-taxonomy/.

2. Mary Forehand, "Bloom's Taxonomy," Emerging Perspectives on Learning, Teaching, and Technology University of Georgia Department of Educational Psychology and Instructional Technology, 2005, accessed July 10, 2016, http://epltt.coe.uga.edu/index.php?title=Bloom%27s_Taxonomy.

3. Todd Coopee, "Tinkertoys," Toy Tales, March 14, 2016, accessed June 9, 2016. https://toytales.ca/tinker-toys/.

4. Sandra Ruppert, "Critical Evidence: How the Arts Benefit Student Achievement," National Assembly of States Arts Agencies, 2006, accessed August 4, 2016, http://nasaa-arts.org/Publications/critical-evidence.pdf.

5. Lisa Tsui, "Cultivating Critical Thinking: Insights from an Elite Liberal Arts College," *JGE: The Journal of General Education* 56, no. 3–4 (2008), 202, accessed December 5, 2016, Academic Search Premier, EBSCOhost.

6. Tsui, "Cultivating Critical Thinking," 206, 208.

7. D. W. Breneman, "Are We Losing Our Liberal Arts Colleges?," *AAHE Bulletin* 43, no. 2 (1990): 3, ERIC, accessed July 5, 2016, https://eric.ed.gov/?id=ED339260; Vicki Baker, Roger Baldwin, and Sumedha Makker, "Where Are They Now? Revisiting Breneman's Study of Liberal Arts Colleges," *Association of American Colleges and Universities* 98, no. 3 (Summer 2012), accessed July 9, 2016, https://www.aacu.org/publications-research/periodicals/where-are-they-now-revisiting-brenemans-study-liberal-arts.

8. Armstrong, "Bloom's Taxonomy."

9. Cathy Davidson, "What U.S. Can Learn from Finland, Hong Kong on Tests Equity," *Washington Post*, January 12, 2012, accessed August 9, 2016, https://www.washingtonpost.com/blogs/answer-sheet/post/what-us-can-learn-from-finland-hong-kong-on-tests-equity/2012/01/11/gIQAlVqttP_blog.html.

10. Plato, *Republic*, "Book X," in *Critical Theory since Plato*, ed. Hazard Adams, trans. Benjamin Jowett (New York: Harcourt, 1971), 35–37.

11. William Wordsworth, "Preface to *Lyrical Ballads*," 1802, in *The Romantic Period*, vol. D of *The Norton Anthology: English Literature*, ed. Stephen Greenblatt (New York: Norton, 2012), 297; Robert Doran, *The Theory of the Sublime from Longinus to Kant* (Cambridge: Cambridge University Press, 2015), 27.

12. Horace, "Ars Poetica," in *Critical Theory since Plato*, ed. Hazard Adams, trans. E. C. Wickham (New York: Harcourt, 1971), 73; Sir Philip Sidney, *An Apology for Poetry*, 1595, ed. Forrest G. Robinson (Indianapolis: Bobbs-Merrill, 1980), 26–28; Aristotle, *Poetics*, in *Critical Theory since Plato*, ed. Hazard Adams, trans. S. H. Butcher (New York: Harcourt, 1971), 51.

13. Oscar Wilde, *The Decay of Lying* (New York: Sunflower, 1902; originally published 1889), 2; W. K. Wimsatt and Monroe C. Beardsley, "The Intentional Fallacy," in *Critical Theory since Plato*, ed. Hazard Adams, trans. S. H. Butcher (New York: Harcourt, 1971), 1015.

14. Barry Oreck, "Artistic Choices: A Study of Teachers Who Use the Arts in the Classroom," *International Journal of Education and the Arts* 7, no. 8 (2006), 4, accessed November 8, 2016, http://files.eric.ed.gov/fulltext/EJ807864.pdf.

15. Stephanie Overman, "Fighting the Stress of Teaching to the Test: Educators Cope with Test Stress in Unique Ways," National Education Association, accessed Aug. 6, 2016. http://www.nea.org/tools/fighting-stress-teaching-to-Test.html.

16. Lauren Knight, "Art Education in Finland and the United States: A Qualitative Inquiry into Teacher Perceptions," thesis, Scholarly Workshops at Georgia University, Georgia State University, 2014, 35, accessed Aug. 6, 2016. http://scholarworks.gsu.edu/cgi/viewcontent.cgi?article=1174&context=art_design_theses.

17. Jeffrey Scheuer, "Critical Thinking and the Liberal Arts: We Neglect Them at Our Peril," American Association of University Professors. (November–December 2015), accessed June 30, 2016, https://www.aaup.org/article/critical-thinking-and-liberal-arts#.V3RG09Q8KrU; Tara Shoemaker Holdren, "Using Art to Assess Reading Comprehension and Critical Thinking in Adolescents," *Journal of Adolescent & Adult Literacy* 55, no. 8 (2012), 700, accessed Oct. 28, 2016, http://www.jstor.org/stable/41827770.

18. "Reinvesting in Arts Education: Winning America's Future through Creative Schools," May 2011, 39, President's Committee on the Arts and the Humanities, Knight Foundation, accessed July 3, 2016. http://www.pcah.gov/sites/default/files/photos/PCAH_Reinvesting_4web.pdf (site discontinued).

19. Aristotle, *Nicomachean Ethics, Book I*, trans. W. D. Ross, Internet Classic Archive, accessed June 20, 2016, http://classics.mit.edu/Aristotle/nicomachaen.1.i.html.

20. Robert M. Hutchins, *The Great Conversation: The Substance of a Liberal Education*, vol. I of Great Books of the Western World (Chicago: William Benton, 1952), https://archive.org/details/greatconversatio0030336mbp.

21. Robert Frost, "The Star Splitter" (1923), in *The Poems of Robert Frost*, Modern Library of the World's Best Books (New York: Random House, 1930), 200–203, accessed August 2, 2016, https://archive.org/details/poemsofrobertfro029898mbp.

Bibliography

Aristotle. *Nicomachean Ethics. Book I*. Translated by W. D. Ross. The Internet Classic Archive. http://classics.mit.edu/Aristotle/nicomachaen.1.i.html. Accessed June 20, 2016.

Aristotle. *Poetics*. In *Critical Theory since Plato*, edited by Hazard Adams. Translated by S. H. Butcher, 48–66. New York: Harcourt, 1971.

Armstrong, Patricia. "Bloom's Taxonomy." Vanderbilt University: Center for Teaching. Accessed June 7, 2016. https://cft.vanderbilt.edu/guides-sub-pages/blooms-taxonomy/.

Baker, Vicki, Roger Baldwin, and Sumedha Makker. "Where Are They Now? Revisiting Breneman's Study of Liberal Arts Colleges." *Association of American Colleges and Universities* 98, no. 3 (Summer 2012). http://www.aacu.org/publications-research/periodicals/where-are-they-now-revisiting-brenemans-study-liberal-arts. Accessed July 9, 2016.

Breneman, D. W. "Are We Losing Our Liberal Arts Colleges?" *AAHE Bulletin* 43, no. 2 (1990): 3–6. ERIC. Accessed 5 July 2016. https://eric.ed.gov/?id=ED339260.

Coopee, Todd. "Tinkertoys." Toy Tales. March 14, 2016. https://toytales.ca/tinker-toys/. Accessed June 9, 2016.

Davidson, Cathy. "What U.S. Can Learn from Finland, Hong Kong on Tests Equity." *Washington Post*, January 12, 2012. https://www.washingtonpost.com/blogs/answer-sheet/post/what-us-can-learn-from-finland-hong-kong-on-tests-equity/2012/01/11/gIQAlVqttP_blog.html. Accessed Aug. 9, 2016.

Doran, Robert. *The Theory of the Sublime from Longinus to Kant*. Cambridge: Cambridge University Press, 2015.

Forehand, Mary. *Emerging Perspectives on Learning, Teaching, and Technology*. Edited by Michael Orey. University of Georgia: Department of Educational Psychology and Instructional Technology. http://epltt.coe.uga.edu/index.php?title=Bloom%27s_Taxonomy. Accessed July 10, 2016.

Frost, Robert. "The Star-Splitter." 1923. *The Poems of Robert Frost*. Modern Library. New York: Random House, 1930. Accessed 2 Aug. 2016. https://www.poetryfoundation.org/poems-and-poets/poems/detail/44273.

Holdren, Tara Shoemaker. "Using Art to Assess Reading Comprehension and Critical Thinking in Adolescents." *Journal of Adolescent & Adult Literacy* 55, no. 8 (2012): 692–703. http://www.jstor.org/stable/41827770. Accessed 28 Oct. 2016.

Horace. *Ars Poetica*. (Art of Poetry). In *Critical Theory since Plato*, edited by Hazard Adams. Translated by E. C. Wickham, 67–75. New York: Harcourt, 1971.

Hutchins, Robert M. "Liberal Education: 'The Great Conversation.'" 1952. Center for the Study of Great Ideas: A Syntopical Approach to the Great Books and Practical Philosophy. http://www.thegreatideas.org/libeducation.html. Accessed Sept. 1, 2016.

Knight, Lauren. "Art Education in Finland and the United States: A Qualitative Inquiry into Teacher Perceptions." Thesis. Scholarly Workshops at Georgia University, Georgia State University, 2014. Accessed Aug. 6, 2016. http://scholarworks.gsu.edu/cgi/viewcontent.cgi?article=1174&context=art_design_theses.

Longinus. "On the Sublime." In *Critical Theory since Plato*, edited by Hazard Adams. Translated by W. R. Roberts, 76–102. New York: Harcourt, 1971.

Oreck, Barry. "Artistic Choices: A Study of Teachers Who Use the Arts in the Classroom." *International Journal of Education and the Arts* 7, no. 8 (2006): 1–19. Accessed November 8, 2016. http://files.eric.ed.gov/fulltext/EJ807864.pdf.

Overman, Stephanie. "Fighting the Stress of Teaching to the Test: Educators Cope with Test Stress in Unique Ways." National Education Association. http://www.nea.org/tools/fighting-stress-teaching-to-Test.html. Accessed Aug. 8, 2016.

Plato. *Republic*. "Book X." In *Critical Theory since Plato*, edited by Hazard Adams, 19–41. Translated by Benjamin Jowett. New York: Harcourt, 1971.

"Reinvesting in Arts Education: Winning America's Future through Creative Schools." Knight Foundation. May 2011. President's Committee on the Arts and the Humanities. http://www.pcah.gov/sites/default/files/photos/PCAH_Reinvesting_4web.pdf. (site discontinued).

Ruppert, Sandra. "Critical Evidence: How the Arts Benefit Student Achievement." National Assembly of States Arts Agencies. 2006. http://www.nasaa-arts.org/Publications/critical-evidence.pdf. Accessed Aug. 4, 2016.

Scheuer, Jeffrey. "Critical Thinking and the Liberal Arts: We Neglect Them at Our Peril." American Association of University Professors. November–December 2015. Accessed June 30, 2016. https://www.aaup.org/article/critical-thinking-and-liberal-arts#.V3RG09Q8KrU.

Sidney, Sir Philip. *An Apology for Poetry*. 1595. Edited by Forrest G. Robinson. Indianapolis: Bobbs-Merrill, 1970.

Tsui, Lisa. "Cultivating Critical Thinking: Insights from an Elite Liberal Arts College." *JGE: The Journal of General Education* 56, no. 3–4 (2008): 200–227. Academic Search Premier, EBSCOhost. Accessed December 5, 2016.

Wilde, Oscar. *The Decay of Lying*. New York: Sunflower, 1902. Originally published 1889.

Wilmstatt, W. K., and Monroe C. Beardsley. "The Intentional Fallacy." In *Critical Theory since Plato*, edited by Hazard Adams, 1015–22. New York: Harcourt, 1971.

Wordsworth, William. "Preface to *Lyrical Ballads*." 1802. In *The Romantic Period*. Vol. D of *The Norton Anthology: English Literature*, edited by Stephen Greenblatt, 292–304. New York: Norton, 2012.

CHAPTER 9

Developing a More Student-Sensitive Approach in the Liberal Arts

LAWRENCE SLEDGE

When I was a young college professor three years out of graduate school and teaching at Tennessee Technological University in Middle Tennessee, one of my sophomore literature students approached me about his dislike of literature courses and how he felt that they were useless to him because he was a physics major. He was good at physics and had an almost straight-A grade point average. He had done two summer internships at Bell Labs and said that he was ready to get down to business with the courses in his major. I then informed him of the curriculum rules of the school, which required that he take the class or not graduate. He relented and did the work that was required of him in the class, but he held his opinion about the class being a waste of his time, so he asked me to debate him publicly over the issue.

We debated each other in the auditorium; many of my colleagues were there and many of his friends. Of course, I won the debate. By the time he was a senior, he had met the girl of his dreams, who happened to be an English major. They later married, and once, when I saw them at a local Kroger store, he smiled and told me that he had been blind about the importance of English in his life. He told me that he had developed a habit of reading literature, which made his life less boring and routine and made him a well-rounded scientist and husband. This experience with this scientifically gifted student turned liberal arts appreciator made me more cognizant of the liberal arts versus sciences debate. Of course, the other non-liberal-arts programs such as business and technology in general have become part of the debate.

Ultimately, this experience moved me toward the realization, as indicated by other evidence and examples to follow, that the liberal arts are needed for the survival and function of a global society now altered by both the benefits and potential threats created by evolving technology; people trained in the liberal arts have developed temperaments that make them suited to dealing with potentially dangerous situations that require diplomatic solutions. This means that colleges and universities should use a more student-sensitive approach in keeping students in the liberal arts and make them aware that, as the evidence shows, the career benefits of liberal arts majors can be quite rewarding and lucrative.

Meanwhile, there has been a sentiment that society is evolving globally and that technological development has played a profound part in this global evolution. More people around the world have access to technology such as cell phones, laptops, and iPads, and within an instant ideas and information can be shared thousands of miles from their origin. Advanced technology is on its way to becoming the norm worldwide. People can use their iPhones to check their company emails and voicemails, and they can see the faces of those to whom they speak with the use of technology such as Skype. They can also keep an eye on their homes while they are out of town.

Along with all of this technological advancement have come social changes in some cases. For instance, part of the Arab Spring resulted from protestors' use of social media. As a result, those in power in those countries began to crack down on and inhibit the use of social media. This means that technology has made people around the world closer together. The problem is that not all people use technology for the good of mankind; some often use it to cause harm to others. Few would disagree that organizations such as ISIS, the Taliban and Al-Qaeda have made use of technology to cause harm.

These are frightening times in which we live, and many people in the United States think that we need more college students in STEM programs so that our country will not be left vulnerable to attacks from outsiders and those within our borders. In addition the United States has fallen behind other countries when it comes to performance in STEM programs and the graduation of engineers and scientists. It is understandable that some might be alarmed about the United States' shift from being the number one scientific power in the world to where it stands today, but this should not mean that liberal arts programs are no longer valuable to the United States and the world as a whole.

With all that is occurring today on a global scale, liberal arts are needed to counteract the potential for inhumanity to one's fellow humans. From what is happening in the Middle East between Israel and the West Bank to Turkey and the Kurds, North and South Sudan, Syria and other places, the bloodshed of war has not solved the differences of nations the way that diplomacy can. Struggle for sovereignty often causes war between two nations. To assist in the resolution of these conflicts, we must be more aware of the value of the contribution of people with critical thinking skills and the freedom of mind and spirit to think outside the box. Liberal arts students acquire these skills due to the nature of their curriculum.

For instance, English and psychology students are required to think critically about human motivation. English majors do it relative to characters in works of fiction that they have to analyze, and psychology majors do it in evaluating human behavior. A much more frightening place this world would be and would have been without people in power who had the skills to be rational in times of national and global crisis and conflict. People with technological know-how and the power to cause mass destruction need to be schooled in the humanities and liberal arts to keep their minds and spirits free enough to be rational and apprehensive about waging war that leads to human suffering or death.

Along with the idea that our country might be losing its scientific and economic status in the world is the view that students who graduate with a liberal arts degree are not as employable or job ready as those who graduate with STEM degrees. Alistair Cox, in his LinkedIn article "The Unemployable Graduate Crisis and How We Can Fix It," points out that there is a shortage of people graduating in the digital and STEM fields. He argues, "Sad to say but I've seen at first hand how many schools, universities and colleges are unable to provide students with worthwhile career advice that allows all the options available for on-going education and where this can realistically take them."[1] He attributes much of student unpreparedness for the workforce to colleges and universities made up of only education professionals who are not insightful enough to advise students regarding careers outside of their own fields.

Cox also argues that prospects for employment vary relative to course and college. "Our political leaders should instead encourage universities to focus on providing the skills that will be vital to driving employment, businesses and our economies."[2] He proposes that universities and colleges lower the cost of STEM courses to encourage more students to take them. He is not advocating doing away with liberal arts programs, but he claims to want graduates to be ready for the job market.

A similar view of the state of liberal arts education is expressed by Victor E. Ferrall, who in his article "Valediction for the Liberal Arts" says that many college students are graduating with more debt and are not able to find jobs that pay enough money to get rid of this debt. He sees problems like this as being the reason for the decline of students enrolled in liberal arts programs. Ferrall goes on to say, "There no longer is a reason to believe the decline of liberal arts education will be stayed or reversed"; however, "the liberal arts provided the platform from which U.S. students developed reasoning and analytical skills that led them to become critical thinkers and able and eager to distinguish opinions from facts and prejudices from truths."[3] He presents here what he thinks is a nostalgic view of the prominent role liberal arts have played in American and world society, and, ironically, he does not present an effective argument for the cutting of liberal arts programs. This is because people with a liberal education continue to achieve success and make contributions to society, while liberal arts programs are not given proper credit for producing successful graduates.

For instance, Nathan Lindsay, in his article "Enhancing Perpetual Learning: The Nexus between a Liberal Arts Education and the Disposition toward Learning," points out that colleges and universities in this country are increasingly expected to indicate the value of the liberal arts curriculum. This means that the utility of liberal arts degrees is assessed more frequently in the name of accountability and justification for funding with the possibility of programs being cut. He also points out that some scholars such as Pascarell, Wolniak, Seifert, Cruce, and Blaich have examined the empirical benefits of a liberal arts education, such as whether the best liberal arts education is obtained by enrolling in certain types of colleges or universities, choosing certain liberal arts majors, or having certain types of educational experiences.[4]

For Lindsay, liberal arts education proponents, such as the Association of American Colleges and Universities (AACU), believe that "students in the liberal arts are nurtured to develop habits of mind and body that lead to continued learning and wellbeing for themselves and society." The AACU, according to Lindsay, believes that a liberal arts education "'fosters a well-grounded intellectual resilience and a disposition toward lifelong learning, and an acceptance or responsibility for the ethical consequences of our ideas and actions.'"[5]

In "The Living Arts: Comparative and Historical Reflections on Liberal Arts Education," Sheldon Rothblatt says that a "liberal education strengthens the mind and furnishes it with perspective judgement, independence and a tolerance of other viewpoints."[6] This attests to the value, usefulness, and relevance of a liberal arts education to the world we live in today. Not only are liberal arts degrees useful, but many liberal arts graduates have made successes out of their degrees.

George Anders acknowledges examples of liberal arts degree success in his article "That 'Useless' Liberal Arts Degree Has Become Tech's Hottest Ticket." Anders points out that Slack Technologies, a technology company with team-based messaging software, has a value of $2.8 billion. He focuses on people who have enabled the company to thrive with the skills they acquired from their liberal arts degrees. As an example, Anna Pickard, a thirty-eight-year-old editorial director for the company, earned a degree in theater. According to Anders, Pickard came into tech after winning recognition for her video game writing, blogging, and cat impersonations, and now she is a top-earning member of the company making tremendous contributions to its success. She had gotten, according to Anders, tired of unsuccessfully going to auditions to act.[7]

Not only does Anna Prickard have a liberal arts degree, says Anders, but so does her boss, Stewart Butterfield, the cofounder and CEO of Slack Technologies. Butterfield earned degrees in philosophy and the history of science and says that philosophy taught him to follow through on an argument and to write clearly, which helps a person conduct successful meetings. Butterfield also said that studying the history of science taught him how people believe something is true only to find out it is not.[8]

Another example of liberal arts success is Debbie Konkle-Parker, a health care professional and researcher who works in the infectious diseases division at the University of Mississippi Medical Center in Jackson. Konkle-Parker earned an undergraduate degree in liberal arts; her major was educational psychology. This degree required her to take a number of electives in the humanities and liberal arts. In her mind, these liberal arts courses, more so than the technological courses for her medical training, prepared her for some of the difficulties and challenges that come in dealing with patients, some of whom are terminally or mentally ill. She indicated that a medical professional has to deal not only with the individual patient but with the family of the patient.[9] Undoubtedly, liberal arts degrees have value.

Since the evidence indicates the value of liberal arts degrees, liberal arts institutions and programs have the self-saving responsibility of making themselves more attractive to prospective students. This task for liberal arts schools and programs means a redefinition of the liberal arts, particularly through teaching. After having taught at the university level for a number of years, I know that what goes on in the classroom can make or break a student. Some college instructors have taught for thirty years or more, published books, and read papers at academic conferences. These teachers often have colleagues who feel that they are done with their formative phase of teaching and that there is nothing new for them to learn about teaching.

This mind-set, unfortunately, can cause problems for some students, especially those who come to college not fully prepared or who feel culturally isolated. These students need to be encouraged and socially and intellectually nurtured in the classroom. For instance, in *Culturally Responsive Teaching: Theory, Research and Practice*, Geneva Gay discusses how teachers can make culturally different students feel welcome in their classrooms. The empowering nature of culturally responsive teaching makes it easier for students to "be better human beings and more successful learners." These empowered students become more competent academically and more confident personally. According to Gay, this indicates that trust building makes students more successful, because they then believe they can do the work. Geneva Gay also argues in "Preparing for Culturally Responsive Teaching" that culturally responsive teaching improves the academic success of a student body that is ethnically diverse. A major way to enhance culturally responsive teaching is the training of teachers in programs so that they can graduate "with the knowledge, attitudes and skills needed to do this."[10]

In "Student-Centered Teaching: Making It Work," Charles R. Nuckles discusses what he sees as a student-sensitive approach to teaching. He says that, while teaching at a two-year technical school, he had observed that some teachers had come across as authoritative in their approaches to teaching, and he felt that students intimidated by this approach would be too much so to ask for help. In his classes Nuckles passed out what he called an "interests and background" form on which he asked students to indicate whether they needed help with anything such as "tests, writing or public speaking." Nuckles said that a student wrote on the form that he needed help with tests, and the student thanked him, saying that no one had ever asked him that before.[11]

In addition, Nuckles says that "humanistic education values the student as a whole person, a person who deserves to be treated with respect." He defines student-centered education as the teacher's being oriented to the student as learner. This student-centered teaching includes in his observation the teacher's behavior, beliefs, attitude, and system of values. He also says that student-centered teaching includes the teacher's recognition of the importance of individualized instruction in line with the individual differences among students.[12]

Heraldo V. Richards, Ayanna F. Brown, and Timothy B. Forde focus on this issue in "Addressing Diversity in Schools: Culturally Responsive Pedagogy." They write that the increase in students of diverse background in classrooms of the twenty-first century makes it necessary to have more culturally responsive pedagogical approaches to teaching. Meeting this challenge requires that teachers apply culturally responsive as well as theoretically sound pedagogy. This entails a student-sensitive approach to the classroom, where students do not feel culturally or academically isolated. An inclusive pedagogical approach to teaching enhances these students' chances of staying in college, something those of us in the liberal arts should consider.[13]

Rahima C. Wade continues this discussion about student-sensitive teaching in her article "Service-Learning for Multicultural Teaching Competency:

Insights from the Literature for Teacher Educators." Wade stresses the importance of effective teacher training in culturally diverse settings because of the differences in the background of some of the teachers and the students in their classrooms.[14] All teachers, including those at the college and university levels, need to take a student-sensitive approach so that potential liberal arts majors are less likely to feel alienated to the point of giving up and dropping out.

In the realm of student-sensitive teaching in her article "Toward a Theory of Culturally Relevant Pedagogy," Gloria Ladson-Billings says that if students are to benefit from culturally relevant teaching, they need to keep their cultural integrity along with academic excellence.[15] Cultural relevance does not apply just to minorities but to people from any ethnic background. In attracting and keeping students, liberal arts programs and schools must be ever sensitive to the needs of students in the classroom. Other than teaching effectiveness, liberal arts schools and programs can attract students and expand their programs in additional ways.

Some of these ways can become clearer with a little common sense. For instance, in "Career Preparation and the Liberal Arts," the Council of Independent Colleges (CIC) provides information on how its member institutions combine career preparation with the liberal arts. The CIC writes that students are required to take a liberal arts core of courses along with majors in liberal arts and professional fields. This arrangement enables students to choose from a combination of majors, double majors, and "concentrations to prepare themselves for post-graduate jobs and lifelong learning." The CIC also mentions the establishment of both professional degree programs with substantial liberal arts components and "liberal arts degree programs that integrate career readiness, internships and other experiential learning opportunities, and career preparation activities designed to supplement the liberal arts curriculum."[16]

Kristian Pickering, a full professor of English at Tennessee Technological University and director of the professional writing program, has shown a notable decrease in the number of English majors and the humanities in general. To address this issue Tennessee Tech has hosted panels that looked at prospective jobs for students who major in English. Some alumni attend these panels and discuss what they have achieved after graduating with their English degrees. Pickering also says that they have made efforts to broaden their graduate school options for students by the use of "fast track." This allows students to take a few graduate hours while they are undergraduates. In addition, the school has used concentrations in creative writing and professional communication to increase the size of its graduate program.[17]

In line with the idea of the important role that the liberal arts play in preparing students for the real world, Susannah Snider, writer and personal finance editor for *U.S. News and World Report*, spotlights Shannon McNay in her article "Get the Best Return on Investment for Your Liberal Arts Degree." In 2006 McNay graduated from Northern Kentucky University with a degree in English and then found employment as a waitress, a teller at a bank, and a Wall Street office manager. None of these jobs gave McNay the chance to use her writing skills, so she took a chance as a freelance writer for an organization known as ReadyForZero, which provides clients online tools to help with debt management and credit protection. Starting as an intern, McNay rose through the ranks of the company to become community manager, which enabled her to use her writing skills on the company's blog in addition to managing its social media and engaging in marketing and customer outreach. McNay went on to say that her liberal arts degree was worth the cost.[18]

According to Snider, experts say that a career path such as McNay's is common for people with a major in liberal arts, but the experience they get before landing the ideal job makes them skilled and ready once they "find their professional footing." At this point, they are apt to have substantial paychecks that indicate their worth to the organization for which they work. Snider also points out that a report by the Association of American Colleges and Universities indicates that graduates with degrees in humanities and social sciences tend to earn $2,000 more per year than their professional or preprofessional peers. The report focused on graduates around the age of fifty-six to sixty. According to Snider, Patrick Kelly, a senior associate with the National Center for Higher Education Management Systems, reports that a liberal arts degree, regardless of the major, is a good investment.[19]

While acknowledging the fact that students face rising college costs that are twice as much for out-of-state students, Snider suggests ways for students to make their liberal arts degrees pay off. She suggests that students could choose a minor that could make them more marketable, think about their career choice earlier, and go to visit the career services office. This could give students more perspective about their future and how they could use their liberal arts degree. For Snider, liberal arts majors have the "soft skills" that focus on engineering and beyond needed by companies.[20] Here again is a testament to the important role that the liberal arts play in the workplace.

Jarrett Carter concurs with this viewpoint in his article "Demanding More Liberal Arts Graduates." Carter believes that "liberal arts remain at the center of necessary leadership development and communication skills." He points out that the Education Advisory Board, in its report "Reclaiming the Value of Liberal Arts for the 21st Century," encourages institutions of higher learning to establish stronger bonds "between traditional majors in the arts and professional disciplines" and argues that these institutions should market liberal arts opportunities and successes more effectively. Carter also mentions Stephen Teske, a consultant and researcher with the Education Advisory Board, who has a bachelor's and a doctoral degree in history. According to Carter, Teske makes the case that the liberal arts prepares students to do more than just one thing in more than just one career. The problem is that some students have more of a challenge in recognizing the career path that is right for them.[21]

In Carter's interpretation of Teske, not only should students start thinking about their careers early in their matriculation but universities and colleges should be more helpful in assisting students in the liberal arts to "shape ideas about outcomes" and "match their classroom experiences in ways which are also attractive to employers."[22] The beauty of this practice is that it fills in professional perception gaps that students might have about moving from college degree to the job market. If students have a good idea of what they need to do before graduation and what they are qualified for, then the transition is smoother, and less time is spent looking for suitable employment.

Chris Teare is senior associate director of admissions at Drew University in Madison, New Jersey. In his article "STEM Study Starts with Liberal Arts," Teare argues that the liberal arts are the basis for and predecessor of STEM fields. He attended St. John's College, a liberal arts school, and credits his remarkable success to the liberal arts curriculum. Teare notes all the great books he read, along with other parts of the liberal arts program at St. John's, which he feels made him a well-rounded thinker. He asserts that great thinkers in the liberal arts such as Hobbes, Locke, Rousseau, Euclid, and Harvey are a large part of the foundation upon which the STEM fields are based.[23]

For instance, Teare shows that Euclid, with his geometric proof that "A squared plus B squared equals C squared," had training in the liberal arts, which led to his contribution to mathematics and geometry and the other discoveries that followed. Likewise, William Harvey, who lived during the time of Shakespeare and developed a theory on the circulation of blood, helped to lay part of the foundation for STEM fields and current medical knowledge.[24] Even mathematics is a language based on and growing out of this brilliant discourse, and the scholars who came after these thinkers have carried the torch to the present.

The liberal arts should not be written off as being irrelevant and inessential to the continued growth of STEM fields. Liberal arts departments should be steadfast and determined to make it known to the naysayers that the liberal arts are still needed. The world needs thinkers who can continue the scholarly tradition of discourse that has led to great discoveries. One must keep in mind that over time society changes. Part of this evolution indicates the increasing global and ethnically diverse relevance of colleges and universities and what they offer the public.

In critical times organizations need to look at themselves phenomenologically. The US no longer has the lead with math and science that it once had. The cost of a college education is increasing at a rate beyond the ability of many students to pay. Students from marginalized communities, though not all, often come to college unprepared. These students need a teacher, a department and a school that makes them feel welcome, relevant, and important. Our liberal arts departments and colleges need to make themselves known for the value of their offerings alongside and within today's world of science and technology. Critical times call for the use of critical thinking. In other words, one must think like liberal arts majors.

Notes

1. Alistair Cox, "The Unemployable Graduate Crisis and How We Can Fix It," LinkedIn, September 8, 2016, www.linkedin.com/pulse/unemployablegraduate.

2. Cox, "Unemployable Graduate Crisis."

3. Victor E. Ferrall, "Valediction for the Liberal Arts," *Inside Higher Education*, January 27, 2015, http://www.indisehighered.com/views/2015/01/27/essay-offers-valdiction-liberalarts.

4. Nathan Lindsay, "Enhancing Perpetual Learning: The Nexus between a Liberal Arts Education and the Disposition toward Lifelong Learning," ASHE Research Paper, November 2008.

5. Lindsay, "Enhancing Perpetual Learning."

6. Sheldon Rothblatt, *The Living Arts: Comparative and Historical Reflections on Liberal Arts Education* (Washington, DC: Association of American Colleges and Universities, 2003).

7. George Anders, "That 'Useless' Liberal Arts Degree Has Become Tech's Hottest Ticket," *Forbes*, July 29, 2015, http://www.forbes.com/sites/georgeanders/2015/07/29/liberal-arts-degree.

8. Anders, "That 'Useless' Liberal Arts Degree," 12.

9. Debbie Konkle-Parker, personal interview, July 16, 2016.

10. Geneva Gay, *Culturally Responsive Teaching: Theory, Research, and Practice* (New York: Teachers College Press, 2010), 34; Geneva Gay. "Preparing for Culturally Responsive Teaching," *Journal of Teacher Education* 53, no. 2 (2002), 108.

11. Charles R. Nuckles, "Student-Centered Teaching: Making It Work," *Adult Learning* 11, no. 4 (2000).

12. Nuckles, "Student-Centered Teaching."

13. Heraldo V. Richards, Ayanna F. Brown, and Timothy B. Forde, "Addressing Diversity in Schools: Culturally Responsive Pedagogy," *Teaching Exceptional Children* 39, no. 3 (2007), 64.

14. Rahima C. Wade, "Service-Learning for Multicultural Teaching Competence: Insights from the Literature for Teacher Educators," *Equity & Excellence in Education* 33, no. 3 (2000), 23.

15. Gloria Ladson-Billings, "Toward a Theory of Culturally Relevant Pedagogy," *American Education Research Journal* 32, no. 5 (1995), 160.

16. Council of Independent Colleges, "Career Preparation and the Liberal Arts: Council of Independent Colleges Project on the Future of Independent Higher Education," July 2015, 7, https://eric.ed.gov/?id=ED569212.

17. Kristian Pickering, personal interview, August 31, 2016.

18. Susannah Snider, "Get the Best Return on Investment for Your Liberal Arts Degree," *U.S. News and World Report*, November 19, 2014, http://www.usnews.com/education/best-colleges/paying-for-college/articles/2014/11/19/get-the-best-return-on-investment-for-your-liberal-arts-degree.

19. Snider, "Get the Best Return."

20. Snider, "Get the Best Return."

21. Jarrett Carter, "Demanding More Liberal Arts Graduates," EducationDive, July 22, 2016, www.educationdive.com/news/why-tech-industriesare-demanding-more-liberal-arts-graduates/423093/.

22. Carter, "Demanding More Liberal Arts Graduates."

23. Chris Teare, "STEM Study Starts with Liberal Arts," *Forbes*, August 5, 2015, http://www.forbes.com/sites/christeare/2015/08/05stemstudy-starts-with-liberal-arts/#722cbff87b8a.

24. Teare, "STEM Study Starts with Liberal Arts."

Bibliography

Anders, George. "That 'Useless' Liberal Arts Degree Has Become Tech's Hottest Ticket." *Forbes*. http://www.forbes.com/sites/georgeanders/2015/07/29/liberal-arts-degree. July 29, 2015.

Carter, Jarrett. "Demanding More Liberal Arts Graduates." www.educationdive.com/news/why-techindustries-are-demanding-more-liberal-arts-graduates/423093/. July 22, 2016.

Council of Independent Colleges. "Career Preparation and the Liberal Arts: Council of Independent Colleges Project on the Future of Independent Higher Education." July 2015. https://eric.ed.gov/?id=ED569212.

Cox, Alistair. "The Unemployable Graduate Crisis and How We Can Fix It." LinkedIn. September 8, 2016. www.linkedin.com/pulse/unemployable-graduate.

Ferrall, Victor E. "Valediction for the Liberal Arts." *Inside Higher Ed*, January 27, 2015. https://www.insidehighered.com/views/2015/01/27/essay-offers-valediction-liberal-arts.

Gay, Geneva. *Culturally Responsive Teaching: Theory, Research, and Practice*. New York: Teachers College Press, 2010.

Gay, Geneva. "Preparing for Culturally Responsive Teaching." *Journal of Teacher Education* 53, no. 2 (2002): 106–116.

Ladson-Billings, Gloria. "Toward a Theory of Culturally Relevant Pedagogy." *American Education Research Journal* 32, no. 5 (1995): 160.

Lindsay, Nathan. "Enhancing Perpetual Learning: The Nexus between a Liberal Arts Education and the Disposition toward Lifelong Learning." ASHE Research Paper, November 2008.

Nuckles, Charles R. "Student-Centered Teaching: Making It Work." *Adult Learning* 11, no. 4 (2000): 5.

Richards, Heraldo V., Ayanna F. Brown, and Timothy B. Forde. "Addressing Diversity in Schools: Culturally Responsive Pedagogy." *Teaching Exceptional Children* 39, no. 3 (2007): 64.

Rothblatt, Sheldon. *The Living Arts: Comparative and Historical Reflections on Liberal Education.* Washington, DC: Association of American College and Universities, 2003.

Snider, Susannah. "Get the Best Return on Investment for Your Liberal Arts Degree." *U.S. News and World Report*, November 19, 2014. www.usnews.com/education/best-colleges/paying-forcollege/articles/2014/11/17/get-the-best-return-on-investment-for-your-liberal-arts-degree.

Teare, Chris. "STEM Study Starts with Liberal Arts." *Forbes*, August 5, 2015. http://nevagewww.forbes.com/sites/christeare/2015/08/05/stem-study-starts-with-liberalarts/#722cbff87b8a.

Wade, Rahima C. "Service-Learning for Multicultural Teaching Competency: Insights from the Literature for Teacher Educators." *Equity & Excellence in Education* 33, no. 3 (2000): 21–29.

WRITING
AND THE
LIBERAL ARTS

CHAPTER 10

Conversation in the Writing Center

Developing Student Rhetorical Awareness, Critical Thinking, and Translingual Dispositions

TATIANA GLUSHKO AND KATHI R. GRIFFIN

If we were to define what writing means today, we might rely on how Kathleen Blake Yancey, past president of the National Council of Teachers of English (NCTE), describes it in her 2009 report "Writing in the 21st Century." For Yancey, people write to participate in "community groups," often via digital technology, and they learn to write, as apprentices, in collaboration with others. Thus, writing becomes an "unfolding activity" that often happens right in front of our eyes, an activity in which attention to form and correctness is secondary to the participation in the making of meaning through conversation.[1]

Even before Yancey defined writing for the twenty-first century as citizen participation, a group of experts on literacy education from the US, the United Kingdom, and Australia, dubbed the New London Group, called for a new understanding of what literacy, and hence writing, means: "Literacy educators and students must see themselves as active participants in social change, as learners and students who can be active designers—makers—of social futures."[2] Although the idea of designing futures seems, well, futuristic, what resonates with us in this definition is the shift from reception of knowledge to participation in the making, or creating, of knowledge and meaning, which for writing center practitioners like us implies taking an active part and engaging in conversation with students in the practice of writing, intentionally focused on developing their authority as writers and our own credibility as scholars. In this article, we seek to highlight writing centers, often viewed outside the field of writing studies as marginal places where writing is corrected rather than practiced, as central to the fulfillment of this pedagogical goal predominantly through conversation. We emphasize how centers respond to the pragmatics of students' lives in the changing social environment when they engage students in intellectual conversations about writing, embrace collaborative rather than regulatory, hierarchical approaches to education, and foster translingual dispositions.

Since the early twentieth century, writing labs, clinics, and centers have provided time and space for diverse student populations as they also responded to changing educational and social contexts and definitions of knowledge to better support individual student-writers. Early writing labs relied on medical metaphors in defining their practices and were considered sites of "remediation," "fix-it shops." They used prescriptive methods of instruction in a context where knowledge was defined as "exterior to us and directly accessible" and "individually derived and held," and the definition of writing focused on the solitary writer.[3]

In the latter half of the twentieth century, knowledge came to be defined as socially constructed through language, which is closely tied to identity. Recognizing this connection in *Students' Right to Their Own Language*, researchers criticized writing pedagogy that focuses on error as indicator of an individual's ability or inability, a pedagogy that reinforces the stigmatization of dialects different from Standard Written English (SWE) and that prevents students from "becoming fully, richly literate." With metaphors of remediation no longer relevant, writing labs became writing centers to address issues in student writing that go beyond grammar and point toward rhetorical problems, as well as toward social issues related to class, ethnicity, gender, and race. Yet among the public and even in academia, conversations about correction and grammar in writing persist.[4] In our recent study of reflection forms, which students complete after each tutorial in our writing center, we found that 38 percent of students still focused on grammar as they used words like "error," "fix," and "correct" when describing their writing.

The view of writing as a production of grammatically correct texts that follow a particular format (e.g., the ubiquitous five-paragraph essay) fits the purpose of standardization within the current audit culture and predominantly monolingual ideology. The danger inherent in this view is that it leads to a narrow understanding of literacy, and education in general, as a "carefully restricted project" that serves strictly utilitarian purposes of passing a standardized exam or preparing for a job and ignores human and citizen aspirations that go beyond that purpose.[5] Thus, we have the responsibility to engage in ongoing conversations about the teaching of writing on our campus, in our field, and in education, as we also respond to social issues that result from digitalization, audit culture, and globalization—to find new ways to describe to audiences outside our center and represent what we do and how we do it.

To introduce the idea of writing support for students in twenty-first-century terms, we need to move beyond the notion of help and remediation and toward describing writing in college as joining a new discourse community. To support student writers who transition to a new discourse community means to invite them to participate in intellectual conversations, as academics and experts in other fields do, and create an environment where they can do that without fear or judgment.

When students, faculty, administrators, and even parents ask us to describe what we do in the writing center, we say we "provide an environment for intellectual engagement outside the classroom" based on the Jackson State mission statement. However, many students and their instructors, not only in our university, still think of the writing center as a place where we help students correct errors and, perhaps, work on the organization of ideas—in other words, that we mainly provide *help*. We are struck by the emphasis on "help" in an academic setting and by the reductive view of writing, especially in light of the theory and best practices accumulated in the field of composition and writing studies.[6]

Help implies ineptness on the part of students who come to the center. *Help* also implies that the work of the writing center is supplemental to classroom experiences rather than central to students' development as writers and to their education. In *Good Intentions*, Nancy Grimm explains, "To say that we are helping [students] in writing conferences erases the historical contingencies that position some of us as helpers of Others, masks the power relations involved, and positions students as needing our beneficence." Instead of thinking of students who step into our center as needing help, we think of them as newcomers who join our discourse community and who may yet be unfamiliar with practices of our community.[7] By inviting them into a conversation about their writing, we also invite them to become part of the academic community and participate in knowledge making.

It is through conversation that students develop ideas and deepen their understanding of issues. In "Peer Tutoring and the 'Conversation of Mankind,'" a seminal writing center text, Kenneth Bruffee states, "Our task must involve engaging students in conversation at as many points in the writing process as possible," and make this conversation "similar in as many ways as possible to the way we would like them eventually to write." During one-to-one conversations in the writing center, we ask students questions that allow them to think critically, to reflect on their experiences and their writing processes, and to connect to their ideas. Thus, we share our epistemology with other disciplines, particularly in the liberal arts. For example, when we ask students what they are working on, why they are interested in their topic, why it is important, who might be interested in reading what they are writing, we allow them to explore their ideas, understand the purpose of their writing, think about their audience, and become aware of strategies that academics and experts in other professions use to communicate.[8]

With their emphasis on conversation and reflection, writing centers also offer immense "liberatory possibilities" as they demystify the process of writing and democratize it by inviting students and faculty to consider how their vernacular languages, rhetorical strategies, and genres can be used in academic and professional domains. In this regard, writing center pedagogy is innovative and has the potential for engaging students in ways that increase their confidence and persistence. In our study of student language on reflection forms, students' language suggests they experience greater understanding of and lessened resistance related to reading and learning and to writing.[9] For example, some students resolved to "read the whole story," "refer back to writing styles that the social work department gave out," "participate more in class," "write a few pages more than required," and "write every day." It is unlikely that students had never been encouraged to read or write more, but a conversation in the writing center allowed them to understand the significance of reading and writing for their own education, thus transforming them from passive recipients of information to more active learners.

Equally important, during face-to-face interactions, students can begin to see their writing as relevant in the public sphere. By providing a context outside the classroom and an audience other than their instructor, writing centers provide a space for students to begin thinking about their learning experiences as "personally meaningful" and to "stand by their work in a public way," instead of an exercise in pleasing the teacher and thus developing "compliance and discipline" instead of "creativity, ingenuity, and self-reliance."[10]

As we stress the importance of conversation about ideas in developing students as writers, we cannot ignore instructors' concerns about correctness and grammar. We do not ignore these issues but situate them in the rhetorical/cultural context of students and their audiences. However, we are more interested in what these concerns reveal about our culture and educational system and how the two influence our views on writing. Writing centers often serve as contact zones, where tensions and conflicts experienced by students—particularly first-generation students, basic writers (BW), and English language learners (ELL)—become apparent as they emerge in conversation. Students' home languages and habits of mind acquired earlier may clash with those of academe. Errors that we as faculty encounter in student writing and too often deem as a deficiency are often, in fact, indications of students' attempts to mesh their own language with academic discourse that is new to them. Their errors are manifestations of exploratory language and of attempts to appropriate unfamiliar syntax and vocabulary. When supported by a nonhierarchical, nonregulatory pedagogy, these errors may become points for discussion, for learning to solve problems, communicate effectively, and negotiate differences—abilities expected from college graduates in any field.[11]

In one-to-one conversations with peer tutors in the writing center, students have an opportunity to practice writing without fear of error or shame for using dialects that differ from SWE. We use conversation to invite students to think about the language they use in relation to their purpose, audience, and social context rather than one standard of correctness. For example, by asking students, "What are you trying to say here?" instead of merely correcting them, we can create space to talk about rhetorical strategies academics employ to achieve our goals and discuss how these strategies are different from or similar to ones students use in their home discourse communities.[12] As students reflect on their rhetorical preferences and compare them to strategies they are learning in college, they develop a greater awareness of rhetorical, sociocultural, and linguistic expectations that they might have to negotiate as they transition into discourse communities new to them.

When writing is judged in terms of correctness only, a complex practice of writing is reduced to regulatory terms of inputs and outputs (i.e., student learning outcomes). These terms, as anthropologist Marilyn Strathern notes, bear "the cultural stamp of accountability, notably assessments which are likened to audit." In higher education, audit (which originated in finance and accounting) has transformed into outcomes-based education (OE), retaining corporate language and practices. Having firmly established itself in higher education, audit perpetuates the "banking concept of education" criticized by Paolo Freire in *Pedagogy of the Oppressed*, as it reduces student learning to "receiving, filing, and storing the deposits." Even when learning outcomes include more than passive reception of knowledge (e.g., Bloom's taxonomy), the idea of prescribing what students will learn leaves little room for constructing knowledge through "invention and re-invention" and through "restless, impatient, continuing, hopeful inquiry human beings pursue, in the world, with the world, and with each other."[13]

In "Giving Place to Unforeseeable Learning," Claudia Ruitenberg offers three reasons why the idea of measurable outcomes that perhaps serves well the purposes of "economic utility and productivity" applies poorly to education and particularly, we argue, the humanities. First, focus on outcomes is contradictory to the nature of education when education is viewed as a process of entering new academic or professional communities. In this process, what is most important is to "give newcomers a place" that "invites and welcomes them into traditions." This is especially important for students who are "least prepared for college" and whose home dialects differ from SWE. Applying Jacques Derrida's concept of unconditional hospitality to education, Ruitenberg posits that educators receive students, who are very much like guests, into academic tradition, into which the educators themselves have been received. According to her, prescribing what students should learn, as OE seeks to do, runs counter to the idea of academia as a welcoming, hospitable place. The kind of space Ruitenberg describes—*khôra*—resonates with descriptions of writing centers as welcoming spaces, "safe houses" particularly within contact zones. But such spaces also invoke power struggle and marginalization, even when it comes to physical spaces writing centers occupy on campuses.[14]

Second, the demand for measurable outcomes and resulting practices of assessment and evaluation hardly leave room for student-faculty interaction. As Michele Eodice, Anne Ellen Geller, and Neal Lerner posit, meaningful writing experiences require opportunities for interaction with passionate, caring faculty. Yet the working conditions of composition instructors, like large class sizes, in audit culture often cause, if not require, faculty to resort to formulaic and regulatory actions and focus on format, correctness, and rubrics in their response to student writing.[15] To counter this trend, we have to create more time and space for meaningful interaction between students and instructors, between students and peers, places like writing centers.

Third, by setting predetermined, fixed goals, OE moves attention away from individual students, their prior and current educational experiences, and does not take into consideration "unexpected" outcomes or collateral learning. In our recent study of student language on reflection forms completed at the end of each tutorial in the writing center, students who came to revise their papers wrote in their reflection that they realized the need to read more and surprisingly to revisit departmental guidelines. In other words, conversation in the writing center allowed students to make sense of required readings and see value in them.[16]

While articulating student learning outcomes (SLO) may help to set some goals for a course or program, stating fixed, measurable objectives does not seem to fit well when we focus on human experience, and in our case on how students develop as writers, especially if we consider one-to-one, peer-to-peer and nonhierarchical conversation as essential to this development. Relationships within audit cultures are "hierarchical and paternalistic." Those who are assessed are the sources for collecting data rather than interlocutors, relationships contrary to the ones necessary for intellectual engagement and for developing ideas, for individual agency, for developing critical thinking and writing—relationships we value both in the writing center and in the liberal arts.[17]

In an audit culture, Mary Soliday and Jennifer Seibel Trainor argue, students experience writing as a "process of rules and regulations" and are "unable to see the rhetorical purposes of the assignments" and "the opportunities for authorship they provide." Rather than teaching and learning environments, classrooms become places of "economic exchange," where students adhere to rules and regulations and in return receive desired grades. Regulation permeates students' experiences with learning so much so they "may expect to be regulated."[18] Among students who come to the writing center, more often we hear regulatory expectations. When, instead of giving answers, we ask questions about student writing, some resist, feeling confused and uncertain about what to do next. We provide support to these students as they struggle with a shift from thinking about correctness to thinking about their ideas.

Instead of regulating students' experiences with writing in terms dictated by audit culture, educators in the twenty-first century need to consider the kinds of experiences and practices that would allow students to move closer to developing rhetorical authority. Students need an environment designed to allow them to experience tolerance, especially in the context of error and uncertainty, time to engage with others and ideas, and opportunities to reflect on their experiences. These habits of mind would help students develop "rhetorical and twenty-first-century skills" described in the Framework for Success in Postsecondary Writing developed by the Council of Writing Program Administrators, the National Council of Teachers of English, and the National Writing Project.[19]

Even though the framework presents students experiences in "fixed terms," as Chris Gallagher points out, it offers a different way to talk about student writing, as it places emphasis on writing experiences that allow students to develop habits of mind leading to success over time instead of predetermined outcomes within a limited time frame. It seems that in this framework, accountability and transparency, principles on which audit is based, can then be exercised not through regulation, metrics, and rubrics, but through the "power of artisanal 'building' and 'making.'" However, the same of goals of accountability and transparency can be achieved through peer observation and feedback, reflection on the experiences of teaching and learning, allowing both instructors and students to tell their stories in their own voices about how their "learning [and teaching] unfolds."[20] Instructors can observe each other's classes and share their observations; students can provide feedback to each other.

In college, students encounter dialects, rhetorical practices, and habits of mind often new to them. Even at our historically black university (HBCU), students arrive from different regions and have increasingly diverse needs, backgrounds, and abilities. Like some students who arrive at Jackson State University (JSU), Tatiana A. Glushko, who was born and grew up in Russia, came to the US to study in a graduate program. In her first year, she also worked in the writing center, where she was concerned about how she, a non-native speaker of English, would be able to speak to and write for faculty who were native speakers and tutor students, also native speakers, in writing. At that time, good writing for her meant good grammar and organization. She was worried whether she would be able to recognize errors in student writing and correct them. Her initial focus on error, however, gave way to other concerns as she found herself immersed in a new culture and a dialect of English she could hardly understand at times because it was different from the one she had learned in Russia.

Yet being from a different culture and having a background in teaching English as a Foreign Language (EFL) afforded her a unique position from which she worked with students on their writing: Glushko did not own English. (She began to develop that sense of ownership later.) Nor did she think she had authority to tell students how to use their language. Even though she had taught English in Russia for ten years before coming to the US, here she was in the role of learner rather than teacher. Students who came to the center, on the contrary, owned the language and, she thought, had ultimate authority in how to use it.

When tutoring students in the writing center, Glushko came across grammatical forms and expressions in their writing that were different from what she had learned. She would point to those differences and ask, "Is this how you usually say it here? This is different from how I learned." If she had trouble understanding a student's writing, she would say, "I am not sure what you are saying here. Could you please explain what this means?" Students, understanding that she came from another culture, would explain with enthusiasm the meaning of expressions or what they meant to say in their paper, sometimes accompanying their explanation with a cultural commentary.

Encounters in the writing center, such as Glushko's, offer students and faculty glimpses into the linguistic diversity of the US, a perspective often overlooked in conversations about writing. As we become a global community, the importance to consider linguistic and cultural diversity in academia, business, and sciences, particularly in the realm of digital communication, is increasing, and the teaching of writing may require new approaches. When Glushko was a student and was tutoring in the writing center, she was engaging in what she later learned to be called translingual practices.[21] Through one-to-one conversation, she was learning to negotiate cultural and linguistic differences and finding new writing pedagogies that later, upon reflection, would become more clear and intentional.

Research on multilingual writers helps us to think of the writing center as a place for dialogue, where writers from all social, cultural, and linguistic backgrounds engage in conversation about their writing, speaking, or research projects with trained tutors. This research also points us toward practices that would enable these speakers and writers to articulate their ideas and to negotiate differences while also developing their agency and rhetorical authority. In the nonhierarchical context of the writing center, tutors do not act as teachers; in a sense they become "brokers" who help prepare students to "negotiate the competing discourses" among academic audiences worldwide. When working with multilingual writers, "[tutors] are called upon to assist with language and rhetorical issues," so they must develop rhetorical skills such as listening, asking critical questions, and responding. To learn to engage writers across cultural and disciplinary differences, tutors also must learn to reflect on ways of using language and to "draw on a range of language resources to negotiate differences."[22]

As a translingual "community of practice," each writing center functions within its own sociocultural and educational context, and within each context, participants generate "knowledge, theories, and policies from practices," a process of negotiation that requires a heuristic system. At an HBCU, our writing center serves as both a contact zone and a safe house. In "'Tryin to Make a Dolla Outa Fifteen Cent': Teaching Composition with the Internet at an HBCU," Teresa M. Redd describes the composition program at Howard University, stating, "HBCUs are 'contact zones' where African American traditions sometimes collide with academic traditions." A translingual perspective, Bruce Horner explains, relies on reflection, "an inevitable if not always fully realized feature of all language practice," a feature we work to realize in the writing center. When language is understood as an "always emerging outcome of practice," rather than a "tool of thought or medium of its communication" as it functions within a monolingual ideology, translingual practices allow students to change "how [they] perceive themselves in the world," which has "clear political consequences." If we view language differently, as emerging rather than full of errors, and if we engage students in conversation about their language, their "agency [as] language users" can increase. Horner points out that agency is "not the same thing as mastery," which is something we all work on throughout our careers.[23]

In a global culture with various Englishes in use, monolinguals, Horner argues, will be at an increasing disadvantage as "communicative effectiveness" rather than "conformity to standards" will require a translingual disposition and thus rhetorical flexibility. He explains, "By posing, and giving students practice in posing, questions about difference," much as we do in writing centers, we engage students in practices that encourage a multilingual perspective and engage them in conversations that allow them to experience, develop, and reflect on their rhetorical authority.[24]

In higher education, we have been looking to technology for innovation in teaching and learning, such as online courses and tutorials, plagiarism software, and new learning platforms. Amidst this increasing reliance on technology, are we really giving students, and their instructors, access to meaningful human interaction that education requires? This question resonates with issues raised by Sherry Turkle in her recent book *Reclaiming Conversation: The Power of Talk in a Digital Age*. Turkle, an MIT endowed chair, clinical psychologist, and sociologist, argues that our reliance on devices, such as cell phones, has led to a decline in empathy and the ability for self-reflection. A recent study that measured the level of empathy among college students from the cell-phone generation noted a 40 percent decline in the past twenty years. Turkle advocates for work spaces designed for face-to-face conversations and reminds us that perfectly written emails rarely spark ideas, but one-to-one conversations, when we give our full attention to another person, do. Learning is not only cognitive but also emotional. Emotional responses to learning are more likely to occur when students and instructors share a physical space, which is hard to achieve by sitting in front of a computer.[25]

In her interview in the *Atlantic*, Turkle talks about the power of conversation and reflection—two main practices we rely on in the writing center—as a way of "reclaiming ourselves" and calls this kind of conversation "privileged." We were particularly struck by Jonathan Franzen's review of Turkle's book in the *New York Times*, in which he suggests that solitude and self-reflection, and conversation itself, are becoming luxuries available only to a few who have the power and the privilege to disconnect from their devices and to afford a "technological Sabbath," like the late Steve Jobs, who did not allow devices at his dinner table. Instead, he engaged in conversation with his family and friends about things far from technology. Or like Tristan Harris, who until recently worked as design ethicist and product philosopher at Google, and who, as Turkle says, "distinguishes between time on our devices and time well spent." As we read this, we began to wonder if our insistence on students' using technology might put them at a disadvantage and create further disparities in educational experiences. When we do not enlarge pedagogical spaces that provide opportunities for students to engage in conversation and reflection, we create another kind of inequality in education, just like those that existed before by the lack of access to technology.[26]

Digital capability as one of the goals of higher education may be important for effective communication in most professions, but as Helen Beetham reminds us, "to create social value from personal capability," it is not enough to "simply mak[e] oneself attractive to graduate recruiters." In most professions, she argues, effective communication will require "critical digital literacy," "a capacity to question both the resources involved and the larger purposes for which technologies offer themselves as the means."[27] To use technology to communicate effectively, students need to develop their rhetorical authority, linguistic flexibility, and translingual disposition to maintain relationships across distances, which may be difficult to do without opportunities to validate their own language through writing and through meaningful conversation and reflection.

In the field of writing centers, we recognize the tension between the long-held view of writing centers as proofreading shops and our practices that engage students in conversation about their writing. To build our credibility as a place of scholarly engagement, we must move beyond assessment toward research. Research about writing centers has primarily been anecdotal, so to extend evidence of our effectiveness and relevance to an audience outside our field, we must look toward empirical research, which for us means crossing sociolinguistic barriers in much the same way students do. Challenged by increasing public scrutiny and financial austerity, institutional administrators are pushing for accountability reported in numbers, and the field of writing studies itself has called for research that is replicable, aggregable, and data-driven (RAD).[28]

As writing centers seek ways to demonstrate their relevance to their universities' missions and strategic plans, directors have to be intentional about their institutional discourse, borrowing the language of administration, making the language of audit culture—words like "retention" and "strategic plan"—part of their vocabulary. However, as Maggie Berg and Barbara K. Seeber remind us in *The Slow Professor*, quoting Collini, "the more we talk the language of Prodspeak the more we have to live by it." While it is useful to know "Prodspeak," we must also use our own language to center conversations with "others" in the values we hold as a discipline. This requires using translingual practices and taking time for deliberation, "reflection and dialogue."[29]

Over the past three years, we have worked to develop a methodology that will allow us to capture the complexity of our work in the writing center, a work that cannot be replaced by software. We also took time to reflect on what has made writing centers resilient and relevant and discovered that the deliberate practices that account for the success of experts in most fields are precisely the same we use in our writing center. For example, psychologist Angela Duckworth explains that students are more likely to be successful and resilient if they have what she calls "grit," passion and perseverance.[30] Hard work that leads to success involves, according to Duckworth, deliberate practice with 100 percent concentration, one-to-one tutoring with focus on areas of weakness, immediate feedback focused on students' ideas rather than errors, and reflection on feedback and progress in relation to goals—all of which students experience in the writing center.

While the primary role of writing centers remains to support students, we also engage faculty in conversation about and reflection on their own writing processes and on using writing in their teaching, asking them questions that would allow them to hear different ways of thinking and talking about writing, to think critically about their own writing. To sustain the work of writing centers and to support faculty across the curriculum, campuses need writing programs to create environments that also provide opportunities for faculty to participate in conversations about writing and teaching writing in their fields. Kathi Griffin remembers a conversation with a biology professor who described her frustration as she tried to teach her seniors to write a literature review: "It's a good assignment; it's something they will have to write when they get to medical school." Griffin asked, "Do you have your students read literature reviews?" "Yes, from the time they begin as biology majors." Griffin then asked if she had identified elements specific to the genre for her students along the way, to which she replied, "No, I haven't." After making a list of elements together, the professor revised her assignment and reported significant improvements in her students' writing. In the twenty-first century, conversations about writing, about help, correctness, and accountability, about rhetorical similarities and differences across disciplines and cultures must directly inform teaching and learning on college campuses.

Notes

1. Kathleen Blake Yancey, "Writing in the 21st Century," Report from the National Council of Teachers of English, NCTE, 2009, http://www.ncte.org, 5, 7.

2. Courtney Cazden, Bill Cope, Norman Fairclough, Jim Gee, et al., "A Pedagogy of Multiliteracies: Designing Social Futures," *Harvard Educational Review* 66, no. 1 (1996), 64.

3. Elizabeth H. Boquet, "'Our Little Secret': A History of Writing Centers, Pre- to Post Open Admissions," *College Composition and Communication* 50, no. 3 (1999), 468;

Andrea Lunsford, "Collaboration, Control, and the Idea of a Writing Center," in *The St. Martin's Sourcebook for Writing Tutors*, ed. Christina Murphy and Steve Sherwood, 36–42 (New York: St. Martin's Press, 1995), 37.

4. Staci Perryman-Clark, David E. Kirkland, and Austin Jackson, *Students' Right to Their Own Language: A Critical Sourcebook* (Boston: Bedford/St. Martin's, 2015); see John U. Ogbu, "Literacy and Schooling in Subordinate Cultures: A Case of Black Americans," in *Literacy in Historical Perspectives*, ed. Daniel P. Resnick, 129–53 (Washington, DC: Library of Congress, 1983); David Bartholomae, "Inventing the University," in *Perspectives on Literacy*, ed. Eugene R. Kintgen, Barry M. Kroll, and Mike Rose, 273–85 (Carbondale: Southern Illinois University Press, 1988); Glynda Hull and Mike Rose, "'This Wooden Shack Place': The Logic of an Unconventional Reading," *CCC* 41, no. 3 (1990): 287–98; Gloria Ladson-Billings, "Reading between the Lines and beyond the Pages: A Culturally Relevant Approach to Literacy Teaching," *Theory into Practice* 31, no. 4 (1992): 312–20; Russell K. Durst, *Collision Course: Conflict, Negotiation, and Learning in College Composition* (Urbana, IL: National Council of Teachers of English, 1999); Teresa M. Redd, "Keepin' It Real: Delivering College Composition at an HBCU," in *Delivering College Composition: The Fifth Canon*, ed. Kathleen B. Yancey (Portsmouth, NH: Boynton/Cook, 2006); Vershawn Ashanti Young, *Your Average Nigga: Performing Race, Literacy, and Masculinity* (Detroit: Wayne State University Press, 2007); Vershawn Ashanti Young, "Keep Code-Meshing," in *Code-Meshing as World English: Pedagogy, Policy, Performance*, ed. Vershawn Ashanti Young and Aja Y. Martinez, 139–45 (Urbana: National Council of Teachers of English, 2011); Vershawn Ashanti Young, "Should Writers Use They Own English?," in *Writing Centers and the New Racism: A Call for Sustainable Dialogue and Change*, ed. Laura Greenfield and Karen Rowan, 61–72 (Logan: Utah State University Press, 2011); H. Samy Alim and Geneva Smitherman, *Articulating While Black* (New York: Oxford University Press), 2012; Mike Rose, *Lives on the Boundary: A Moving Account of the Struggles and Achievements of America's Educationally Underprepared* (New York: Penguin, 1990), 210–11; see Mina P. Shaughnessy, *Errors and Expectations: A Guide for the Teacher of Basic Writing* (New York: Oxford University Press, 1977); Elaine Maimon, "Talking to Strangers," *College Composition and Communication* 30, no. 4 (1979): 364–69; Gesa Kirsch, "Students' Interpretations of Writing Tasks: A Case Study," *Journal of Basic Writing* 7, no. 2 (1988): 81–90; Linda Flower, "Rhetorical Problem Solving: Cognition and Professional Writing," in *Writing in the Business Professions*, ed. Myra Kogen, 3–36 (Urbana, IL: NCTE, 1989); Carol Severino, "Where the Cultures of Basic Writers and Academia Intersect: Cultivating the Common Ground," *Journal of Basic Writing* 11, no. 4 (1992): 4–15; Laura Greenfield and Karen Rowan, *Writing Centers and the New Racism: A Call for Sustainable Dialogue and Change* (Logan: Utah State University Press, 2011); Dana Goldstein, "Why Kids Can't Write," *New York Times*, August 2, 2017, https://www.nytimes.com/2017/08/02/education/edlife/writing-education-grammar-students-children.html?mcubz=0.

5. See Ed White, "My Five-Paragraph-Theme Theme," *College Composition and Communication* 59, no. 3 (2008): 524–25; Cazden et al., "Pedagogy of Multiliteracies," 61.

6. Linda Adler-Kassner and Elizabeth Wardle, *Naming What We Know: Threshold Concepts of Writing Studies* (Logan: Utah State University Press, 2015).

7. Lisa Ede, "Writing as a Social Process: A Theoretical Foundation for Writing Centers?" *Writing Center Journal* 9, no. 2 (1989): 3–13; Nancy M. Grimm, *Good Intentions: Writing*

Center Work for Postmodern Times (Portsmouth, NH: Boynton/Cook, 1999); Patricia Bizzell, *Academic Discourse and Critical Consciousness* (Pittsburgh: University of Pittsburgh Press, 1994).

8. Kenneth Bruffee, "Peer Tutoring and the 'Conversation of Mankind,'" in *Landmark Essays on Writing Centers*, ed. Christina Murphy and Joe Law, 87–98 (New York: Routledge, 1995), 91; Jeffrey Scheuer, "Critical Thinking and the Liberal Arts," *Academe* (November-December 2015): 35–39, https://www.aaup.org/article/critical-thinking-and-liberal-arts#.WK8wH2_sKM8; Bartholomae, "Inventing the University"; Bizzell, *Academic Discourse and Critical Consciousness*; Gerald Graff and Cathy Birkenstein, *They Say/I Say: The Moves That Matter in Academic Writing* (New York: Norton, 2010).

9. Boquet, "Our Little Secret," 466; Kathi R. Griffin, Tatiana Glushko, and Daoying Liu, "Rhetorical Awareness of Student Writers at an HBCU Writing Center," *Praxis* 16, no. 2 (2019): 55–58.

10. David Gooblar, "Produce Thinkers, Not Docile Workers," *Pedagogy Unbound*, September 1, 2015, https://chroniclevitae.com/news/1118-produce-thinkers-not-docile-workers.

11. Mary Louise Pratt, "Arts of the Contact Zone," *Professions* 91 (1991): 33–40; Bizzell, *Academic Discourse and Critical Consciousness*; Courtney B. Cazden, *Classroom Discourse: The Language of Teaching and Learning* (Portsmouth, NH: Heinemann, 1988); Bartholomae, "Inventing the University"; Rose, *Lives on the Boundary*; see Graff and Birkenstein, *They Say/I Say*.

12. Jamila J. Lyiscott, "3 Ways to Use Liberation Literacies in Your Classroom This Fall" (blog), August 25, 2016, http://jamilalyiscott.com/2016/08/25/3-ways-to-use-liberation-literacies-in-your-classroom-this-fall/; Redd, "Keepin' It Real," 79–80.

13. Marilyn Strathern, *Audit Cultures: Anthropological Studies in Accountability, Ethics, and the Academy* (London: Routledge, 2000), 2; Chris Shore and Susan Wright, "Coercive Accountability: The Rise of Audit Culture in Higher Education," in *Audit Cultures: Anthropological Studies in Accountability, Ethics, and the Academy*, ed. Marilyn Strathern, 57–89 (London: Routledge, 2000); Chris W. Gallagher, "The Trouble with Outcomes: Pragmatic Inquiry and Educational Aims," *College English* 75, no. 1 (2012): 42–60; Mary Soliday and Jennifer Seibel Trainor, "Rethinking Regulation in the Age of the Literacy Machine," *College Composition and Communication* 68, no. 1 (2016): 125–51; Paulo Freire, *Pedagogy of the Oppressed*, trans. Myra Ramos (London: Penguin, 1970), 53.

14. See Ann Gardiner, "Democratizing Space in the Writing Center," *Connecting Writing Centers across Borders* (blog), February 1, 2017, https://www.wlnjournal.org/blog/2017/02/democratizing-space-in-the-writing-center/; Tatiana Glushko and Kathi Griffin, "A Writing Center to Envy," *Connecting Writing Centers across Borders* (blog), April 10, 2015, https://www.wlnjournal.org/blog/2015/04/a-writing-center-to-envy/; see Michele Eodice, Anne Ellen Geller, and Neal Lerner, *The Meaningful Writing Project: Learning, Teaching, and Writing in Higher Education* (Boulder: University Press of Colorado, 2016), ch. 5, 108–29.

15. See Ede, "Writing as a Social Process," 4; Michael Murphy, "Head to Head with EDX? Toward a New Rhetoric for Academic Labor," in *Contingency, Exploitation, and Solidarity: Labor and Action in English Composition*, ed. Seth Kahn, William B. Lalicker, and Amy Lynch-Biniek (Fort Collins, CO: WAC Clearinghouse, 2017), https://wac.colostate.edu/books/contingency/; John Dewey, *Experience and Education* (New York: Touchstone, 1938).

16. Griffin, Glushko, and Liu, "Rhetorical Awareness of Student Writers at an HBCU Writing Center"; Shore and Wright, "Coercive Accountability," 59.

17. Shore and Wright, "Coercive Accountability"; Soliday and Trainor, "Rethinking Regulation," 126.

18. Soliday and Trainor, "Rethinking Regulation," 125; Council of Writing Program Administrators, National Council of Teachers of English, and National Writing Project. Framework for Success in Postsecondary Writing, 2011, http://wpacouncil.org/framework.

19. Gallagher, "Trouble with Outcomes," 52.

20. Soliday and Trainor, "Rethinking Regulation," 129, 145; Helen Beetham, "Designing Learning for an Uncertain Future," in *Rethinking Pedagogy for a Digital Age: Designing for 21st Century Learning*, ed. Helen Beetham and Rhonda Sharpe, 258–81 (New York: Routledge, 2013).

21. A. Suresh Canagarajah, "Introduction," in *Literacy as Translingual Practice: Between Communities and Classrooms*, ed. A. Suresh Canagarajah (New York: Routledge, 2013); and A. Suresh Canagarajah, "Teacher Development in a Global Profession: An Autoethnography," *TESOL Quarterly* 46, no. 2 (2012): 258–79; Angela Creese and Adrian Blackledge, "Translingualing in the Bilingual Classroom: A Pedagogy for Learning and Teaching?," *Modern Language Journal* 94 (2010): 103–15; Min-Zhan Lu and Bruce Horner, "Translingual Literacy and Matters of Agency," plenary address, Penn State Conference on Rhetoric and Composition: Rhetoric and Writing across Language Boundaries, State College, Pennsylvania, 2012; Paul Kei Matsuda, "Second Language Writing in the Twentieth Century: A Situated Historical Perspective," in *Exploring the Dynamics of Second Language Writing*, ed. Barbara Kroll, 15–34 (New York: Cambridge University Press, 2013).

22. Ben Rafoth, *Multilingual Writers and Writing Centers* (Boulder: University Press of Colorado, 2015); Canagarajah, "Teacher Development," 272, 276; Canagarajah, qtd. in Rafoth, *Multilingual Writers*, 81; Bruce Horner, Min-Zhan Lu, Jacqueline Jones Royster, and John Trimbur, "Language Difference in Writing: Toward a Translingual Approach," *College English* 73, no. 3 (2011): 303–21; Glenda Hull and Mike Rose, "'This Wooden Shack Place': The Logic of an Unconventional Reading," *College Composition and Communication* 41, no. 3 (1990): 287–98; Seth Kahn, William B. Lalicker, and Amy Lynch-Biniek, eds., *Contingency, Exploitation, and Solidarity: Labor and Action in English Composition* (Fort Collins, CO: WAC Clearinghouse, 2017), 312–13, https://wac.colostate.edu/books/contingency/.

23. Teresa M. Redd, "'Tryin to Make a Dolla Outa Fifteen Cent': Teaching Composition with the Internet at an HBCU," *Computers and Composition* 20 (2003): 359–73; Bruce Horner, "Reflecting the Translingual Norm: Action-Reflection, ELF, Translation, and Transfer," in *A Rhetoric of Reflection*, ed. Kathleen Blake Yancey, 105–24 (Boulder: University Press of Colorado, 2016), 105, 108, 111, 115.

24. Sherry Turkle, *Reclaiming Conversation: The Power of Talk in a Digital Age* (New York: Penguin, 2015).

25. Maggie Berg and Barbara K. Seeber, *The Slow Professor: Challenging the Culture of Speed in the Academy* (Toronto: University of Toronto Press, 2016); Lauren Cassani Davis, "The Flight from Conversation," *The Atlantic* (2015), https://www.theatlantic.com/technology/archive/2015/10/reclaiming-conversation-sherry-turkle/409273/.

26. Jonathan Franzen, "Sherry Turkle's 'Reclaiming Conversation,'" *New York Times*, September 28, 2015, http://www.nytimes.com/2015/10/04/books/review/jonathan-franzen-reviews-sherry-turkle-reclaiming-conversation.html?_r=0; Davis, "Flight from Conversation"; see Beetham, "Designing Learning," 264, 266.

27. See Beetham, "Designing Learning," 269; Sarah Liggett, Kerri Jordan, and Steve Price, "Mapping Knowledge-Making in Writing Center Research: A Taxonomy of Methodologies," *Writing Center Journal* 21, no. 2 (2011): 50–88.

28. Muriel Harris, "Making Our Institutional Discourse Sticky: Suggestions for Effective Rhetoric," *Writing Center Journal* 30, no. 2 (2010): 47–71.

29. Berg and Seeber, *Slow Professor*, x, 64; see Murphy, "Head to Head," 72.

30. Angela Duckworth, *Grit: The Power of Passion and Perseverance* (New York: Scribner, 2016); see Kathi R. Griffin and Tatiana Glushko, "Caught between the Promise and the Past: A View from the Writing Center," *Composition Studies* 44, no. 2 (2016): 167–71.

Bibliography

Adler-Kassner, Linda, and Elizabeth Wardle. *Naming What We Know: Threshold Concepts of Writing Studies*. Logan: Utah State University Press, 2015.

Alim, H. Samy, and Geneva Smitherman. *Articulating While Black*. New York: Oxford University Press, 2012.

Bartholomae, David. "Inventing the University." In *Perspectives on Literacy*, edited by Eugene R. Kintgen, Barry M. Kroll, and Mike Rose, 273–85. Carbondale: Southern Illinois University Press, 1988.

Beetham, Helen. "Designing Learning for an Uncertain Future." In *Rethinking Pedagogy for a Digital Age: Designing for 21st Century Learning*, edited by Helen Beetham and Rhonda Sharpe, 258–81. New York: Routledge, 2013.

Beetham, Helen, and Rhonda Sharpe. Introduction to *Rethinking Pedagogy for a Digital Age: Designing for 21st Century Learning*, edited by Helen Beetham and Rhonda Sharpe. New York: Routledge, 2013.

Berg, Maggie, and Barbara K. Seeber. *The Slow Professor: Challenging the Culture of Speed in the Academy*. Toronto: University of Toronto Press, 2016.

Bizzell, Patricia. *Academic Discourse and Critical Consciousness*. Pittsburgh: University of Pittsburgh Press, 1994.

Boquet, Elizabeth H. "'Our Little Secret': A History of Writing Centers, Pre- to Post-Open Admissions." *College Composition and Communication* 50, no. 3 (1999): 463–82.

Bruffee, Kenneth. "Peer Tutoring and the 'Conversation of Mankind.'" In *Landmark Essays on Writing Centers*, edited by Christina Murphy and Joe Law, 87–98. New York: Routledge, 1995.

Canagarajah, A. Suresh. "Introduction." In *Literacy as Translingual Practice: Between Communities and Classrooms*, edited by A. Suresh Canagarajah. New York: Routledge, 2013.

Canagarajah, A. Suresh. "Safe Houses in the Contact Zone: Coping Strategies of African-American Students in the Academy." *College Composition and Communication* 48, no. 2 (1997): 173–96.

Canagarajah, A. Suresh. "Teacher Development in a Global Profession: An Autoethnography." *TESOL Quarterly* 46, no. 2 (2012): 258–79.

Cazden, Courtney B. *Classroom Discourse: The Language of Teaching and Learning.* Portsmouth, NH: Heinemann, 1988.

Cazden, Courtney, Bill Cope, Norman Fairclough, and Jim Gee, et al. "A Pedagogy of Multiliteracies: Designing Social Futures." *Harvard Educational Review* 66, no. 1 (1996): 60–92.

Council of Writing Program Administrators, National Council of Teachers of English, and National Writing Project. Framework for Success in Postsecondary Writing. 2011. http://wpacouncil.org/framework.

Creese, Angela, and Adrian Blackledge. "Translinguaing in the Bilingual Classroom: A Pedagogy for Learning and Teaching?" *Modern Language Journal* 94 (2010): 103–15.

Dewey, John. *Experience and Education.* New York: Touchstone, 1938.

Duckworth, Angela. *Grit: The Power or Passion and Perseverance.* New York: Scribner, 2016.

Durst, Russell K. *Collision Course: Conflict, Negotiation, and Learning in College Composition.* Urbana, IL: National Council of Teachers of English, 1999.

Ede, Lisa. "Writing as a Social Process: A Theoretical Foundation for Writing Centers?" *Writing Center Journal* 9, no. 2 (1989): 3–13.

Eodice, Michele, Anne Ellen Geller, and Neal Lerner. *The Meaningful Writing Project: Learning, Teaching, and Writing in Higher Education.* Boulder: University Press of Colorado, 2016.

Flower, Linda. "Rhetorical Problem Solving: Cognition and Professional Writing. In *Writing in the Business Professions*, edited by Myra Kogen, 3–36. Urbana, IL: NCTE, 1989.

Franzen, Jonathan. "Sherry Turkle's 'Reclaiming Conversation.'" *New York Times*, September 28, 2015. http://www.nytimes.com/2015/10/04/books/review/jonathan-franzen-reviews-sherry-turkle-reclaiming-conversation.html?_r=0.

Freire, Paolo. *Pedagogy of the Oppressed.* Translated by Myra Ramos. London: Penguin, 1970.

Gallagher, Chris W. "The Trouble with Outcomes: Pragmatic Inquiry and Educational Aims." *College English* 75, no. 1 (2012): 42–60.

Goldstein, Dana. "Why Kids Can't Write." *New York Times*, August 2, 2017. https://www.nytimes.com/2017/08/02/education/edlife/writing-education-grammar-students-children.html?mcubz=0.

Gooblar, David. "Produce Thinkers, Not Docile Workers." *Pedagogy Unbound*, September 1, 2015. https://chroniclevitae.com/news/1118-produce-thinkers-not-docile-workers.

Graff, Gerald. *Beyond the Culture Wars: How Teaching the Conflicts Can Revitalize American Education.* New York: W. W. Norton, 1993.

Graff, Gerald, and Cathy Birkenstein. *They Say/I Say: The Moves That Matter in Academic Writing.* New York: Norton, 2010.

Greenfield, Laura, and Karen Rowan. *Writing Centers and the New Racism: A Call for Sustainable Dialogue and Change.* Logan: Utah State University Press, 2011.

Griffin, Kathi R., and Tatiana Glushko. "Caught between the Promise and the Past: A View from the Writing Center." *Composition Studies* 44, no. 2 (2016): 167–71.

Griffin, Kathi R., Tatiana Glushko, and Daoying Liu. "Rhetorical Awareness of Student Writers at an HBCU Writing Center." *Praxis* 16, no. 2 (2019): 55–58

Grimm, Nancy M. *Good Intentions: Writing Center Work for Postmodern Times.* Portsmouth, NH: Boynton/Cook, 1999.

Harris, Muriel. "Making Our Institutional Discourse Sticky: Suggestions for Effective Rhetoric." *Writing Center Journal* 30, no. 2 (2010): 47–71.

Horner, Bruce. "Reflecting the Translingual Norm: Action-Reflection, ELF, Translation, and Transfer." In *A Rhetoric of Reflection*, edited by Kathleen Blake Yancey, 105–24. Boulder: University Press of Colorado, 2016.

Horner, Bruce, Min-Zhan Lu, Jacqueline Jones Royster, and John Trimbur. "Language Difference in Writing: Toward a Translingual Approach." *College English* 73, no. 3 (2011): 303–21.

Hull, Glenda, and Mike Rose. "'This Wooden Shack Place': The Logic of an Unconventional Reading." *College Composition and Communication* 41, no. 3 (1990): 287–98.

Kahn, Seth, William B. Lalicker, and Amy Lynch-Biniek, eds. *Contingency, Exploitation, and Solidarity: Labor and Action in English Composition*. Fort Collins, CO: WAC Clearinghouse, 2017. https://wac.colostate.edu/books/contingency/.

Kirsch, Gesa. "Students' Interpretations of Writing Tasks: A Case Study." *Journal of Basic Writing* 7, no. 2 (1988): 81–90.

Ladson-Billings, Gloria. "Reading between the Lines and beyond the Pages: A Culturally Relevant Approach to Literacy Teaching." *Theory into Practice* 31, no. 4 (1992): 312–20.

Lerner, Neal. "Choosing Beans Wisely." *Writing Lab Newsletter* 26, no. 1 (2001): 1–5.

Liggett, Sarah, Kerri Jordan, and Steve Price. "Mapping Knowledge-Making in Writing Center Research: A Taxonomy of Methodologies." *Writing Center Journal* 21, no. 2 (2011): 50–88.

Lu, Min-Zhan, and Bruce Horner. "Translingual Literacy and Matters of Agency." Plenary address, Penn State Conference on Rhetoric and Composition: Rhetoric and Writing across Language Boundaries. State College, Pennsylvania, 2012.

Lunsford, Andrea. "Collaboration, Control, and the Idea of a Writing Center." In *The St. Martin's Sourcebook for Writing Tutors*, edited by Christina Murphy and Steve Sherwood, 36–42. New York: St. Martin's Press, 1995.

Lyiscott, Jamila J. "3 Ways to Use Liberation Literacies in Your Classroom This Fall" (blog). August 25, 2016. http://jamilalyiscott.com/2016/08/25/3-ways-to-use-liberation-literacies-in-your-classroom-this-fall/.

Maimon, Elaine. "Talking to Strangers." *College Composition and Communication* 30, no. 4 (1979): 364–69.

Matsuda, Paul Kei. "Second Language Writing in the Twentieth Century: A Situated Historical Perspective." In *Exploring the Dynamics of Second Language Writing*, edited by Barbara Kroll, 15–34. New York: Cambridge University Press, 2013.

Murphy, Michael. "Head to Head with EDX? Toward a New Rhetoric for Academic Labor." In *Contingency, Exploitation, and Solidarity: Labor and Action in English Composition*, edited by Seth Kahn, William B. Lalicker, and Amy Lynch-Biniek. Fort Collins, CO: WAC Clearinghouse, 2017. https://wac.colostate.edu/books/contingency/.

Ogbu, John U. "Literacy and Schooling in Subordinate Cultures: A Case of Black Americans." In *Literacy in Historical Perspectives*, edited by Daniel P. Resnick, 129–53. Washington, DC: Library of Congress, 1983.

Perryman-Clark, Staci, David E. Kirkland, and Austin Jackson. *Students' Right to Their Own Language: A Critical Sourcebook*. Boston: Bedford/St. Martin's, 2015.

Pratt, Mary Louise. "Arts of the Contact Zone." *Professions* 91 (1991): 33–40.

Rafoth, Ben. *Multilingual Writers and Writing Centers*. Boulder: University Press of Colorado, 2015.

Redd, Teresa M. "Keepin' It Real: Delivering College Composition at an HBCU." In *Delivering College Composition: The Fifth Canon*, edited by Kathleen B. Yancey. Portsmouth, NH: Boynton/Cook, 2006.

Redd, Teresa M. "'Tryin to Make a Dolla Outa Fifteen Cent': Teaching Composition with the Internet at an HBCU." *Computers and Composition* 20 (2003): 359–73.

Rose, Mike. "The Language of Exclusion: Writing Instruction at the University." In *Cross-Talk in Comp Theory*, edited by Victor Villanueva, 547–69. Urbana: National Council of Teachers of English, 2003.

Rose, Mike. *Lives on the Boundary: A Moving Account of the Struggles and Achievements of America's Educationally Underprepared*. New York: Penguin, 1990.

Ruitenberg, Claudia. "Giving Place to Unforeseeable Learning: The Inhospitality of Outcomes-Based Education." In *Philosophy of Education 2009*, edited by Deborah Kerdeman. Urbana, IL: Philosophy of Education Society, 2010.

Scheuer, Jeffrey. "Critical Thinking and the Liberal Arts." *Academe* (November–December 2015): 35–39. https://www.aaup.org/article/critical-thinking-and-liberal-arts#.WK8wH2_sKM8.

Severino, Carol. "Where the Cultures of Basic Writers and Academia Intersect: Cultivating the Common Ground." *Journal of Basic Writing* 11, no. 4 (1992): 4–15.

Shaughnessy, Mina P. *Errors and Expectations: A Guide for the Teacher of Basic Writing*. New York: Oxford University Press, 1977.

Shore, Chris, and Susan Wright. "Coercive Accountability: The Rise of Audit Culture in Higher Education." In *Audit Cultures: Anthropological Studies in Accountability, Ethics, and the Academy*, edited by Marilyn Strathern, 57–89. London: Routledge, 2000.

Soliday, Mary, and Jennifer Seibel Trainor. "Rethinking Regulation in the Age of the Literacy Machine." *College Composition and Communication* 68, no. 1 (2016): 125–51.

Strathern, Marilyn. *Audit Cultures: Anthropological Studies in Accountability, Ethics, and the Academy*. London: Routledge, 2000.

Turkle, Sherry. *Reclaiming Conversation: The Power of Talk in a Digital Age*. New York: Penguin, 2015.

White, Ed. "My Five-Paragraph-Theme Theme." *College Composition and Communication* 59, no. 3 (2008): 524–25.

Yancey, Kathleen Blake. "Writing in the 21st Century." Report from the National Council of Teachers of English. NCTE. 2009. http://www.ncte.org.

Young, Vershawn Ashanti. "Keep Code-Meshing." In *Code-Meshing as World English: Pedagogy, Policy, Performance*, edited by Vershawn Ashanti Young and Aja Y. Martinez, 139–45. Urbana: National Council of Teachers of English, 2011.

Young, Vershawn Ashanti. *Your Average Nigga: Performing Race, Literacy, and Masculinity*. Detroit: Wayne State University Press, 2007.

Young, Vershawn Ashanti. "Should Writers Use They Own English?" In *Writing Centers and the New Racism: A Call for Sustainable Dialogue and Change*, edited by Laura Greenfield and Karen Rowan, 61–72. Logan: Utah State University Press 2011.

CHAPTER 11

Translingualism, Transhistoricism, and Shakespeare in a Freshman Seminar

ERIC J. GRIFFIN

Therefore paucas palabras, *let the world slide*. Sessa!
—WILLIAM SHAKESPEARE, *The Taming of the Shrew*[1]

Even as a growing chorus of leaders in the business, medical, and technology sectors affirm that training in fields associated with the liberal arts is a strong predictor of job success and career longevity, the flight from traditional humanities majors such as English, history, philosophy, classical and modern languages proceeds apace. Students and their parents appear either immune to or unaware of pronouncements such as "That 'Useless' Liberal Arts Degree Has Become Tech's Hottest Ticket," or "Liberal Education ... Is the Life and Breath of Medicine," or even, "When businesses go hunting for CEOs or managers, they will say ... I'm looking for a liberal arts grad."[2]

At the same time, colleges and universities with strong liberal arts traditions are themselves—doubtless in response to changing perceptions of student need, imagined workplace requirements, parental guarantees of job security, and dwindling market share—busily modifying curricula in an effort to demonstrate ongoing relevance in a culture no longer convinced that higher education is worth the money. Observing that today's student has changed, and fearing that yesterday's knowledge has lost relevance in the age of information, faculty and administrators search desperately for magic pills that will engage today's distracted student-consumers. Where many descry the doom of liberal education, Nicolas Lemann sees in this moment of uncertainty an opportunity for reinvention, arguing that our historical moment calls for a new "methods-based, rather than a canon-based, curriculum," designed to inculcate "a suite of intellectual skills that together would empower a student to be able to acquire and understand information across a wide range of fields, and over the long term."[3]

Changing times and changing students may indeed call for new pedagogical approaches. A problem arises, however, in that the current enthusiasm for curriculum redesign arrives at a moment in which student preparedness, whether for college-level courses or for the workplace, is widely perceived to be hitting unprecedented lows, even as simultaneous pressure grows not merely to retain underprepared students but to graduate them in a timely, more cost-effective manner.[4] This is to say that in an era during which students have further to go in order to attain desired language competencies, fewer resources—in terms of faculty devoted to freshman- and sophomore-level instruction and the number of contact hours allotted for acquiring (or remediating) basic skills—are being allotted to their development. Student attainment is thus limited by a convergence of social and institutional constraints.

In order to situate these widespread concerns in relation to the realities of twenty-first-century classroom practice, this essay will take as exemplary a recent case of curriculum reform at my home institution, Millsaps College. Historically Mississippi's premier liberal arts institution, Millsaps, following national trends, has moved toward an emphasis on skills-based student learning outcomes (SLOs) of the sort Lemann champions, and away from the college's former emphasis on developing multiple levels of "consciousness." Whereas the previous general education core viewed as an intrinsic good the goal of developing "*habits of mind* the college considers essential in the development of mature scholars and productive citizens," the new "Compass curriculum" seeks to inculcate *skills* and *tools* "designed to develop the general abilities of a liberally educated person" (my emphasis).[5]

What follows describes my own efforts as a professor of literature to design a freshman general education course that attempts, in line with the current emphasis on skills-based outcomes, to teach basic interpretive methods, research abilities, and writing skills, while also validating my students' prior experience. In thinking through these complex goals, I have found most helpful the principles and processes that in recent years have come to be associated with *translingualism*. I argue, therefore, that, given the contradictions of the present moment—wherein, on the one hand, liberal arts expertise may be viewed as a desirable commodity, while on the other, instructional hours devoted to the acquisition of liberal arts abilities are declining—translingual approaches to pedagogy may offer the readiest way to achieve the goals of the new curricula, particularly as they apply to the enhancement of such traditional outcomes as improved oral and written communication, the development of research skills, and the procedures of evidence-based argument.

Developed in association with increasingly globalized ESL settings, *translingualism*, as Min-Zhan Lu and Bruce Horner suggest, treats semiotic modes and cultural/linguistic histories "as always emergent, in process (a state of becoming), and their relations as mutually constitutive." Further developing the concept, Juan C. Guerra adds that translingualism "reflects the belief that every student needs to develop a critical awareness about what language does, rather than what it is, in the context of very specific circumstances informed . . . by a critical awareness of the choices made in the context of . . . various competing . . . approaches to language difference." Accordingly, classrooms become "translingual contact zones" wherein awareness of available linguistic choices is emphasized more than the "correctness" of the English—or more precisely, the *Englishes*—being spoken and written in class.[6] Translingual theory thus suggests that approaches to instruction that view student language use in terms of deficiency and correction are not likely to be productive, especially in multicultural class settings.

Although Jackson, Mississippi, is commonly thought of as being more biracial than multicultural (in the sense that metropolitan centers as large and diverse as New York, Chicago, Los Angeles, and other major US cities are multicultural), the past twenty years have seen Jackson experience significant demographic shifts. The growth of its Asian, Hispanic, Eastern European, North African, and other immigrant communities has resulted in increasing diversity in our college and university classrooms. And a growing African American middle class has seen enrollment from that community rise from 8 to 10 percent of the student body to around 20 percent at Millsaps, a relatively expensive private institution. Given this changing, far less binary institutional setting, regarding student preparedness—including the writing and communication skills students may or may not be bringing to college—in terms of "deficiencies to be remedied" risks generating adversarial relationships between teachers and students. Translingual perspectives allow us to valorize who students are, acknowledge their widely differing cultural and educational experiences prior to college, and then shift the focus away from who they are and where they are from in order that students might begin to envision the skills they will need to achieve the goals they wish to attain for themselves.

This shift in pedagogical mind-set is particularly well suited to the many curricular objectives demanded of the fast-moving writing seminars recommended by curriculum maps designed to speed students toward their preferred majors. Called "Connections," the Millsaps version of a "new core" freshman communication course is intended to focus on both speaking and writing skills in the manner of a traditional rhetoric class. But in place of the *transdisciplinary* orientation common to most rhetoric courses, the class foregrounds a specific disciplinary and historical period focus. This requires individual instructors to bring their own professional training and expertise to bear on a topic in ways that "connect" students with a particular historical topic they should have encountered in the year-long freshman survey of culture and history—entitled Our Human Heritage (OHH)—in which all students should be concurrently enrolled. In other words, Connections is a freshman-level rhetoric course tasked with teaching the principles of audience, occasion, and purpose. But it is also, at the same time, a period-specific topics course.

The charges of this rhetorical-historical encounter are as follows: to build the written and oral communication skills necessary to succeed in college as in a traditional rhetoric course; to guide students into developing their own research topics by introducing them physically to the college library and its staff; to acquaint students with the various print, electronic resources, and search engines the college library makes available to them; to teach students how to organize bibliographic materials and present research findings in the manner typical of the traditional, thesis-focused term paper; to introduce the rhetorical principles of arrangement and argumentation necessary to craft a credibly written academic paper; and to practice the abilities required to present this work before an audience, including offering basic guidance in how to employ the digital technologies appropriate to the multimodal presentations now in favor.

These are all worthy goals, and in spirit the Connections SLOs are not so different from what any general education curriculum would hope to achieve. However, this new kind of core directs instructors to accomplish its objectives in an institutional context in which the total number of hours spent on critical reading, writing, and speaking instruction has been reduced from the previous program's twenty semester hours to the new curriculum's twelve. It would thus be an understatement to say that *a lot* rides on the Connections seminar, which now provides the *only* dedicated writing instruction students are guaranteed by the college, and in which they are required to produce four artifacts that will be collected in a portfolio and assessed independent of classroom context.[7]

Reflecting upon this mountain of curricular objectives in light of the increasingly diverse character of the Millsaps student body—a significant number of whom would, by traditional standards, be considered underprepared—and recognizing that the design of our new core gives scant attention to any effective system of remediation, I was led to consider translingual practice as an alternative mode of thinking about approaching written and oral communication. At the same time, I struggled to imagine how I could entertain the course's rhetorical objectives in a specific historical context.

The requirements of this new, historical-rhetorical/rhetorical-historical encounter brought me in mind of the way translingual theorists borrow the notion of the *contact zone* from cultural anthropology. In the liminal, transitional space of the contact zone, different languages converge in ways that require acts of double translation. These indeterminate spaces can often produce new, sometimes surprising or unforeseen meanings. But there are historical dimensions to contact zones as well. For not only do we bring different languages with us into such liminal spaces, we also bring with us histories born of divergent backgrounds and experiences. Therefore, in addition to weighing the various linguistic backgrounds of my students, I would need to view their historical sensibilities as *emerging* or *in process* as well. Within the contact zone of my Connections class, translingual encounters would likely be unfolding alongside and in relation to *transhistorical* ones.[8] If, rather than focusing on deficiencies, I could view writing as being in a state of *becoming*—by taking students where they are, and helping them to identify and adjust their own rhetorical habits—so would I need to accept their limited awareness of historical continuity and change, not so much as an obstacle to be overcome or content area to be learned, but as an opportunity to engage in an intergenerational and intercultural dialogue.

As a Renaissance scholar, all of this reflection on the relationships between language and history and culture inspired me to fall back upon the one touchstone with which I could be certain that virtually all of my students would have at least some passing familiarity, William Shakespeare's *Tragedy of Romeo and Juliet*. Since I began teaching in 1991, I have yet to encounter a college or university student (including most of the home-schooled) who has not suffered through a ninth-grade *Romeo and Juliet* unit. Therefore, in order to shape a classroom environment wherein I might function more as facilitating participant than as a perceived authority on all things Shakespeare, we begin the semester by recalling experiences of high school Shakespeare—both my students' experiences and my own. Together, we take an inventory of what we know collectively about Shakespeare himself: who he was (or may have been), what works are known to the various members of the class, what film and pop culture versions of his plays we may have in common. While reflecting upon why we think Shakespeare is still being read (or forced upon us) four hundred years after his death, we also begin having discussions about *when* he wrote by taking stock of the kinds of cultural and historical commonplaces they associate with the era in which Shakespeare lived and worked, making "connections" between our class and their study of the Renaissance in Our Human Heritage. Throughout these initial discussions, I attempt to validate what the students know and feel, and encourage them to take ownership of Shakespeare at whatever level they are capable of articulating.[9]

Beginning, then, where we all began, Connections returns to *The Tragedy of Romeo and Juliet*. Our focus initially tends toward the "timeless," transhistorical qualities commonly associated with the play. As we recall what students know from their prior study, such as how its character relationships or archetypes may (or may not) continue to be "relatable," students teach each other (and they teach me) what they know. I seed our acts of recollection and recovery by introducing two short videos. The first is a documentary, *Finding Shakespeare*, produced in 2008 by a Millsaps student who, as a college senior studying Shakespeare, returned to her own high school alma mater to recapture on film the experience of encountering Shakespeare for the first time—in, of course, the ninth-grade *Romeo and Juliet* unit.[10] Finding that little has changed since they undertook their own nearly identical exercise four years ago, Connections students can see in the film their "earlier selves" grappling with Shakespearean language. This linguistic encounter, especially, sparks many to remember the difficulty of simply trying to navigate the verbal density of the play—how it was a struggle for them even to discern the bare bones of Shakespeare's plot.

In response to the problem of "Shakespearean language"—which inevitably inspires students to ask such questions as, "Why is this language so confusing?" or "Why doesn't Shakespeare just say what he means?" or "How am I supposed to read this 'Old English?'"—I introduce our second visual artifact, a YouTube video by Chris Coutts called *Romeo + Juliet l33t*, a cartoon adaptation of the play into an early version of SMS or "textspeak," complete with Baz Luhrmann's suggestive 1996 *Romeo + Juliet* film score. The point of this SMS exercise, which confronts issues of communication head-on, is twofold. In addition to underscoring the transhistorical omnipresence of the play, Coutts's reduction of Shakespearean language into SMS virtually demands that we reflect upon the importance of context to understanding, how the secondary "texting" language in which we have all become steeped may trouble the status of Standard English, as well as how SMS itself suggests numerous interpretive possibilities.[11] Again, the purpose is not to judge or criticize student practice but to emphasize the rhetorical principles of audience, occasion, and purpose. As we consider how particular kinds of understandings are possible in SMS, while others are not, we also begin to raise questions about linguistic change across space and time. While we can agree that textspeak has its uses—many of them quite comical—to juxtapose Coutts's jarringly funny SMS paraphrases with passages of the Shakespearean text is to foreground the differences between the instrumental rapidity of the ubiquitous communicative mode students employ so constantly, and Shakespeare's highly figurative and luxuriant poetry.

This discussion about "SMS Shakespeare" becomes the basis of our first Connections writing assignment, produced in class at the end of the first week. While an important goal of the course is to foster attention to specific detail and the overall importance of close reading to the study of literature and the advancement of evidence-based argument, I also want simply to get my students writing early, often, and in a variety of modes.[12] I therefore provide three speeches from *Romeo and Juliet* with which they are already familiar: the sonnets delivered by Shakespeare's Chorus to begin acts 1 and 2, and Juliet's famous "Come, gentle night" soliloquy from act 3, scene 2. In juxtaposition with Coutts's variants, these passages provide an early opportunity to explore the poetic richness of Shakespeare's language and the range of meanings that get lost in SMS translation. As it nudges students into moving beyond mere plot summary and impressionistic notions about the meaning of the play as a whole, the assignment—an exercise in the most essential interpretive skill of my own discipline, close reading—requires them to refer to specific moments in their chosen text, and to describe in writing how individual words, phrases, and images indicate specific issues they know to be concerns of the play.

To foreground the translingual and transhistorical perspectives of the course, I try to offer my students a "Will in the World," a Shakespeare who was once as they are now, a young writer learning to attune himself to the possibilities of verbal expression and to the necessities of rhetorical purpose. After all, like many of them, Shakespeare may be perceived as having been an outsider, someone provincial, who, motivated to succeed, acquired the skills necessary to thrive in the professional theatrical environment he chose to enter, and a young person who, to adapt Guerra, developed "a critical awareness about what language does," as opposed to "what it is," who saw the possibilities of language in the "context of very specific circumstances."[13] From this perspective Shakespeare may be seen to embody translingualism as we experience it in the contact zone of our Connections encounter.

An example of this "translingual Shakespeare" occurs in the opening lines of *The Taming of the Shrew* (one which appears above as this essay's epigraph), the play we turn to following our opening week's focus on *Romeo and Juliet*. As spoken by Christopher Sly to the hostess of a country inn in the play's Induction, here is the full quote:

SLY   I'll feeze you, in faith.
HOSTESS   A pair of stocks, you rogue.
SLY   You're a baggage. The Slys are no rogues. Look in the Chronicles—we came in with Richard Conqueror, therefore, *paucas palabras*, let the world slide. *Sessa!*"[14]

Clearly, the language voiced by Sly and this hostess does not the represent the high eloquence for which Shakespeare is commonly remembered. Rather, the language with which he opens *The Taming of the Shrew* reflects the sort of speech the young playwright would have heard among "the commons," perhaps in the rural Warwickshire community from whence he came. Here, in these provincial voices, Shakespeare reveals something of the character of the English language as spoken by everyman and everywoman, circa 1592.

These five opening lines plunge us into an argument in process. Christopher Sly has apparently refused a demand that he pay his tab at the hostess's inn, where he seems already to have imbibed a considerable quantity of ale. The two are trading threats. Sly tells the hostess that he will "feeze" her; she then threatens him with a "pair of stocks" and calls him a "rogue." He, in response, calls her "a baggage" and counters with "The Slys are no rogues."[15] In these simple lines Shakespeare has set a conflict in motion, which provides our point of entry into the play's argument. While students certainly know the word "baggage" (though they might never have considered the implications of its being employed as an insult), and might also have some sense of the word "rogue," it is less certain that they will understand the significance of the "stocks" with which Sly is threatened. And the meaning of the word "feeze"—even with the help of the standard marginal gloss, "I'll fix you"—remains a mystery.

At this point I introduce the class to the *Oxford English Dictionary*, projecting the OED internet portal on screen at the front of the class.[16] Calling for a volunteer, we look up "feeze," a word which appears in Old English by 890 CE, when it meant "to drive off, or away," "to put to flight," or "to frighten away." As we discover that in Shakespeare's day "feeze" had come to mean "impel," and that his phrase, "I'll feeze you," had come to suggest something like "to do for," or "'settle the business of' (a person, a person's pride, etc.)," we also learn from the OED that other playwrights of Shakespeare's day used "feeze" to mean "to beat, or flog." And so the significance of Sly's threat comes gradually into focus. At the same time, Shakespeare's opening lines have given us the opportunity to raise the issue of historical change in language. The pedagogical aim here is not to regress into philological curiosity for its own sake; rather, the exercise serves to demonstrate the instability of linguistic meaning across time, suggesting that the language we speak is changing too, that what might be obvious in one age or to one generation can present a mystery to another, and that there are times when it might be necessary to temper our use of idioms if we want to be understood by others.

Reading on, it becomes clear that Christopher Sly is making claims (albeit rather dubious ones) in defense of his family origins: "The Slys" being "no rogues." Doing another OED search we find that in the sixteenth century, "rogue" meant not so much a "dishonest or unprincipled person" (in the way it does today), or someone or something "acting in an aberrant or unpredictable way" (as in the current phrases, "rogue state" or "going rogue"). Rather, in Shakespeare's day "rogue" connoted a social class and was related to vagrancy, idleness, or homelessness. In response to the hostess's order to leave her establishment, then, Sly is asserting his right, as an Englishman, to remain in her public house because his family had "come in," that is, they had emigrated, some five hundred years earlier, "with Richard Conqueror."[17]

Of course, just as it is common knowledge today (although the assumption is not always borne out by classroom discussion), "everyone" knew then that it was William the Conqueror who had prevailed in the 1066 Battle of Hastings and established French rule, not some conqueror named Richard. This alerts us that Shakespeare embeds in this line a joke on Christopher Sly. His untutored (and intoxicated) condition is revealed, even as he assures the hostess asking him to leave her premises that "in the Chronicles" his family heritage can be verified. "Therefore," Sly goes on, as a consequence of this official history, which he associates with national identity, he may, "*paucus palabras*, let the world slide."[18]

"*Paucas palabras*," today spelled *pocas palabras*, means now as it did then, "few words." And as many students will recognize, the phrase Sly speaks here is not from his own national language at all, but from Spanish. His phrase "let the world slide" is somewhat ambiguous, too. It may mean something like "let it be," "the heck with it," "it doesn't concern me," "let the world turn," or maybe even our own saying, "let it slide," a phrase originating in the sixteenth century still in use today. But the meaning of "*Sessa!*"—the word with which Sly dismisses his interlocutress—is a bit tougher to discern. In this case even the OED is not much help. It says that "Sessa!" is an obsolete exclamation of uncertain meaning.[19] It could signify "says I," which is sort of how it sounds. Or it could be a transliteration of the French word *cessez*, meaning "cease!"

Or, since "sess," as the dictionary tells us, was a dialect word used to call dogs to dinner, and because Sly is about to be set upon by a gentleman's brace of hunting dogs, his word may both cue the entry of the lord and his hounds *and* provide a neat bit of dramatic foreshadowing. Then again, "sessa" could signify something else altogether, perhaps a slang word, the meaning of which has been totally forgotten over time.

Among the many things this short example reveals, then, is the always already translingual nature of the English language—how unstable English is, how it is now and always has been in flux, how it changes across time and region, how several dialects can cross each other, and how it can reveal, if we go back a few generations, that all of us are, like Christopher Sly, from somewhere else. And just like the English language of today, Shakespeare's English was peppered with Spanish loan words like "paucas palabras" and French ones like "sessa." Such "foreign" antecedents run through the evolving "American" language we all imbibe daily. It also demonstrates how some words and phrases stick due to repeated usage, while others don't; how the vocabularies we use mark us as being of a place and a space and a time; and how this confluence can trouble effective communication.

To help students see that, like the dialects and sociolects they speak, language is always in a state of becoming, is to help them to see that different social settings can demand from them different ways of speaking. But it is not to suggest that one way of speaking is inherently "better" than another. Unpacking brief passages like this one in class can open productive, nonjudgmental discussions about how our linguistic heritages mark us, as Shakespeare's language marks Christopher Sly, as hailing from particular regions, social classes, educational backgrounds, and moments in history. Therefore, although there is neither time nor space to explore the issue here, linguistic encounters like the one we have just explored can also help to introduce questions of Renaissance difference. Such discussions thus further the historical aims of the Connections curriculum as well.

Students know intuitively that their generation and its various culture groups possess their own ways of speaking, and that the multiple social spheres they each inhabit require of them different vocabularies. And translingual encounters like the one that opens *The Taming of the Shrew* can help make the merely intuitive present, allowing students to glimpse several concrete examples of how language changes across time, space, and culture. However, encounters with broader questions of historical continuity and change can be somewhat difficult to engineer in an era characterized by presentism in the extreme. Indeed, the historical moment through which we are currently passing may be characterized by what Andrew Keen and others have called "the tyranny of the now." As Keen observes, we inhabit a world for which "the Internet was supposed to have created a civil environment for discussion," but, ironically, it often reveals itself as a "parochial, narrow, selfie-centric universe" that places us in a "perpetual present."[20]

The cast of mind that has been shaped by Keen's "tyranny" makes it increasingly difficult to pose deep historical questions for audiences consumed by the digital now. And the utility of studying history, let alone the pleasures of doing so, like the pleasures of studying literature, appears to be more difficult to market and promote than ever before.[21] Therefore, we must grant the continuing attractions of the transhistorical Shakespeare so often presented in public culture via live performance, media representation, and classroom discussions. But we must aim at the same time to demonstrate the interdisciplinary productiveness of bringing traditional literary and historical methods together. For to do so is to offer students a glimpse of both Shakespeare's apparent "timelessness"—a quality already attributed to his works when the First Folio was published in 1623—while also showing the difference it can make to situate Shakespeare in the Renaissance context in which he lived and wrote.

In a manner very like the way Guerra, Lu, and Horner conceive their classrooms as translingual contact zones, then, I also imagine Connections as a zone of *transhistorical* contact. Inevitably, we approach the past through the lenses available to us in the present. Since students quite commonly tend to imagine their own subject positions as "natural," viewing the present as the historical center from which their own orientations and inclinations, including their digital ones, radiate outward to encompass past, present, and future, it makes sense to highlight—in much the way we do their various linguistic heritages—the presentist perspectives that encompass them. But whereas the coupling of textbook narratives with primary source readings may once have been sufficient to attract students to the humanities disciplines, it no longer appears that they are doing so in an era in which the culture of the book is being displaced by the multiplying media platforms that command attention in alternative ways. In the world of the selfie, it would appear that in order to be effective, our more traditional pedagogical methods must be annexed, at least in part, to digital mediation and a sense of real-time identity.

In the interest of "connecting" with collective as well as individual selves, I attempt in class to approach these concerns in terms of the multiple generational perspectives—the students', their parents' or grandparents', and my own—which we bring into focus by foregrounding Shakespeare's relationship to various kinds of contemporary media productions *and* to primary source readings that reveal a range of cultural attitudes that were present in Shakespeare's day. Having witnessed the collision of past and present in the translation of Shakespearean language into SMS, I attempt to orchestrate similar encounters via any number of available film adaptations of the plays. Even as we discover the translingualism lurking in *The Taming of the Shrew*'s Induction, for example, scenes from "Shakespeare movies," which are multiplying with each passing year, may be employed to approach the dynamics and aesthetics of historical change.

For example, the already aging Touchstone production *Ten Things I Hate about You* (1999), starring the late Heath Ledger (who remains a student favorite), and the classic Franco Zeffirelli production of *Taming of the Shrew* (1967), which famously featured Elizabeth Taylor and Richard Burton, may easily be juxtaposed to offer a transhistorical encounter. In the Zefffirelli production, the filmmaker's highly detailed representation of Renaissance Italy and his reliance on language that is almost solely Shakespeare's provide rich opportunities for discussing cultural and historical differences between the early modern world and the society represented in *Ten Things*. What is more, discussion of the 1999 film presents an opportunity to foster the historical consciousness objectives of Connections in ways that might not previously have been thought relevant. For although there is much that students can recognize in the late-twentieth-century Seattle High School of the film, with its emphasis on pop-rock, grunge, and reggae, its lack of smart phones, and even its culture of "dating," this world too appears distant to undergraduates viewing it two decades later.

Because the present media landscape offers so many platforms wherein students may experience film, television, video game, and even amateur YouTube productions of Shakespeare, we may easily juxtapose traditional "Renaissance" representations with "modern-day" adaptations. This operation may be repeated with a difference in relation to each play we take up. While obvious film pairings such as Oliver Parker's *Othello* (1996) and Tim Blake Nelson's *O* (2001) remain useful, more distant or oblique appropriations of Shakespearean archetypes such as those offered by *Richard III* and *Macbeth*, which are marvelously deployed in such recent hit series as *House of Cards* and *Game of Thrones*, may also be examined in class. Again, the aim of each juxtaposition remains the same: to foreground the persistence and continuing relevance of Shakespearean archetypes, to awaken student consciousness with respect to how these archetypes get reworked in ways that reveal historical difference, and, as important, to coordinate in each case appropriate exercises involving the active examination of and participation in the Shakespearean text.

Finally, to push our discussions of transhistorical continuities toward questions of historical change, with each new play we encounter, we add to the mix primary-source readings of the sort made available by such resources as *The Norton Shakespeare* and *The Bedford Companion to Shakespeare*, which add yet another layer of historicity to our contact zone. By reading specific expressions of cultural practice or historical belief from the Renaissance, students become aware of multiple historical perspectives on issues that may matter to them individually, whether in relation to present concerns regarding economics, race, gender, sexuality, religion, nationality, or any number of important social issues. And it is from these period encounters that the extended research essay required of Connections students gets generated. For the final course assignment is to build a thesis-driven research project that either puts one of Shakespeare's plays into conversation with a later Shakespearean adaptation (such as a film of their choice) or makes an argument about an issue that was important in Shakespeare's day by examining one of his plays in relation to additional Renaissance primary sources they will also have encountered in class.

Observing evolving linguistic phenomena in a historical setting somewhat closer to our own than Shakespeare's England, John Trimbur has provided an overview of the evolution of language in the history of the United States. By including in his survey the "dialects, pidgins, and creoles born out of the travel and expansion of settlers," Trimbur demonstrates our "tendency to forget [our own] heritage as a linguistically diverse nation."[22] Although the linguistic heritage of which Trimbur speaks may be observed in any locale, Mississippi offers a tremendously fruitful case in which to audit language adaptation and change. This is so because linguistic processes like those currently being speeded along by globalization and digitization have been at work here since the Renaissance.

For even as Shakespeare was putting a dialect of sixteenth-century English into the mouths of Christopher Sly and his hostess, Europeans and Africans were arriving to encounter the Native American languages that give us place-names like the one by which our state is known. Among the phenomena that make Mississippi storytelling traditions so rich is the fact that Mississippians have long been navigating the linguistic processes coming to be associated with translingualism. We can hear them in the work of signature writers like William Faulkner and Richard Wright, Margaret Walker and Eudora Welty, and in the newer voices of Natasha Trethewey, Jimmy Kimbrell, C. Liegh McInnis, Beth Ann Fennelly, and Katie Simpson Smith, who have flourished as writers by tapping into translingual processes. For each of these writers in their way has developed, to call upon Guerra's formulation a final time, "a critical awareness of the choices made in the context of ... various competing ... approaches to language difference."[23]

The implications of conceiving language instruction translingually mean that, pedagogically speaking, we ought to concern ourselves with cultivating in students the awareness that they will inevitably encounter in life occasions upon which and for which it will be incumbent upon them to ensure that they not be misunderstood by others who may stand outside their immediate language community or social group. Students who are freed to think more about audience, occasion, and purpose, and less about peer group identification and the mystifications of "correct language," can begin to reflect upon the multiple possibilities of communicative acts, how language can be harnessed to work for them in specific situations, what language can help them to do and to accomplish. It is at this point that they begin to write and speak purposively—that is, to further their own goals and interests more than simply to please their elders, or to earn a grade.

As teachers of language, let us not decry the barbarians at the classroom gate or long for the good old days of Standard English (that never really were). A more generative and hopeful pedagogy lies down the path of translingualism. To accord students their own linguistic agency is not to say that "correction"—perhaps more properly conceived as guidance—has no place in college writing and speaking instruction. One can always learn to write and speak more effectively, and pointing out ways of doing so must always be an aim of good pedagogy. It may be even more important, in a world growing ever more complex and interconnected, to point students toward understandings of what language can do, and how, depending upon the goals they envision for their own futures, they can benefit from acquiring the skills needed to make words work for them. Awaiting the twenty-first-century student are global vistas as unimaginable to us as our world was to the Renaissance. And while it is to be granted that few have ever been born with linguistic aptitudes as apparently innate as William Shakespeare's must have been, like the country boy from Stratford, today's students can learn the communication skills that life, careers, and an ever-changing world will require of them. Let others try to keep the gate. Communicatively speaking, our task ought to be to offer them a way forward.

Notes

1. William Shakespeare, *The Taming of the Shrew* (Induction 1: 4–5). All quotations are from *The Norton Shakespeare*, ed. Stephen Greenblatt et al. (New York: W. W. Norton, 1997).

2. George Anders, "That 'Useless' Liberal Arts Degree Has Become Tech's Hottest Ticket," *Forbes*, August 17, 2015; Leslie Henderson, Glenda Shoop, and Lisa V. Adams, "Why Get a Liberal Education? It Is the Life and Breath of Medicine," *U.S. News and World Report*,

August 15, 2016; Judy Samuelson, executive director of the Aspen Institute's Business and Society Program, quoted in Yoni Appelbaum, "Why America's Business Majors Are in Desperate Need of a Liberal Arts Education," *The Atlantic*, June 28, 2016.

3. James Atlas, "Is College Education Even Worth It Anymore?," *Town & Country*, July 10, 2018; Ellen Ruppel Shell, "College May Not Be Worth It Anymore," *New York Times*, May 16, 2018; Nicholas Lehmann, "The Case for a New Kind of Core," *Chronicle Review*, November 27, 2016.

4. "Employers and College Faculty Report Gaps in Recent Graduates' Preparedness in New National Survey," Achieve, https://www.achieve.org/employers-and-college-faculty-report-gaps-recent-graduates%E2%80%99-preparedness-new-national-survey (accessed September 4, 2018).

5. Specifically, the former model fostered "reasoning, communication, historical consciousness, and social and cultural awareness." Millsaps College, "Compass Curriculum," http://www.millsaps.edu/academics/compass-curriculum.php (accessed February 20, 2017).

6. Min-Zhan Lu and Bruce Horner, "Translingual Literacy, Language Difference, and Matters of Agency," *College English* 75, no. 6 (2013), 587; Juan C. Guerra, "Cultivating a Rhetorical Sensibility in the Translingual Writing Classroom," *College English* 78, no. 3 (January 2016), 228; A. Suresh Canagarajah, *Translingual Practice: Global Englishes and Cosmopolitan Relations* (London: Routledge, 2013), especially "Theorizing Translingual Practice," 19–34.

7. According to a recent College Composition and Communication Conference (CCCC) Position Statement, "electronic portfolios (e-portfolios) have become a viable institutional tool to facilitate student learning and its assessment. E-portfolios can be "web-sensible"—a thoughtfully arranged collection of multimedia-rich, interlinked, hypertextual documents that students compose, own, maintain, and archive on the Internet or in other formats. Web applications designed to support e-portfolio composition can offer additional opportunities for providing structure, guidance, and feedback to students, and can provide students with opportunities to connect selectively with multiple audiences."

8. OED. Transhistorical. Having significance that transcends the historical; universal or eternal.

9. Doug Downs and Liane Robertson, "Threshold Concepts in First Year Composition," in *Naming What We Know: Threshold Concepts of Writing Studies*, ed. Linda Adler-Kassner and Elizabeth Wardle, 105–21 (Logan: Utah State University Press, 2015).

10. Amy Marsalis, *Finding Shakespeare*. Produced for Eric J. Griffin, instructor, English 3340: Shakespeare and Film, Millsaps College, Jackson, MS. 2008.

11. Chris Coutts, *Tales for the L33T—Romeo and Juliet: 2011 Deluxe HD Remix of Fury*; The noun "SMS," or "short message service," entered the OED in 1991, with a verb form arriving in 1996. "Leetspeak," which the OED prefers, was recognized in 1996, although "textspeak" appears to be the noun preferred by practitioners. Whereas SMS has sometimes been characterized as a subset of English, it has also demonstrated tremendous cross-cultural adaptability.

12. See Lehmann, "Case for a New Kind of Core"; and Ayanna Thompson and Laura Turchi, *Teaching Shakespeare with Purpose: A Student-Centered Approach* (London: Bloomsbury Arden Shakespeare, 2016), 14–16, 130–34.

13. Reflecting my own disciplinary training in New Historicism and my continuing commitment to historicist practices, I refer here to Stephen Greenblatt, *Will in the World: How Shakespeare Became Shakespeare* (New York: W. W. Norton, 2004); Guerra, "Cultivating a Rhetorical Sensibility," 228.

14. William Shakespeare, *Taming of the Shrew*, in *The Norton Shakespeare*. Edited by Stephen Greenblatt et al. New York: W. W. Norton, 1997. Induction 1, 3–5.

15. Shakespeare, *Taming of the Shrew*, Induction 1, 1–3.

16. For the utility of the "OED exercise," see Thompson and Turchi, *Teaching Shakespeare with Purpose*, 47–49.

17. Thompson and Turchi, *Teaching Shakespeare with Purpose*, 47–49.

18. Thompson and Turchi, *Teaching Shakespeare with Purpose*, 47–49.

19. *Oxford English Dictionary*, s.v. "sessa," obs., an exclamation of uncertain meaning; or possibly < French *cessez* 'cease!,'" accessed October 5, 2016.

20. Quoted in Steven Slon, "The Internet Has Failed Us," *Saturday Evening Post*, July/August 2015.

21. Lynn Hunt's recommendations in "Against Presentism," *Newsletter of the American Historical Association* (May 2002), are even more relevant than they were fifteen years ago.

22. John Trimbur, "Linguistic Memory and the Uneasy Settlement of U.S. English," 21–22.

23. Guerra, "Cultivating a Rhetorical Sensibility," 228.

Bibliography

Anders, George. "That 'Useless' Liberal Arts Degree Has Become Tech's Hottest Ticket." *Forbes*, August 17, 2015. https://www.forbes.com/sites/georgeanders/2015/07/29/liberal-arts-degree-tech/#7e6708c5745d (accessed February 20, 2017).

Appelbaum, Yoni. "Why America's Business Majors Are in Desperate Need of a Liberal Arts Education." *The Atlantic*, June 28, 2016. https://www.theatlantic.com/business/archive/2016/06/why-americas-business-majors-are-in-desperate-need-of-a-liberal-arts-education/489209/ (accessed September 4, 2018).

Atlas, James. "Is College Education Even Worth It Anymore?" *Town & Country*, July 10, 2018. https://www.townandcountrymag.com/society/money-and-power/a22037810/the-cost-of-college-is-too-high/ (accessed September 4, 2018).

Canagarajah, Suresh. *Translingual Practice: Global Englishes and Cosmopolitan Relations*. London: Routledge, 2013.

College Composition and Communication Conference (CCCC). Position Statement. "Electronic Portfolios: Principles and Practices" (November 2007, revised March 2015). http://www.ncte.org/cccc/resources/positions/electronicportfolios (accessed February 26, 2017).

Coutts, Chris. *Tales for the L33T—Romeo and Juliet: 2011 Deluxe HD Remix of Fury*. https://www.youtube.com/watch?v=pYLHpg5HwZo (accessed February 20, 2017).

Downs, Doug, and Liane Robertson, "Threshold Concepts in First Year Composition." In *Naming What We Know: Threshold Concepts of Writing Studies*, edited by Linda Adler-Kassner and Elizabeth Wardle, 105–21. Logan: Utah State University Press, 2015.

"Employers and College Faculty Report Gaps in Recent Graduates' Preparedness in New National Survey." Achieve. https://www.achieve.org/employers-and-college-faculty

-report-gaps-recent-graduates%E2%80%99-preparedness-new-national-survey (accessed September 4, 2018).

Flaherty, Colleen. "Liberal Arts College Students Are Getting Less Artsy." *Inside Higher Ed*, February 21, 2017. https://www.insidehighered.com/news/2017/02/21/liberal-arts-students-fears-about-job-market-upon-graduation-are-increasingly (accessed February 26, 2017).

Greenblatt, Stephen. *Will in the World: How Shakespeare Became Shakespeare*. New York: W. W. Norton, 2004.

Guerra, Juan C. "Cultivating a Rhetorical Sensibility in the Translingual Writing Classroom." *College English* 78, no. 3 (January 2016): 228–33.

Henderson, Leslie, Glenda Shoop, and Lisa V. Adams. "Why Get a Liberal Education? It Is the Life and Breath of Medicine." *U.S. News and World Report*, August 15, 2016. https://www.usnews.com/news/articles/2016–08–15/why-get-a-liberal-education-it-is-the-life-and-breath-of-medicine (accessed August 6, 2018).

Hunt, Lynn. "Against Presentism." *Newsletter of the American Historical Association*, May 2002 (accessed February 1, 2017).

Jameson, Frederic. *The Historical Unconscious: Narrative as a Socially Symbolic Act*. Ithaca: Cornell University Press, 1982.

Lehmann, Nicholas. "The Case for a New Kind of Core." *Chronicle Review*, November 27, 2016. http://www.chronicle.com/article/The-Case-for-a-New-Kind of/238479?cid=cr&utm_source=cr&utm_medium=en&elqTrackId=f72583b6e5e94170bc90e4f0cbe42e8b&elq=7ee4238087a84e5492ad723da8d20fe9&elqaid=11612&elqat=1&elqCampaignId=4588 (accessed February 25, 2017).

Lu, Min-Zhan, and Bruce Horner. "Translingual Literacy, Language Difference, and Matters of Agency." *College English* 75, no. 6 (2013): 582–602.

Marsalis, Amy. *Finding Shakespeare*. Produced for Eric J. Griffin, instructor, English 3340: Shakespeare and Film, Millsaps College, Jackson, MS. 2008.

McDonald, Russ, ed. *The Bedford Companion to Shakespeare: An Introduction with Documents*. Boston: Bedford/St. Martin's, 2001.

Millsaps College. "Compass Curriculum." http://www.millsaps.edu/academics/compass-curriculum.php (accessed February 20, 2017).

Millsaps College. "Core Curriculum (for Students Admitted prior to Fall 2015)." http://www.millsaps.edu/academics/core-curriculum.php (accessed February 20, 2017).

The Oxford English Dictionary. http://www.oed.com.ezproxy.millsaps.edu/.

Shakespeare, William. *The Norton Shakespeare*. Ed. Stephen Greenblatt et al. New York: W. W. Norton, 1997.

Slon, Steven. "The Internet Has Failed Us." *Saturday Evening Post*, July/August 2015. http://www.saturdayeveningpost.com/2015/07/27/health-and-family/tech/internet-failed-us.html (accessed February 21, 2017).

Thompson, Ayanna, and Laura Turchi. *Teaching Shakespeare with Purpose: A Student-Centered Approach*. London: Bloomsbury Arden Shakespeare, 2016.

Trimbur, John. "Linguistic Memory and the Uneasy Settlement of U.S. English." In *Cross-Language Relations in Composition*, edited by Bruce Horner, Min-Zhan Lu, and Paul Kei Matsuda, 21–41. Carbondale: Southern Illinois University Press, 2010.

CHAPTER 12

The Liberal Arts Faculty Writing Boot Camp

PRESELFANNIE W. MCDANIELS, BYRON D'ANDRA OREY,
RICO D. CHAPMAN, AND MONICA FLIPPIN WYNN

In 2012 D'Andra Orey stepped down from the position of chairperson of the Department of Political Science at Jackson State University (JSU), and he attempted to reclaim his track of conducting and publishing on serious research topics in his field of study. He soon discovered that what he had was much more work than he knew how to organize, streamline, and keep up with. A few months later, he experienced a brief boot camp writing experience with colleagues during one of his research-based trips away from JSU. This eye-opening experience sparked in him the idea that this experience should be duplicated at his home institution. He considered what C. M. Badenhorst et al. acknowledge in their article "Writing Relationships: Collaboration in a Faculty Writing Group": "For many academics, the challenge of navigating the competitive discourse demands of conducting research and publishing journal articles, while at the same time coping with teaching and administrative loads, often leads to anxiety and stress."[1]

In January of 2013, Orey shared his recently gained information on the effectiveness of faculty writing boot camps in publication productivity with two colleagues in the College of Liberal Arts at Jackson State University. From that "parking lot" conversation, the idea for an interdisciplinary liberal arts faculty writing boot camp was born. In addition he shared in detail the recent experience he had had participating in a faculty writing boot camp and the positive results from that experience. He wanted his colleagues who were moving toward administrative positions and the promotion and tenure process to gain from the boot camp experience. The ideas he shared coincided perfectly with the research on boot camp productivity and purpose.

According to scholar Ashley Sanders, the faculty writing boot camp has a number of major objectives:

1) Create space and time in our schedules to make significant progress on writing goals
2) Develop goal-setting skills
3) Increase the writers' awareness of their own process through writing logs
4) Share writing resources
5) Determine sustainable writing habits
6) Offer both camaraderie and accountability.[2]

In addition to the objectives of the boot camp, faculty must consider how the boot camp can aid them in meeting challenges that might deter their writing productivity.

On this aspect, Sanders suggests, "Writing can be such an *isolating task*, whose very isolation may deter us from starting or progressing toward our goals. The other obstacle we often face is a *lack of accountability* once we leave the classroom for the desert of ... writing." As Sanders sees it, "Writing boot camps address both challenges by providing a space and time in which to work on writing projects alongside others doing the same and setting a schedule with periodic, brief meetings to report on goals, challenges, and progress." The boot camp setting is definitely ideal for accountability. Commitment to reporting goals and progress can keep participants on track to meet their short-term and long-term production goals. In addition the boot camp structure can be absolutely conducive to productivity, both in physical and virtual meeting spaces. "For those conducted in person, a boot camp provides a quiet, distraction-free space in which to work on your writing project for a set period of time." Sanders adds, "The beauty of boot camps is that they are flexible and can be tailored to the needs of the participants. What is common to all of them, though, is a "git 'er done" attitude and an atmosphere of mutual support and encouragement. We're all in this together, and it's nice to know there are others in the trenches with us, especially when the going gets tough."[3]

In this chapter, the members chronicle, discuss, analyze, and reflect on a two-year time span in an interdisciplinary liberal arts writing boot camp experience at JSU. In this examination (and reflective exercise), the four boot camp participants focus on issues of accountability, customization, sustainability, and production that resulted from the JSU boot camp experience. The accountability discussion deals with the actual writing, feedback, and camaraderie of the participants. Customization deals with the fitting and refitting of the structure of the boot camp in order to maintain the experience. Sustainability deals with longevity and the importance of the boot camp experience to processes of mentorship, evaluation, tenure, and promotion. Lastly, the production conversation deals with the report on participants' submitted goals and accomplishments and the measured success of the boot camp experience as a whole. What follows are reflections on these aspects of the experience.

"Joy and pain, like sunshine and rain." That epigraph, based on the lyrics of Maze, a popular band, epitomizes the art of writing. Writing by nature can be a lonely experience. It often involves finding a quiet space and engaging in dialogue with one's inner self. The experience can be frustrating and painful. Indeed, there is an age-old adage that it is okay to talk to oneself; however, it is not okay to answer oneself. For writers, this is known as writer's block. Once writer's block kicks in, procrastination is soon to follow. One might even characterize the experience as dreadful. The experience, however, need not be such. Rather than finding a secluded space, divorced from society, it is possible to link with others who might experience the same anxieties. As with teaching, many colleagues continue to possess anxieties about writing, primarily due to the pressures of delivering a successful product. This section examines the role of colleagues in holding one another accountable. Here, accountability is accomplished by developing and adhering to a firm set of rules for writing and the creation of an assessment tool.

Writing boot camps consist of members of a support group who share the difficulties of managing their writing schedules. As was the case with a physical exercise boot camp, a time is designated, a location is chosen, and members assemble with one goal in mind—to write. Unlike the exercise boot camp, in this case of the faculty writing boot camp, one is not led by a commander. One is simply joined by others and left to accomplish the assignments. As a professor, each boot camp participant assigns writings to the faculty-students. Unlike in classroom assignments, the professor (in the role of faculty writing boot camp participant) takes on the role of the student again. Prior to writing, each individual is asked to submit a set of goals, stating what she or he intends to accomplish (short-term and long-term). Because the group agrees to a set time to write, the participants are forced to develop realistic goals that can be accomplished during that time frame.

This is one of the most important elements of the process. Let us explain. One of the problems associated with writer's block is that writers often see "the elephant" and agonize about how to "eat the elephant." As the adage goes, the most effective way is to "eat it one bite at a time." Allow me to make this more relevant to the topic at hand: in the case that one follows the regimen of meeting regularly in the writing boot camp, it forces him or her to develop small tasks, which ultimately accumulate to successfully produce the larger target product. Here, accountability involves submitting goals prior to writing, as a part of the writing boot camp rules. It forces one to write or think in a logical way about how the project will proceed and to follow a linear structure for production.

While accountability is often determined by being marked as present or absent, ultimately one has to hold himself or herself accountable for completing his or her own assignments. The assembly of the writing group (similar to a support group model) denotes that each member has a writing production problem. Once the problem is admitted, the next step is to address this problem. Here, for each participant involved in the group, writing is the solution.

Writing boot camp members being in one space, such as writing in the same room, works best for D'Andra Orey. When writing away from the group, in one's office, for example, one can be faced with endless distractions. In Orey's case, more often than not, when he wrote in his solitary space, even though at the same time as other group members, he felt like he was not writing with the group at all. There is something about witnessing others write that forces you to stay focused, knowing that you have committed to completing a set of self-assigned goals. There have been cases, however, when Orey has written away from the group and has had success. For example, in a Twitter summer boot camp sponsored by the Center for University Scholars at JSU, writers were given time slots to write, and during the breaks they were asked to tweet their progress. Some boot camps are firm and highly structured. In addition to setting goals, one must submit updates on progress. Ultimately, one is expected to complete the final product. One means of accountability is to require a formal receipt of the submission of the final product. In the JSU boot camp, a simple acknowledgment stating that a manuscript has been submitted will suffice.

The proper environment is also important when writing, as this aspect intersects with accountability. In addition to the physical space, there is an unwritten rule that talking and other distractions such as loud headphones are prohibited. To be sure, talking is natural; however, each member is expected to respect the limited time that has been allocated to complete their submitted goals. Lastly, another means of holding participants accountable is to offer opportunities for peer review sessions. This gives members the opportunities to brainstorm and to get feedback from other members. The potential downside is that, arguably, members join a boot camp because of difficulties in managing their time. That said, these members view time as currency. Hence, some members may not view this approach as an efficient use of their time.

The structure of the JSU liberal arts writing boot camp was intended to fit the needs and schedule of full-time faculty members in the College of Liberal Arts at Jackson State University. Upon initial formation of the boot camp, each member had a combination of teaching and administrative duties that made the organization of time crucial to meeting writing goals and ensuring productivity. The boot camp participants' goal was to meet once a week, usually for no less than two-hour blocks. A notice was sent out by the lead organizer to solicit and confirm dates and times. While there was flexibility in the arrangement allowing for unexpected occurrences such as meetings, student issues, and whatever else can go on at a university at the last minute, the group was disciplined about keeping commitments. This is precisely how and why the boot camp was a success.

A valuable component to the structure of the boot camp was the venue. Often the writing venues were in places with adequate lighting, large windows, and ample plugs for electronic devices. In addition, there were plenty of snacks, coffee, and water to stay energized and hydrated to avoid the desire to leave the selected writing venue. When not meeting collectively in person, the group signed in electronically via email. Having a flexible venue option helped to sustain the boot camp when meeting physically became a challenge, especially when one of the members relocated to another state.

The four-member boot camp consists of an interdisciplinary team representing the fields of English, political science, mass communications, and history. Most are mid-career tenure-track or tenured and have held administrative posts at some point. There was a proposal to expand the group, but with some dialogue and a vote, the decision was made to keep the number to a minimum to avoid a large group forming and to minimize distractions and conversations.

The boot camp serves a valuable purpose for one in the process of revising a book manuscript for publication. When time is limited to submit a full working manuscript to a publisher, it is necessary to carve out time to write, especially if teaching and administrative obligations are involved. Obviously, it is important that any manuscript has purpose, that it is clearly written, and that the structure makes sense. Furthermore, "understanding that writing isn't merely the vehicle of one's information. Shape, voice, narrative line, density, length: [one needs] to get these right in order to turn a manuscript into a book."[4] The boot camp requires consistent check-in and progress reports of stated writing goals, which makes tackling large writing goals easier by having smaller objectives to achieve and be held accountable for.

Choosing the right members is critical in developing a writing boot camp. Liberal arts academics are often eccentric persons who have taken the arduous path of being educators of mostly young adults. What many early career academicians fail to realize is that one has also elected to be a professional writer. This may dawn on some tenured and tenure-track professors earlier or later, but the fact remains that once you achieve a tenure-track position, writing becomes part of your life. This is not always envisioned while one is in graduate school pursuing a PhD in any of the liberal arts. It comes as a hard truth for those who may have thought that writing the dissertation would be the last time they would stay up in the wee hours of the night trying to make sense of sources and churn out typed pages. The writing boot camp helps to relieve the loneliness and isolation of the writing process, which also helps to alleviate the anxiety that comes along with meeting writing deadlines. If one is part of a group of colleagues whose goal is to research, write, and publish, the mere fact that one is no longer in it by oneself relieves a great deal of stress associated with the meticulous writing process.

The JSU writing boot camp grew organically out of conversations between colleagues who were already friends or at least knew of each other. They all had different routines to put pen to paper, yet they all came together and wrote. For example, when writing in a common space, it was important for a couple of members to informally chat, catch up, and share some laughs before settling in to write. Rico Devara Chapman, on the other hand, skipped the casual conversations and dove straight in because he knew his routine, and his fellow boot campers knew as well and didn't take offense when he put on headphones and zoned into his writing. The important part is that they were all there to accomplish individual writing goals for that day, and whatever it takes for that to happen they agreed with. When it became difficult for writing goals to be accomplished during the designated boot camp time, editing was the best use of that chosen time.

Editing is an important part of the overall writing process. The boot camp served also as an ideal time to edit one's work after the initial drafts, since there may be times when words do not easily flow onto the paper. Editing is just as important as writing. This is where one revises clumsy sentences and deletes unnecessary flowery language for a clear, concise, and error-free essay. Consequently, "vigorous writing is concise." According to Strunk and White, "a sentence should contain no unnecessary words, a paragraph no unnecessary sentences, for the same reason that a drawing should have no unnecessary lines and a machine no unnecessary parts. This requires not that the writer make all sentences short, or avoid all detail and treat subjects only in routine, but that every word tell."[5]

The benefits of the writing boot camp for historians are many. As the historian in the JSU group, it was important to Rico Chapman that time was used effectively to work systematically and to engage source material and other writers, with that being the only way to write history. The consistency of a writing boot camp allows for the historian to "gain a sense of [one's] own style and interests" that comes from writing more often. Also, when completing drafts it was critical that time was allotted to reflect and gain some perspective on the draft before making revisions. Therefore, proofreading and revising became a vital part of the boot camp, as revision "is an essential part of writing history."[6]

The writing boot camp's structure fit the needs of full-time faculty who were engaged in teaching and administration. Not all boot camps operate as successfully, especially with this amount of flexibility. The looseness of the structure of the boot camp allowed for various adjustments to be made at any given moment, yet the integrity of the boot camp was not diminished. The needs of the boot campers were primary, and the structure was fluid enough to fulfill each individual need.

For Monica Flippin Wynn, the boot camp experience provided scheduled and focused writing times. The times were designated by the group. Then she scheduled the time as she would a regular appointment. There were defined goals and objectives that would be shared, and the administrative boot camp member, while not monitoring her individual progress per se, required a beginning goal and outcome. Ofttimes, in the beginning of the boot camp process, the time provided Flippin Wynn, who had little academic writing experience, with the opportunity to peruse the journals in her discipline and allowed her the time and freedom to generate ideas and develop her research identity and position. The fear she felt about writing and the tenure process subsided with every session and soon gave way to a desire to put pen to paper and write.

The fear and apprehension surrounding beginning the writing process is not unusual for early-career faculty members. What happens too often is that junior faculty somehow believe that the writing sequence required for academic writing is similar to the writing process for completing a dissertation. In fact, as Boice suggests, most times new faculty members have had little exposure to academic writing, and, as Page, Edwards, and Wilson argue, they have no idea of the time and commitment required to produce scholarly material for publication. Furthermore, this new "faculty persona" and all its duties and responsibilities are quite overwhelming, so it is not unexpected that finding time to begin the writing process is often not a high priority for new faculty members.[7]

For Flippin Wynn's early career as a faculty member, the boot camp was a crucial building block in her tenure dossier toolkit, because it provided so many tangible essentials in one opportunity. She was not concerned with carving out time to write and organize, because the boot camp provided focused and scheduled appointment times. It was flexible if she needed to enter and leave again because of a prior appointment, but, as there were sometimes several scheduled writing times during the week, she got some focused time in every week, dedicated to writing and preparing her tenure portfolio.

The boot camp experience also provided unofficial mentors. Since two of the boot camp members were already tenured, Flippin Wynn could submit questions, ask for reviews, and observe as the two more experienced boot campers utilized the boot camp for grant writing and developing new fields of interest. Having access to colleagues who had completed the process was crucial as she navigated her way.

The race for tenure becomes a reality once the tenure-track position has been secured. Often, academic departments may not provide mentors or have a formal process in place for early-career faculty members. They may not provide collaborative writing options or insight into developing a holistic work-life balance, yet the boot camp experience familiarized Flippin Wynn with guidelines and protocol to successfully integrate herself into the university culture.

The transition from junior faculty to mid-career faculty can also be a difficult evolution. Mirsa and Lundquist suggest that mid-career faculty have extreme difficulty finding time to do research and write, because of the added responsibilities after getting through the tenure process. In addition they argue that "although deadlines related to teaching, advising and committee meetings are externally imposed, [...] most research deadlines are internally imposed. Thus, research gets pushed farther and farther back in the queue."[8]

Boot camps can offer these faculty members the sustainability, comprehensive vision, collegiality, and focused time to become inspired with the writing process again, and to refocus and reestablish research identities and perspectives. Several leading institutions utilize boot camps to revitalize the mid-career faculty and to increase retention and decrease faculty and academic burnout, but often these are limited or scheduled for one day.[9] When the workshop or boot camp is completed, faculty members return to previous behavior, thus continuing to cancel or postpone individual writing and research time in favor of more external appointments and other requests on their time.

Having completed the tenure process, the boot camp option remains a priority for Flippin Wynn to continue her research and writing agenda, work collaboratively with fellow boot campers, and remain motivated and engaged in the academic community. Recently she participated in a different type of boot camp writing experience. This writing group is associated with a fellowship, and the mentees meet each week with one of the researchers and write at least thirty minutes based on a goal or task to complete. The writing option provides a clear time frame to reach a specific goal or objective. It also provides weekly time for individual writing tasks.

Faculty are hired at institutions where they must stay relevant and publish within their disciplines. As job duties increase, finding the time or the motivation to continue or expand research agendas is difficult at best. The sustainability of the boot camp has also provided the members with some external benefits. As one participates in the writing boot camp, time-management skills increase. Organization and focus increase, and, especially after publishing your content or getting tenure, confidence in the writing process increases. Willingness to work and mentor junior faculty and graduate and undergraduate faculty soars, as one has real-time examples and experiences that can help others with their productivity, writing focus, and motivation.

Hence, writing boot camps or writing teams are an excellent opportunity to remain vibrant and creative in the academy. The sustainability of the boot camp is dependent upon the motivation and dedication of the individual members in specific boot camp groups as well as individual desires to remain consistent and present in the discipline and specific area of study. This boot camp experience, if cultivated and maintained, can be an influential source for productivity and motivation throughout the academic career of a faculty member. However, that depends on the colleagues involved and the boot camp environment. This boot camp has survived tenure, promotions, and changing locations. The ability to communicate and continue the process through viral and digital options suggests that indeed a boot camp with the right tangible entities can be sustainable.

Preselfannie McDaniels has considered the results of the JSU boot camp experience and, in that process, knows that some experts might consider the boot camp experience a failure. The four members sat down physically together and wrote only twice. Several times there were two or three people, but at some point that got derailed by administrative duties, family life, travel periods, and the fact that two actually do most of their writing (and send emails) between 2:00 and 4:00 a.m. This is similar to what C. M. Badenhorst et al. contend about their experience: "What became clear early on in the project was that the writing group provided support in areas other than research and writing. One issue that surfaced continually was work/life balance. Members discussed their teaching, committee work and other issues that impact on academic work." They continue: "Members continued to attend the group because they found support for their research and writing, and the group helped them to negotiate the academic culture in the Faculty."[10] This is echoed in sentiments expressed by each of the members of the JSU boot camp.

But for those who would consider the JSU boot camp experience a failure based on the experience of meeting times and spaces, they might have a hard time accounting for the productivity successes: Chapman's book (summer 2016), McDaniels's coedited book (spring 2016), Flippin Wynn's book contract and promotion, and Orey's funded National Science Foundation grant from which the research produced is already gaining national recognition. They might not be able to account for a combined twenty-one conference and invited scholarly presentations during one boot camp year, while 30 percent of those presentations were made with students in collaborative research projects.

Some might also consider the JSU experience the greatest restructured boot camp effort of all time, as well, for when the group graded itself a few months into the experience and made a grade of "D," D'Andra Orey came up with the idea to restructure by becoming a virtual boot camp of sorts: electronically submitting goals and accomplishments on a schedule. As one can ascertain from the productivity record, the virtual restructuring turned out to be quite successful. In addition the administrative member of the boot camp charted goals, accomplishments, and evaluations. Based on that evidence, the JSU group was able to look back and evaluate their successes, thereby making this chapter about the JSU boot camp experience possible.

Notes

1. Cecile M. Badenhorst, Sharon Penney, Susan Pickett, Rhonda Joy, Jacqueline Hesson, Gabrielle Young, Heather McLeod, Dorothy Vaandering, and Xuemei Li, "Writing Relationships: Collaboration in a Faculty Writing Group," *AISHE-J* 5 (2013), 1002.

2. Ashley Sanders, "Writing Boot Camps," blog from GradHacker and Matrix, *Inside Higher Ed*, May 11, 2014.

3. Sanders, "Writing Boot Camps."

4. William Germano, *From Dissertation to Book* (Chicago: University of Chicago Press, 2005), 8.

5. William Strunk Jr. and E. B. White, *The Elements of Style* (New York: Longman, 2000), 23.

6. William Kelleher Storey, *Writing History: A Guide for Students* (Oxford: Oxford University Press, 2013), 5, 31, 122.

7. Robert Boice, *Advice for New Faculty Members: Nihil Nimus* (Boston: Allyn and Bacon, 2000); C. Steven Page, Susan Edwards, and Judi H. Wilson, "Writing Groups in Teacher Education: A Method to Increase Scholarly Productivity," *Journal of the Southeastern Regional Association of Teacher Educators (SRATE)* 115 (2012), 31.

8. Joya Misra and Jennifer Lundquist, "Making Time for Research," *Inside Higher Education*, January 15, 2016, https://www.insidehighered.com/advice/2016/01/15/tips-help-midcareer-faculty-members-find-time-research-projects-essay.

9. "IU Bloomington Faculty Taking Part in 'Boot Camp' for Academic Success," *IU News Room*, May 28, 2013, http://newsinfo.iu.edu/news-archive/24283.html.

10. Badenhorst et al., "Writing Relationships," 10015, 10018.

Bibliography

Badenhorst, Cecile M., Sharon Penney, Sarah Pickett, Rhonda Joy, Jacqueline Hesson, Gabrielle Young, Heather McLeod, Dorothy Vaandering, and Xuemei Li. "Writing Relationships: Collaboration in a Faculty Writing Group." *AISHE-J* 5 (2013): 1001–26.

Boice, Robert. *Advice for New Faculty Members: Nihil Nimus*. Boston: Allyn and Bacon, 2000.

Germano, William. *From Dissertation to Book*. Chicago: University of Chicago Press, 2005.

"IU Bloomington Faculty Taking Part in 'Boot Camp' for Academic Success." *IU News Room*, May 28, 2013. http://newsinfo.iu.edu/news-archive/24283.html.

Misra, Joya, and Jennifer Lundquist. "Making Time for Research." *Inside Higher Education*, January 15, 2016. https://www.insidehighered.com/advice/2016/01/15/tips-help-midcareer-faculty-members-find-time-research-projects-essay.

Page, C. Steven, Susan Edwards, and Judi H. Wilson. "Writing Groups in Teacher Education: A Method to Increase Scholarly Productivity." *Journal of the Southeastern Regional Association of Teacher Educators (SRATE)* 22 (2012): 29–35.

Sanders, Ashley. "Writing Boot Camps." Blog from GradHacker and Matrix. *Inside Higher Ed*, May 11, 2014.

Storey, William Kelleher. *Writing History: A Guide for Students*. Oxford: Oxford University Press, 2013.

Strunk, William Jr., and E. B. White. *The Elements of Style*. New York: Longman, 2000.

SOCIAL ISSUES
AND THE
LIBERAL ARTS

CHAPTER 13

You Can't Say That

Warnings, Political Correctness, and Academic Freedom

RASHELL R. SMITH-SPEARS

Early in her professional career, a professor at one of the nation's postsecondary institutions taught a first-year writing class that focused on the Black image in the media. As part of the course content, she wanted to show Spike Lee's *Bamboozled* (2000), a film that explores the history and lasting effects of minstrelsy in America through a modern-day actor who dons blackface makeup. The professor believed that viewing the film would be beneficial for her students for several reasons: (1) it would allow them to have some idea of how decisions about media content are made by the power brokers in the industry; (2) it would expose them to the history of minstrelsy in American culture, a subject with which they were quite unfamiliar; (3) it would challenge them to contemplate the construction of Black identity in the face of oppressive societal forces; (4) it would familiarize them with the concept of satire; and (5) it would teach them how to engage with popular culture as more than entertainment, but rather as text that must be considered with a critical eye. However, this professor was told that *Bamboozled* might be "too much for them," and instead Lorraine Hansberry's *A Raisin in the Sun* should be shown. The film version of Hansberry's play is an acceptable and canonical text that could address some of the issues that she wanted to present to her students, but not all. Nonetheless, she was young and untenured in the profession, and *A Raisin in the Sun* is what her class studied.

Diversity in the form of culture, politics, and technology, among other areas, causes us to explore the world through new lenses and with new approaches. It allows for an encounter with concepts and individuals that expand our own values and understandings so that we can produce new and tested ideas for the community. Certainly, diversity is a necessary and valuable part of a well-developed educational experience. While this can be beneficial and expanding, it can serve as a double-edged sword, producing challenges that threaten the academic endeavor. These threats manifest as trigger warnings as well as an ideology-based push for political correctness. Such manifestations pose a challenge to academic freedom and influence those of us in the academy to refocus our priorities.

The story of the young professor is illustrative of an infringement upon her academic freedom. As the college classroom is a space for the free exploration and expression of ideas, any subject can and should be examined through a critical and intellectual lens. This assessment is supported by former American Association of University Professors president Cary Nelson. In a 2010 article in *Inside Higher Ed*, Nelson explains that "academic freedom means that both faculty members and students can engage in intellectual debate without fear of censorship or retaliation." Furthermore, it "means that both faculty members and students can make comparisons and contrasts between subjects taught in a course and any field of human knowledge or period of history." Also, academic freedom gives both students and faculty the right to express their views—in speech, in writing, and through electronic communication, both on and off campus without fear of sanction, unless the manner of expression substantially impairs the rights of others or, in the case of faculty members, those views demonstrate that they are professionally ignorant, incompetent, or dishonest with regard to their discipline or fields of expertise.[1]

Similarly, Robert Ivie explains it as "unfettered scholarly inquiry, a scholar's fundamental right of research, publication, and instruction free of institutional constraint." This freedom is designed to allow for innovation and progress, and thus it is an imperative in the college setting. Since the origination of the concept in the mid-twelfth century at the University of Bologna, scholars have relied on academic freedom to pursue new knowledge or espouse dissent without the fear of persecution or administrative retribution. Faculty as well as students engage with the university as a place in which they are allowed and encouraged to investigate multiple perspectives of a subject, even if one perspective has been accepted as the leading one.[2] This level of intellectual pursuit demands that it be unfettered by financial or political concerns, because those elements have a way of hindering Truth. The college classroom is about seeking Truth, even when it becomes uncomfortable for the faculty, the students, or the administration. This pursuit is the way toward new ideas, new inventions, and new understandings of our reality. Of course, at times this pursuit of knowledge has involved controversial content, ideas that challenged the status quo, that pushed against boundaries of political or socioeconomic comfort or that simply called for paradigm shifts, all of which necessitated intellectual autonomy.

According to Scott Bass and Mary Clark in "The Gravest Threat to Colleges Comes from Within," not only scholars have benefited from this freedom to pursue their intellectual passions, but also society. "Basic research that appears to have little practical application has helped cure disease, led to breakthroughs in science, and fostered understanding of the world. Presentation of counterculture perspectives, art, and literature has contributed to the next generation of leaders' understanding of social and political movements." In fact, "many of the things we take for granted were once controversial, even heretical."[3] Without the freedom to pursue such passions, not only would students suffer, but society would be left without its benefits.

Our current society has struggled with its own controversial content as well as questions about the most appropriate means by which to handle it. In 2015 Wheaton College professor of political science Larycia Hawkins posted on Facebook that Christians and Muslims worship the same God. She then daily donned a hijab in solidarity with Muslim women. Administrators at Wheaton College, an evangelical Christian school, immediately took steps to suspend and eventually fire the tenured professor. They claimed that by not distinguishing the differences between Islam and Christianity, Hawkins violated their code of conduct. By 2016 Hawkins and Wheaton officials had reached an agreement that included her no longer teaching at the school.

In another case that speaks to issues of academic freedom, Steven Salaita was given a conditional job offer as a tenured associate professor in the American Indian Studies program at the University of Illinois at Urbana-Champaign. The offer was rescinded when attention was brought to a series of pro-Palestinian tweets Salaita made about the Israeli-Palestinian conflict. Considerable pressure was placed on the then-chancellor, Phyllis Wise, by external groups to terminate the offer made by the department and interim dean of the College of Liberal Arts and Sciences.

Both examples involved tenured professors whose political views were controversial and thus were at odds with the administration. In each instance their academic freedom was challenged, and not only did Hawkins and Salaita suffer for it, but so did the educational enterprise. According to the *Chicago Tribune*, Wheaton College has lost donors and has suffered damage to its reputation. The media storm surrounding Salaita's case has garnered both a negative light for the University of Illinois at Urbana-Champaign and censure from the AAUP. Surely, these situations have given pause to other faculty across the country as they research subjects that may not be favorable to their administrations.

But, even as we contend with such administrative and sometimes legislative challenges to freedom in academia, another threat has arisen. Deriving from within the classroom, trigger warnings and hyper-political-correctness are well intentioned but, if unchecked, can function to shackle academic freedom, which stifles intellectual inquiry and academic rigor.

In the debate concerning trigger warnings, its definition moves along a wide spectrum. The understanding of its meaning and its attendant effects vary between and within student groups, professors, administration officials, and the nonacademic community. Basically, trigger warnings are alerts to students that course content might be upsetting, "trigger" a recurrence of past trauma, or cause symptoms of post-traumatic stress disorder. Objectionable content can range from issues of suicide in Virginia Woolf's *Mrs. Dalloway* to images of war in a film or photography to scenes of domestic violence and sexual assault in textbooks and lecture notes. These warnings originated in the blogosphere among feminist blogs and forums with a concern for victims of rape and sexual abuse, advising them that the posted content could contain retraumatizing material. This warning provided them with the option to avoid it.

Quoting Andrea Smith, feminist scholar Angela M. Carter explains that these warnings were "'a part of a complex of practices within the anti-violence movement' working to recognize 'that we are not unaffected by the political and intellectual work that we do' and that 'the labor of healing has to be shared by all.'"[4] In the last decade, however, these warnings (sometimes called "content warning" to avoid reference to the violence of the word "trigger") have moved beyond cyberspace and entered the college classroom.

At the University of California-Santa Barbara there has been a formal call for them by the student government, but other schools are also publicly contending with this issue. These institutions include Oberlin College, Rutgers University, the University of Michigan, George Washington University, Scripps College, and Wellesley College, among other schools. While students at these colleges and universities have called for trigger warnings, the National Coalition Against Censorship found in its nonscientific survey of eight hundred members of professional associations for professors of literature and art that few schools have a policy about trigger warnings.[5] Without a formal school policy, individual professors are left to determine how they want to handle students' requests for these trigger warnings.

At first glance, honoring requests for such warnings seems obvious and simple. The goal of educators is to convey information and concepts that will better the student, not harm them. With more diverse populations entering college than ever before, and according to a 2009 article in *Pediatrics* journal, with more people experiencing violence in their lives, issuing trigger warnings seems to be sensitive and decent. Further data from the National Survey of Children's Exposure to Violence indicates "more than 60 percent of children from birth to 17 years, experience victimization." The rates are higher for African Americans, with black people being three times more likely to be victims of robbery and five times more likely to be victims of homicide. In terms of sexual violence, one in five women and one in seventy-one men will experience rape or sexual assault. Lastly, the National Center for Education Statistics assesses that "schools have more nontraditional students, including veterans who have fought and killed in war."[6]

Certainly, students are entering the college classroom with emotional memories and traumas that professors have no way of being knowledgeable of, so issuing warnings about certain course content provides access to a space for students to process the course content. Angela M. Carter says trigger warnings function by "lessening the power of the shock and the unexpectedness, and granting the traumatized individual agency to attend the affect and effects of their trauma."[7] Moreover, requests for trigger warnings demonstrate students' agency in their educational experience. Claiming their right to avoid being confronted with traumatizing material is an assertion of their personhood and acknowledgment that learning is a cooperative exercise that involves more than just the professor feeding the student information. Additionally, some would argue that as paying individuals, students absolutely have the right to speak to the content to which they are exposed.

Providing further evidence that trigger warnings should be issued by professors, Carter argues that the popular understanding of trigger warnings and trauma itself is faulty. Retraumatization is not merely discomfort about a subject matter. When one has suffered a trauma, to be triggered is to mentally and physically re-experience a past trauma in such an embodied manner that one's affective response literally takes over the ability to be present in one's bodymind. When this occurs, the triggered individuals often feel a complete loss of control and disassociation from the bodymind. This is not a state of injury, but rather a state of disability.[8]

To be sure, to be triggered when one has experienced a trauma actually produces a psychosomatic response beyond the individual's control. Carter argues that we must reconceptualize trauma as a disability, and rather than place it within a marginalizing binary of disabled and able-bodied, we must "reimagine what education can look like" when we do not other those with disabilities.[9] In this way, to not issue a trigger warning strangles the educational process for students, placing restrictions on their access to content because of their disability (the trauma). So the trigger warning enhances the academic freedom of such students rather than limiting them.

The task before professors, then, becomes not only understanding what trigger warnings are but also how to accommodate requests for them. Carter's argument to use them seems reasonable, but for many professors confronted with requests, the task is not as clear as warning traumatized students that they may be retraumatized. Sometimes students are asking to be exempt from the content in some form because it is uncomfortable. This exemption could entail not being present during the discussion of sensitive topics; being assigned alternative assignments; or not having the content discussed at all. Each of these accommodations in some way affects the academic climate and, to an extent, freedom of the classroom.

In a 2015 *Chronicle of Higher Education* article, Robin Wilson discusses the story of one professor at UC-Berkley who teaches a master's-level course on social-welfare policy. In the class he regularly pushes students who are both in favor of abortion and opposed to the death penalty to consider inconsistencies in their arguments. Some students indicated on the teacher evaluations that they were offended. Because administration uses these evaluations to measure faculty performance, to avoid negative consequences the professor eliminated his lecture on abortion altogether. His fear, he acknowledged, is that "sensitivity has become a more important criterion than intellectual challenge when it comes to the way administrators review a professor's performance."[10] In this instance, and others like it in which professors feel they must eliminate course content, the academic climate suffers, because students are not exposed to important content and are not called upon to interrogate their perspectives. At this point trigger warnings have lost their benign and beneficial intent, to become harmful.

What is considered inappropriate or insensitive can vary. Often people speak of trigger warnings in regard to discussions of war or sexual violence, but the desire for warnings is more inclusive. Students want to be warned about—and/or exempted from—discussions of racism, classism, sexism, heterosexism, ableism, religion, sexuality, and topics that could be deemed immoral by the student, such as foul language. The efforts to circumvent such topics represent a shift in the expectations of the college classroom. Rather than seeking academic rigor and intellectual engagement, students seek safety.

Initially the call for safe spaces came from members of the privileged class who wanted to be shielded from charges by marginalized people. As people with power, they used the notion of the safe space as an authoritative way to silence voices that acknowledged perspectives of the world that not only challenged their own but held them complicit in the marginalization of others. Feminist scholar bell hooks explains, "Indeed, exposing certain truths and biases in the classroom often created chaos and confusion. The idea that the classroom should always be a "safe," harmonious place was challenged. It was hard for individuals to fully grasp the idea that recognition of difference might also require of us a willingness to see the classroom change, to allow for shifts in relations between students."[11]

Today, the classroom has changed, and the call for safe spaces is coming from the marginalized groups. However, much like those privileged groups who used safe spaces to silence others, groups are still being silenced by safe spaces. Students claim a right to be safe not only from hostile and violent verbal assaults but also from offensive and uncomfortable discussions. While the former is certainly understandable, the latter works to shut down a significant portion of intellectual discussion.

Moreover, Greg Lukianoff, a constitutional lawyer, and Jonathan Haidt, a social psychologist, argue that this push for "safe spaces" assumes a psychological fragility on the part of American college students and gives primacy to emotional well-being. By allowing students to "hide out" in these spaces and avoid unpleasant subjects or uncomfortable realities, academic institutions are providing a disservice to the students and the institutions themselves. Lukianoff and Haidt warn that by indulging students in these trends of safe spaces and trigger warnings, "they are teaching them a kind of hypersensitivity that will lead them into countless conflicts that will damage their careers and friendships along with their mental health."[12] In this way they are opting out of diversity of thought to be assuaged by the comfort of the familiar, an act which is popularly known as confirmation bias. With confirmation bias, people are open only to information that supports their already-held beliefs and tend to reject evidence that challenges their beliefs. Eventually, as Lukianoff and Haidt seem to suggest, this may lead to an eschewing of diversity at all that will hinder human relationships.

This shift toward protecting students from anything offensive or upsetting adheres to a sense of hyper-political-correctness that can be dangerous to the educational enterprise. Ironically, political correctness began as a concept that would help fight discrimination and myopic thinking. Through the act of being inclusive in one's language, one would be prompted to think more inclusively and move beyond biased or intolerant behavior. Unfortunately, students (and in some cases, professors) have sometimes failed to critically assess situations and instead fall back on a political correctness based on ideology. DeBard and Eberly assert, "When advocacy, no matter how well intended, is driven by ideology, it is dangerous." The danger can result in what

Lukianoff and Haidt call *vindictive protectiveness*, a cultural impulse in which individuals "must think twice before speaking up, lest they face charges of insensitivity, aggression, or worse."[13]

In 2015 student activists at Yale University bullied and harassed two faculty members, Nicholas and Erika Christakis, because Erika challenged the suggestions distributed by the administration for nonoffensive Halloween costumes, inviting everyone to consider a discussion of the suggestions through an intellectual lens. Erika, a researcher in early childhood development, wrote in a reply to the administration: "Have we lost faith in young people's capacity—in your capacity—to exercise self-censure, through social norming, and also in your capacity to ignore or reject things that trouble you?" Students were especially angered when she wrote: "Nicholas says, if you don't like a costume someone is wearing, look away, or tell them you are offended. Talk to each other. Free speech and the ability to tolerate offense are the hallmarks of a free and open society."[14] The student protestors felt that in telling students to "look away" from offensive costumes, these professors were providing license to the wearers and working to perpetuate unsafe spaces for offended individuals. Many in the heated controversy seemed to ignore the call for discussion and intellectual engagement.

In response to the incidents of vindictive protectiveness much like the Yale controversy, popular comedians such as Chris Rock and Jerry Seinfeld have declared that they will not perform on college campuses anymore. These declarations are due to their inability to freely perform their craft, which uses humor to make social commentary. Often comedians, like some political speakers, are censored and protested by college students demanding political correctness. In an interview with Frank Rich, Rock said that college students are "too conservative . . . in their social views and their willingness not to offend anybody. Kids raised on a culture of 'We're not going to keep score in the game because we don't want anybody to lose.'" Rock explains that the climate on college campuses will not even allow for one to "be offensive on your way to being inoffensive."[15] These are only two examples of how an atmosphere of hyper-political-correctness has infiltrated the college campus, but these examples are not anomalies. Encouraged by the belief that there is a correct way to think about a subject, students can be offended by any divergent viewpoints and feel that they should not be subjected to them.

DeBard and Eberly, in "Diversity for All: Opening Perspectives on Campus," explain that this political correctness, in its inception a tool to fight against limiting diversity and now becoming pervasive on college campuses, has skewed "critical thinking into acceptable thinking. . . . The result is the exclusion of thought rather than its inclusion." The practice of challenging held beliefs to push for critical introspection is lost and its value diminished. This loss is unfortunate, as the American college system is considered one of the leaders in knowledge production, according to a study of five hundred top world universities conducted by Shanghai Jiao Tong University.[16]

Cultural studies scholar Henry Giroux cites the study. "Offering faculty a substantial measure of academic freedom and students the opportunity to learn within *a culture of questioning and critical engagement* [emphasis mine]," Giroux argues, "American higher education strongly affirms, at least in principle, the knowledge, values, skills and social relations required for producing individual and social agents capable of addressing the political, economic, and social injustices that diminish the reality and promise of a substantive democracy at home and abroad."[17] The college classroom is charged with being the site of new inquiry that functions to shape our local and global communities for the better. Additionally, it is here that students learn to be more than consumers of information, but rather producers of knowledge themselves. This type of intellectual engagement is possible, however, only when academic freedom is a reality and not beholden to the misguided tenets of hyper-political-correctness.

This type of political correctness and the trigger warnings that emerge from it can be dangerous and diminishing for students; however, for adjunct, term, and nontenured faculty, it is especially troubling. While the UC-Berkeley professor mentioned earlier was a tenured faculty member and feared only what he termed a "ding" in his file, faculty with probationary status would have much more to lose if they received negative feedback from students about their behavior in the classroom. In his article "Student Entitlement," Stephen Lippmann argues that the instability of adjunct and term faculty positions may force faculty members to make choices between presenting their academic content as they deem appropriate and appeasing students to keep them happy and thus to keep their jobs.[18]

The professor discussed in the beginning of this article who attempted to present *Bamboozled* in class was early in her career and not tenured, and thus felt she had to accept the suggestion of showing *A Raisin in the Sun* rather than the content that she believed to be the more intellectually appropriate. Lippmann explains that in such incidents, "these pressures are exacerbated by a heightened emphasis on student evaluations. . . . [Furthermore], these developments have fueled the student-as-customer mantra, which in turn accentuates the faculty role as employee rather than professional."[19] When students begin to see themselves as the customer (as many colleges and universities encourage them to do intentionally or unintentionally), they begin to perceive the college and the institution as a commodity that must respond to their needs and desires.

Hunter Rawlings, president of the Association of American Universities, agrees, stating: "If colleges are responsible for outcomes, then students can feel entitled to classes that do not push them too hard, to high grades and to material that does not challenge their assumptions or make them uncomfortable. Hence, colleges too often cater to student demands for trigger warnings, "safe rooms," and canceled commencement speakers." Certainly, the recent discourse on academia in the popular culture posits college simply as a means to a financial end, and a costly one at that. It becomes a matter of course, then, that if students view college as an economic exchange, for their money, they expect to be satisfied with the product. It is unfortunate that the product is not always intellectual enlightenment, but rather affirmation that does not challenge their views, and grades that will lead to a degree. Lippman writes that "students now see professors less as intellectual leaders who are to be respected and more as simply gatekeepers (even impediments) on the students' path to educational completion and the desired better job."[20] Not only do these adjusted roles for the students and the faculty have an effect on the intellectual atmosphere of the classroom, but they also could affect faculty job satisfaction, which will still affect the intellectual climate.

So, we are faced with a dilemma in this new century of technology, diversity, political correctness, student entitlement and budgetary concerns: how do we remain true to the intellectual goals of the academic classroom while creating a safe, inclusive space for the learners who enter it? It is imperative that we seek and find solutions so that we can continue to produce engaged, critically thinking graduates who will help to shape a better, more compassionate world. We are charged, student and faculty, with the responsibility of reassessing our understanding of trauma so that we can address the issue of difference safely and re-triggering better. An administrator at Lasell College in Massachusetts argues that we are moving beyond the "sage-on-the-stage" model of education and that "students are becoming more proactive in their own education," which includes asserting their rights to have warnings about course content, university speakers, and ideas and events that they are exposed to on the college campus.[21]

Lippman suggests that faculty need to be "re-socialized into the world of today's students" to gain a better understanding of their orientations and expectations of education." However, as DeBard and Eberly assert, it is still "one of the challenges of higher education to push students to learn in new ways that do not come easily." Underscoring this idea, the American Association of University Professors (AAUP) released a statement in 2014 on trigger warnings: "The presumption that students need to be protected rather than challenged in a classroom is at once infantilizing and anti-intellectual. Some discomfort is inevitable in classrooms if the goal is to expose students to new ideas, have them question beliefs they have taken for granted, grapple with ethical problems they have never considered, and more generally, expand their horizons so as to become informed and responsible democratic citizens."[22]

Assuming we all want to do what is right for our students and the enterprise of learning, this is a topic that demands serious consideration. Certainly, the subject of trigger warnings and political correctness and their effects on academic freedom will remain a significant issue for the academic institutions as it calls for adjustments on the part of administration, students, and faculty. Change is never easy. For many, the solution is to maintain the educational enterprise as it has been, in which the student comes into the academic environment and accept it as is. Students must adjust to the professor rather than the other way around. But this method is becoming ineffective and irrelevant as more students are expecting more student-focused practices, and institutions are working to accommodate those expectations. However, the questions and concerns that arise because of it must be addressed. We must find a balance between the needs of the students and the demands of academic freedom. Take note: you have been warned.

Notes

1. Giroux, Henry A. "Academic Freedom under Fire: The Case for Critical Pedagogy," *College Literature* 33, no. 4 (2006), 31.

2. Giroux, "Academic Freedom," 31; Scott Bass and Mary L. Clark, "The Gravest Threat to Colleges Comes from Within," *Chronicle of Higher Education*, October 16, 2015.

3. Bass and Clark, "Gravest Threat."

4. Angela M. Carter, "Teaching with Trauma: Warnings, Feminism, and Disability Pedagogy," *Disability Studies Quarterly* 35, no. 2 (2015), 5.

5. Ingrid Sturgis, "Warning: This Lesson May Upset You," *Chronicle of Higher Education* 62, supp., March 18, 2016: 33–35.

6. Sturgis, "Warning," 33–35.

7. Carter, "Teaching with Trauma," 10.

8. Carter, "Teaching with Trauma," 4.

9. Carter, "Teaching with Trauma," 7.

10. Robin Wilson, "Students' Requests for Trigger Warnings Grow More Varied," *Chronicle of Higher Education*, September 14, 2015.

11. Carter, "Teaching with Trauma," 8.

12. Greg Lukianoff and Jonathan Haidt, "The Coddling of the American Mind, *The Atlantic*, September 2015, 7–8.

13. Robert DeBard and Charles G. Eberly, "Diversity for All: Opening Perspectives on Campus," *About Campus*, 2014, 11; Lukianoff and Haidt, "Coddling of the American Mind," 7.

14. Conor Friedersdorf, "The Perils of Writing a Provocative Email at Yale," *The Atlantic*, May 16, 2016.

15. Frank Rich, "In Conversation with Chris Rock," *New York Magazine*, December 1, 2014.

16. DeBard and Eberly, "Diversity for All," 10; Giroux, "Academic Freedom under Fire."

17. Giroux, "Academic Freedom under Fire," 2.

18. Stephen Lippmann, Ronald E. Bulanda, and Theodore C. Wagenaar, "Student Entitlement: Issues and Strategies for Confronting Entitlement in the Classroom and Beyond," *College Teaching* 57, no. 4 (2009): 202. doi: 10.1080/87567550903218596.

19. Lippmann, "Student Entitlement," 202.

20. Hunter Rawlings, "College Is Not a Commodity. Stop Treating It Like One," *Washington Post*, June 9, 2016; Lippmann, "Student Entitlement," 200.

21. Carter, "Teaching with Trauma," 8; Sturgis, "Warning."

22. Lippmann, Bulanda, and Wagenaar, "Student Entitlement," 202; DeBard and Eberly, "Diversity for All," 10; Wilson, "Students' Requests for Trigger Warnings."

Bibliography

Bass, Scott, and Mary L. Clark. "The Gravest Threat to Colleges Comes from Within." *Chronicle of Higher Education* 62, no. 7, October 16, 2015.

Carter, Angela M. "Teaching with Trauma: Warnings, Feminism, and Disability Pedagogy." *Disability Studies Quarterly* 35, no. 2 (2015): 1–21.

DeBard, Robert, and Charles G. Eberly. "Diversity for All: Opening Perspectives on Campus." *About Campus* 19, no. 3 (2014): 9–16.

Friedersdorf, Conor. "The Perils of Writing a Provocative Email at Yale." *The Atlantic*, May 16, 2016. https://www.theatlantic.com/politics/archive/2016/05/the-peril-of-writing-a-provocative-email-at-yale/484418/.

Giroux, Henry A. "Academic Freedom under Fire: The Case for Critical Pedagogy." *College Literature* 33, no. 4 (2006): 1–42.

Lippmann, Stephen, Ronald E. Bulanda, and Theodore C. Wagenaar. "Student Entitlement: Issues and Strategies for Confronting Entitlement in the Classroom and Beyond." *College Teaching* 57, no. 4 (2009): 197–204. doi: 10.1080/87567550903218596.

Lukianoff, Greg, and Jonathan Haidt. "The Coddling of the American Mind." *The Atlantic*, September 2015, 7–8.

Medina, Jennifer. "Warning: The Literary Canon Could Make Students Squirm." *New York Times*, May 18, 2014.

Nelson, Cary. "Defining Academic Freedom." *Inside Higher Ed*, December 21, 2010.

Pashman, Manya B. "Wheaton College Could Face Long-Term Fallout over Professor Controversy." *Chicago Tribune*, February 22, 2016.

Rawlings, Hunter. "College Is Not a Commodity. Stop Treating It Like One." *Washington Post*, June 9, 2016.

Rich, Frank. "In Conversation with Chris Rock." *New York Magazine*, December 1, 2014.

Sturgis, Ingrid. "Warning: This Lesson May Upset You." *Chronicle of Higher Education* 62, supp., March 18, 2016, 33–35.

Wilson, Robin. "Students' Requests for Trigger Warnings Grow More Varied." *Chronicle of Higher Education* 62, no. 3, September 14, 2015.

CHAPTER 14

Not All Apples Are Red

KATRINA BYRD

In a kindergarten classroom twenty children sit quietly at long wooden-topped tables. A white sheet of paper with the shape of an apple outlined in thick black ink is in front of each student. "All apples are red," the teacher says as she places one crayon labeled brick red beside each student. When one child raises her hand and says, "Not all apples are red," she is scolded. "Yes, they are," the teacher says angrily. She towers over the child staring down at her briefly—a signal that the conversation is over. At the end of the day, twenty pictures of brick red apples adorn the classroom wall, and one student is left feeling confused about what she was taught about apples and the fact that she had seen apples in a variety of colors in the grocery store.

At home the child speaks to her mother about the teacher's saying all apples are red. "Mama, can I take a green apple and a yellow apple to school tomorrow?" she asks. "No!" her mother says angrily and accuses the child of challenging the teacher's authority. "You just trying to know more than the teacher," the mother says to the child, who feels she's done something wrong by voicing a provable fact.

In exploring the reasons why a liberal arts education is undervalued by parents and students, my goal with this paper is to discuss the preparation of global learners, the history of American education, and the conflict between the search for meaning and the desire for marketable skills, while taking a look at the life and work of Nina Simone.

The conflict between the search for meaning and the desire for marketable skills is clear and present in today's society. Lots of lip service is given to thinking outside the box or fostering creativity, but little voice is given to rearranging the roles in the classroom so that students and teachers can enter collaborative, information-sharing educational structures that lead to intellectual learning. Training produces workers who are a part of a systemic way of life. Liberal arts education produces lifelong learners, critical thinkers, and people who can use that education to create meaning. Nina Simone, notable black song writer, performer, and activist, referred to her work as an activist as more important than her training as a concert pianist. Simone's ability to encapsulate the human spirit in her music during a time of civil unrest went well beyond the skill for which she was trained.

In her autobiography *I Put a Spell on You*, Simone talks of how she'd always been aware of prejudice but hadn't been directly affected by it. Politics and race weren't talked about in her home as a child. When she spoke out about racial inequality with her song "Mississippi Goddam" on her debut album *Nina Simone in Concert* (live recording, 1964), it was the beginning of her civil rights work.

"Mississippi Goddam" was written in response to the murder of Medgar Evers on June 12, 1963, and the September 15, 1963, bombing of the 16th Street Baptist Church in Birmingham, Alabama. The bombing killed four young girls and injured one. For Simone, who spent so much of her early years at home or at church (safe places), this brutality against black people who only wanted equality was too much for her to take. After the murder of Medgar Evers, Simone found herself in a state of rage. In *I Put a Spell on You* she writes, "Suddenly I realized what it was to be black in America in 1963, but it wasn't an intellectual connection of the type Loraine had been repeating to me over and over—it came as a rush of fury, hatred and determination."[1]

Simone wanted to kill. Armed with a load of tools and other things, she went to her apartment, where she tried to make a gun. When her husband discovered her working fervently on what would prove to be a senseless effort, he suggested she use her music to express her feelings. After Simone calmed herself, she returned to her studio and turned her anger into her first civil rights song, "Mississippi Goddam." After writing it Simone knew there was no turning back. She was a classically trained musician who had high standards for her music. She had a great disrespect for popular music and protest songs. To her they were "simple." For Simone, putting the life of a man like Medgar Evers into a tune was somehow not good enough. After the first live performance of "Mississippi Goddam" at the Village Gate in New York, she gained a new respect for activism and how it informed her classical training.

Simone had to choose between a skill she'd learned since childhood and her passion for giving a voice to an oppressed people. The conflict between earning money and following her passion was present because the American educational system had a history of skill-based, do-as-you're-told training with a primary focus on earning money.

Preparing critically thinking, purpose-driven, and lifelong learners should be the goal of any education system. Unfortunately, much of our society's education system is rooted in what Paulo Freire, author of *The Pedagogy of the Oppressed*, calls the "banking system." According to Freire, "the banking system: is a product of teacher-student relationships which are narrative in character." In this system an all-knowing teacher speaks about physical existence as if it were stationary. The task, as the teacher sees it, is to "fill" students with information of this "narration content." This information is far removed from truth. The words are devoid of their power and only serve the purpose of the all-knowing teacher. According to Freire, "A careful analysis of the relationship of the teacher-student relationship at any level, inside or outside the school, reveals its fundamentally narrative character." For Freire, "this relationship involves a narrating Subject (the teacher) and patient, listening objects (the students). The contents, whether values or empirical dimensions of reality, tend, in the process of being narrated, to become lifeless and petrified. Education is suffering from narration sickness."[2]

This relationship is at the crux of the American education system. It blocks learning that comes from the sharing of knowledge, creativity, and a connection to the information being shared. This "narrated" version of education also leads to a "narrated" version of life. For the kindergarten girl in the opening of this paper, her exchange with the teacher over the color of apples is just one of many where she finds herself in direct conflict with the "narrated" education model. In junior high she is told that she is not as smart as the other students when she makes B's on her Spanish test even though she is the most fluent speaker in her class. In high school she is told that she isn't smart, because she is unable to grasp the principles of trigonometry. When she has to drop out of college after the third year for poor grades, she is once again told she isn't smart. "School isn't for everyone," several people say to her and then encourage her to get a job. The young woman knows in her heart that she's smart, talented, and creative, but she doesn't understand why she continues to fail. Defeated by her inability to thrive in an unforgiving system that refuses to accept her as she is, she tries to conform. She gets a job making minimum wage as a secretary in a small certified driver's license training office.

The "narrative" education offers a one-size-fits-all version of education. It is the equivalent of going to a restaurant that serves only sugary desserts, leaving no other options for customers who want meat or vegetables. It is like having one story told from only one point of view. The narrator of that story tells it, tells the reader how to feel about it, then requests a response from the reader that the narrator then measures. While it is important for students to know that five times five is twenty-five, it is more important that they are given the opportunity to explore why five times five is twenty-five. When this information is presented in a static form that the student is expected to commit to memory, record, and repeat, they have no true connection to what they've learned, and the information is in danger of only being available for temporary use.

With this method of teaching, students lose their human qualities and become mere objects to be filled with knowledge by an all-knowing and all-powerful teacher. As a result education becomes a system of "deposits." As Paulo Freire points out, "education thus becomes an act of depositing, in which the students are the depositories and the teacher is the depositor. Instead of communicating, the teacher issues communiques and makes deposits which the students patiently retrieve, memorize and repeat." This is Freire's banking concept of education, "in which the scope of action allowed to the students extends only as far as receiving, filtering and storing the deposits."[3]

In this system students have little to no room to invest in their own educational experience, evaluate its usefulness, or determine how what they have learned relates to their lives. When students are denied the opportunity to bond with their education, they grow into adults who have no relationship with information before them. On a cool November morning, I went to the doctor's office. When I was done, I caught a ride with a girl I knew from college. In the car she asked if I would mind if she stopped at the gas station to get a pack of cigarettes. I told her I didn't mind. She turned into the parking lot of the gas station and parked in front of pump number 5. She exited the vehicle and slammed the door behind her. Unbeknownst to the girl who had disappeared through the door of the gas station, the car started to roll backward, with me sitting in the passenger seat. Frantically I searched for the emergency brake, hoping it would be located in the center of the car directly behind the automatic gears. It was not. The car, despite my efforts to try and stop it, slammed into a concrete barrier at the back of the parking lot.

As I told this story to a friend later that week, she looked at me confused and asked, "Why were you looking for the emergency brake?" I was shocked by her question. It took me a second to answer. "To stop the car," I said. This woman in her early fifties, who had been driving since she was sixteen, stood stunned and said, "I never realized that the emergency brake would stop the car." To her, the emergency brake had only one use, which was extra support for her vehicle when it was parked on a slope. It had never occurred to her that the emergency brake could be used to stop the car when the regular brakes were inaccessible or inoperable.

When the information is presented, the teacher already has the one answer that she wants the students to grasp. There's no room for discussion or questions in this concept. In a talk at the Millsaps Principals' Institute on June 14, 2016, Steve Barkley, author of *Instructional Coaching with the End in Mind*, explained that higher learning takes place when a student leaves a course with more questions than she had when she started the class.[4]

In their quest to build an educational system that preserves democracy and embraces equality, the framers of the American educational system failed to educate thinkers. They were successful, however, in creating a system rooted in conformity and inequality. The idea to educate to conform has filtered into present society. Students are unaware that they play a role in their own education. Many students can articulate that one day they want to be rich or have a big house, but unfortunately it is not realized that "one day" is directly related to today's actions. They want to be doctors, lawyers, nurses, rap stars, high-profile sports figures, and movie stars, yet they are clueless about the work involved in achieving success in any profession. Their ignorance is a direct result of America's educational practices rooted in the "banking system."

This system steers students toward uniformity rather than guiding them on the path toward critical thinking, collaboration, and self-evaluation. There is no room for creativity or freedom of expression. As a result, students are not aware of the usefulness of the information presented to them in the classroom. For many students, what they learn in the classroom stays in the classroom. Many students find their educational experience limited in a system of enmeshment where everyone has a specific role. The teacher's role is omniscient and is not to be questioned, while the student has the role of respondent who repeats information taught to her by the teacher. This limited student investment in education presents a disconnect between what students do in the classroom and the end product, and it creates a disconnect between memorization in the classroom and the practical use of the information in the real world.

Politicians like Thomas Jefferson viewed the education of Americans as vital to democracy. According to Sarah Mondale and Sarah Patton, editors of *School: The Story of American Public Education*, Jefferson's ideas were radical for his time. During this time only wealthy men were offered the luxury of an education. Though his ideas about providing what he described as equal schools were radical, Jefferson remained true to his cause to no avail. Between 1779 and 1817, his bill was up for ratification three times, and every time it was defeated. His argument was that Americans needed to be literate in order to cast informed votes for worthy leaders. His education system would also be an arena for the training of future leaders. Author and journalist Nicholas Leman explained Jefferson's "two tiered system." Leman suggests that "Jefferson's system was a little bit of universal education with two purposes. One to give people the democratic basis, and two to be a kind of staging area or an audition site for this small group of national aristocrats who would then be given full-dress university education and then serve the country as he had done."[5] For this cause Jefferson fought for an education system that included everyone. His definition of everyone, however, was lacking.

Jefferson championed a system to prepare white males for college and eventual upward mobility in American society. For white females, he advocated educating them only for marriage and motherhood. According to *School: The Story of American Public Education*, the founders of the American education system encountered many issues as they attempted to construct an education system for all on an equal basis. One major issue in the 1800s during the Common School Movement was religion.

Between 1820 and 1840, Horace Mann, one of the original education reformers who was the secretary of the state board of education in Massachusetts, did a great deal by way of creating a system that he felt embraced equality for all. Incidentally, this was a system similar to that of Thomas Jefferson's idea in the late 1700s. After doing extensive investigation into the condition of schools, Mann fought for safer facilities, comfortable school furniture, adequate teachers, and textbooks. In his quest to provide education rooted in equality, Mann neglected to construct a system that embraced equal religious practices. For Mann, equal schools were defined as schools that taught Protestant beliefs. Bishop John Hughes, a Catholic Irish immigrant, challenged Mann, arguing that taxpayer dollars should be filtered into a school system that incorporated other religious beliefs into its teaching, but the American public disagreed. After other religious sects began requesting public funding for their prospective schools, the issue was put up for debate. In 1841 the Great Debates took place. One church historian described the debates as a "man against a whole army of people." Despite his minimal support, Hughes continued to push the issue. In 1859 Hughes was appointed archbishop of New York and was in a position to create a national system of Catholic schools.[6]

During the 1840s, while the primary topic of debate was providing equal education for all, the issues related to religion and politics were prominently discussed. The issue of race was not configured into the "equality for all" design of America's education system. According to Patton and Mondale, African Americans and other oppressed groups viewed education as vital in their struggle toward freedom. Because of this belief, African Americans tested the limits of equality in the American education system. In 1849 a judge ruled against the parents of Sara Roberts, a five-year-old African

American girl whose parents sought to enroll her into a white school because of the poor condition of the black schools. Roberts argued that his daughter should be permitted to enroll into white schools because the public schools were operating under the idea that they were "free to all."[7]

Politics, religion, and oppressed groups shaped the ideas of the American education system during the course of American history. As a result, the education system has centered on conformity rather than individualism. Politicians and groups plagued by oppression have found the American education system a prime topic of debate. Each group desired power over America's education system in an attempt to manipulate young minds into reflecting their desired beliefs. Unfortunately, the idea of educating individual thinkers was not figured into the structuring of the education system. As a result, the American education system reveals a history rich with the seeds of conformity, which have shaped the legacy of American society. This legacy continues to live on in our education system in today's society. According to noted author and educator Theodore Sizer in his book *Places for Learning, Places for Joy*, today's schools continue to be rooted in the basic principles that fueled the education system of the past: "today's schools continue on yesterday's model."[8]

Power, inequality, and conformity have filtered into today's educational system, creating a clash with liberal arts education. A higher value is placed on skills-based learning. Parents don't want to pay for an education that won't result in marketable skills and a good job. Liberal arts education is also devalued because of a narrow-minded view of success, which is usually measured in financial terms.

Preparing global learners flexible enough to embrace the universal themes of learning the basics while simultaneously developing critical thinking, creativity, and other elements that a liberal arts education has to offer begins with an investment in learning by both the teacher and the student. Barkley says "teaching is a team sport."[9] He goes on to explain how teachers from different classes should work together sharing ideas and tips on how to implement more-effective methods in working collaboratively with their students. This idea of shared responsibility and shared accountability in the classroom is another issue that contributes to the devaluing of a liberal arts education, because it challenges the power structure in the "one teacher who knows it all" learning model. Students' being active participants in their own education and teachers' working together to sustain an educational environment geared toward collaboration and critical thinking attack the power structure of the "banking system" model, which reigns supreme in many educational settings.

Though America has long nurtured power-centered classrooms, it is viewed by other countries as a country that values a liberal arts education. In his *In Defense of a Liberal Education*, Fareed Zakaria writes, "Around the world the idea of a broad-based 'liberal' education is closely tied to the United States and its great universities and colleges. But in America itself, a liberal education is out of favor."[10] This chronic way of providing a power-centered, skills-based education is at the center of the liberal arts crisis. Students who are accustomed to being told what to do, when to do it, and how to do it become adults who expect someone to tell them what to do and when to do it.

According to Paulo Freire, a response to the rigid, dehumanizing "banking system" is to restructure the teacher and student roles in this educational model. The redistribution of power opens the door to collaborative learning. Freire writes, "Knowledge emerges only through invention and re-invention, through the restless, impatient, continuing, hopeful inquiry human beings pursue in the world, with the world, and with each other."[11]

On the college level, addressing the liberal arts crisis is a matter of challenging students and parents to think critically and to make an investment in a system that they deem useless. Parents don't want to pay for an education that appears not to lead to a secure job. As a result one question—What can you do with a liberal arts degree?—becomes front and center in the discussion of what should be their child's focus of study. Parents feel justified in steering their children away from the liberal arts path because they feel that it doesn't offer a secure career. In reality, a person with a liberal arts degree can choose any career path she or he desires: science, math, creative writing, CEO of Amazon, or the founder of companies like Facebook. In the day-to-day grind of a job, a person will need to know how to communicate effectively verbally and through writing. As professions change, employees must be able to learn new skills. This is true in science, dance, writing, technology and any field of study a person wants to pursue.

One misconception is that a liberal arts education just teaches students to think. A liberal arts education also teaches students how to write. Growing up, I always wrote stories, but I wrote them when the mood struck. When I finished a story, I considered it done. I was in for a rude awakening when I enrolled at Millsaps College. During the first semester, I found myself frustrated when my professor took a look at my first essay and said, "This is a great first draft." She handed the paper back to me. My first reaction was one of shock, but I soon realized that writing involved more than putting words on paper. As I went through the revision process, writing and rewriting the essay, I came to embrace the writing process and my writing improved.

This process aided me in organizing my ideas and sharpening my skills as a writer. Another virtue of a liberal arts education is verbal communication. Unlike the narrative education that Freire describes, the liberal arts education offers students the opportunity to discuss what they have learned. And, last but not least, a liberal arts education builds strong research muscles. The idea is not for students to know all the facts, but rather, that they are equipped with the proper skills to find the information that they need when they need it.

Once a friend who taught second grade told me that on the first day of class, she spent an hour letting the students know that she was the boss in that class. "I'm gonna treat you like you act," she said. "If you act like a fool, then that's how um gone' treat ya." She went on to tell me that she walks the classroom, looking each of them in the eye and daring them to say a word. I wondered why this process had to take an hour. "Because they have to know the rules," she said to me. Then I wondered why this hour-long intimidation process couldn't be swapped for an active learning experience. "You're not a teacher," she said. "You just don't understand."

Taking the step from a more traditional education, to one in which students are expected to engage in active learning, involves a change in teacher training and expected goals. Most importantly it requires a major transformation in the thought process of educators. Teachers must understand learning as a shared, continuous process. This line of thinking will enable them to be more open-minded to a training process that embraces this concept.

As educators debate the topic of education reform in the twenty-first century, they can propose many reasons why reform won't work. One reason, as noted by Seymour B. Sarason in his book *The Predictable Failure of Education Reform*, is power in the classroom. Since the beginning of schools, teachers have reigned supreme in the classroom. According to Sarason, the powerlessness that many students feel can result in loss of desire for learning. "When one has no stake in the way things are, when one's needs or opinions are provided no forum, when one sees oneself as the object of unilateral actions, it takes no particular wisdom to suggest that one would rather be elsewhere."[12]

Sarason believes that the power issue can be solved by acknowledging students' feelings and opinions. This acknowledgment gives the students part ownership of the classroom, and most importantly, it gives them ownership of the learning experience. According to Sarason, power is one of the main issues of the classroom, and it is the first one attended to in the school year. In fact a teacher's power warrants a reputation among the students. Sarason describes an example in an inner-city school he visited; he describes an incident where he saw a nine-year-old climb the wall. The school was old, with exposed stream pipes, which enabled youngsters to climb to the ceiling. After noticing the teacher's lack of control over the student and the class, Sarason addressed the child: "Next year you will be in Mrs. Espito's classroom. Is that the way you will act there?" The student had little to no reaction before responding, "I would never do it in her classroom. She would kick the shit out of me."

Sarason says that this was somewhat of an extreme case. Unfortunately, it is not an uncommon situation in the school system. In his book, Sarason concludes that sharing the learning experience with students creates an environment of learning where students' interest is at a much higher level than in classrooms where they are sitting and memorizing on a daily basis. Sarason also states that "using the criterion of academic achievement, the cooperative, small group approach is as effective as the conventional one and more often than not, is superior."[13]

In order to relinquish power in the classroom, teachers must be properly trained in a facilitative cooperative learning experience. The idea of teachers as all-knowing and students as subordinates must end to facilitate change. This was the case in the transformation of Thayer Junior High in the early 1980s. Sizer describes this transformation in his book *Horace's Hope*. Before the arrival of Dennis Linky, a founder of the "award winning middle school in Shoreham Wading River on Long Island, New York" in the 1970s, Thayer Junior High was plagued by truancy, a high dropout rate, violence, and apathy from students, faculty, and the community in Winchester, which it served. Linky started this transformation by first acknowledging the faculty, students, and surrounding community and letting them know that they played a key role in the success of the school.

Sizer notes that Linky made cosmetic changes to the actual structure and surrounding grounds. He also made changes in the curriculum. Sizer states that nineteen more courses were implemented. These courses were designed to help students work collectively and individually on problem solving and critical thinking skills. The teachers, Sizer notes, were made to feel a part of the transformation as well. First, Linky worked alongside them, acknowledging their talents, skills, and input as vital in promoting a proactive learning environment for their students. According to Sizer, each year Linky gave teachers a blank notebook and asked that they write him a letter every Wednesday of the week. He would then read each letter and respond to them. The response to these changes was overwhelming. The school has experienced a significant decline in dropout rate, violence, and truancy.[14]

During the course of history, the American education system has reflected the political, religious, and economic tone of our society at any given time.

In the early 1800s, education was offered only to rich white males. After the Common School Movement, the education system began to recognize that religion played a major role in educating students. Everyone needed a school that would reflect their religious beliefs. According to Sizer in *Places of Learning, Places of Joy*, it was not until after World War II that the American economy shifted from technical to scientific. As a result, people called for reform in the education system. In the 1960s, however, during the civil rights struggle, college students called for a change that would allow them to abandon conformity and enter into a diverse learning experience in and outside of the classroom.[15]

No approach is guaranteed to transform the rigid educational system that has been present all through American history. Transforming people who are used to being told what to think into people who engage in critical thinking is not going to happen tomorrow. There needs to be a change in the preparation of students so that they can be better equipped as they have to choose between a skills-based career and their search for meaning. In the case of Nina Simone, who grew to become a voice of the civil rights movement with her music, the search for meaning came out of her rage and disgust for the violence against and oppression of Black people. To embrace her life of purpose, Simone had to change her feelings about protest songs, and she had to change her views about her audiences. Addressing the liberal arts crisis in K–12 means that we need to create teacher and parent partnerships and abandon the antiquated "narrated" education model. On the college level, students need to be redirected and exposed to a liberal arts education that offers writing, collaboration, and effective research skills and recognizes diverse learning styles.

Notes

1. Nina Simone, *I Put a Spell on You*. (New York: Da Capo Press, 1992), 89.

2. Paulo Freire, *Pedagogy of the Oppressed* (New York: Continuum, 1989), 57.

3. Freire, *Pedagogy of the Oppressed*, 58.

4. Stephen G. Barkley, "Culture of Coaching," Millsaps Principals' Institute, Conference for Principals, June 14, 2016, Northwest Rankin High School, keynote.

5. Sarah Mondale and Sarah Patton, eds., *School: The Story of American Public Education* (Boston: Beacon Press, 2001), 23.

6. Mondale and Patton, *School*, 23, 44.

7. Mondale and Patton, *School*, 44.

8. Theodore R. Sizer, *Places for Learning, Places for Joy: Speculations on American School Reform* (Cambridge: Harvard University Press, 1973), 4.

9. Barkley, "Culture of Coaching."

10. Fareed Zakaria, *In Defense of a Liberal Education* (New York: W. W. Norton, 2016), 1.

11. Gabrielle Micheletti, "Re-Envisioning Paulo Freire's 'Banking Concept of Education,'" *Inquiries Journal*, accessed Sept. 2, 2016.

12. Seymour Sarason, *The Predictable Failure of Education Reform* (San Francisco: Oxford, 1990), 83.

13. Sarason, *Predictable Failure of Education Reform*, 89.

14. Sizer, *Places for Learning*.

15. Sizer, *Places for Learning*.

Bibliography

Barkley, Stephen G. "Culture of Coaching." Millsaps Principals' Institute, Conference for Principals, June 14, 2016, Northwest Rankin High School, keynote.

Freire, Paulo. *Pedagogy of the Oppressed*. New York: Continuum, 1989.

Micheletti, Gabrielle. "Re-Envisioning Paulo Freire's 'Banking Concept of Education.'" *Inquiries Journal*, Sept. 2, 2016.

Mondale, Sarah, and Sarah Patton, eds. *School: The Story of American Public Education*. Boston: Beacon Press, 2001.

"Nina Simone." Bio.com. A&E Networks Television.

Pak, Eudie. "On Nina Simone's 80th Birthday, Eight Interesting Facts." Bio.com. A&E Network Television. February 21, 2013.

Sarason, Seymour. *The Predictable Failure of Education Reform*. San Francisco: Oxford, 1990.

Simone, Nina. *I Put a Spell on You*. New York: Da Capo Press, 1992.

Sizer, Theodore R. *Places for Learning, Places for Joy: Speculations on American School Reform*. Cambridge: Harvard University Press, 1973.

Zakaria, Fareed. *In Defense of a Liberal Education*. New York: W. W. Norton, 2016.

CHAPTER 15

Liberal Arts and Humanities as "Molders of Consensus" in the Public Arena

THOMAS M. KERSEN

In 1986 I enrolled as a cadet at the New Mexico Military Institute in Roswell, New Mexico. My first undergraduate courses were art, biology, and English composition. I still have fond memories of the art class. Later, after fighting in the Gulf War, I returned to my duty station in Germany. Soon after, I earned an associate's degree in liberal arts from City-Wide Colleges of Chicago (Europe). At Fort Carson I decided to leave the regular army and pursue my bachelor's degree in some type of physical or biological science. I planned to return to the regular army and go through Officer Candidate School (OCS). Two things happened: first, I found out that I enjoyed the social sciences more than the physical sciences. Furthermore, I was really doing well in my new sociology major, and I realized that to get the full potential of a sociology education, I would need to get a PhD. Second, I met my future wife. Thus, for much of my professional life, I have been either a product or a producer of liberal arts knowledge.

Some decades later I wrote an article for the *Journal of Applied Social Science* about the role that the social sciences and, more broadly, liberal arts and humanities should have in public life. One aspect of our collective identity that my past article allowed me to explore is the unique position we have as advocates for critical thinking. And such was the thinking of Martin Luther King, who suggested that social scientists should be "molders of consensus." The particular issue King was urging social scientists to advocate for was civil rights.[1] However, his idea applies to any social issue and fits well within the broader scope of liberal arts and humanities disciplines.

Martin Luther King, whose background was in sociology, was interested in how we need to demonstrate that the personal problems a common person suffers have linkages to wider social issues usually beyond their control. This notion is called the "sociological imagination," according to C. Wright Mills.

The liberal arts vision is more relevant than ever, because few people in the public know or trust what we teach and study.[2]

Making people aware that their personal problems are linked to greater social issues is important. However, that is not the only task liberal arts educators must pursue to fulfill Reverend King's vision of molders of consensus. We need to exploit our methodological skills and liberal arts and humanistic vision to empower individuals and communities. Given the right tools, groups and communities can identify and solve their own issues as they arise. Recognizing the wisdom organic to a group or community is a valuable resource in community resource building. Often people possess a sociological imagination and an appreciation of the fact that nothing in the social world is very simple. How aware people are of their liberal arts/humanities perspective is a question rarely addressed.

It has been difficult for me to put into words what liberal arts and humanities mean to me. I have written on this subject so many times I was worried I would turn this latest effort into a dry, academic treatise. So, I asked my wife what she thought the value of her liberal arts education was. She told me that it allowed her to see that any issue has more than one side to it. In other words, nothing in social reality can be reduced to a black-and-white perspective. Encouraged by my wife's feedback, I asked other people with a liberal arts background what they thought the value of their major was. A woman who graduated from a small liberal arts college forty-five years ago echoed my wife's sentiments.

Another alumna from the same liberal arts college wrote of her sociology degree: "It served me well. I went into journalism, spending 17 years at a number of Mississippi newspapers. . . . I was able to analyze situations, ask tough questions and bring curiosity to my big stories. . . . My education taught me how to think." A retired Exxon public relations official wrote how liberal arts taught her how to think critically and helped her with her job. Other people pointed out how liberal arts and humanities fostered personal creativity and seeing the "big picture."

Focusing on how liberal arts fosters and strengthens interaction between people and groups, one fellow wrote that he gained "exposure to more types of people, and hence, a broader group of free thinkers." A high-level public education official in Mississippi wrote that "the liberal arts are the knowledge that connect us to our humanity . . . it is my study of liberal arts that gives me the aspiration [to contribute to making the world a better place to live]." Other respondents mentioned how liberal arts gave meaning to their lives.

Echoing my informants, major entrepreneurs are recognizing the value of a liberal arts and humanities background. David Kalt, founder of Reverb.

com, wrote in the *Wall Street Journal*, "While we've hired many computer-science majors that have been critical team members, it's noncomputer science degree holders who can see the forest through the trees. For example, our chief operating officer is a brilliant, self-taught engineer with a degree in philosophy from the University of Chicago." As Kalt describes him, "He has risen above the code to lead a team that is competitive globally. His determination and critical-thinking skills empower him to leverage the power of technology without getting bogged down by it. His background gives him the soft skills—the people skills—that make him stand out as someone who understands our customers and knows how to bring the staff along." And there is scholarly support for Kalt's view that liberal arts majors do well in terms of critical thinking, problem solving, and other skills.[3]

From this unscientific query of liberal arts alumni and supporters, I gained some useful insights. First, most people mentioned how liberal arts made them better thinkers, perhaps because liberal arts majors do well at critical thinking, particularly recognizing and solving problems, as Derek Bok, Richard Arum, Josipa Roska, and other scholars argued. The other benefit was being part of an inclusive, broadminded community. However, no one specifically addressed what types of people liberal arts graduates tend to be. Also overlooked is the process by which liberal-arts-minded people become catalysts for progressive social change.

According to Paul Ray and Sherry Anderson, for much of our history, there have been two cultural groups who have competed for power in American life. One group are the traditionalists, people who are drawn toward nostalgia and see community as something lost. They make up a quarter of the population. The traditionalists are culturally conservative and tend to see the world in black-and-white terms. They were not very interested in the past, but that has changed, especially since the elections of Presidents Clinton and Obama. They have definite views about family, church, and community. Traditionalists favor patriarchal arrangements at various levels, public regulation of private behavior, and law and order over civil liberties. They believe rural living is the only true American way of life. They hold dim views of foreigners and are strong supporters of owning weapons.[4]

Around another 50 percent are called the "moderns," according to Ray and Anderson. Some famous moderns are people such as Isaac Asimov, Ernest Hemingway, and Madonna. Typically, moderns have a more urban outlook than traditionalists. They value achievement and are driven by technology. They love lots of choices and consider big as beautiful.[5]

While the traditionalists and moderns have battled each other, a third group, "cultural creatives," emerged from the cultural turmoil of the 1960s and 1970s. Cultural creatives (CCs) often share the same worldview as many graduates and professors in liberal arts and humanities. They are open-minded, sometimes eccentric, and love to travel. Their pluralistic outlook and acceptance of ambiguity makes them cosmopolitan in orientation. They do not watch much television but do listen to National Public Radio more than other people do. They know who Garrison Keillor is and get his jokes. They are heavily involved in the arts and culture.[6]

CCs have a knack for what Robert Persig in *Zen and the Art of Motorcycle Maintenance* calls lateral knowledge. He wrote that lateral knowledge is "knowledge that's from a wholly unexpected direction, from a direction that's not even understood as a direction until the knowledge forces itself upon one. Lateral truths point to the falseness of axioms and postulates underlying one's existing system of getting at truth."[7]

More recently, scholars such as historians and sociologists term lateral knowledge as "sideways thinking." This way of thinking involves "extracting unintended or unexpected long-term consequences from apparently isolated and eccentric events." I happen to think this is one of the more interesting and exciting facets of a cultural creative. Lateral thinking exposes societal contradictions, something Paulo Freire termed "conscientization."[8]

Unlike the traditionalists and the moderns, CCs rarely have a sense of social solidarity. This lack of a sense of group identity is also observed in liberal arts and humanities fields such as sociology. Interestingly, when they do gather together, many of them have a hard time realizing that there are so many like-minded people. This lack of a sense of solidarity is one of the major obstacles for CCs.[9]

At first blush, it may not be apparent why the United States Department of Agriculture (USDA) would be interested in the "creative class" as well as related concepts such as cultural amenities, but these indicators are signs of positive community development. Citing Richard Florida's *Rise of the Creative Class*, the USDA reported on its website that large numbers of creative workers are "strongly associated with new firm formation and high-tech specialization in metropolitan areas." Eric Weiner argued the same: that creative people fostered communities of genius. Based on my computations, the percentage of cultural creatives for Hinds County, where the city of Jackson is, has declined from 21.7 percent in 2000 to 18.9 percent from 2007 to 2011. On the other hand, during the same period, the percentage of creative workers to all workers slightly increased in Mississippi and the United States.[10]

All three cultural groups have reacted to social realities in different ways. The traditionalists tend to reject modernity in favor of nostalgia. The original counterculturals, traditionalists seek to reconfigure society back to some

SHARE OF CREATIVE WORKERS TO ALL WORKERS			
	1990	2000	2007–11
Hinds County, MS	20.2%	21.7%	18.9%
Mississippi	15.3	18.1	19.1
United States	21.1	23.9	25.0
Source: Economic Research Service, USDA 2016			

preindustrial ideal. In the South, traditional-minded evangelicals during frontier times viewed themselves as countercultural in that they were often at odds with elite planters and the modernist ideals the planters tended to have.[11]

Moderns, with the winds of industrialism and modernity at their backs, perhaps even as far back as five hundred years, gained the upper hand against traditionalists. Moderns accept technological progress and have a greater reliance on science to explain things. They seek to demystify the mystical, tame the wild, and comfort the masses with ready-made deterministic formulas and cost-benefit-analysis worldviews. It is this worldview that is overly rationalistic, bureaucratic, and formal.

Ray and Anderson describe traditionalists and the moderns in dichotomous terms. One choice is to retreat into nostalgia. The other choice is to rely on progress and technology to save us from ourselves. The third group, the cultural creatives, provides another path to deal with modernity. They synthesize and adapt to emerging social issues. They also create a social space for exploration and problem solving, more so than the other two groups. CCs tend to be more reflective than traditionalists; however, they recognize the value of science and technology.[12]

The late Ernst Borinski, professor of sociology at Tougaloo College, epitomizes the idea of what a cultural creative is. From an early age he was a polymath who challenged people and conventional ways of thinking. He fled Nazi Germany because of his Jewish background. Because of his cultural awareness, he was an asset in World War II, while serving in the United States Army in North Africa. Later, he became a long-serving professor in Jim Crow era Jackson, Mississippi. His unique insider/outsider perspective as well as his sense of humor helped bring groups together to address social issues.[13]

Borinski became so well known that he was able to bring to Jackson influential people such as labor leader Ralph Bunche and other social activists and thinkers. The sociological perspective, which is a liberal arts outlook, was useful according to Borinski, in his address at Millsaps College in 1972, because "we may have possibly to create a new breed of social scientist, who can look at society in terms of multiple perspectives and who would on the basis of the perspectives use a social context for his research which will make his research relevant, applicable to the social reality, and an instrument of creative social change."[14] Borinski's message highlights the values of a liberal arts education.

James Surowiecki wrote in *The Wisdom of Crowds* that there were four conditions necessary for a crowd to be wise. The first is *diversity*: that is, allowing and fostering different perspectives within a group. The second condition is *independence*, or the ability for group members to explore and question things independent of pressures of group conformity and peer pressure. The third condition is *decentralization*, or generating ideas and solutions to issues rather than relying on a centralized, oftentimes hierarchical decision-making process. Lastly, there needs to be some way of making sense of everything by collecting and analyzing information, or, using Surowiecki's term, *aggregation*.[15] One of my main contentions is that liberal arts and humanities answer each of these conditions, which enables us to be the molders of consensus that we need to be. Indeed, many of the respondents I referred to earlier in this paper pointed out several of these qualities.

Not only is diversity important in the university and other formal settings, it is important in decision making for groups that are small.[16] Interdisciplinary collaboration is a hallmark of liberal arts and humanities. Scholars should work in an interdisciplinary fashion when dealing with social problems rather than in isolated disciplines. As a collective entity, we offer more than any one expert usually can. It is in this space that allows people to explore and brainstorm issues.

Even more important, when diverse people congregate in certain spaces, creativity and innovation flourish. Such is the case in the academic world when scholars from diverse disciplines come together and share their knowledge and experiences with one another. Early in the twentieth century, Herman Schmalenbach described an area in which people recognize a "mutual sense of belonging." This recognition is one of the reasons why CCs want to be part of something larger than themselves. Even if they are not in positions of power, they realize that they have influence as members of a "huge cloud of sympathetic supporters," to use Ray and Anderson's terms.[17]

Later, Sara Evans and Harry Boyte, as well as Francesca Polletta, discussed "free spaces" where people congregated who possessed a liberal arts and/or humanistic spirit. Evans and Boyte defined them as "the environments in which people are able to learn a new self-respect, a deeper and more assertive group identity, public skills, and values of cooperation and civic virtue. Put simply, free spaces are settings between private lives and large-scale institutions where ordinary citizens can act with dignity, independence, and vision." Such a space allows for CCs to broker solutions between traditionalists and moderns. This is done by revitalizing our concepts regarding the past and future. Elders offer wisdom that guides younger generations. Their stories carry forward our collective understanding of the world and our place in it. Moderns provide the tools of technology. Likewise, consider Elijah Anderson's term "cosmopolitan canopy," which allows for a community that nestles members and pushes them to excel.[18]

Free spaces and cosmopolitan canopies are dynamic and intrinsically democratic. They are not tied to "direct control of dominant groups, are voluntary participated in, and generate the cultural challenge that precedes or accompanies political mobilization." These areas are where diverse groups of people meaningfully interact with one another. Freedom of expression is a key element of free spaces. I believe that wherever liberal arts and humanities people congregate, there is a cosmopolitan canopy. This free space does not even need to reside on campus. For example, Tougaloo College professor Ernst Borinski's popular integrated discussion group during the height of Jim Crow in the center of Jackson did the same as a popular Jackson bar called Birdland, a place for Jackson State University professors and others to relax, mingle, and foster creativity. Such places are a vital ingredient in helping mold consensus.[19]

To me, independence is crucial to free inquiry and problem solving. Surowiecki wrote that independence prevents people making the same mistakes and fosters information. Independence is important to both the scholar and people in the wider community. Despite the value independence offers to academia, the trend away disempowering faculty is worrisome. Robert Lynd noted all the way back in 1954 how "university trustees and Liberty Leaguers" were weakening the professoriate. Furthermore, William Leuchtenberg noted in response to the rise of social science, elites fomented anti-intellectualism to shore up and consolidate power.[20]

Of note, various allied entities, such as the Mississippi State Sovereignty Commission and various state higher education boards of trustees, have scrutinized the institutions in the South over time. Such scrutiny affects professors and administrators to the extent that they are censored or self-censor. Administrative and political micromanagement forces scholars and teachers to lead dual lives: one as an academic and one as a marginalized person. Oftentimes, the latter subsumed the former. This even extended to classroom instruction and books adopted for courses. Early sociology courses at historically black colleges and universities faced scrutiny and led one researcher to declare that "the introductory course in sociology in Negro Colleges and universities is safe for sociology."[21] It seems that liberal arts courses such as introductory sociology needed careful oversight to maintain the status quo.

Likewise, for many in the public, elites in government, business, and the media set the agenda too often without feedback from the public. To foster a sense of independence in the community, elites need to share power and decision making with people in the community. Cosmopolitan places facilitate that process. What is exciting is that liberal arts and humanities scholars are often at the forefront of such endeavors that help shape individual and group life for the better.

Another facet of the centralization of academic life is the rise of departmentalization. Campbell contended that as scholars, we do ourselves and the general public a disservice when we establish disciplinary visions that become impermeable to what is going on in related fields. Bok argued that scholars need to be more collaborative. One example of collaboration in teaching is writing across the curriculum, where scholars from various departments share insights with students about the fundamentals needed to write about any topic.[22]

Related in some ways to independence is decentralization. The ability for different groups and individuals to manage their work is a key feature of the academic life or even for ordinary citizens. However, the trend in governance both in academia and the public arena is toward greater centralization. Standardized formats for syllabi, teaching, and research protocols are common throughout universities in the United States. This trend inhibits creativity and critical thinking. Furthermore, accountability rhetoric popular among many politicians and administrators suggests that higher education is a means to an end and not an end in itself. It is common to hear people question the utility or value of a particular discipline. In response, politicians and administrators are imposing metrics on things that often defy quantification or commodification.[23]

How an institution makes sense of information and solutions is the key task of aggregation. One issue is the process of gathering information. What are the assumptions? For example, consider the notion that professors, workers in other industries, and community leaders must somehow adhere to projections or goals that they had no input in creating. Such expectations even defy what we know about our institutions and communities. For instance, assuming that student-eligible population growth can be projected in a continuous, upward linear way may not be the reality for an area. We miss the peaks and troughs that a cyclical model would more accurately predict.

Yet recruitment goals continue to climb in a linear fashion at too many institutions. Such is the risk when public goods and services are regarded as commodities.

Another issue of aggregation is that institutional leaders seek outside consultants rather than seeing value in using the organic knowledge base that exists within the institution. Blindly chasing after metrics is what Harvey Graff referred to as administrative malpractice.[24] How many times have professors and staff witnessed large sums of money going to an outside firm that produces a report that tells them what they already know or, even worse, ignores the complexities of context and history?

Recently, I attended a public discussion about how to improve the lives of people in Mississippi and the city of Jackson in particular. The talk featured a panel of successful young people who lived in the area. Many of the panelists were expatriates who returned to Mississippi. Some major points they discussed were ending the brain drain out of Jackson and Mississippi, restoring a sense of collective identity for the area, and rebuilding our human, social, physical, and cultural infrastructure.

Of course, much of the reason why people leave Mississippi is economics. On the other hand, it was noted in the meeting, and I agree, from my observations and readings, many Mississippian leaders do not foster a sense of collective good. "If you do not like it," they say, "leave." This leads to a self-fulfilling prophecy in terms of ensuring Mississippi's continued last place in most state-level indicators. We should have a vested interest in seeing everyone succeed. Creativity is critical. Creative folks make life more than tolerable; they make it a joy. Creativity breeds further creativity and becomes a dynamo of innovation and forward thinking. This type of community attracts millennials and many other types of people. It is inclusive and inherently democratic.

Restoring our sense of community is hard, because it involves talking about and doing something in regard to all forms of oppression. This is something we have been unwilling to do so far. Oppressive legislation, symbols, and rhetoric thwart that effort and repel many people from perhaps considering Mississippi as their home. The precipitating factor to make all these ideas a reality is instilling in each of us a sense of urgency that something needs to be done. As molders of consensus, we can change this situation.

Once there is a critical mass, things will change. Overall, I felt the love that many of the panelists and the attendees had for Mississippi. To paraphrase former governor William Winter at that event, the raw material of building community is creating and strengthening our connections with one another. Cosmopolitan canopies create and deepen those connections. More broadly, when we gain a sociological perspective, we see ourselves as part of something greater than any one individual. Furthermore, no one person can fix the issues before us, but they are fixable when we work together.

One take-away for academics like myself is that many people in the public need more information. Participants at the public discussion wanted more facts and insights about all the processes and dynamics involved with migration and other sociological and demographic factors within the state. That means that we academics need to provide the best ideas, data, and practices to meet the needs of the public.

Creative people tend to be reflective, critical thinkers. Often they rely on lateral or sideways thinking, where they recognize the transformative nature of epiphanies and point out social contradictions. The liberal arts and humanities are well suited to expose and question day-to-day societal assumptions. Creative people see things in the everyday world that other people filter out. More importantly, creative people are more aware of the limits of their knowledge, yet seek to expand those boundaries.

Liberal arts and humanities dominate the cultural creative class. As such they value free expression, even if it is from people they disagree with. They are able to make the connection between the individual and societal structures and trends. Focusing on connections, context, and meaning is important to humanities people. Finally, they agree that to fulfill Martin Luther King's vision, they must be an active force for progressive change.

Notes

1. Martin Luther King, "The Civil Rights Movement Needs the Help of Social Scientists," *Journal of Social Issues* 24, no. 1 (1968): 2–12.

2. C. Wright Mills, *The Sociological Imagination* (Oxford: Oxford University Press), 1959; Sally Hillsman, "The Policy Relevance of Sociology," *Footnotes* 43 (2015): 2, 4; Alvin Bertrand, "Social Traps: The Achilles Heel of Sociology and Sociologists," *Sociological Forum* 2 (1979): 83–91.

3. David Kalt, "Why I Was Wrong about Liberal Arts Majors," *Wall Street Journal*, June 1, 2016. Accessed January 2017. http://blogs.wsj.com/experts/2016/06/01/why-i-was-wrong-about-liberal-arts-majors/; Derek Bok, *Our Underachieving Colleges: A Candid Look at How Much Students Learn and Why They Should Be Learning More* (Princeton: Princeton University Press, 2006); Louis Menand, "Thinking Sideways: The One-Dot Theory of History," *New Yorker*, March 30, 2015, accessed March 2015, http://www.newyorker.com/magazine/2015/03/30/thinking-sideways; Richard Arum and Josipa Roksa, *Academically Adrift: Limited Learning on College Campuses* (Chicago: University of Chicago Press), 2011.

4. Paul Ray and Sherry Anderson, *The Cultural Creatives: How 50 Million People Are Changing the World* (New York: Harmony Books, 2001); Zygmunt Bauman, *Community* (Cambridge: Polity Press, 2001); Alan Touraine, *Critique of Modernity* (New York: Wiley, 1995).

5. Ray and Anderson, *Cultural Creatives*.

6. Kevin Hetherington, *New Age Travelers: Vanloads of Uproarious Humanity* (New York: Cassell, 2000); Anthony Appiah, *Cosmopolitanism: Ethics in a World of Strangers* (New York: W. W. Norton, 2006); Eric Weiner, *The Geography of Genius: A Search for the World's Most Creative Places from Ancient Athens to Silicon Valley* (New York: Simon and Schuster, 2016).

7. Persig, Robert M. *Zen and the Art of Motorcycle Maintenance: An Inquiry into Values* (New York: Harper Collins, 2000), 106.

8. Philip Jenkins, "Sideways into Sociology," *American Sociologist* 29, no. 3 (1998): 5–8; Menand, "Thinking Sideways"; Robert Merton, "Insiders/Outsiders: A Chapter in the Sociology of Knowledge," *American Journal of Sociology* 78 (1978): 9–47; Paulo Freire, *Pedagogy of the Oppressed* (New York: Bloomsbury, 2013); Joe Feagin and Hernán Vera, *Liberation Sociology* (Boulder: Paradigm, 2008)

9. Herbert Gans, "Sociology in America: The Discipline and the Public," *American Sociological Review* 54 (1989): 1–16.

10. United States Department of Agriculture Economic Research Service. "Creative Class County Codes: Documentation," 2017, https://www.ers.usda.gov/data-products/creative-class-county-codes/documentation/; Weiner, *Geography of Genius*.

11. Randy Sparks, *Religion in Mississippi* (Jackson: University Press of Mississippi, 2001), 35.

12. Ray and Anderson, *Cultural Creatives*; see also C. P. Snow, *The Two Cultures and the Scientific Revolution* (New York: Cambridge University Press), 1959.

13. Thomas Kersen, "Insider/Outsider: The Unique Nature of the Sociological Perspective and Practice," *Journal of Applied Social Science* (2016): 104–12.

14. Ernst Borinski, Talk in Millsaps College, Tougaloo College, 1972, Jackson, Mississippi Department of Archives and History, Box 7 Folder 13, p. 7.

15. James Surowiecki, *The Wisdom of Crowds* (New York: Doubleday, 2004).

16. Surowiecki, *Wisdom of Crowds*.

17. Allison Adams, "Helping Professors Find Time to Think," *Chronicle of Higher Education*, December 5, 2016, accessed January 2017. http://www.chronicle.com/?cid=UCHETOPNAV; Herman Schmalenbach, *On Society and Experience*, trans. Gunther Luschent and Gregory Stone (Chicago: University of Chicago Press, 1977); Ray and Anderson, *Cultural Creatives*.

18. Sara Evans and Harry Boyte, *Free Spaces: The Sources of Democratic Change in America* (New York: Harper and Row, 1986), 17; Francesca Polletta, "'Free Spaces' in Collective Action," *Theory and Society* 28 (1999): 1–38; Elijah Anderson, *The Cosmopolitan Canopy: Race and Civility in Everyday Life* (New York: W. W. Norton, 2011).

19. Polletta, "Free Spaces," 1; Anderson, *Cosmopolitan Canopy*; Evans and Boyte, *Free Spaces*; Jimmie Bell, interview by Thomas Kersen, September 5, 2013, "Over 50 Years of Sociology at Jackson State Mississippi," unpublished oral history.

20. Surowiecki, *Wisdom of Crowds*; Robert Lynd, *Knowledge for What? The Place of Social Science in American Culture* (Princeton: Princeton University Press, 1954); William Leuchtenberg, "Anti-intellectualism: An Historical Perspective," *Journal of Social Issues* 11 (1955): 8–17.

21. Jesse Singal, "Why Some of the Worst Attacks on Social Science Have Come from Liberals," *New York Magazine*, December, accessed December 2015, http://nymag.com/scienceofus/2015/12/when-liberals-attack-social-science.html; Michael Shermer, "Is Social Science Politically Biased?" *Scientific American*, March 1, 2016, accessed September 2016, http://www.scientificamerican.com/is-social-science-politically-biased?/; Bertram Doyle, "The Introductory Course in Sociology in Negro Colleges and Universities," *Journal of Educational Sociology* 7, no. 1 (1933), 36, accessed February 2015, http://www.jstor.org/stable/2961506.

22. Donald Campbell, "Ethnocentrism of Disciplines and the Fish-Scale Model of Omniscience," in *Interdisciplinary Relationships in the Social Sciences*, ed. Muzafer Sherif and Carolyn Sherif (Chicago: Aldine, 1959); Bok, *Our Underachieving Colleges*; Adams, "Helping Professors Find Time to Think."

23. John Sides, "Why Congress Should Not Cut Funding to the Social Sciences," *Washington Post*, June 10, 2015, accessed June 2015, https://www.washingtonpost.com/blogs/monkey-cage/wp/2015/06/10/why-congress-should.

24. Harvey Graff, "How Misguided University Policies Are Harming the Humanities, Arts and Sciences," *Inside Higher Ed*, December 18, 2015, accessed December 2015, https://www.insidehighered.com/print/views/2015/12/18/how-misguided-university-policies.

Bibliography

Adams, Allison. "Helping Professors Find Time to Think." *Chronicle of Higher Education*, December 5, 2016. Accessed January 2017. http://www.chronicle.com/?cid=UCHETOPNAV.

Anderson, Elijah. *The Cosmopolitan Canopy: Race and Civility in Everyday Life*. New York: W. W. Norton, 2011.

Appiah, Anthony. *Cosmopolitanism: Ethics in a World of Strangers*. New York: W. W. Norton, 2006.

Arum, Richard, and Josipa Roksa. *Academically Adrift: Limited Learning on College Campuses*. Chicago: University of Chicago Press, 2011.

Bauman, Zygmunt. *Community*. Cambridge: Polity Press, 2001.

Bell, Jimmie. Interview by Thomas Kersen. September 5, 2013. "Over 50 Years of Sociology at Jackson State Mississippi." Unpublished oral history.

Bertrand, Alvin. "Social Traps: The Achilles Heel of Sociology and Sociologists." *Sociological Forum* 2, no. 2 (1979): 83–91.

Bok, Derek. *Our Underachieving Colleges: A Candid Look at How Much Students Learn and Why They Should Be Learning More*. Princeton: Princeton University Press, 2006.

Borinski, Ernst. Talk in Millsaps College. Tougaloo College, Jackson. Mississippi Department of Archives and History, Box 7, Folder 13, 1972.

Campbell, Donald. "Ethnocentrism of Disciplines and the Fish-Scale Model of Omniscience." In *Interdisciplinary Relationships in the Social Sciences*, edited by Muzafer Sherif and Carolyn Sherif, 3–21. Chicago: Aldine, 1969.

Delanty, Gerard. *Community*. New York: Psychology Press, 2003.

Doyle, Bertram. "The Introductory Course in Sociology in Negro Colleges and Universities." *Journal of Educational Sociology* 7, no. 1 (1933): 30–36. Accessed February 2015. http://www.jstor.org/stable/2961506.

ERS, Economic Research Service. *Creative Class Codes*. US Department of Agriculture. September 2016. Accessed September 2016. http://www.ers.usda.gov/data-products/creative-class-county-codes.aspx.

Evans, Sara, and Harry Boyte. *Free Spaces: The Sources of Democratic Change in America*. New York: Harper and Row, 1986.

Feagin, Joe, and Hernán Vera. *Liberation Sociology*. Boulder: Paradigm, 2008.

Freire, Paulo. *Pedagogy of the Oppressed*. New York: Bloomsbury, 2013.

Gans, Herbert. 1989. "Sociology in America: The Discipline and the Public." *American Sociological Review* 54: 1–16.

Graff, Harvey. "How Misguided University Policies Are Harming the Humanities, Arts and Sciences." *Inside Higher Ed*, December 18, 2015. Accessed December 2015. https://www.insidehighered.com/print/views/2015/12/18/how-misguided-university-policies.

Hetherington, Kevin. *New Age Travelers: Vanloads of Uproarious Humanity*. New York: Cassell, 2000.

Hillsman, Sally. "The Policy Relevance of Sociology." *Footnotes* 43, no. 1 (2015): 2, 4.

Jenkins, Philip. "Sideways into Sociology." *American Sociologist* 29, no. 3 (1998): 5–8.

Kalt, David. "Why I Was Wrong about Liberal Arts Majors." *Wall Street Journal*, June 1, 2016. Accessed January 2017. http://blogs.wsj.com/experts/2016/06/01/why-i-was-wrong-about-liberal-arts-majors/.

Kersen, Thomas. 2016. "Insider/Outsider: The Unique Nature of the Sociological Perspective and Practice." *Journal of Applied Social Science*, 10, no. 1, 104–12.

King, Martin Luther. "The Civil Rights Movement Needs the Help of Social Scientists." *Journal of Social Issues* 24, no. 1 (1968): 2–12.

Leuchtenberg, William. "Anti-intellectualism: An Historical Perspective." *Journal of Social Issues* 11, no. 3 (1955): 8–17.

Lynd, Robert. *Knowledge for What? The Place of Social Science in American Culture*. Princeton: Princeton University Press, 1954.

Menand, Louis. "Thinking Sideways: The One-Dot Theory of History." *New Yorker*, March 30, 2015. Accessed March 2015. http://www.newyorker.com/magazine/2015/03/30/thinking-sideways.

Merton, Robert. 1972. "Insiders/Outsiders: A Chapter in the Sociology of Knowledge." *American Journal of Sociology* 78, no. 1: 9–47.

Merton, Robert. *On Theoretical Sociology: Five Essays, Old and New*. New York: Free Press, 1967.

Mills, C. Wright. *The Sociological Imagination*. Oxford: Oxford University Press, 1959.

Persig, Robert M. *Zen and the Art of Motorcycle Maintenance: An Inquiry into Values*. New York: Harper Collins, 2000.

Polletta, Francesca. "'Free Spaces' in Collective Action." *Theory and Society* 28, no. 1 (1999): 1–38.

Ray, Paul, and Sherry Anderson. *The Cultural Creatives: How 50 Million People Are Changing the World*. New York: Harmony Books, 2001.

Schmalenbach, Herman. *On Society and Experience*. Translated by Gunther Luschent and Gregory Stone. Chicago: University of Chicago Press, 1977.

Shermer, Michael. "Is Social Science Politically Biased?" *Scientific American*, March 1, 2016. Accessed September 2016. https://www.scientificamerican.com/article/is-social-science-politically-biased/.

Sides, John. "Why Congress Should Not Cut Funding to the Social Sciences." *Washington Post*, June 10, 2015. Accessed June 2015. https://www.washingtonpost.com/blogs/monkey-cage/wp/2015/06/10/why-congress-should.

Singal, Jesse. "Why Some of the Worst Attacks on Social Science Have Come from Liberals." *New York Magazine*, December 2015. Accessed December 2015. http://nymag.com/scienceofus/2015/12/when-liberals-attack-social-science.html.

Snow, C. P. *The Two Cultures and the Scientific Revolution*. New York: Cambridge University Press, 1959.

Sparks, Randy. *Religion in Mississippi*. Jackson: University Press of Mississippi, 2001.

Surowiecki, James. *The Wisdom of Crowds*. New York: Doubleday, 2004.

Touraine, Alan. *Critique of Modernity*. New York: Wiley, 1995.

United States Department of Agriculture Economic Research Service. "Creative Class County Codes: Documentation." 2017. https://www.ers.usda.gov/data-products/creative-class-county-codes/documentation/.

Weiner, Eric. *The Geography of Genius: A Search for the World's Most Creative Places from Ancient Athens to Silicon Valley*. New York: Simon and Schuster, 2016.

THE AFRICAN AMERICAN EXPERIENCE AND THE LIBERAL ARTS

CHAPTER 16

Historical Memory and the Meredith Monument at Ole Miss

ROBERT E. LUCKETT JR.

Members of the Southern Historical Association (SHA) who attended the 1963 annual meeting in Asheville, North Carolina, witnessed a most astonishing address. As president of the SHA that year, James Silver damned the Jim Crow South, where he had lived since joining the history department at the University of Mississippi (Ole Miss) in 1936. Not much more than a year after the riots that accompanied James Meredith's integration of Ole Miss in October 1962, Silver, a liberal arts faculty member, characterized white Mississippi as a "Closed Society" committed to thwarting the cause for racial equality at all costs.[1]

Silver's words went well beyond the walls of that academic gathering and led to his exile from the South. For his part, Silver could no longer hold his tongue in the face of diehard white resistance to civil rights, and white Mississippians could not stomach such criticism from a state employee, even if he did have tenure. Those whites could not engage an open, honest discussion about their racist social system. To do so would have compelled them to recognize that the efforts of activists had weakened Jim Crow and forced a reluctant federal government to act on behalf of civil rights. And, while activists forced their hand, Silver, a scholar of the highest sort, called racists out. In turn, bigotry in Mississippi evolved, and a brand of conservative politics emerged that avoided explicit issues of race while implicitly maintaining white power.

Due in large part to the Meredith crisis, some segregationists realized that, to maintain their prerogatives, whites needed to ditch the line-in-the-sand defiance that had characterized resistance to black advancement since Reconstruction. If they were to retain power, they had to abandon unconcealed racism and acquiesce to some activist demands. Historian Joe Crespino, a modern liberal arts scholar, claims that "strategic accommodation" fueled "practical segregation" in Mississippi, as Sovereignty Commission director Erle Johnston termed it. Practical segregation protected racial power but avoided the minefield of race as an open topic.[2]

It was not a new strategy but an ascendant one amongst segregationists after the deadly debacle Mississippi governor Ross Barnett created during the Meredith crisis. By shifting the talking points from race, the advocates of white supremacy created the illusion that they had changed and rejected open resistance to racial progress. In that sense, Silver's attack correctly analyzed and condemned the racist intentions of white leaders as a subtler system of racist politics, committed to white supremacy, emerged as the leading brand of conservatism in Mississippi after 1962.

And so Mississippi continued to be a "closed society." Whites could not tolerate a legitimate examination of race relations, and others continued to pose a threat to civil rights advocates. But, rather than a physical, violent rejection in the name of Jim Crow, an environment was created whereby Silver "chose" to leave for the University of Notre Dame. His absence meant that white leaders more easily crafted a system of white hegemony without as much informed dissent from a scholarly community rooted in the liberal arts. Of course, activists offered a challenge, but new, more efficient strategies rebranded white supremacy.

That brand of "practical segregation" has dominated Mississippi for the past six decades. The Ole Miss community is one place where that has been apparent, as that institution has struggled to deal with its past in an open and honest way, one meant to heal its wounds and welcome a new day of inclusion on its campus. Much of that reason in Oxford has been due to the lack of institutional support for the type of academic analysis that the liberal arts are based on. In the eyes of any oppressive power structure, the danger of an education that stresses critical and analytical thinking and writing is how such an education and those skills can call into question the foundation of that power structure. Outspoken products of such an education are better scared away, as in the case with James Silver, or brushed aside, as in the case of more modern efforts to examine the historical legacy of Ole Miss and its role in white supremacy.

By the end of the twentieth century, the timing seemed right to bring that conversation to light. In November 1995, a folklore class in the Southern Studies program at Ole Miss broached the need for a civil rights memorial on campus, both to remember what had happened and to spur dialogue. The group sought to memorialize the oppressive and brutal reality of Mississippi's history as well as the determination and courage of those who fought that oppression.

In the context of the modern debate over monuments, this story reveals the type of democratic, local participation and liberal arts scholarship that can drive public history to be at its best, but it also reflects the type of resistance to facts, especially those that make us uncomfortable, which plagues American discourse today. A liberal arts program and its participants initiated this effort at Ole Miss and brought to the brink of fruition a monument that challenged its visitors to think deeply about the past and how it continues to impact the present. This type of deep thinking and critical analysis is the hallmark of the best liberal arts education. At the same time the leader of that research institution, saddled no doubt with pressures from the state's elite, who were not that different from those of the 1960s, shattered the process that had led to such a remarkable possibility for the Ole Miss campus. He silenced the voices that challenged the status quo, much as Silver had been silenced, and, in their place, he left a staid and deficient marker to the past that obscures more than it reveals.

Led by John T. Edge, members of the Southern Studies Students Association met with Shawn Clark and the Black Graduate and Professional Student Association at the outset of the Spring 1996 term. Their goal was to forge plans for "an artistic commemoration of the struggle for equal educational opportunity in Mississippi. The work will challenge viewers to reflect upon their role in the struggle and to consider the future of civil rights as a whole." At that time, the most notable artwork on campus was a giant statue of a Confederate soldier. Soon thereafter, Clark and Edge were surprised when Chancellor Robert Khayat told them that "the University supports your project and would like to assure its quality and aesthetic control by inviting competitive bids that reflect a variety of architectural ideas." Although he foreshadowed later efforts to "control" the project, Khayat pledged his support.[3]

Members of the newly founded Civil Rights Commemoration Foundation (CRCF) initiated bimonthly meetings, drafted their first mission statement, and hired a consultant, Lyn Kartiganer. Some supporters questioned whether hiring a professional advisor for a grassroots movement was paradoxical, but Kartiganer had worked with indigenous movements before and proved indispensable. In a memorandum to Khayat, foundation members asked for "financial support and administrative assistance" and declared that "this project will send an important message that the University of Mississippi is dealing directly and sensitively with its past."[4] That effort proved long and elusive.

Yet at first Khayat agreed and proposed that the monument be "placed ... in the center of what is now known as the Ellipse." The Ellipse is a prominent and symbolically important part of the Ole Miss campus, sitting between the

J. D. Williams Library and the Lyceum, which houses the chancellor's office. The Lyceum stood at the heart of the riots and bears the scars of the bullets of 1962. As Nadine Cohodas put it, the Ellipse was "a fitting location, halfway between the university's seat of power and the house of study—a reminder of where Ole Miss has been and where it is striving to go."[5] Liberal arts students and scholars know the significance of how we study and commemorate the past, the powerful, the oppressed, and the future.

Although a national press push led to early donations and some momentum, more tangible support for the project failed to materialize from the Ole Miss administration. The initial issue was money. The CRCF proposed a basement bottom price of $150,000 for the memorial and applied for half of those funds from the National Endowment for the Arts (NEA) in 1997. But the grant required having $75,000 in matching funds in place by April 1. John T. Edge hoped to raise a portion of that at a campus speech by Myrlie Evers, widow of slain civil rights leader Medgar Evers and chairwoman of the NAACP. For the remaining funds, he turned to three groups: "the university community, university alumni and a consortium of business persons."[6] He went to the chancellor for help in that process. Although Khayat had endorsed the foundation's mission from the start, when it came to actual dollars, he wavered.

On February 18, 1997, Provost Gerald Walton reported "that we have no University funds to commit to the project, but [...] the Chancellor has given his full commitment to seeking private money." Nonetheless, on February 28, an Ole Miss press release claimed that the university had agreed to be the guarantor for the $75,000 in matching NEA funds. Several high-ranking university administrators were livid when they read the news, and Walton set the record straight with a Memphis reporter. "The University of Mississippi is not contributing any of the funds to this activity. I explained that we have simply said we are committed to seeking private money."[7] Walton then tried to clarify the matter with the CRCF.

In an interoffice memorandum, Walton told Edge that Ole Miss was trying to get private donations in place, "making the raising of funds a high priority, but it needs to be understood that we will simply have to reject the NEA money, should it become available, if we have not been able to raise the needed funding in time." Edge and the CRCF were not to be deterred. By October, they returned to Khayat, who replied less than enthusiastically. "'I hope you recall that, in our first discussion, when I told you we would support the initiative ... I advised you that I could not offer any University resources for this project.'" The chancellor claimed that the CRCF could meet its goal through private sources but offered little help in so doing.[8]

Edge was baffled by Khayat's response. "This is NOT what we were told [original emphasis]." Edge pointed out that Khayat had agreed to "act as a guarantor for the NEA application," but, as a liberal arts student, Edge understood what he was up against. In an update to the NEA Review Committee, Edge described ongoing problems with the school's troubled racial history and reported that Ole Miss "remains embroiled in a fight over the divisive symbols associated with its past. Recent efforts to restrict the waving of Confederate flags at university events have proven only marginally successful. Yet, the ongoing debate over symbols has provided a great forum for discussion of inclusive, evocative symbols like the sculpture we will commission." A statue in Oxford of William Faulkner, Edge remarked, had been criticized for being "a product of what folks around here call 'the good ole boy network,'" rather than a grassroots effort like the one he was leading, which had produced "approximately half of the $75,000" needed in matching funds for the memorial.[9] His appeal did not sway the grant reviewers at the NEA, and, a few months later, the CRCF received discouraging news.

The NEA awarded just $9,000. By 1999 the foundation requested a one-year extension on its NEA grant "in order for additional funds to be raised in support of the project." In addition to searching for more money, the CRCF needed the time for Susan Glisson—an assistant professor of Southern Studies and assistant director of the then newly founded William Winter Institute for Racial Reconciliation—to take over the job as project director.[10] The next three years became a struggle for the CRCF to get its funding in place and build its civil rights monument.

In 2001 William Doyle published *An American Insurrection*, a history of the Meredith crisis written for a popular audience. He ended the book with a notable reproach: "Today, there are no monuments to James Meredith or to the men of the Mississippi National Guard on the campus of the University of Mississippi, no buildings or statues or scholarships bearing their name. But if you look very closely, and if you know where to look, you can still see bullet marks in the great columns of the Lyceum." By 2001 the CRCF was not much closer to making a civil rights memorial a reality, but Gerald Walton, then provost emeritus, sent letters to alumni "to secure approximately $100,000." In his fundraising plea, he marveled at the same phenomenon that caught Doyle's attention: the only reminder of the 1962 Meredith crisis was a plaque in the dorm room where Meredith lived. "Many of us believe we should do more."[11]

Six months later, the CRCF began looking for jurors to select the winning design and sought artistic bids for the first "permanent civil rights monument in Mississippi." After the August 10 deadline for submissions, the five-member jury "of visual arts professionals" would select five finalists and then a winning design. That design was to be completed and installed by September 2002: the fortieth anniversary of Meredith's admission. More significantly, the renamed Civil Rights Commemoration Initiative (CRCI) announced that it had raised $125,000, including a $75,000 African American Heritage Grant from the Mississippi Department of Archives and History and $20,000 in matching funds from the William Winter Institute for Racial Reconciliation. That left $25,000 to be raised.[12] Still, the CRCI faced more setbacks.

First, Chancellor Khayat sought more control and insisted that he "and/or the Provost will have dinner with the jurors" before their final selections. While that move was problematic, Lynn Kartiganer expressed another concern. In July 2001 she worried about the lack of proposals with the deadline for submissions coming in August. In her mind, it had to be one of three things: the short amount of time provided for submissions, the lack of press coverage after the press release, and the relatively small budget of $150,000 for such a project. She did hope that there would be "quality" submissions if not a high "quantity" and that "a(nother) fairy godmother" might appear with more money.[13] At the time, that looked like wishful thinking at best.

The CRCI pushed back the deadline for submissions to January 4, 2002. The final selection was rescheduled for the fortieth anniversary of the Meredith crisis, and the installation was not going to happen until April 2003. Susan Glisson noted that Gloria Kellum and the university administration were "disappointed with the number of applicants, not the quality.... These kinds of important competitions get twice the number of applications than what we received." In addition, administrators liked the idea of a year-long celebration "of reconciliation" to end with the project installation in April 2003.[14] As the liberal arts teach us, it is easier to celebrate than to question but not necessarily more productive for the public good.

By February 2002 the CRCI named its five finalists from more than four hundred proposals: Terry Adkins of Brooklyn, Marcus Akinlana of New Orleans, Meredith Bergmann of New York City, Willie Birch of New Orleans, and Dennis Oppenheim of New York City. Things were in full swing for the CRCI, but the university's leadership remained less than enthusiastic and faltered again in helping to raise the rest of the money.[15] But when the chancellor tried to take over the selection process from the panel of jurors, the CRCI faced a critical turning point.

In the end, Khayat wanted to pick the winner from the finalists, and Kartiganer blasted the Ole Miss leader. "By far the wisest thing the Chancellor could do is to take a hands-off approach to the actual selection of the artwork." From the beginning, Ole Miss had agreed to a selection process that did not include Khayat, and, in relation to the professional artists who sat on the jury, Khayat had "no credible basis on which to make a decision." In fact, having the committee make the decision freed Khayat from criticism that was bound to come with the selection.[16] More than a concern over funding, Khayat's attempt to take control reflected what later appeared to be a desire to tone down an explicit discussion of race and human rights, much in the vein of practical segregationists who sought to silence James Silver in 1963.

Not knowing the accuracy of her projections, Kartiganer predicted problems if Khayat "subverts this thorough, fair, professional selection process. ... All the good intentions and the fact of the University's willingness after nearly forty years to take the huge step of erecting a civil rights commemorative artwork will be negated." She closed on an important note: Ole Miss could have erected such a monument through an internal process at any time but had not. Now, someone else was doing what should have happened. That argument seemed to convince the university "to stand by the jury's selection," and, for the time being, Khayat backed off.[17]

On May 6, 2002, the five-member jury recommended Terry Adkins's design for the monument. In words that embody the spirit of the liberal arts, his "proposed artwork perfectly captures the dignity of the memorial. The work is universal. It does not specifically address the admission of James Meredith to the University of Mississippi. Therefore, it opens this experience to other people who may have felt disenfranchised in other contexts." Adkins's blueprints included twin bell towers, connected by a flower bed in the middle of the Ellipse. Supported by columns, each bell had the word *Overcome* engraved on it. Along with one of four words at the top—*Henceforth, Freedom, Justice,* and *Forevermore*—one of four quotations was etched in glass under each tower: "Teach in Fear No More, Learn in Fear No More, Insist in Fear No More, Unite in Fear No More." The selection committee believed that Adkins's proposal had "a spiritual, abstract, philosophical" connection to the library as well as the Lyceum and had the potential to make Ole Miss "the most visible representative of full access to higher education throughout Mississippi."[18] As many praised the selection, the design and wording provided the opportunity for Khayat to take over.

Tupelo's *Northeast Mississippi Daily Journal* described "a striking design ... [that] makes a bold statement about rapid change for the good." The project was reason for "celebration" in Mississippi, where "many monuments in our state glorify mistakes and defeats, representing collectively for most Mississippians something objectionable and painful." Gloria Kellum urged Ole Miss to move ahead and commented that, thanks to Edge, Glisson, and

Kartiganer, "this dream has finally been fulfilled."[19] It was an exciting moment but too soon to celebrate. At that point, the memorial stalled, and, over the next three years, everything fell apart.

Warning signs had appeared in the monument's initial stages. Foremost, Khayat's hesitancy was rooted in issues that had kept any reminder of the 1962 events off the Ole Miss campus. In some ways Khayat was tied to the same racial atmosphere that had hampered chancellors at Ole Miss before him and that had driven the agenda of practical segregationists and silenced past critics and scholars like James Silver. Khayat faced a state regime that avoided explicit discussions of race to maintain the tranquility that cushioned white power. It all foreshadowed the drawn-out, frustrating conclusion to ten years of hard work by the CRCI.

Both the artist and the CRCI began to express frustrations. Susan Glisson complained that she had been asking Adkins for weeks "for a schedule for installation and he's yet to provide it." In turn, Adkins shot off to Edge about Ole Miss administrators. "I am so through with this.... If this is so important, the Chancellor should make time for it."[20] In a series of other e-mails, Adkins complained about being delayed, not having been paid, and not launching the project at all. Worst of all, he did not feel like it was going to be possible to make the original deadline.

Issues on that front boiled over when, in a move that smacked of practical segregation, Khayat expressed concerns with Adkins's design and its feasibility within the existing budget. In particular, Khayat did not like the size of the design and decided that the word *fear* was not appropriate for the memorial and should be replaced with the word *respect*. In addition, Khayat wanted to remove a drawing of the state of Mississippi "from the glass doors," all of which was going to happen, Adkins noted, "without my consent."[21] The artist jumped on the chancellor for his unilateral decisions that were not Khayat's to make, in Adkins's mind.

Adkins informed the architect, Jim Eley, that nothing should be changed without his approval as the artist. "I WILL NOT CHANGE ANY OF THE WORDING ON THE DOORS AND THE IMAGE OF THE STATE MUST REMAIN ON THE DOORS AS WELL [original emphasis]." Not mincing words, Adkins ranted, "I think that the chancellor's suggestion of the word 'respect' to be a natural given that is quaint and southern gentleman bullshit.... If the image of the state is not contained in them for any reason, then there is sabotage afoot. Please inform the chancellor's office that no changes can be made without my approval and that I stand firm on all wording as described above."[22] Although unfiltered, Adkins's criticism hit close to the mark.

Khayat's rejection of the word *fear* mirrored, whether subconsciously or not, a white power structure erected by practical segregationists who bristled at direct reflection, as imagined in liberal arts disciplines, on racial problems but maintained white power. On this point, Glisson and the other members of the CRCI were "on the same page with" Adkins and told the chancellor's office that any changes had to be cleared by him.[23] While challenging, the budgetary issues opened the door for Khayat to thwart the entire process.

Jim Eley, the memorial's architect, raised serious questions when he declared "that the design can't be built for less than 175k minimum and he really advocates for 200–225k. The implication is that Terry [Adkins] was naive or duplicitous to suggest that it could be built for the 100k we have and which the prospectus mandates." Glisson and Edge needed to either raise more money or ask Adkins to change the design. Knowing the unlikelihood of Adkins's conceding substantive changes and rather than abandoning the project, they tried to raise another $75,000 for the memorial, but they had to once again delay the October 2003 dedication.[24]

By April 2004 all involved saw that progress was "stalled," but, unbeknownst to the CRCI, Khayat moved ahead. Not heeding Adkins's threats, the chancellor hoped to alter the design without the artist's permission, but, when the university's general counsel, Lee Tyner, advised against it, Khayat began thinking about scrapping the project and issuing his own proposal.[25] Unless Adkins acceded to changes, Glisson and Edge faced a chancellor determined to see his version of a memorial erected on campus.

By June, Adkins had not changed his mind about alterations and advised Glisson that he "cannot budge from my initial proposal in terms of location or scale. I will not be intimidated by the threat of not building the monument at all as that is just an old boy ploy to get me to commit to moving it and reducing the size." Moreover, Adkins retorted, "I will absolutely not shrink from this position in any way nor compromise my vision for a monument that will outlive the chancellor and his abortive effort. If he would like to go down in history as one who perpetuated the very same attitudes that created the necessity for the memorial to be built in the first place, then that is up to him." Adkins was happy to tell Khayat that in person and "expose this to the media in a big way," possibly through the *New York Times*.[26]

A month later Glisson drafted a "'compromise'" that addressed Khayat's "four areas of concern: safety, cost, wording, and visual placement in the Ellipse." As for safety, anxiety about the size of the glass doors, especially in hurricane-force winds, meant that Adkins had to reduce "the scale of the design by 20%," but that solved the cost dilemma. In addition, Glisson felt that Adkins would agree to move the design a few feet farther away on the

Ellipse than originally planned.[27] The wording was the most problematic. In the liberal arts, language matters.

Glisson remarked that "concern [was] expressed that the word 'fear' communicates a negative impression," but she and the CRCI agreed with Adkins that it "actually depicts the victorious triumph of freedom effected on the UM [Ole Miss] campus." Whether Khayat agreed was another matter, but Glisson felt they had "adequately addressed the concerns enumerated to us" and that everyone should get on board for a groundbreaking ceremony.[28] Despite a modicum of progress, when the Fall 2005 semester began, the project was no closer to completion.

On October 4, 2005, the chancellor thanked Edge and Glisson but regretted that their differences could not be resolved. As chancellor, he decided that "the process has dragged on for too long, and it is time for the memorial to be built. Therefore, we have asked an architect to provide a design that preserves the themes of open doors and that can be completed within this academic year."[29] In so doing, Khayat rejected a grassroots, democratic movement that expressed the complexity of racial progress and had taken the better part of the previous decade. In its place he prepared to build his version of a civil rights monument in a matter of a few months.

Khayat's decision set off a firestorm. For Glisson, *fear*, "though painful, sadly represents what many African Americans have felt in this state. To fail to acknowledge those experiences is a grave disservice both to them and to the future." Glisson complained that Khayat was thwarting a long, inclusive, and juried process. Now "one person will choose how best to memorialize the civil rights movement and the university's unique significance. It is dangerous when one person is invested with so much power; inevitably the voices of others are left out and ignored."[30] Others raised similar concerns with Khayat's plan.

The editorial board of the school paper, the *Daily Mississippian*, attacked the school's administrators. "Our university has not only failed itself in its inability to put up the memorial, it has failed to honor the legacy of the civil rights movement. . . . It has seemed obvious from the very beginning that officials at the Lyceum and some alumni have not wanted this memorial's construction." More than that, the editors noted, "they are seeking not only to hide the awful past, they seek to whitewash them entirely." The opinion editor published his own assault on Khayat's decision. "As a student body, we should support and push for the original memorial. If we don't, we have yet again failed to form a synthesis of Southern identity and to come to terms with the past, no matter how dark or painful those memories are."[31] Surprisingly harsh, those views came from an organization not always recognized for its racial progressivism.

John T. Edge offered the loudest salvo in the *Daily Mississippian*. In his account, he argued that, "owing to its peculiar and poignant history, Ole Miss should memorialize the struggle for equal access to education." Edge was "stunned" by Khayat's decision and how he had "objected to the use of the word 'fear' in the inscription upon the doors of the artwork. You told me you objected to its placement on the axis, at the center of the ellipse, that same axis that bisects the Confederate Memorial at the prow of our campus. I strongly disagree with your rationale. I think it's deeply flawed."[32] He then saved his most strident criticism for last.

Although Edge could not do much, he wrote, "I would say to shirk from the word 'fear' when paying homage to a struggle for equal access to education during which two people were shot and killed—within sight of your office window—is an act of denial." Edge continued, "I would tell you that it does a disservice to James Meredith and a host of others who first stepped on this campus with trepidation. I would tell you that it denies the students of today—black and white—their history." Edge suggested that Khayat solicit civil rights activists, folks who were there in 1962, "and students—for students will be the inheritors of *this* struggle to erect an appropriate memorial, not to mention *that* struggle for equal access to education [original emphasis]."[33] Edge called out Khayat's actions and the perpetuation of a status quo so like the 1960s.

Of course, not everyone disagreed with Khayat. Andrew Mullins, executive assistant to the chancellor, noted, "Nobody loved that campus more than Robert Khayat." As Mullins remembered it, Khayat was "100%" in support of the civil rights monument from the start, but, along with the funding difficulties, Khayat was suspicious of the original design for aesthetic purposes. According to Mullins, Khayat believed that Adkins's design did not fit the campus; it was too big. While Khayat "didn't like the word 'fear,'" it was not a "die in the ditch issue." As Mullins saw it, Khayat implemented the redesign and was more than willing to take any blame.[34]

Valeria Ross, an assistant dean of students, got involved after the original design had been rejected, due to architectural problems, as she understood it. At one point, it seemed there would not be any monument at all, and she wanted to respond to student concerns about the absence of a memorial. She invited faculty members to speak with students about their "emotions," and the students expressed frustration with all points of view. Some wanted the original design, and others wanted something else. After those meetings, her committee concluded there should be more evidence about the history of the integration of the university.³⁵

Faced with questions, Khayat tried to explain his thought process to John T. Edge and rehashed his four areas of concern: location, design, message, and "aspirational words." As for the first, Khayat insisted that "we did not want to place anything on the walk between the Lyceum and Library," a statement that stood in contrast to his earlier willingness to erect a monument there. In terms of the design, Khayat believed that "two 15-foot stone archways are not compatible with the architecture of the campus" and that there needed to be a clearer explanation about "the role of Ole Miss in the integration of higher education." As for the wording, Khayat admitted, "I balked on the words 'Teach in Fear No More,' 'Fear No more.' I think the words should be strong and positive: such as 'Freedom—Truth—Courage—Respect—Honor—Opportunity.'" It did not matter that those words, not to mention the means through which they had been chosen, obscured a message that had been agreed upon through long and open debate, another hallmark of the liberal arts.³⁶ With that said, Khayat turned to his design.

Less than two weeks after Khayat rejected the old proposal, Gloria Kellum presented the plan for the new memorial at a student meeting. The *Daily Mississippian* reported, "University administrators, led by Chancellor Robert Khayat, have passed a new proposal similar to the original but without the far-reaching democratic process evident in the first." Expressing some sense of surprise, the reporter noted that a student leader, Twuan Samuel, answered questions about the new proposal and "closed the meeting after posing a single question to the audience: How many of them are in favor of the new plans for the Civil Rights monument? No one raised a hand."³⁷ Khayat also had to explain himself to alumni and donors to the memorial.

That task was complicated, since he had to clarify why he rejected the old design and describe the reasoning behind the artwork that he had chosen to sit on the Ellipse but now off the central axis between the Library and the Lyceum. He explained that "the new hand-carved limestone memorial will be approximately 17 feet tall and will be surrounded by a low wall." In addition, the monument's message was not going to be abstract. "On one side a panel will explain Ole Miss' role in the integration of higher education and the South. Another panel will have inspirational quotes from historical figures of the 1960s and one-word quotes will be placed on the monument's upper stonework." Finally, Khayat noted, "A life-sized statue of James Meredith modeled after a 1962 photograph will be placed on the sidewalk." It was a tasteful, politically muted design.³⁸

Khayat did not foresee the backlash to the Meredith sculpture itself. Some people did not want to honor a man who, in 1989, had worked for Jesse Helms, the notorious segregationist from North Carolina, and had supported former Ku Klux Klansman David Duke as he ran for public office in Louisiana. Glisson warned that "it's always dangerous to put people on pedestals.... It's better to think of heroic moments instead of simplifying people into good guys or bad guys."[39] Terry Adkins offered deeper criticism and defended his proposal.

Asking Khayat to reconsider his choice, the artist detailed how the word *fear* had been inspired by Meredith's 1966 "March Against Fear." As Adkins saw it, neither Khayat nor Jim Eley had the artistic and activist credentials to interpret a civil rights memorial. On the offensive, Adkins argued, "The new memorial plan that you have proffered is aesthetically inappropriate and of little consequence.... Its unbefitting location and makeshift inelegance render the new plan a morbid exercise in conservative nodding." If such a monument were built, Adkins believed, it was going to be a blight on Khayat's legacy.[40] To no one's surprise, Khayat moved forward.

On October 1, 2006, Ole Miss held its "Civil Rights Monument Dedication," but Adkins was no longer the artist. Instead, Jim Eley stood behind the design. Rod Moorhead, a white Ole Miss graduate and "sculptor from Oxford who grew up on the Ole Miss campus," had created the Meredith statue. John Lewis, the civil rights activist and member of the US House of Representatives from Georgia, gave the keynote. Meredith attended with his son Joseph, who received a PhD in business exactly forty years after his father graduated. Joseph Meredith spoke at the ceremony along with Morgan Freeman, and they delivered a rousing tribute.[41]

For Andrew Mullins, the unveiling was a "moving ceremony," and the monument has been a huge success as a "gathering point for visitors to campus," promoting interaction and dialogue around race. In Mullins's view, its existence is a credit to Khayat, who saw it to fruition, and Khayat did so forgiving what many considered the "insubordinate" behavior of Glisson and Edge. Twaun Samuel insists "its presence is important. Regardless of how far detached these generations may be from those times, it is there, and it is a destination that speaks to the origin of the black experience at Ole Miss. It is a place minority students and all students can visit and reflect."[42] On the other hand, Terry Adkins had his own interpretation.

With his penchant for overreaction, Adkins claimed that "the dedication of the monument to the new reign of hypocrisy at Ole Miss should be a cause for sheer embarrassment and grief instead of celebration. The menacing will of Chancellor Khayat has prevailed in the erection of an ignorantly orchestrated disgrace to the field of contemporary public art." He called the new monument a product of "the mentality of incestuous cronyism," and, while he praised Glisson and Edge, Adkins hammered Khayat for "his insular, inflexible outlook and oppressive tactics [that] are the familiar protocol of business as usual in the white supremacist South. If I were a bell, I would toll in mourning on October 1, 2006."[43] Although harsh, Adkins's words got at what white leaders had been doing for forty years in Mississippi. Khayat undermined sincere, intellectual reflection on race and racism and left a monument that celebrated progress rather than attempting to understand the strife that had made progress possible in the first place.

Ole Miss historian Charles Eagles describes the controversy surrounding the monument in the last chapter of *The Price of Defiance*, an encyclopedic account of the Meredith crisis. For Eagles, the "disagreement over the word *fear* captured the essence of the conflict." As he sees it, *fear* represented "the feelings of black people" during Mississippi's Jim Crow era. "To omit *fear* to create a more optimistic, hopeful perspective would allow people, particularly whites, to celebrate progress without facing the realities both of black life and of the past actions of whites. The struggle, therefore, signified a battle over the state's history, who would determine its content, and how to honor it."[44] For Eagles, the fact that the Chancellor won that "battle" was apparent in the "aspirational" quotations on the four bronze plates at the monument site.

Along with quotations from Myrlie Evers, William Winter, and Chancellor Khayat, the monument has a poor paraphrase of a passage from James Meredith's memoir, *Three Years in Mississippi*: "Always, without fail, regardless of the number of times I enter Mississippi, it creates within me feelings that are felt at no other time ... joy ... hope ... love. I have always felt that Mississippi belonged to me and one must love what is his." Removed from that quote and replaced with the ellipses are Meredith's comments about another feeling that the state of Mississippi aroused in him: "Sadness because I am immediately aware of the special subhuman role that I must play, because I am a Negro, or die. Sadness because it is the home of the greatest number of Negroes outside Africa, yet my people suffer from want of everything in a rich land of plenty, and, most of all, they must endure the inconvenience of indignity."[45] The selective editing created the same effect that removing the word *fear* from the monument had had.

For those reasons, Eagles argues that, despite "all its success, the 2006 celebration betrayed the limitations of the racial change that had occurred at the university and in the state."[46] From a noted liberal arts scholar, that commentary is an admonition for Khayat and those people who have touted triumph and obscured struggle. The forces of white hegemony that pushed James Silver out of the state evolved into the series of events that led Khayat to erect his Meredith monument on the Ole Miss campus. Both were underscored by the same power-preserving impulses. The advocates of practical segregation would have stood and applauded such an outcome, while the proponents of liberal arts inquiry must continue to demand more.

Notes

1. James Silver, Presidential Address before the Southern Historical Association, Asheville, North Carolina, 7:00 p.m., November 7, 1963, "Mississippi: The Closed Society," "Silver, James W. 1963" folder, Minor Papers, Box 13, MSU.

2. Joseph Crespino, *In Search of Another Country: Mississippi and the Conservative Counterrevolution* (Princeton: Princeton University Press, 2007), 4, 19, 30.

3. Memorandum, the Civil Rights Commemoration Foundation to Robert Khayat, June 4, 1996, "The Civil Rights Commemoration Foundation" folder 3, CRCI Papers, Box 2, Ole Miss, p. 3; Letter, John T. Edge to Robert Khayat, February 1, 1996, "Correspondence February, 1996" folder 4, CRCI Papers, Box 3, Ole Miss; Letter, Robert Khayat to John T. Edge, February 16, 1996, "Civil Rights Monument Meetings" folder 10, CRCI Papers, Box 1, Ole Miss; and John T. Edge, Civil Rights Memorial Timeline: Highlights, "Notes" folder 2, CRCI Papers, Box 1, Ole Miss, p. 1.

4. Letter, Ari Frede to John T. Edge, April 4, 1996, "Correspondence April, 1996" folder 6, CRCI Papers, Box 3, Ole Miss, pp. 1, 2; Memorandum, The Civil Rights Commemoration Foundation to Robert Khayat, June 4, 1996. "The Civil Rights Commemoration Foundation" folder 3, CRCI Papers, Box 2, Ole Miss, p. 1.

5. John T. Edge, Civil Rights Memorial Timeline: Highlights. "Notes" folder 2, CRCI Papers, Box 1, Ole Miss, p. 1; Nadine Cohodas, *Band Played Dixie: Race and the Liberal Conscience at Ole Miss* (New York: Free Press, 1997), 264.

6. "Newspaper Articles" folder 22, CRCI Papers, Box 5, Ole Miss; Rheta Grimsley. "Civil Rights Statue Worth Effort of Ole Miss Students," *Atlanta Journal-Constitution*, November 17, 1996. "The Atlanta Journal Constitution" folder 4, CRCI Papers, Box 5, Ole Miss; Letter, John T. Edge to Robert Khayat, February 12, 1997, "Correspondence February, 1997" folder 13, CRCI Papers, Box 3, Ole Miss, p. 1.

7. Memorandum, Gerald Walton to Don Fruge, October 30, 1997, "Correspondence October, 1997" folder 16, CRCI Papers, Box 3, Ole Miss, pp. 1, 2.

8. Memorandum, Walton to Fruge, October 30, 1997, folder 16, CRCI Papers, Box 3, p. 2; E-mail, John T. Edge to Charles Alexander, October 25, 1997, "Correspondence October, 1997" folder 16, CRCI Papers, Box 3, Ole Miss.

9. E-mail, Edge to Alexander, October 25, 1997, folder 16, CRCI Papers, Box 3; Memorandum, Gerald Walton to Don Fruge, October 30, 1997, "Correspondence October, 1997" folder 16, CRCI Papers, Box 3, Ole Miss, p. 2; and Memorandum, John T. Edge to NEA Review Committee, November 17, 1997, "Correspondence November, 1997" folder 17, CRCI Papers, Box 3, Ole Miss.

10. Letter, Ronald Borne to Whom It May Concern, June 30, 1999, "Correspondence June, 1999" folder 27, CRCI Papers, Box 3, Ole Miss.

11. William Doyle, *An American Insurrection: The Battle of Oxford, Mississippi, 1962* (New York: Doubleday, 2001), 318; Letter, Gerald Walton to Harold Burson, January 17, 2001, "Correspondence January, 2001" folder 39, CRCI Papers, Box 3, Ole Miss.

12. Press release, "UM Group Seeks Artwork for Proposed Civil Rights Memorial: Permanent Monument Would Be the First of Its Kind in State," May 25, 2001. "Correspondence July, 2001" folder 45, CRCI Papers, Box 3, Ole Miss, pp. 1, 2; Letter, Elbert Hilliard to Robert Khayat, September 21, 2001, "Correspondence September, 2001" folder 47, CRCI Papers, Box 3, Ole Miss.

13. E-mail, Lyn Kartiganer to John T. Edge, Vanessa Bliss, and Susan Glisson, April 27, 2001, "Correspondence April, 2001" folder 42, CRCI Papers, Box 3, Ole Miss, p. 1; E-mail, Lyn Kartiganer to John T. Edge, Vanessa Bliss, and Susan Glisson, July 11, 2001, "Correspondence July, 2001" folder 45, CRCI Papers, Box 3, Ole Miss, p. 1.

14. E-mail, Vanessa Bliss to Susan Glisson, Gloria Kellum, Lyn Kartiganer, and John T. Edge, August 21, 2001, "Correspondence August, 2001" folder 46, CRCI Papers, Box 3, Ole Miss, pp. 1, 2; E-mail, Susan Glisson to Vanessa Bliss, Lyn Kartiganer, and John T. Edge, August 21, 2001, "Correspondence August, 2001" folder 46, CRCI Papers, Box 3, Ole Miss.

15. E-mail, Mary Beth Lasseter to John T. Edge, February 4, 2002, "Correspondence February, 2002" folder 2, CRCI Papers, Box 4, Ole Miss; Letter, Iby Albriton to John T. Edge, March 2002, "Correspondence March, 2002" folder 3, CRCI Papers, Box 4, Ole Miss; E-mail, Jason Dean to Gloria Kellum, April 12, 2002, "Correspondence April, 2002" folder 4, CRCI Papers, Box 4, Ole Miss; E-mail, Mary Beth Lasseter to Gloria Kellum, April 24, 2002, "Correspondence April 2002" folder 4, CRCI Papers, Box 4, Ole Miss.

16. John T. Edge, Civil Rights Memorial Timeline: Highlights, "Notes" folder 2, CRCI Papers, Box 1, Ole Miss, p. 2; E-mail, Lyn Kartiganer to John T. Edge and Susan Glisson, April 25, 2002, "Correspondence April 2002" folder 4, CRCI Papers, Box 4, Ole Miss.

17. E-mail, Kartiganer to Edge and Glisson, April 25, 2002, Folder 4, CRCI Papers, Box 4; John T. Edge, Civil Rights Memorial Timeline: Highlights, "Notes" folder 2, CRCI Papers, Box 1, Ole Miss, p. 2.

18. Memorandum, CRCI Selection Panel to Civil Rights Commemoration Initiative, May 6, 2002, "Correspondence May, 2002" folder 5, CRCI Papers, Box 4, Ole Miss; Terry Adkins, CRCI Memorial Proposal: University of Mississippi, April 27, 2002, "Photographs" folder 12, CRCI Papers, Box 1, Ole Miss, p. 2.

19. Nash Molpus, "Civil Rights Memorial Design Selected," *Southern Register*, Fall 2002, pp. 1, 4, "The Southern Register" folder 16, CRCI Papers, Box 5, Ole Miss; "Claiming the Future: UM Monument Honors Idealism and Courage," *Northeast Mississippi Daily Journal*, July 20, 2002, "Open Doors Celebration Background Materials" folder 16, CRCI Papers, Box 1, Ole Miss; Memorandum, Gloria Kellum and Brian Reithel to Carolyn Staton, May 31, 2002, "Correspondence May, 2002" folder 5, CRCI Papers, Box 4, Ole Miss.

20. E-mail, Susan Glisson to Lyn Kartiganer and John T. Edge, October 3, 2002, "Correspondence October, 2002" folder 10, CRCI Papers, Box 4, Ole Miss, pp. 1–3; E-mail, Terry Adkins to John T. Edge, October 10, 2002, "Correspondence October, 2002" folder 10, CRCI Papers, Box 4, Ole Miss.

21. E-mail, Terry Adkins to Susan Glisson, undated, "Correspondence May, 2003" folder 15, CRCI Papers, Box 4, Ole Miss.

22. E-mail, Adkins to Glisson, undated, folder 15, CRCI Papers, Box 4.

23. E-mail, Susan Glisson to Terry Adkins, May 28, 2003, "Correspondence May, 2003" folder 15, CRCI Papers, Box 4, Ole Miss; E-mail, Susan Glisson to Terry Adkins, May 29, 2003, "Correspondence May, 2003" folder 15, CRCI Papers, Box 4, Ole Miss.

24. E-mail, Susan Glisson to John T. Edge, June 9, 2003, "Correspondence June, 2003" folder 16, CRCI Papers, Box 4, Ole Miss; E-mail, John T. Edge to Susan Glisson, June 10, 2003, "Correspondence June, 2003" folder 16, CRCI Papers, Box 4, Ole Miss; E-mail, Susan Glisson to John T. Edge, June 10, 2003, "Correspondence June, 2003" folder 16, CRCI Papers, Box 4, Ole Miss; E-mail, Susan Glisson to John T. Edge, July 9, 2003, "Correspondence July, 2003" folder 17, CRCI Papers, Box 4, Ole Miss.

25. E-mail, Peter Frost to John T. Edge, April 27, 2004, "Correspondence April, 2004" folder 19, CRCI Papers, Box 4, Ole Miss; E-mail, Donna Patton to Lee Tyner, October 5, 2004, "Correspondence October, 2004" folder 22, CRCI Papers, Box 4, Ole Miss; E-mail, Susan Glisson to John T. Edge, October 12, 2004, "Correspondence October, 2004" folder 22, CRCI Papers, Box 4, Ole Miss; E-mail, Lee Tyner to Donna Patton, October 15, 2004, "Correspondence October, 2004" folder 22, CRCI Papers, Box 4, Ole Miss.

26. E-mail, Terry Adkins to Susan Glisson, June 30, 2005, "Correspondence June, 2005" folder 28, CRCI Papers, Box 4, Ole Miss; E-mail, Susan Glisson to John T. Edge, June 30, 2005, "Correspondence June, 2005" folder 28, CRCI Papers, Box 4, Ole Miss.

27. E-mail, Susan Glisson to John T. Edge, July 28, 2005, "Correspondence July, 2005" folder 29, CRCI Papers, Box 4, Ole Miss

28. E-mail, Glisson to Edge, July 28, 2005, folder 29, CRCI Papers, Box 4.

29. Memorandum, Robert Khayat to John T. Edge, October 4, 2005, "Correspondence October, 2005" folder 32, CRCI Papers, Box 4, Ole Miss.

30. E-mail, Susan Glisson to Victoria Hiles, October 5, 2005, "Correspondence October, 2005" folder 32, CRCI Papers, Box 4, Ole Miss.

31. "We Have Not Overcome," *Daily Mississippian*, October 5, 2005, p. 2, "The Daily Mississippian 2005" folder 2, CRCI Papers, Box 5, Ole Miss; Brandon Niemeyer, "Forging a Past for Everyone," *Daily Mississippian*, October 11, 2005, p. 2, "The Daily Mississippian 2005" folder 2, CRCI Papers, Box 5, Ole Miss.

32. John T. Edge, "Khayat's Rationale in Rejecting Civil Rights Memorial Design a 'Disservice to James Meredith' and Others," *Daily Mississippian*, October 7, 2005, p. 3, "The Daily Mississippian 2005" folder 2, CRCI Papers, Box 5, Ole Miss.

33. Edge, "Khayat's Rationale," October 7, 2005, p. 3, folder 2, CRCI Papers, Box 5.

34. Andrew Mullins, interviewed by author, March 4, 2009, Jackson, Mississippi.

35. Valeria Ross, interviewed by author, March 3, 2009, Oxford, Mississippi.

36. Letter, Robert Khayat to John T. Edge, October 11, 2005, "Correspondence October, 2005" folder 32, CRCI Papers, Box 4, Ole Miss, pp. 1, 2.

37. Alexis Lognion, "Panel Addresses Student Concerns," *Daily Mississippian*, October 18, 2005, pp. 1, 4, "The Daily Mississippian 2005" folder 2, CRCI Papers, Box 5, Ole Miss, pp. 1, 4.

38. Letter, Robert Khayat to Donald Summers, November 3, 2005, "Correspondence November, 2005" folder 33, CRCI Papers, Box 4, Ole Miss, pp. 1–2.

39. Brian Doyle, "Additions Made to Memorial," *Daily Mississippian*, October 28, 2005, pp. 1, 4, "The Daily Mississippian 2005" folder 2, CRCI Papers, Box 5, Ole Miss, p. 1; Jerry Mitchell, "Plans for Meredith Statue Criticized: Critics Question Civil Rights Legend's Politics after Leaving Ole Miss," *Clarion-Ledger*, November 4, 2005, pp. 1A, 3A, "The Clarion-Ledger" folder 6, CRCI Papers, Box 5, Ole Miss, pp. 1A, 3A.

40. Terry Adkins, "Artist Defends Memorial," *Daily Mississippian*, November 10, 2005, p. 2, "The Daily Mississippian 2005" folder 2, CRCI Papers, Box 5, Ole Miss.

41. The University of Mississippi, Civil Rights Monument Dedication, October 1, 2006, "Civil Rights Monument Dedication; October 1, 2006" folder 11, CRCI Papers, Box 1, Ole Miss, pp. 4, 7.

42. Mullins interview; Twaun Samuel, e-mail to author, April 7, 2009, in possession of the author.

43. Terry Adkins, "If I Were a Bell," *Daily Mississippian*, September 26, 2006, p. 2, "The Daily Mississippian 2006" folder 3, CRCI Papers, Box 5, Ole Miss.

44. Charles Eagles, *The Price of Defiance: James Meredith and the Integration of Ole Miss* (Chapel Hill: University of North Carolina Press, 2009), 436–41.

45. Eagles, *Price of Defiance*, 441.

46. Eagles, *Price of Defiance*, 442.

Bibliography

Civil Rights Commemoration Initiative (CRCI) Papers. University of Mississippi (Ole Miss).

Cohodas, Nadine. *The Band Played Dixie: Race and the Liberal Conscience at Ole Miss*. New York: Free Press, 1997.

Crespino, Joseph. *In Search of Another Country: Mississippi and the Conservative Counterrevolution*. Princeton: Princeton University Press, 2007.

Doyle, William. *An American Insurrection: The Battle of Oxford, Mississippi, 1962*. New York: Doubleday, 2001.

Eagles, Charles W. *The Price of Defiance: James Meredith and the Integration of Ole Miss*. Chapel Hill: University of North Carolina Press, 2009.

Silver, James W. *Mississippi: The Closed Society*. New York: Harcourt Brace and World, 1966.

Wilson Minor (Minor) Personal Papers. Mississippi State University (MSU).

CHAPTER 17

[Re]Engineering a New Liberal Arts Experience

Future Studies and HBCUs

JOSEPH MARTIN STEVENSON, DAWN BISHOP McLIN,
AND KAREN C. WILSON-STEVENSON

This "re-engineering" chapter discusses the utility of futurism and the applicability of futures studies for modern-day liberal arts at the nation's historically black colleges and universities (HBCUs). The term "re-engineering" is used here and defined as redesigning, refocusing, and reconceptualizing liberal arts education with the thematic threads of future studies in the modern higher education curriculum. Our purpose as enthusiasts, advocates, and proponents of re-engineered liberal arts is to introduce a new enculturation for liberal arts thinking, learning, and teaching. The closest reference found by the authors that connects futures to liberal arts was by Carl Bereiter in the often-studied book *Liberal Education in a Knowledge Society*. He references "futuristic business literature" and summarizes this as the "flood of publications from organizational theorists, management consultants, economists, futurologists, and diverse social scientists that take as a backdrop the rapid rate of technological change, ... digitization, globalization, outsourcing ... to a knowledge-based economy and the need for constant innovation."[1]

Like Bereiter, who offered a new perspective for thinking about liberal arts education, we offer a new paradigm for HBCUs and other institutions of higher learning based upon the precept and principles of futurism. Futurism is the forward-thinking ability to position for the future, and the acumen to prepare for the future based on data-driven informatics and other forecasting analytics from trends throughout the world. The methods of futurism and futures studies employ data-driven decision-making skills for lifelong critical and creative thinking needed in all facets of life. Metaphorically, in the HBCU community, this is called "Sankofa," which means looking forward and backward simultaneously. Some of these methods and their transdisciplinary teaching taxonomies include environmental scanning, historical analysis, scenario analysis, visioning, brainstorming, polling, gaming, and others. While this chapter focuses on the utility, relevance, and application of "futures studies" in liberal arts education and not necessarily the "future" of liberal arts education, profiling certain references from the literature does provide a fundamental backdrop. Maryville University points out on its website that liberal arts institutions can survive pressing transformational forces, but it will require an ability to adapt.[2]

Among the challenges, forces, and impacts mentioned are evolving landscape, financial challenges, social impact, technical teaching demands, critical thinking imperatives, workforce demands, marketplace shifts, emerging technology, and interdisciplinary competition between the sciences and the humanities and other areas inside and outside the classroom amid changing political times. We believe the nature of futures studies can help to achieve this adaptation as the result of its analytical methodologies. The website highlights a number of the same driving forces and counterforces with suggestions on how to adapt in today's environment. Some of these same forces and challenges were highlighted during the 2012 conference at Lafayette College on The Future of the Liberal Arts College in America and Its Leadership Role in Education Around the World. The forum suggested that "by virtue of their scale and their focused mission, liberal arts colleges are especially well-positioned to lead in developing new approaches for an uncertain future."[3] Again, we believe that futures studies should be one of those approaches to consider.

Commenting on how liberal arts education has impacted Canada as well as the US, the report by Universities Canada entitled "The Future of the Liberal Arts" observes, "The liberal arts college helps us navigate disruptive change and build an innovative, prosperous, and inclusive Canada." We believe this to be true for the US, particularly given the country's politically and culturally divisive climate. Studying the impact of the manifestation from this sociological climate change through the lens of futures studies may be a healthy and forthcoming experience for students and faculty. Finally, William Darden, president of Dickinson College, made some sapient observations at New York University in his presentation "The Future of Liberal Arts Colleges." He surmised that "liberal arts colleges are unique American institutions that were created to fulfill a distinctively American approach to higher education. The challenge facing our institutions today is to successfully adapt their historical purpose to the complex world of the 21st century."[4]

Although the literature applies the liberal arts experience by institutional classification or thematic thread within a curriculum, we believe futures studies can be implemented at a designated or classified liberal arts college and within an identified curriculum at a larger university. This unique chapter discusses futures studies for future HBCU stakeholders, as well as for next-generation thought-leaders in liberal arts fields. We say "unique" because the chapter is different from others relative to content, context, and subtext—often a way to foster, nurture, and harvest liberal arts thinking. In addition, the chapter reviews some examples of futuring methods for both faculty and students studying liberal arts in HBCUs, suggestions of "quadrivium" and "trivium" blending for consideration in liberal arts. A conceptual framework in this chapter is the introduction of a bridging between professorial teaching and student learning relationship-building to foster the uniqueness of futures studies in liberal arts teaching and learning. This process has been successfully applied by J. M. Stevenson at several liberal arts institutions of higher learning, specifically, York College/New York City; Stockton College (now Stockton University)/New Jersey; and Tougaloo College/Mississippi. The framework was also introduced at liberal arts Miles College in Alabama. Concrete examples for building relationships between faculty and students can be driven by following and framing guided practices from: (a) futures studies frameworks, (b) faculty teaching overarches, and (c) student learning outcomes as denoted in the figure below:

The FTOs are meant to be general thematic threads, whereas the SLOs should be conceptualized to be more specific to an action-driven verb, such as "create," "develop," "project," "innovate," "hypothesize," or "forecast."

HBCUs, from the mid-1800s to the present day, have played a foundational and fundamental role in the African American community and in the historical development of the liberal arts from an African American lens. Without question, American HBCUs have served as the primary pipeline for historically freed slaves to access higher education during the founding period of many of these institutions. Providing this type of historical access during a postslavery era also anchored the institutions' spiritual mission, which provided the genesis for the campuses to serve as the freedom-fighting venues in the civil rights movement and the impetus for the institutionalization of social justice throughout historical agrarian, industrial, and information societies.

HBCUs often sustain their existence and longevity within a struggling economy and an intensifying academic marketplace through a legacy attractive to the next generation. By focusing on the future and the past, the traditional HBCU becomes anchored in a cyclical history with returns on investments from moving toward the future while being grounded in the past. And, futurism can be thematically threaded throughout the HBCU

A	B	C
Tenet	Tenet	Tenet
Futures Studies Frameworks(FSF)	Faculty Teaching Overarches(FTO)	Student Learning Outcome(SLO)
Scanning	Significant Changes	Conduct a literature review of future trends in liberal arts curriculum
Trend Analysis	Nature, Cause, Speed	Study the major variables that impact the nature, the speed, and the causes of liberal arts curriculum changes
Scenarios	Future Development	Create a future scenario for a student who is a major in liberal arts but has a specific interest in the sciences and humanities
Polling	Collecting Viewpoints	Collect and compare male and female points of view on how the environment will impact gender in the future
Brainstorming	Generating Ideas	Conduct a brainstorming activity that facilitates the generation of ideas to create innovations in teaching and learning in the liberal arts
Historical Analysis	Anticipating Outcomes	Describe how historical events in civil rights can contribute to an analysis of future events in civil rights amid a climate of national division, adversity, and diversity
Gaming	Simulating Situations	Create a game simulation that could be an app on a phone to foster critical thinking in the liberal arts
Visioning	Creating Desirable Futures	Describe how a review of past events and current situations can help an organization identify specific ways to plan for the future

liberal arts curriculum as well as in the sciences and the professions. The recommendations for all HBCUs are to engage "future diversification."

In today's fiercely competitive academic market, HBCUs will survive, thrive, and progress in their market share only if and when there is liberal arts teaching and learning that includes a cutting-edge forward-thinking curriculum. By diversifying the liberal arts curriculum with futurism and futuring methods, HBCUs can distinguish their uniqueness, brand, identity, and instructional delivery in the liberal arts market. The future student-scholar enrolled at an HBCU can also seek learning opportunities by building on the heritage of HBCUs and by becoming research literate in futurism during the undergraduate experience, in and out of the classroom and at the freshman, sophomore, junior, and senior levels. In order for this to occur, the faculty must take on the role of mentor, virtuoso, and provocateur (MVP)—guiding the student through the tenets and research paradigms, and toward future positioning. The Socratic teaching or probing method might be considered in this inquiry process by posing questions like: What if? How can we predict or forecast? Where could the data trend take us? When could we expect? Or what is more likely or less likely to occur? Indeed, many African Americans contributed to agrarian advancements in agriculture, industrial progress in manufacturing growth, and information expansion from technological breakthroughs in America.

In setting the stage for this new campus culture, HBCUs should consider modern innovations that can foster futurism, as in accelerated learning models, modes, and modalities to survive the fierce academic marketplace. Futurism and research literacy can utilize innovative time frames, through a program, for example, of three-year degrees within an accelerated and compressed time frame. Increased academic rigor makes better economic sense in today's climate, given intensifying public concern about financial aid default, student debt, student dropout rates, and degree relevance in the global job market.

The liberal arts at HBCUs should exhaustively document how innovative student engagement will meet societal needs and workforce demands and provide market-ready students to support industry imperatives, economic development, job creation, and emerging global workforce requirements. To do all of this, HBCU leaders must master the fundamentals of conciliatory leadership with faculty that is manifested through shared governance, trans-disciplinary alliances, and community-spirited coalitions on and off campus. This will truly manifest the nature, context, and intent of the transdisciplinary learning and teaching for future liberal arts. The future-oriented HBCU must both maintain and modify its mission with cutting-edge modernization integrated with futurism. The liberal arts at HBCUs must maintain their commitment, dedication, and focus on those who most want, deserve, and need higher education—the underserved, the underrepresented, the underutilized, the impoverished, the voiceless, and the marginalized—but within a context that bridges futurism and research across liberal arts disciplines in an era of increased competition and accelerated change.

The more modernized liberal arts mission at HBCUs should have futurism central to its core curriculum. Classroom instruction, from and through FSFs, FTOs, and SLOs, should center on futuring methods to empower students to develop their own mission statements and visionary strategies for futuring. Futuring methods can serve as a catalytic force to create campus-based methodologies for seeking answers to social injustice, inequality, imbalance, inequity, marginalization, and disparity, as well as to resolve other elements of the natural and physical life that require investigative, scientific, exploratory, diagnostic, evidenced-based, and data-driven decision making. The future venues where most HBCU graduates arrive—the world of work, professional schools, and graduate education—are increasingly requiring this type of cognitive competence. There is no reason futurism could not be systemically, synergistically, and sequentially integrated with a more pronounced presence in the liberal arts curriculum with a future context guided by student and faculty collaboration.

The liberal arts at HBCUs must engage faculty as MVPs, students, and others in our new learning community of practice in all dimensions of scholarly research via futures studies: analysis, inquiry, innovation, investigation, fact-finding, probing, theorization, examination, innovation, experimentation, and exploration. The ultimate challenge for catalytic leaders, especially in the future-oriented HBCU, is to translate and transition relevant research in futurism into real-life action for permanent and sustainable positive change, thereby improving the human condition in a modern world widely wounded, broadly broken, terribly troubled, and profoundly perplexed. This means the redefined liberal arts curriculum at HBCUs must embody a culture for students and faculty that is more futuristic, innovative, invigorating, ingenious, entrepreneurial, creative, and investigative in the classroom and throughout the academic community.

The faculty MVP—mentor, virtuoso, and provocateur—guides the future positioning in the complex world described above. The future-oriented HBCU should build on the past to provide a foundation for forecast. The excitement experienced by newly freed slaves and the electricity that was created by civil rights advocates will always be a part of the history for the incubation of HBCUs. Liberal arts HBCUs must now build on another foundation to propel the institution to sustainability through the creative engagement of scholarly research and the empowerment of futuring skills among the students and the faculty.

Futurism should be the constant and common denominator in today's undergraduate curriculum at HBCUs, and the undergirding pedagogical theme should be critical thinking with futurism methodology as a foundation for much-needed, looping-back learning that connects the past, the present, and the future. This epistemological revelation can be experienced, nurtured, and navigated from the arts to anthropology; economics to engineering; music to mathematics; theater to technology; and social sciences to behavioral sciences like politics, psychology, geography, history, and many other areas in humanities. Some futuring methods for transdisciplinary teaching encompass environmental scanning, scenario analysis, polling, and gaming.

HBCU students can apply environmental scanning to identify significant or substantive changes in an environment within or around an organization. For instance, the HBCU campus could be a laboratory of learning from which students and faculty conduct an environmental scan as part of futuring. Cornish suggests that "scanning focuses mainly on trends—changes that occur through time—rather than events, changes that occur very quickly and generally are less significant for understanding the future."[5]

The use of scenario analysis is quite common in many college classrooms where students and faculty work together to discuss hypotheses and other hypothetical situations for real-life situations and relevant conditions. Scenarios provide pathways to creative thinking that are generated from brainstorming. Cornish writes, "The future development of a trend, a strategy, or a wildcard event may be described in the story or outline form. Typically, several scenarios will be developed so that decision makers are aware that future events may invalidate whatever scenario they use for planning purposes."[6]

Regarding polling, Cornish offers that it is "collecting people's views on the future and other topics. Data may be collected through face-to-face conversation, telephone interviews, and questionnaires sent by electronic or ordinary mail. Delphi polling, popular among futurists, uses a carefully structured procedure to generate more-accurate forecasts."[7] Students with a particular interest in qualitative research methodology may find the polling method effective for interactions in focus groups or other informal settings. Nowadays, polling can be done through different types of social media as well as other instruments that are available through internet navigation and web access. Polling can also be conducted from both informal and formal questionnaires and printed survey instruments (quantitative and qualitative) to generate information for understanding forecasts and anticipated projections in academic study. Some academics and social demographers who work on areas related to public policy and opinion use the Delphi method. Students and faculty at HBCUs might consider the polling method to learn more about differing opinions on sensitive subjects such as inclusion, diversity, gender, sexual orientation, race, age, culture, and ethnicity.

Cornish defines gaming as "the simulation of a real-world situation by means of humans playing different roles. In war games, real soldiers may become actors in a mock battle, which helps them to understand what actual combat is like and helps generals to test out alternative strategies and tactics they may later use."[8] Students with an acumen for game simulation through computer technology could work with others in theater to conceptualize simulations from real-world situations. This type of technological and human interaction is quite often engaging for students who enjoy interdependent human dynamics in social settings. Psychology students could use this in regard to post-traumatic stress disorder symptom management and treatment of mental disorders.

Another method that Cornish has conceptualized for liberal arts majors is the essence of brainstorming reality, which has been cited in the *Harvard Business Review* by Gregersen as "a process for recasting problems in valuable new ways." He adds, "brainstorming for questions rather than answers makes it easier to push past biases and venture into uncharted territory."[9] This method might find particular application at HBCUs where racial or other biases could be inherent in the teaching of liberal arts curriculum. Other methods include modeling, which could be applied through computer simulation; trend analysis, which examines the nature, speed, and cause of a trend; historical analysis, which uses historical events to anticipate outcomes of event developments; and visioning, which is the creation of systematic visions for positioning of desirable futures.

Faculty who lead discussions about the creative journey of positioning for the future should encourage collaborative futures research in the undergraduate experience. Service learning can be a major component for collaboration between faculty and students. As both the world within the academy and the society that surrounds it more intensely blend the disciplines, collaborative futures research can be revealing, rewarding, and reflective. Creativity taught and learned, dimensions of these areas can be found in today's disciplines such as art, communications, sociology, criminal justice, nursing, public health, social work, literature, philosophy, geography, theater, mathematics, and many other disciplines across the arts, sciences, and professions. In the scholarship, "trivium" is defined as the usage of language, logic in thinking, and the ways of persuasion through speech that empower people to understand a subject matter. In that regard, "quadrivium" is the connection of mathematics to meanings found in numbers, geometrical spaces, musical counting, and other arithmetical proportions. All of these areas have impactful meaning in past, present, and future engagement of the modern liberal arts. What follows are some transdisciplinary examples for aligning the historical fourteenth-century "seven liberal arts" of quadrivium and trivium with modern-day interpretations and applications. In modern-day interpretations, all of the areas below are either directly or indirectly related to the past references of trivium—grammar, rhetoric, and dialectic—and quadrivium—arithmetic, geometry, astronomy, and music.

Art students might collaborate with anthropology students on collecting Native American images to determine the varying cultural interpretations in the future. Students could assemble these images and ask members of a Native American community to assess the different meanings as they relate to their future lives and their community. Students could conduct qualitative focus groups in this community and later administer a quantitative survey to validate the gathered data about the different interpretations. Using Table 1.0, scenarios (3) in column A, along with columns B (FTO) and C (SLO), could be considered. Communication students could collaborate with others who are studying sociology to analyze different case studies about the portrayal of different cultural groups in the media and to forecast trends. Students could study these case studies from the internet or from print journals or print media and then create scenarios from brainstorming. Each case study should be examined for common and contrasting points of view.

Students might also select particular televised broadcasts to examine images, perceptions, optics, and portrayals of different people. These students could develop their own case studies for future students in the disciplines. Brainstorming (5) in column A with tenets in columns B (FTO) and C (SLO) could be applied. Criminal justice students might analyze case studies about high-risk youth and then survey local youth to determine whether their behavior is dissimilar or the same for future development. Nursing students could conduct interviews with teenage mothers to determine whether their lifestyles and eating habits either contrast or are in concert with revelations from literature reviews. A follow-up survey to verify the data from the interviews could be formulated to continue the investigation. Scanning (1) in column A, combined with tenets in B (FTO) and C (SLO), might be useful in the areas of nursing and criminal justice.

Students who study public health and social work should be involved too. Economics students might conduct focus groups with or surveys of targeted populations to determine patterns of consumer behavior, comparing global markets to local markets, for instance. Other economics students might collaborate with history majors to trace the history of economic thought from medieval civilization to modern times and then project future thought for modern times. The result of this historical examination might compare the application of economics in urban settings with marginalized populations.

Trend analysis (2) in column A (FTO) and B (SLO) or historical analysis (6) in column A along with the accompanying tenets in column B (FTO) and C (SLO) could be considered.

Literature, linguistics, and language students might study areas of Greek mythology and conduct focus groups with people from the Delta or Appalachian culture to determine future relevance. Other students in English could assemble different analyses of poetry and survey non-English majors to determine the extent to which they embrace the art and future interpretation of poetry. Philosophy students and others in the humanities could create case studies based on the comparison of readings from the "Black books" and the "classics." Their findings might be examined and captured for developing a futuristic hip-hop genre with music majors. In another possibility, humanities students might compare Russian literature to Japanese literature and translate different cultural meanings. These meanings could be incorporated in a survey for other students to complete to determine the appreciation of the comparisons. Historical analysis (6) or polling (4) with accompanying tenets could be completed in this instance.

Geography majors might study the human elements behind the devastation of Katrina by conducting on-site surveys and making follow-up observations concerning human experiences and then create different scenarios for future preparation. Geographic information systems (GIS) could provide data from a helicopter point of view to examine different patterns within the regions of devastation. The examination of climatic variations could enhance data revelations, and forecasting techniques might provide the basis for future planning. Gaming (7) in column A with the tenets in columns B (FTO) and C (SLO) could be generated here.

Math students could collaborate with political science majors to conduct surveys or focus groups about mathematical relevance as perceived by middle-school students in rural settings. Psychology students might join in this collaborative to determine the extent to which self-concept is linked to academic performance in mathematics and might craft a futures-oriented model for instruction. And theater students might develop productions based on an analysis of case studies from families who experience agricultural life at the turn of the century. Aging farmers could provide short stories about their experiences, and these experiences could be crafted into the design and development of theatrical productions. Visioning (8) in column A could be imagined into the related tenets in columns B (FTO) and C (SLO) here.

These are just a few futures-aimed examples for the utilization of focus groups, surveys, interviews, observations, and other instruments that can be used to collect data for further analysis and in-depth examination. Certainly, students are not expected to master all of the domains and dimensions of qualitative and quantitative research in a futures context, but they should apply these methodologies and compare their treatments during future-oriented methods. FTOs and SLOs can be empowering and provide the wherewithal. Faculty, as MVPs, should lead all of these research endeavors with their students to secure and sustain the appropriate guidelines for human subject research, if needed. Here, too, students should be involved to learn about the ethical and legal dimensions of conducting research. As mentioned by Michael P. Grady, the dimension of quantitative research is embedded in a purpose for prediction and control or cause and effect, while the purpose of qualitative research is to understand, describe, and interpret behavior. On the other hand, quantitative instrumentation typically uses tests and instruments, and the research of data collection is primary to quantitative methodology. The condition of qualitative research is conventionally conducted under natural dimensions, but quantitative research is conducted under more-controlled conditions.[10] Both quantitative and qualitative components could be integrated in futures studies, especially as undergraduates prepare for graduate or professional school. This is being exemplified and modeled at Miles College in Alabama.

In either case, students should embrace futuring as a cognitive tool and decision-making technique. Their vocabulary and level of understanding of futurism should grow over time, from understanding the fundamentals of a futures hypothesis to the selection of research approaches that could lead to correlational, experimental, causal-comparative research in liberal arts postgraduate or professional study, where the core of liberal arts grounding is often manifested. From the futuring experience, students could become increasingly aware of the development for random sampling, pilot studies, and measurements from certain instruments used to apply research methodologies. Understanding the basics behind verifying and validating data is critical to empirical research and evidence-based learning. All students should examine the perplexities and complexities of life that are hidden behind the numbers of quantitative research or the words of qualitative research. As mentioned earlier, the development of young scholars as futurists is an embryonic and cyclical process with students culminating their experiences from judgment and reasoning in the first several years of college to vocational connections later. The development of students expands across personal, academic, and professional stages, moving from understanding the foundations of research, to the fundamentals of research, to the refinement of research toward higher and wider orders of literacy.

Futuring should filter throughout the undergraduate experience. Exit interviews of students to determine their levels of futures literacy might serve the institution well in determining academic effectiveness and instructional efficiency. Becoming research literate will empower our students to make sound decisions, assess situations based on assembled data, resolve conflicting points of view, make choices, and choose alternatives substantiated by evidence and supported with data derived from quantitative and qualitative treatments of research. Finally, given the much-anticipated and predicted retirement, attrition, and exodus of the American professoriate, and the severe shortages of scientific researchers, college and university leaders should leverage the undergraduate curriculum to nurture students as first responders to this national crisis and empower students as next-generation futurists.[11]

This is an opportunity for HBCUs to encourage students to be futurists in today's higher education environment and the world arena. Whether students seek to be artists, activists, catalysts, liberators, change agents, investigators, pioneers, entrepreneurs, explorers, or innovators, HBCUs should also encourage them to build a foundation from futures studies and futurism. Indeed, today's HBCUs are strongly positioned to grow new generations of creators who anchor their work with pioneering thoughts that are sparked by imagination, sustained by perseverance, and endured by clarity of vision. The continued focus of HBCUs should be to empower student scholars to be forward-thinking leaders, without losing sight of their history (Sankofa) and not relegate them to institutionally banal and pedagogically conventional learning experiences that contribute to the status quo or become institutions that marginalize, devalue, or compromise the importance of historical and future contributions of African Americans.

Training HBCU students in futures acumen could lead to much-needed innovative business plans to boost changing economies of scale, new standards for ethical behavior, new cultural understanding in the physical and biological worlds, health innovations, educational innovations, new poverty research revelations for marginalized populations, new frontier techniques for emerging technologies, new entrepreneurial product development, and new scientific explorations in our vast, infinite universe. Futuring empowers undergraduate students to be thought-leaders from data-driven decision making and creative analysis for practical application in all of these areas.

HBCUs are no longer isolated to the local neighborhood and regional needs. HBCUs should react and respond to the new national agenda and global milieu and studying futures, anchored in profound FTOs and SLOs, or be empowering in this regard. In the new global academy, HBCUs must now respond to global demands and create pathways to careers that are workforce ready and industry relevant. Thus, they must continue to be locally responsive but globally responsible to new dimensions of academic life. Moreover, HBCUs need to work on being less competitive with one another and more collaborative with sharing resources by combining efforts for mutual mission benefit. The liberal arts disciplines at HBCUs need to do more together than apart. Public and private institutions, including non-HBCUs, can collaborate on regional and national needs in order to meet larger global imperatives. A central focus on futures studies across all liberal arts, especially at smaller, boutique liberal arts HBCUs like Miles College, Wiley College, Edward Waters College, and Tougaloo College, could have a powerful national influence throughout the nation's South. Liberal arts through the lens of futurism can be instrumental in this process, this development, and this manifestation.

HBCUs are not just measured ultimately by what their students do while they are enrolled on campuses. HBCUs are measured by what students do after they leave the campus, and again, studying futures can be empowering to this end. HBCUs must train students in futuring methods, data-driven, diagnostic, and prescriptive decision making before they graduate, in an effort to empower them with the research literacy they will need in the workplace or graduate school. The ability to compile, analyze, and judge data is critical to the lifelong adult learning of our students—personally, academically, professionally. In addition, with our usual academic aims for higher-order achievement in the curriculum, HBCUs must ignite creativity and stimulate the innovative thinking that this country needs. This, of course, will require students, staff, faculty, and administrators to move with a spirit of collaboration.

Whatever we have lost, forgotten, forgone, and been stripped of can be reclaimed, revived, preserved, and manifested through futures studies and the art and science of futurism. HBCUs must modernize their missions by moving forward with continuous retrospection in the evolutionary and revolutionary African dimensions of the Sankofa. Time is of the essence and of profound urgency for teaching and learning the liberal arts at HBCUs to re-engineer, reset, and restart with an eye toward the future.

Notes

1. Carl Bereiter, "Liberal Education in a Knowledge Society," in *Liberal Education in a Knowledge Society*, ed. Barry Smith (Illinois: Open Court, 2002), 13.

2. "The Future of Liberal Arts Education," Maryville University online, accessed December 2018, https://online.maryville.edu/liberal-arts-degrees/the-future-of-liberal-arts-education/.

3. "The Future of the Liberal Arts College in America and Its Leadership Role in Education around the World, April 9–11, 2012," Lafayette College online, accessed January 2019, https://sites.lafayette.edu/liberal-arts-conference/.

4. "The Future of the Liberal Arts: Report," Universities Canada online, 2016, https://www.univcan.ca/the-future-of-the-liberal-arts-report/; William Darden, "The Future of Liberal-Arts Colleges," 2008, https://steinhardt.nyu.edu/scmsAdmin/uploads/002/619/The%20Future%20of%20Libera%2323E3FC.pdf.

5. Edward Cornish, *Futuring: The Exploration of the Future* (World Future Society, 2004).

6. Cornish, *Futuring*, 78–79.

7. Cornish, *Futuring*, 79.

8. Cornish, *Futuring*, 79.

9. Gregersen, Hal. "Brainstorming: Focus and Questions, Not Answers, For Breakthrough Insights," *Harvard Business Review*, March–April 2018, 67.

10. M. P. Grady, *Qualitative and Action Research: A Practitioner Handbook* (Bloomington, IN: Phi Delta Kappa Intl., 1998).

11. Joseph Martin Stevenson, "Action Research, Liberal Arts Dimensions, the Master Student and Managing Knowledge," lecture and paper presented at Jackson State University School of Liberal Arts, 2001.

12. Joseph Martin Stevenson, "Founding Purpose to Future Positioning: Why HBCUs Must Maintain but Modify Mission," unpublished paper, 2008.

Bibliography

Anderson, Lorin, and David Krathwohl. *A Taxonomy for Learning, Teaching, and Assessing: A Revision of Bloom's Taxonomy of Educational Objectives*. New York: Longman, 2001.

Bereiter, Carl. "Liberal Education in a Knowledge Society." In *Liberal Education in a Knowledge Society*, edited by Barry Smith, 11–33 (Illinois: Open Court, 2002).

Bronson, Po, and Merryman, Ashley. "The Creativity Crisis." *Newsweek*. July 19, 2010. www.newsweek.com/2010/07/10/the-creativity-crisis.html.

Cornish, Edward. *Futuring: The Exploration of the Future*. Bethesda, MD: World Future Society, 2004.

Darden, William. "The Future of Liberal-Arts Colleges." 2008. https://steinhardt.nyu.edu/scmsAdmin/uploads/002/619/The%20Future%20of%20Libera%2323E3FC.pdf.

"The Future of the Liberal Arts College in America and Its Leadership Role in Education around the World, April 9–11, 2012." Lafayette College online. Accessed January 2019. https://sites.lafayette.edu/liberal-arts-conference/.

"The Future of Liberal Arts Education." Maryville University online. Accessed December 2018, https://online.maryville.edu/liberal-arts-degrees/the-future-of-liberal-arts-education/.

"The Future of the Liberal Arts: Report." Universities Canada online. 2016. https://www.univcan.ca/the-future-of-the-liberal-arts-report/.

Grady, Michael. *Qualitative and Action Research: A Practitioner Handbook*. Bloomington, IN: Phi Delta Kappa Intl., 1998.

Gregersen, Hal. "Brainstorming: Focus on Questions, Not Answers, for Breakthrough Insights." *Harvard Business Review*, March–April 2018, 64–71.

Helmer-Hirschberg, Olaf. *Analysis of the Future: The Delphi Method*. California: RAND Corporation, 1967. http://www.rand.org/pubs/papers/P3558.

Navarro, Joe. *Louder than Words: Take Your Career from Average to Exceptional with the Hidden Power of Nonverbal Intelligence*. New York: HarperCollins, 2010.

Navarro, Joe, and Marvin Karlins. "Body Language of the Hands: What the Hands Say Is Often Louder than Words!" *Psychology Today*, Jan. 20, 2010.

Navarro, Joe, and Marvin Karlins. *What Every Body Is Saying: An Ex-FBI Agent's Guide to Speed-Reading People*. New York: William Morrow/HarperCollins, 2008. https://www.psychologytoday.com/blog/spycatcher/201001/body-language-the-hands.

Schwartz, Barry. "Intellectual Virtues." *Chronicle of Higher Education* 61, no. 39, June 18, 2015, B6–B9. http://chronicle.com/article/Intellectual-virtues/230965/.

Stevenson, Joseph Martin. "Action Research, Liberal Arts Dimensions, The Master Student And Managing Knowledge." Lecture and paper presented at Jackson State University School of Liberal Arts, 2001.

Stevenson, Joseph Martin. *The Engrossed Entrepreneurial Campus: What Our Nation Needs Now Anew*. Washington, DC: Academica Press, 2007.

Stevenson, Joseph Martin. "Founding Purpose to Future Positioning: Why HBCUs Must Maintain but Modify Mission." Unpublished paper, 2008.

Sukel, Kayt, ed. *The Brain: The Ultimate Guide*. N.p.: Ben Harris, 2015

CONCLUSION

Redefining Liberal Arts Education

Challenges and Opportunities

MARIO J. AZEVEDO

Today, the state of the liberal arts and their future direction needs reflection, open intellectual discussion, and a heightened understanding of student welfare. We are at the crossroads from which we can either go down the slippery road of decline and oblivion or rise to new heights that will make the liberal arts second to none. Notwithstanding the changes that have occurred around the globe over the past centuries, when we have seen our knowledge double every seven years, liberal arts education has, in most part, survived.

As the repository of liberal arts education and the preservers of the arts, we are the first line of defense against ignorance, bigotry, religious intolerance, and xenophobia in the name of freedom, brotherhood, universalism, nonexclusivist humanity, and the pursuit of happiness. Thomas Jefferson once wrote of ignorance: "If a nation expects to be ignorant and free in a state of civilization, it expects what never was, and never will be." The Association of American Colleges and Universities defines liberal arts education as "an approach to college learning that empowers individuals and prepares them to deal with complexity, diversity, and change," emphasizing "broad knowledge of the wider world (that is, science, culture, society), as well as in-depth achievement in a specific field of interest."[1] However, a liberal arts education does much more: it helps the student or the disciple (thus the word "discipline" and its canons) instill a sense of responsibility as well as strong intellectual and practical skills that span all major fields of study.

As Mortimer Adler noted on liberal education, where he clearly differentiated liberal arts from liberal education: "The liberal arts are traditionally intended to develop the faculties of the human mind, those powers of intelligence and imagination without which no intellectual work can be accomplished. Liberal education is not tied to certain academic subjects, such as philosophy, history, language, normally Greek and Latin, literature, music, and art. In the liberal arts tradition, the scientific disciplines, such as mathematics and physics, [were] considered equally liberal, that is, equally able to develop the powers of the mind." The designation of liberal arts comes from the Latin words *liber*, meaning free, and *artes* (*ars*, *artes*, plural), which included philosophy, literature, history, politics or government, languages, ethics, and science, such as mathematics and biology. Hence, at many universities, the sciences tend to be housed in the colleges or schools of arts and sciences.[2]

The learning tools for students in the liberal arts have included the skills for critical thinking and problem-solving, writing, the art of speaking, reading with comprehension, and research. These prepared the individual not just to be successful in a trade or professional career but to be an all-around educated and literate individual. The ultimate targeted outcome of liberal arts is the application of skills learned to benefit the common good, thus the importance of civic learning and the acquisition of a sense of social and individual responsibility. Several distinguished scholars in the liberal arts have shown how the arts can be strengthened to be relevant to the ever-changing times in a college setting and can stress civic engagement to cultivate professional skills, a theme that is said to be closely correlated to vocational pathways within the context and the value of the liberal arts. In our colleges today, the impact of learning on society and vice versa expressed in civic engagement is often neglected when it should stand out as a priority. Civic engagement is characterized by Amy Koritz, Paul Shadewald, and Haddassah St. Hubert as the habit of "working to make a difference in the life of the community" and combining "knowledge, skills, values, and motivation."[3] It means promoting the quality of life in a community through both political and nonpolitical processes. In addition, civic engagement encompasses actions wherein individuals participate in activities of personal and public concern that are both individually enriching and socially beneficial.

In this context the authors recall the study conducted by William Sullivan, which, linking professional identity with public responsibilities, makes the liberal arts more relevant, as it involves several critical apprenticeships: intellectual training, which provides foundational academic knowledge; skills for professional development as practitioners; and an understanding of the complexities and exigencies of the real world, combined with an "apprenticeship of purpose that helps students understand and internalize the ethical standards and larger pubic purposes through which their work serves the public and contributes to the social good."[4]

Critics say that one of the major obstacles to the relevance of the liberal arts has been a tendency on the part of some scholars and artists to focus on the primacy of knowledge for knowledge's sake. In that sense, their academic training "define[s] their professional lives primarily in relation to the disciplinary norms and practices learned in graduate school," neglecting or outright rejecting what is external to "institutional expectations and reward systems."[5] Such a one-sided academic tendency results not only in deficient student training for life outside the walls of the university but in the neglect of community needs, which provide further opportunities for intellectual engagement and growth. Indeed, the resources the community can provide are many, and sitting in the tower and simply looking at the communities below obliterates the responsibility universities have in improving the immediate needs of the communities surrounding them and of others beyond their physical reach.

In earlier times, beginning with the Greeks and the Romans, the teaching of liberal arts was sequential. First taught was the *trivium*, which consisted of grammar, rhetoric, and logic. The *quadrivium* focused on arithmetic, geometry, astronomy, and music. This tradition has continued in Europe, especially in Germany. However, over the years, pessimism has crept slowly into academia.

Recently, Liz Coleman, in "A Call to Re-Invent Liberal Education," wrote: "Liberal arts education no longer exists—at least genuine liberal arts education—in this country." We have "professionalized liberal arts to the point where they no longer provide the breadth of application and the enhanced capacity for civic engagement that is their signature." In fact, in her view, "the expert has dethroned the educated generalist to become the sole model of intellectual accomplishment," the reason why STEM has become so appealing. Coleman adds: "Oversimplification of civic engagement, idealization of the expert, fragmentation of knowledge, emphasis on technical mastery, and neutrality as a condition of academic integrity—is toxic when it comes to pursuing the vital connections between education and the public good, between intellectual integrity and human freedom, which were at the heart [of liberal arts]."[6] Readers and listeners would not disagree that little mastery of skills and a bare minimum of cultural literacy have become the benchmark of many institutions and colleges of liberal arts, even though no dichotomy should exist between studying the classical arts and finding a job.

In other words, knowledge for knowledge's sake is not a waste of time. It is a lifelong human endeavor that makes us complete and fully human. People have often said—wisely, I think—that a half-educated man is more dangerous than a nonliterate man. Today, the impression is that thousands of students are abandoning the liberal arts and rushing to major in the professions and in engineering and technology because of the lucrative returns promised them. However, we in the liberal arts forget that we are the ones who impart skills to them so that they can understand their majors and succeed in their careers. The debate over which is more important—the liberal arts or the natural science disciplines—and which is financially more lucrative for individual sustainability and the common good has gone on for a long time.

The Association of American Colleges and Universities (AAC&U) further informs us that "by coupling a field-specific skill set with the soft skills that form the foundation of a liberal education, liberal arts graduates can nearly double the number of jobs available to them."[7] In fact, humanities students are as prepared for the workforce as their classmates in fields such as business. However, it appears that they do not seem to have higher aspirations for more lucrative careers, possibly due to the way they are conditioned in college regarding the value of liberal arts outside the university.

Colleges will do a much better job preparing liberal arts students for careers and lucrative positions if they are open-minded and employ innovative professors. David Attis, managing director of the Education Advisory Board, notes, for example, that one way to make liberal arts students more competitive is "adding at least one field-specific skill set, including marketing, graphic design, or computer programming." Indeed, experience seems to prove that adoption of some initiatives has done wonders among students seeking employment such as opportunities for integrated career exploration through for-credit courses, career-aligned tracks within liberal arts majors, programs that encourage liberal arts majors to obtain supplementary certificates from on-campus professional schools, and cocurricular opportunities to integrate work experience with academic coursework. For Attis, "It's important to remember that these [salary] metrics average over many students with many different outcomes, backgrounds, and goals." Attis writes, "The university and the major are not the most important factors responsible for graduates' salaries (though they are the easiest to measure)." A 2010 study conducted by the Obama administration estimated that people who held jobs without high school training earned $24,300 per year. With a high school education, that number grew to $33,800, and, with a bachelor's degree, it was $55,700 and went on up to $100,000 with having a professional degree.[8]

A 1977 American survey of CEOs indicated that employers were more focused on the long-term outcomes of education, such as adaptability, than were college students and their parents, who were more concerned with the short-term outcomes of getting a job. Employers are now seeking qualified graduates who have a broad base of knowledge, whose undergraduate experience has granted them "the critical thinking skills, and an understanding and appreciation of diversity, ethical issues, and service to others." Problem-solving skills are learned systematically in the liberal arts, provided by an education that is "a result of the equal development of the right and left side of the brain," according to Bob Murray, dean of enrollment management at Illinois Wesleyan University. Murray further states that *artes liberals* "denote a curriculum that imparts general knowledge and develops the student's rational thought and intellectual capabilities, unlike the professional, vocational and technical curricula emphasizing specialization." Differently put by David Kogler, associate director for admission at Gustavus Adolphus College in Minnesota, "Instead of learning only about business at a business school, a liberal arts degree will teach you about business, the history of business, politics and other areas that influence and shape the world of business."[9]

Writing in 2014, Scott Cohen said: "The liberal arts are in trouble, and have been for a long time," but David Breneman had first mapped out the ongoing transition of liberal arts colleges to more vocationally oriented "professional colleges." Indeed, in 1990 Breneman's study had revealed that there were 212 "true liberal arts colleges," but by 2012, there was a drop to 130. In other words, the human sciences "no longer play the central, cohesive role in the curriculum that they once did."[10]

The statements of politicians like governors Pete McCrory of North Carolina and Rick Scott of Florida have been particularly discouraging. In 2013 McCrory put it crudely: the success of college education "is not based on butts in seats but on how many of those butts can get jobs." Rick Scott said in 2012: "I want money to go to degrees where people can get jobs in this state" and not to liberal arts colleges, which are a luxury. Kentucky governor Matt Bevin advocates subsidizing electrical engineering students but not those enrolled in French literature, just as Marco Rubio, failed presidential candidate, said that the US needed "more welders and fewer philosophers."[11] Apparently, many politicians never received a strong liberal arts education when they attended college, perhaps the reason why they chose politics over other careers.

Sharla Rausch, a PhD psychologist, who led the research in the so-called harder science in the US Department of Homeland Security's Science and Technology Directorate, had a few important comments about the sociobehavioral sciences compared to the natural sciences. Rausch is surrounded daily by all kinds of strategists, scientists, federal agents, psychologists, sociologists, biometric experts, and others, to study devious behavior that can lead to terrorism. On the controversy over the superiority of the so-called harder versus the softer sciences, she says poignantly. "It's [social science] the harder science," meaning the most difficult to understand and research. "Chemicals can predict," she adds. "People are another story."[12] This speaks to the unending debate about the superiority of STEM disciplines.

As Carol Schneider notes, "The challenge now confronting campuses is to turn what have been topical discussions about general education into continuing forums for faculty attention to the curriculum as a whole." However, the danger with episodic curriculum engagements and goals is that "without a continuing dialogue about what a requirement seeks to achieve and how well these goals are being met, an institution's new general education program may soon become little more than a rhetorical artifact of the catalog." In this context, Schneider argues that "the major as a home of liberal learning has many responsibilities, including: an obligation to help students learn a particular field, but an equally important obligation to help their learning across disparate fields."[13] This, I think, is what many liberal arts colleges are lacking. As I tell my history students, especially my honors students, the importance of studying history lies in the ability or skill to link the past with the present, and the present with the past and discern either continuity or disruption.

What are the remedial models that have been advocated in the face of the alleged demise of the liberal arts? I can only point to a few. In an article titled "Taking It to the Streets: Preparing for an Academy in Exile," Johann Neem discusses four models. First is Adam Smith's model developed in his 1776 *Wealth of Nations*, the precursor of the capitalist system we worship today. In his book Adam characterized the faculty as "lazy and ineffective," a fault of our universities. His point was that faculty should get their jobs only once they have proved that they are great lecturers. The second would be the establishment of small, intimate liberal arts colleges, "closer to the original American colleges whose origins can be found in the 17th to 18th century dissenting academies established in England as alternatives to Oxford and Cambridge."[14] This is a difficult task, as we have seen some liberal arts colleges vanish.

The third option has been called the "yoga" liberal arts college, a result of academicians abandoning the university, because the latter has become completely corrupt or vocational, relying on grants from private institutions or the government. The fourth type is one where academics rely solely on philanthropy "in order to create teaching and research centers oriented toward specific themes or goals." The fifth, proposed by Scott Cohen, is the "boutique" liberal arts model. Defying the pernicious impact of the now-trendy "common core," many in the academy contend that it will lead to a collapse of the liberal arts curriculum by "threatening to erode the arts through funneling students into instrumental learning regimes and perpetual assessment, thereby sending colleges and universities a new generation of students who will have had less of a liberal education in high school than perhaps any previous generation of students in this nation's recent history."[15] The last option, which places all blame and responsibility for the demise of the liberal arts on the doorsteps of you and me, asks for a fundamental change in our modus operandi, especially in the classroom.

Leon Botstein, president of Bard College, professor of arts and humanities, music director, and principal conductor of the American Symphony Orchestra, has much to say about the issue. Botstein demonstrates that, over the past fifty years, the winners of the Nobel Prize in science have been individuals with strong backgrounds in the humanities and social sciences as well as the arts, which goes to show that "no breakthroughs and discoveries occur 'without pioneers whose ambitions are fueled by matters outside the realm of science and technology narrowly defined.'" There are no illiterate scientists, and "all the decisive progress in science—the essential bedrock of technological and economic change [he says]—is a high order of literacy." Noting that it is not true that students come to college just to prepare for a job, Botstein points out that most enroll to learn about the challenges of the world and are curious about issues of "the environment, genetic inheritance, disease, poverty, and inequality, even boredom . . ., humor, beauty, communities, and the past."[16]

To Botstein, the problem of the liberal arts has essentially been the "delivery system." He observes that we can beat the "crisis of confidence in the liberal arts and humanities by reforming our teaching and by stopping from preaching. We place the liberal arts in peril by not integrating the sciences and mathematics (and that includes computer science) into the substance of the humanities and social sciences." In fact, he further notes, we need to realize that "the reform that is needed is not cosmetic but fundamental in terms of the organization of faculty and the curriculum. The relevance and utility—let alone the substance—of the liberal arts (which include the sciences) are not in danger. The danger lies only in the way we go about making the case and delivering on the promise of liberal education."[17] I think we at Jackson State University have begun that process seriously with the whole curriculum review in our College of Liberal Arts, but that cannot be done properly in three months. It must continue to be a deliberate, permanent, and engaging process. On the other hand, technology, reflected in cyber learning, if we embrace it correctly, can only enhance the revival and success of liberal arts education. However, for the liberal arts to succeed and survive, they cannot rely entirely on online, impersonalized courses that rob teachers the opportunity to know the students firsthand.

Summarizing what most employers prefer in their workforce regardless of majors, one might list the following priority skills: problem solving, civic knowledge and application in the real world, judgment "essential for contributing to our democratic society," broad knowledge of liberal arts and science, intercultural skills, and awareness of world societies. Employers note that these can be strengthened by applied learning, which may be obtained from internships, theses, dissertations, good writing derived from several courses, group projects, community service, and fieldwork.[18] Thus, job security for liberal arts majors and others enrolled in four-year liberal arts colleges may not be as bleak as often portrayed by politicians and pessimistic academicians, especially those in the so-called hard sciences and by a large number of students' parents.

The reason for the pessimistic forecasts lies also in the way we in liberal arts prepare our students. We often see ourselves as the foundation of excellence, meaning not just that we keep the sacred tradition of providing the fundamental and foundational skills but that we incorporate innovative approaches and teach a set of skills that sharpen and expand the opportunities of success for our students. It is evident now for those who read the relevant literature that the set of extra skills needed to succeed includes critical thinking, effective verbal and written communication, and problem-solving along with such other skills as marketability, business entrepreneurship, general knowledge, adoption of good social media strategies, advanced analysis, basic statistics—similar to those provided to students in public health—exposure to sound socio-behavioral science methodology, and IT networking with similar programs.

Throughout the entire process of preparing liberal arts college students, therefore, one needs to always keep pace with innovative ideas adopted and tried at similar colleges designed to enhance and benefit student opportunities in the workplace. In an article written in *Opinion*, managers of the Higher Education Practice at Huron Consulting Group similarly put the blame on the colleges of liberal arts themselves and not on the politicians or the media. For them, the major culprit in the potential demise of liberal arts colleges is the organizational structure of the colleges. They hold the view that "challenge has less to do with media perceptions or careless politicizing than with traditional organizational structures and curricular approaches of schools of liberal arts." On this, they cite faculty reluctance and inflexibility to meet the changing market expectations, departmental structures that constrain "the evolution of and effectiveness of general-education curricula," and resistance to necessary organizational workaround, such as the creation of interdisciplinary liberal arts centers and institutes to find a home for innovation, "as hubs of cross-discipline engagement, for faculty and students alike."[19]

Unfortunately, in the effort to make liberal arts education relevant and help the students achieve the goal of landing employment, faculty members are usually left out of the equation, when they should be considered one of the most critical factors in any successful innovation in the liberal arts academy. The university must specifically and deliberately address the needs and responsibilities of the faculty in their effort to make liberal arts education relevant and save it from the onslaught it receives daily from politicians and other less informed individuals in the academy. Faculty retooling and varied opportunities for further education in liberal arts are critical elements that guarantee the success of our students. Policies must be made clear to the faculty as well as changes in university classification status, such as JSU moving to the category of a higher research activity institution according to the Carnegie Foundation. Those policies should result in infusion of new resources and announcements of concomitant new directions in pedagogy, research, and service for the twenty-first century.

The reasons for the need of faculty engagement are obvious: "Their colleges are changing, their students are different, their disciplines are expanding and deepening, and their campuses are faced with external forces that require them to leave the lab or classroom and become engaged in the general problems," all of which could result "in more interdisciplinary, collaborative, innovation-friendly campuses," embracing "strategies that make the boundaries of learning more permeable—for everyone, including faculty—better aligned with campus goals." Deliberate attention to faculty roles should result in meaningful and enlightened curriculum reform. Approaches such as retooling faculty would fill the need for academic community involvement "across disciplines, and between the traditionally bounded domains of teaching, research, and service," and would reflect a "fundamentally epistemological position underlying the shift in the locus of education to include the community."[20]

A good example of how to take into account the importance of the needs and involvement of faculty is illustrated by the liberal arts curriculum changes enacted at Hamilton College in Fall 2017, where students have to take and pass either a course or a combination of courses that focuses on "the structural or intellectual hierarchies based on one or more of the social categories of race, class, gender, ethnicity, nationality, religion, sexuality, age, and abilities/disabilities to complete their concentrations or majors." The students have the freedom to choose the class they wish to take, an idea that the majority of the faculty, the students, and the administration were able to buy into. For example, a student in math might wish to enroll in a class that explores the "statistical probability of social mobility of minorities, while a student majoring in physics could take a class that delves into how ideologies and religions look into such topics as the origins or creation of the universe." In spite of these innovations, Hamilton still mandates that its students take three writing-intensive courses in liberal arts and stresses for its students the ability to "identify, understand, and use quantitative arguments in everyday contexts," which requires taking a course in quantitative and symbolic reasoning.[21]

This approach to the emerging, sharpening, and expansion of students' intercollegiate skills can be illustrated through the case of students majoring in engineering, who often see courses in liberal arts as unnecessary requisites, irrelevant to their futures. In reality, however, they do not realize that design is connected to creativity, working together with others, thinking beyond the discipline or out-of-the-box, and an awareness of the need to take into account the socio-behavioral, political, and economic context of any project. As Loni Bordoloi and James J. Winebrake note, "Engineering today needs to help students devise innovative solutions for a complex world while also anticipating their potential unintended consequences," an approach that relies on a liberal arts education and emphasizes critical thinking, effective communication, and cultural understanding, thus helping students see their role in the world as "ethical professionals equipped to define the contours—technical, economic, social, cultural—of the challenges at hand and devise solutions accordingly." Interestingly, on the need for liberal arts skills and those required in technological advances, Steve Jobs once said: "It's in Apple's DNA that technology alone is not enough—that it's technology married with liberal arts, married with the humanities, that yields us the result that makes our hearts sing."[22]

Many universities, including Jackson State University, are proud of their mission of training and preparing global citizens who can compete successfully in today's technological world. These will be civic individuals who will feel and act as true global citizens wherever they might travel or live. In this context, Martha Nussbaum argues that our higher education needs to "build a rich network of human connections in order to shape future democratic citizens who are poised to make decisions based on their understanding of gender, ethnic, racial, sexual, and religious diversity," fostered and nurtured by "cultural self-examination and examination of one's own traditions, thinking as a citizen of the world, and exercising a 'narrative imagination' that allows one to see the world through the eyes of others."[23]

For such liberal arts defenders as Fareed Zakaria, the usefulness of liberal education lies in that it remains relevant no matter which employment one might land in life. In this vein, he advises students that "specific subjects of study are irrelevant to the changes occurring as a result of new technology (i.e., of apps and mobile devices) in our day-to-day work because what was good 10 years ago is probably irrelevant today. What remain constant are the skills you acquire and the methods you learn to approach problems." For Zakaria, "Given how quickly industries and professions are evolving these days, you will need to apply these skills to new challenges all the time. Learning and re-learning, tooling and retooling are the heart of the modern economy."[24]

In Ernest Henninger's opinion, our problem is not that we do not use new technologies. Instead, "the challenge our nation faces is not a lack of technological innovation. The challenge is our unwillingness and inability to anticipate, evaluate and manage our technologies ... In a survey of former pre-engineering students, I got the following response, 'You don't have to know Shakespeare to build a bridge, but you'll build a better bridge if you do.'"[25]

At Xerox in 2002, David Kearns said, "The only education that prepares us for change is liberal education. In periods of change, narrow specialization condemns us to inflexibility—precisely what we do not want. We need the flexible intellectual tools to be problem solvers, to be able to continue learning over time." As Fareed Zakaria has written, "Tasks that have proved most vexing to automate are those that demand flexibility, judgment, and common sense—skills that we understand only tacitly—for example, developing a hypothesis or organizing a closet."[26] With a liberal arts education, we ask critical questions seeking solutions in the tradition of Socrates and other philosophers. Voltaire underscored this point by saying that one can tell a literate man from an ignorant man not by the answers he gives but by the questions he asks.

We are reminded that the community might be a partial solution to our problems. There are observers and experts who think that a college cannot thrive without turning its attention to the community for support for a more relevant problem-solving effort and a higher enrollment number. Ira Arkavey argues, "By focusing on solving universal problems that are manifested in their local communities, institutions of higher learning will be better able to reduce the 'ancient costumes and habitudes' impeding college and university community engagement, advanced research, teaching, learning, and service, and they will be better able to realize Benjamin Franklin and Ernest Boyer's revolutionary vision for a higher education of active engagement and service."²⁷ What we do in the colleges of liberal arts is expose students to humanity's centuries of collective experience and wisdom and let them interject their own experience and wisdom, enabled by their own reflection and their own endowed abilities, which we should try to reinforce systematically in the classroom.

What, then, should we be doing to prepare students for the future so that they may fit in the rapid changes taking place in today's world? Researchers at the Institute for the Future have identified ten skills that graduates will need in order to succeed in the workplace:

1. One will be "sense-making," or higher-level thinking skills that cannot be codified, "or the sense-making skills that help us create unique insights critical to decision-making." Students must reach a level of higher cognition and thinking skills to succeed in the future, and liberal arts educators ought to keep this in mind if they wish to be relevant.
2. Needed as well is what the institute calls social intelligence, or the "ability to connect to others in a deep and direct way, to sense and stimulate reactions and desired interactions." Why? Because "socially intelligent employees are able to quickly assess the emotions of those around them and adapt their words, tone and gestures accordingly," thus gaining different insights and fighting parochialism, exclusivity, and ethnocentric and racial tendencies.
3. Important also is what the Institute for the Future calls "novel and adaptive thinking," defined as "proficiency at thinking and coming up with solutions and responses beyond that which is rote or rule-based."
4. Another important skill for the next decade is cross-cultural competency, which is the "ability to operate in different cultural settings," given that studies have shown that "what makes a group truly intelligent and innovative is the combination of different ages, skills, disciplines, and working and thinking skills that members bring to the table."
5. Computational skills are another must, since many employees are unable to work in the absence of algorithms in the workplace, paralyzing everything that needs to be done to make the workplace work, even when machines break down.
6. Equally important is new-media literacy, which will force people to be "fluent in forms such as video, able to critically 'read' and assess them in the same way that they currently assess a paper or presentation."

7. Next is the need for transdisciplinary collaboration, or "literacy in and ability to understand concepts across multiple disciplines." The authors believe that "the ideal worker of the next decade is 'T-shaped'— they bring deep understanding of at least one field, but they have the capacity to converse in the language of a broader range of disciplines."
8. Students will also need to have a design mind-set that is able to adapt to changes in tasks and to a new environment while they try to innovate it simultaneously.
9. Students will need "cognitive load management," or the "ability to discriminate and filter information for importance, and to understand how to maximize cognitive functioning using a variety of tools and techniques."
10. Lastly, virtual collaboration has become a critical component of any task that needs to be done, including the "ability to work productively, drive engagement, and demonstrate presence as a member of a virtual team," through such activities as micro blogging and social networking in a common field of training and experience.[28]

However, and in conclusion, it is important to remember that, in a college of liberal arts setting, all these needed initiatives require that they be embraced and understood by faculty, administrators, and students alike, where willingness to change is a must; where adaptation to new academic and market demands is considered and met; where the structure is amenable to the abandonment of the silo disciplinary model that perpetuates isolation and parochialism; and where individual perspectives are considered and accepted, if valid and applicable to the complex requirements today.

Notes

1. *Thomas* Jefferson *to Charles Yancey, January 6*, 1816, Manuscript/Mixed Material Library of Congress, https://www.loc.gov/item/mtjbib022264/; Association of American Colleges and Universities, "What Is a 21st Century Liberal Education?," 2007, https://www.aacu.org/leap/what-is-a-liberal-education, 1–4.

2. Mortimer Adler, "Great Ideas from the Great Books," in The Great Ideas Online, Center for the Study of Great Ideas, no. 349 (November 2005). https://www.thegreatideas.org/Tulinwlw/TGIO349.pdf.

3. Amy Koritz and Paul Schadewald, "Civic Professionalism: A Pathway to Practical Wisdom for the Liberal Arts," *Imagining America: Artists and Scholars in Public Life*, 2016: 1–29. https://imaginingamerica.org/wp-content/uploads/CivicProfessionalismWP.pdf, 6.

4. Koritz and Schadewald, "Civic Professionalism," 6.

5. Koritz and Paul Schadewald, "Civic Professionalism," 10.

6. Liz Coleman, "A Call to Re-Invent Liberal Arts" (New York: TED 2009), https://www.ted.com/talks/liz_coleman_a_call_to_reinvent_liberal_arts_education?language=en.

7. "The Art of Employment: How Liberal Arts Graduates Can Improve Their Labor Market Prospects," Burning Glass Technologies, Careers in Focus, August 2013, https://www.burning-glass.com/wp-content/uploads/BGTReportLiberalArts.pdf.

8. David Attis, "Busting Myths about the Liberal Arts," *EAB News*, September 22, 2016, 1–3; Frank Chong, Martha Kanter, Rosemarie Nassif, and Eduardo Ochoa, "Meeting President Obama's 2020 College Completion Goal," Report for the U.S. Department of Education, July 21, 2011, http://www.ed.gov/sites/default/files/winning-the-future.ppt.

9. Bob Murray, "What Are the Liberal Arts?," Illinois Wesleyan University, institutional description, 2016, https://www.iwu.edu/admissions/LiberalArts.html; Shresta Shraddha, "Liberal Arts, Why Not!," *Republica*, September 1, 2016.

10. Scott Cohen, "The Boutique Liberal Arts," *Liberal Education* 100, no. 4 (Fall 2014): 60–69; Edgar Bronfman, "Business and the Liberal Arts," *Inside Higher Ed*, October 17, 2013, 1.

11. "STEM Education Is Vital—But Not at the Expense of the Humanities," *Scientific American*, October 2016, 1–8, https://www.scientificamerican.com/article/stem-education-is-vital-but-not-at-the-expense-of-the-humanities/.

12. John S. Verrico, "A Sociologist Tackles Homeland Security," *ASA Footnotes* 37, no. 5 (May–June 2009), http://www.asanet.org/sites/default/files/savvy/footnotes/mayjun09/sras_0509.html.

13. Carol Geary Schneider, "Challenge and Response: Integrity and AAC&U's Reform Initiatives (1985–1994)," *Liberal Education* 100, no. 4 (Fall 2014): 28–37.

14. Johann Neem, "Taking It to the Streets: Preparing for an Academy in Exile," *Liberal Education* 100, no. 4 (Fall 2014): 54–59.

15. Cohen, "Boutique Liberal Arts."

16. Leon Botstein, "Learning Is Like Sex and Other Reasons the Liberal Arts Will Remain Relevant," *Hechinger Report*, January 8, 2015.

17. Botstein, "Learning Is Like Sex."

18. Hart Research Associates, "Falling Short? College Learning and Career Success," Selected Findings from Online Surveys of Employers and College Students on Behalf of the Association of American College and Universities, 2015, https://www.aacu.org/leap/public-opinion-research/2015-survey-results.

19. Peter Stokes and Chris Slatter, "Liberal Arts, Inflexible Structures," *Inside Higher Education*, September 19, 2016, Opinion/Views, 1–9.

20. P. Jonathan Rossing and Melissa R. Lavitt, "The Neglected Learner: A Call to Support Integrative Learning for Faculty," *Liberal Education* 102, no. 2 (Spring 2016): 34–41.

21. Henry Shuldiner, "The Liberal Arts in the Real World," *Chronicle of Higher Education*, August 5, 2016, 1–4.

22. Loni M. Bordoloi and James J. Winebrake, "Bringing the Liberal Arts to Engineering Education," *Chronicle of Higher Education*, May 1, 2015, A26; "STEM Education Is Vital—But Not at the Expense of the Humanities," *Scientific American*, October 2016, 1–8, https://www.scientificamerican.com/article/stem-education-is-vital-but-not-at-the-expense-of-the-humanities/.

23. Michelle Dawn Whitehead, "Global Learning: Key to Making Excellence Inclusive," *Liberal Education* 101, no. 3 (Summer 2015): 6–13.

24. Fareed Zakaria, *In Defense of a Liberal Education* (New York: Norton, 2015).

25. Ernest Henninger, "STEM Grads Need Broad Education to Succeed in Life," *Lexington Herald Leader*, March 4, 2016, https://www.kentucky.com/opinion/op-ed/article 64126557.html.

26. Association of American Colleges and Universities, National Panel Report, "Greater Expectations: A New Vision for Learning as a Nation Goes to College," 2002; Fareed Zakaria, "Why America's Obsession with STEM Education Is Dangerous," *Washington Post*, March 26, 2015, 1–5.

27. Ira Arkavey, "Creating the Connected Institution: Toward Realizing Benjamin Franklin and Ernest Boyer's Revolutionary Vision for American Higher Education," *Liberal Education* 101, no. 1 (Winter/Spring 2015): 38–47.

28. Anna Davies, Devin Fidler, and Marina Gorbis, "Future Work Skills 2020," Palo Alto, California, Institute for the Future, University of Phoenix Research Institute, 2011, 1–14, https://www.iftf.org/uploads/media/SR-1382A_UPRI_future_work_skills_sm.pdf.

Bibliography

Adler, Mortimer. "Great Ideas from the Great Books." In *The Great Ideas Online*. Center for the Study of Great Ideas, no. 349 (November 2005). https://www.thegreatideas.org/Tulinwlw/TGIO349.pdf.

Arkavey, Ira. "Creating the Connected Institution: Toward Realizing Benjamin Franklin and Ernest Boyer's Revolutionary Vision for American Higher Education." *Liberal Education* 101, no. 1 (Winter/Spring 2015): 38–47.

"The Art of Employment: How Liberal Arts Graduates Can Improve Their Labor Market Prospects." Burning Glass Technologies. Careers in Focus. August 2013. https://www.burning-glass.com/wp-content/uploads/BGTReportLiberalArts.pdf.

Association of American Colleges and Universities. National Panel Report. "Greater Expectations: A New Vision for Learning as a Nation Goes to College." 2002.

Association of American Colleges and Universities. "What Is a 21st Century Liberal Education?" 2007. https://www.aacu.org/leap/what-is-a-liberal-education.

Attis, David. "Busting Myths about the Liberal Arts." *EAB News*, September 22, 2016, 1–3.

Azevedo, Mario. *Africana Studies: A Survey of Africa and the African Diaspora*. Durham, NC: Carolina Academic Press, 2005.

Bordoloi, Loni M., and James J. Winebrake. "Bringing the Liberal Arts to Engineering Education." *Chronicle of Higher Education*, May 1, 2015, A26.

Botstein, Leon. "Learning Is Like Sex and Other Reasons the Liberal Arts Will Remain Relevant." *Hechinger Report*, January 8, 2015.

Bronfman, Edgar. "Business and the Liberal Arts," *Inside Higher Ed*, October 17, 2013, 1.

Buttler, Don. "Selling the (Underappreciated) Value of a Liberal Arts Education," *Ottawa Citizen*, March 15, 2016, 1–6.

Carnevale, Anthony, and Debra Humphreys. "The Economic Case for Liberal Education." Report for the Association of American Colleges and Universities. May 4, 2016. https://www.aacu.org/leap/economiccase.

Chong, Frank, Martha Kanter, Rosemarie Nassif, and Eduardo Ochoa. "Meeting President Obama's 2020 College Completion Goal." Report for the U.S. Department of Education, July 21, 2011. http://www.ed.gov/sites/default/files/winning-the-future.ppt.

Cicarelly, Saundra, J. Noland White. *Psychology*. New York: Pearson Learning Solutions, 2015.

Cohen, Scott. "The Boutique Liberal Arts." *Liberal Education* 100, no. 4 (Fall 2014): 60–69.

Coleman, Liz. "A Call to Re-Invent Liberal Arts." New York: TED 2009. https://www.ted.com/talks/liz_coleman_a_call_to_reinvent_liberal_arts_education?language=en

Davies, Anna, Devin Fidler, and Marina Gorbis. "Future Work Skills 2020." Palo Alto, California: Institute for the Future, University of Phoenix Research Institute, 2011, 1–14. https://www.iftf.org/uploads/media/SR-1382A_UPRI_future_work_skills_sm.pdf.

Falke, Cassandra. "John Henry Newman and Today's Liberal Arts Community." *Modern Language Studies* 36, no. 1 (Summer 2006): 54–60.

Hart Research Associates. "Falling Short? College Learning and Career Success." Selected Findings from Online Surveys of Employers and College Students on Behalf of the Association of American College and Universities. 2015. https://www.aacu.org/leap/public-opinion-research/2015-survey-results.

Henninger, Ernest. "STEM Grads Need Broad Education to Succeed in Life." *Lexington Herald Leader*, March 4, 2016. https://www.kentucky.com/opinion/op-ed/article64126557.html.

Koritz, Amy, and Paul Schadewald. "Civic Professionalism: A Pathway to Practical Wisdom for the Liberal Arts." *Imagining America: Artists and Scholars in Public Life*, 2016: 1–29. https://imaginingamerica.org/wp-content/uploads/CivicProfessionalismWP.pdf.

Murray, Bob. 2016. "What Are the Liberal Arts?" Institutional description. Illinois Wesleyan University. 2016. https://www.iwu.edu/admissions/LiberalArts.html.

Neem, Johann. "Taking It to the Streets: Preparing for an Academy in Exile." *Liberal Education* 100, no. 4 (Fall 2014): 54–59.

Rossing, P. Jonathan, and Melissa R. Lavitt. "The Neglected Learner: A Call to Support Integrative Learning for Faculty." *Liberal Education* 102, no. 2 (Spring 2016): 34–41.

Schneider, Carol Geary. "Challenge and Response: Integrity and AAC&U's Reform Initiatives (1985–1994)." *Liberal Education* 100, no. 4 (Fall 2014): 28–37.

Schneider, Carol Geary. "Making Excellence Inclusive and America's Promise." *Liberal Education* 100, no. 4 (2015): 46–59.

Selingo, Jeffrey J. "The Digital Campus: Tech Innovators 2016." *Chronicle of Higher Education*, April 15, 2016, 13–17.

Selingo, Jeffrey J. "Rebuilding the Bachelor's Degree." *Chronicle of Higher Education*, April 13, 2013, 1–17.

Shraddha, Shresta. "Liberal Arts, Why Not!" *Republica*, September 1, 2016.

Shuldiner, Henry. "The Liberal Arts in the Real World." *Chronicle of Higher Education*, August 5, 2016, 1–4.

Snow, C. P. *The Two Cultures and the Scientific Revolution*. London: Cambridge University Press, 1959.

"STEM Education Is Vital—But Not at the Expense of the Humanities." *Scientific American*, October 2016, 1–8. https://www.scientificamerican.com/article/stem-education-is-vital-but-not-at-the-expense-of-the-humanities/.

Stokes, Peter, and Chris Slatter. "Liberal Arts, Inflexible Structures." *Inside Higher Education*, September 19, 2016, Opinion/Views, 1–9.

Verrico, John S. "A Sociologist Tackles Homeland Security," *ASA Footnotes*. 37, no. 5 (May–June 2009) http://www.asanet.org/sites/default/files/savvy/footnotes/mayjun09/sras_0509.html.

"What Will a Liberal Arts Education Look Like in 50 Years?," *The Atlantic*, August 13, 2014. https://www.theatlantic.com/video/index/376014/what-will-a-liberal-arts-education-look-like-in-50-years/.

Whitehead, Michelle Dawn. "Global Learning: Key to Making Excellence Inclusive." *Liberal Education* 101, no. 3 (Summer 2015): 6–13.

Wong, Frank. "The Search for American Liberal Education." *Liberal Education* 100, no. 4 (Fall 2014): 38–45.

Zakaria, Fareed. *In Defense of a Liberal Education*. New York: Norton, 2015.

Zakaria, Fareed. "Why America's Obsession with STEM Education Is Dangerous." *Washington Post*, March 26, 2015, 1–5.

About the Contributors

WILLIAM D. ADAMS served as tenth chairman of the National Endowment for the Humanities from 2014 to 2017, and as a senior fellow at the Andrew W. Mellon Foundation from 2017 to 2019. He lives in Maine and is working on a book on the French phenomenologist Maurice Merleau-Ponty and the painter Paul Cézanne.

SARAH ARCHINO is assistant professor of art history at Furman University in Greenville, South Carolina. Along with her research on early-twentieth-century American modernism, little magazines, and Dada, she is developing programming to promote the transdisciplinary importance of visual literacy.

MARIO J. AZEVEDO, dean of the College of Liberal Arts at Jackson State University, earned his PhD in history from Duke University and MPH in epidemiology from the University of North Carolina at Chapel Hill. He has more than ten books, over two dozen peer-reviewed articles, and book chapters that focus mainly on the interface between history and health.

KATRINA BYRD received an MFA in creative writing from Mississippi University for Women. A Mississippi Arts Commission Artist Minigrant recipient, Katrina is an emerging writer and playwright. Her most recent work appeared in *Holl & Lane Magazine* and onstage at Bay St. Louis Little Theatre.

RICO D. CHAPMAN is associate professor of history at Clark Atlanta University. He also serves as assistant dean of the School of Arts and Sciences and director of the Humanities PhD Program. His most recent book is titled *Student Resistance to Apartheid at the University of Fort Hare: Freedom Now, a Degree Tomorrow*.

HELEN O. CHUKWUMA is professor of English at Jackson State University. She is a feminist scholar and the first female to be made a professor at the University of Port Harcourt, Rivers State, Nigeria (1993). Her most recent books are *Meeting Points in Black/Africana Women's Literature* (coeditor) and *Achebe's Women: Imagism and Power*.

MONICA FLIPPIN WYNN is assistant vice president at the John N. Gardner Institute for Excellence in Undergraduate Education. She completed her PhD in communications from the University of Oklahoma. Her research interests include racialized portrayals in the media, and instructional technology and student engagement in the classroom.

TATIANA GLUSHKO coordinates the work of the Richard Wright Center for Writing, Rhetoric, and Research at Jackson State University, where she tutors undergraduate and graduate students and trains peer tutors. She also studies rhetorical awareness in students and serves on the board of the Mississippi Writing Center Association.

ERIC J. GRIFFIN is Janice B. Trimble Professor of English at Millsaps College. Whether in the Compass general education sequence or in advanced department seminars, he regularly teaches Shakespeare. As director of Latin American Studies at Millsaps, Griffin also contributes to the college's signature study abroad program Living in Yucatán.

KATHI R. GRIFFIN (PhD, MAT, University of Iowa) is director of the Richard Wright Center for Writing, Rhetoric, and Research, and composition instructor at Jackson State University. Since moving to Mississippi in 1998, Griffin has been actively involved in state and regional conversations about writing, teaching writing, and writing centers.

YUMI PARK HUNTINGTON is assistant professor in the Department of Art and Music at Framingham State University. Specializing in the art history of ancient Peru, she also utilizes archaeology, anthropology, and other disciplines to better understand the artwork, architecture, rituals, and worldviews of multicultural societies from thousands of years ago.

THOMAS M. KERSEN is associate professor of sociology at Jackson State University. Tom is the author of several articles, book chapters, and a forthcoming book about the Ozarks and popular culture. He earned his PhD from Mississippi State University in 2003.

ROBERT E. LUCKETT JR. is associate professor of history and director of the Margaret Walker Center at Jackson State University. His first book is *Joe T. Patterson and the White South's Dilemma: Evolving Resistance to Black Advancement* (University Press of Mississippi, 2015). Robby has three children: Silas, Hazel, and Flip.

FLOYD W. MARTIN is professor of art history at the University of Arkansas at Little Rock. His research interests are primarily in the eighteenth and nineteenth centuries, especially British art and architecture. He is a coeditor of *Formations of Identity: Society, Politics, and Landscape* (2016). He holds degrees from Carleton College, the University of Iowa, and the University of Illinois.

PRESELFANNIE W. McDANIELS is professor of English and dean of graduate studies at Jackson State University. McDaniels has published journal articles and book chapters on her areas of research interest—US women writers, adolescent literature, and service-learning pedagogy—and coedited the collection of essays *Meeting Points in Black/Africana Women's Literature*.

DAWN BISHOP McLIN is tenured professor in the Department of Psychology at Jackson State University. Dr. McLin served as the associate director of Research at the Jackson State University, Mississippi Urban Research Center. She is a past recipient of the National Institute of Mental Health Disparities Research Award.

LAUREN ASHLEE MESSINA is a dancer and choreographer who writes passionately about all things dance. Messina's dance education articles and working artist advice columns have been featured in *Dance! North Texas* magazine, the *MFA Mondays* blog at Frame Dance Productions, and *TheWorkingDancer.com*. Messina performs with the Marigny Opera Ballet in New Orleans.

BYRON D'ANDRA OREY, professor of political science at Jackson State University, researches political psychology and legislative behavior and focuses on race and politics. He earned degrees from Mississippi Valley State University, the University of Mississippi, the State University of New York at Stony Brook, and the University of New Orleans.

KATHY ROOT PITTS received her PhD from the University of Southern Mississippi and teaches composition and literature at Jackson State University. Her research interests include concepts of family trauma and sacred place in Mississippi literature, the intuitive sense of spirituality in literature and the arts, and the serious nature of comedy as depicted by the "heroic laugh."

CANDIS PIZZETTA is associate professor of English and interim dean of the College of Liberal Arts at Jackson State University, where she serves as the general editor of the university's interdisciplinary journal *The Researcher*, and as the coordinator for junior faculty mentoring. Her current research explores the intersection of social reform and women's utopian fiction in nineteenth-century America.

LAWRENCE SLEDGE is instructor of English/professional-technical writing at Jackson State University. He is an alumnus of Tougaloo College (BA, interdisciplinary humanities-music) and the University of Memphis (MA, professional-technical writing). Sledge, a past president of the Mississippi Council of Teachers of English, has a recently published short story, "Ms. Zene's Flowers."

RASHELL R. SMITH-SPEARS, associate professor at Jackson State University, researches African American identity in literature and media. She has published articles on Margaret Walker, L. A. Banks, and *A Different World*, among other subjects. Her creative publications have appeared in *Black Magnolias*, *Sycorax's Daughters*, and *Mississippi Noir*. Smith-Spears earned a BA from Spelman College and a PhD from the University of Missouri–Columbia.

JOSEPH MARTIN STEVENSON is former provost at Jackson State and Mississippi State Valley Universities. He is a graduate of the Futures School in California, where he also served as Provost in Sacramento and Los Angeles. Joseph is an advocate of early exploration of liberal arts and is working on college-bound concepts for K–6.

SERETHA D. WILLIAMS is professor of English and women's and gender studies at Augusta University. She focuses on the work of Margaret Walker (Alexander). Additionally, Dr. Williams is an Emerging Scholar with the Black Book Interactive Project at the University of Kansas.

KAREN C. WILSON-STEVENSON, EMBA, is a higher education and nonprofit executive, advising academic and other leadership on developing strategies, resources, and initiatives to improve equity and effectiveness in education. Karen is a Certified Fund-Raising Executive, completing her EPhD at Jackson State University and is the author of *THEORRY* for undergraduate students.

Index

#MakingofaMovement, 81, 85–86, 88, 90

academia, 134, 138, 140, 151, 186, 192, 214–15, 260
academic freedom, 183–95
accountability, 108, 121, 137–39, 143–44, 170–72, 202, 215
Adkins, Terry, 230–34, 237–38
Adler, Mortimer, 258
Agriculture (USDA), United States Department of, 211–12
algorithm, 269
Alina, Babette, 37
Allen, Danielle, xii, xvii
American Association of University Professors (AAUP), 184–85, 192–93
analytical skills, xi, 14, 37, 39–40, 45, 51, 52n5, 53n15, 76, 95, 97, 100, 102, 111, 120–21, 244; platforms, 120–21; thinking, 37, 102, 226; writing, 226. *See also* critical thinking
Anders, George, 121–22
Anderson, Sherry, 210, 212
anti-intellectualism, 214. *See also* intellectualism
apprehension, 25, 175
apprentices, 133; apprenticeship, 259
Aristotle, x, 110; *Nicomachean Ethics*, 114
Arkavey, Ira, 268
art history, 36–52, 53n10, 57–58, 61, 64–68, 71–78, 78n1, 78n2, 78n6; art historians, 36–40, 51, 71–73, 78n6. *See also* history
ARTstor, 51, 53n16
Association of American Colleges and Universities (AACU), 13, 22n6, 107, 121, 125, 258, 261
audit culture, 134, 138–39, 143

authority, 65, 73, 133, 139–43, 156, 188, 196; power, 188; sources, 107; teachers, 123. *See also* rhetorical authority

Bacon, Francis, 96, 98
Badenhorst, C. M., 169, 177
Baker, Vicki, 107
Baldwin, Roger, 107
banking, 101–2, 137, 198–203; system, 198–203
Barkley, Steve, 200, 202
Barnet, Fiona, 15
basic writers (BW), 136; basic writing, 77
Bass, Scott, 185
Bauerlein, Mark, 4
Bereiter, Carl, 243
Bjork, Olin, 18
Black Lives Matter, 89, 91n6
Blackboard, 36. *See also* learning management systems (LMS)
blog, 20, 25, 29–30, 36, 51, 125; blogging, 29–30, 122, 270
Bloom's Taxonomy, 15–16, 21, 22n6, 104–8, 137
Bok, Derek, 210, 215
boot camp, 169–79; writing boot camp, 169–72, 175–77
Bordoloi, Loni, 267
Borinski, Ernst, 212–14
Botstein, Leon, 264–65
Boyer, Ernest, 268–69
Boyte, Harry, 213–14
Breneman, David (D. W.), 107, 262
Brown, Ayanna F., 123
Bruffee, Kenneth, 135
Butterfield, Stewart, 122

Calhoun, Robert Lowry, 72–73, 79
Calhoun, Thomas, xiii–xiv
canon, 152–53
capitalism, 3; capitalist, 7–8, 263
careers, xi, 7, 40, 76, 108–9, 119–20, 124–26, 142, 152, 165, 173–77, 183, 189, 203, 206, 254, 259, 261–62
Carter, Angela M., 186–88
Carter, Jarrett, 125–26
Catullus, 97
Charney, Noah, 77
Chicago, 78n2, 208; University of Chicago, 7, 210
choreography, 81–90
Christakis, Erika and Nicholas, 190
Christianity and Christians, 84–85, 90, 184–85
citizens and citizenship, x–xvii, 3, 133–34, 153, 193, 214–15, 267
civic life and civic engagement, xi–xvi, 102, 213, 259–60, 265, 267
civil rights, 18, 91n6, 197, 206, 208, 245–48; monument, 225–39
Civil Rights Commemoration Foundation (CRCF), 227–30
Civil Rights Commemoration Initiative (CRCI), 230–34
Clark, Mary, 185
Clark, Shawn, 227
classrooms, 14–17, 21, 24–31, 36, 40, 46, 58, 61, 82–84, 89–90, 96, 99, 100, 104, 107–8, 112–13, 122–26, 135, 139, 153–56, 160, 162, 165, 170–71, 184, 186–93, 196, 200–206, 214, 244, 247–49, 264, 266, 269; college, 184–91, 249; and flipped classrooms, 26–27, 51
cognition, 7, 13, 50, 59, 63, 104, 142, 248, 253, 269–70
Cohen, Scott, 262–63
Cohodas, Nadine, 228
Coleman, Liz, 260
College Art Association (CAA), 37, 52n4
common good, 259, 261
Common School Movement, 206; Horace Mann, 201

communication, 7–8, 57–61, 67, 77, 90, 95–102, 124–25, 141, 143, 154–57, 161, 165, 166n5, 166n7, 184, 204, 265, 267
communications, 27–29, 76, 250–51; mass, 173
community engagement, 268–69
composition courses, 13–14, 17–18, 21, 64, 96, 135, 138, 141, 166n7, 208
Confederate flag, 229; Confederate statue, 227; Confederate Memorial, 235
Conference on the Liberal Arts, ix
conversation, 133–44; intellectual, 134–35
conversational English, 100
Coopee, Todd, 105
Cornish, Edward, 249–50
correctness, 65, 133, 136–39, 144, 154
cosmopolitan canopies, 214–17
Council of Independent Colleges (CIC), 124
course design, 13, 17, 20, 153–56
Coutts, Chris, 157–58, 166n11
Cox, Alistair, 120
Crawford, Caroline, 15–17, 22n6
creativity, 7–8, 37, 40, 104–9, 112–13, 136, 196–202, 209, 213–16, 250, 255, 267
credibility, 133, 143
criminal justice, 71, 250–51
critical thinking, xv, 8, 13–15, 28, 40, 51, 57–61, 66–67, 75, 88, 97, 99, 102, 104, 106–13, 119–21, 127, 133–44, 154–58, 165, 183–84, 189–93, 196–206, 208–10, 215, 217, 226–27, 243–48, 259, 262, 265, 267, 269. *See also* analytical skills
cross-cultural competency, 269
cross-disciplinary practice, xv, 266
cultural creatives, 210–12, 217
cultural literacy, xiii–xv, 260
curriculum, xv–xvi, 5, 7, 8, 15, 22n6, 24–31, 36–37, 40–41, 57–60, 64–67, 75, 84, 105, 118–21, 124–26, 144, 152–55, 161, 205, 215, 243–50, 254–55, 262–66

Daily Mississippian, 234–36
D'Alleva, Anne, 38

dance and dancing, 81–90; dancing the humanities, 81–90
Darden, William, 244
Darwin, Charles, 46–47
deadlines, 174, 176
democracy, xii–xiv, xvi, 191–93, 200–201; citizens, 267; community, 216; hierarchy, 84; ideals, 3, 265; participation, 227; process, 236; society, 265
Dickinson, Emily, 4
digital humanities (DH), 6, 7, 13–21
digital platforms, 26, 51
digital storytelling, 27–29
digital technology, 133, 155
discourse, 5–6, 15, 17, 20, 85, 126–27, 135, 137, 141, 143, 169, 192, 227; community, 135, 137
diversity, xiii, 14, 123, 140–41, 154, 183–84, 189–92, 213, 246, 249, 258, 262, 267
Doyle, William, 229; *An American Insurrection*, 229
During, Simon, 3

Eagles, Charles, 238–39; *The Price of Defiance*, 238–39
economics, xi–xii, 4–8, 85, 101, 107–8, 120, 137–39, 164, 191–92, 205–6, 211–12, 216, 247–51, 264, 267; economy, x–xii, xv, 8, 206, 245, 268. *See also* knowledge economy
Edge, John T., 227–39
Education Advisory Board, 125–26, 261
educational outcomes, 13–19, 24, 26, 51–52, 58, 61, 67, 82, 96, 98, 111, 137–39, 153, 192, 261–62. *See also* student learning outcomes (SLOs)
Eley, Jim, 232–33, 237
English, 4, 13, 15–20, 29, 100–101, 118, 120, 124–25, 133–36, 139–40, 152, 154, 157–61, 164–65, 166n11, 173, 208, 252
English language learners (ELL), 136–37
environment, 8, 45, 48, 83–85, 88, 95, 264; academic and learning, 17–18, 21, 28, 30–31, 37, 58, 63–65, 74, 97–99, 114, 134–35, 139, 144, 156, 158, 162, 172, 177, 193, 202, 205, 213, 226, 244, 246, 249, 254, 270; environmental humanities, 6
error, 60, 100–101, 134–37, 139–42, 144, 174
ethics, 29–30, 37, 53n10, 76, 114, 121, 139, 142–43, 253–54, 259, 262, 267
Evans, Sara, 213–14
Evers, Medgar, 197, 228
Evers, Myrlie, 228, 238

Facebook, 25, 86, 185, 203
faculty: collaboration, 248; engagement, 266
Faulkner, William, 164, 229
fear, 25, 91, 108, 135, 137, 152, 175, 184, 188, 191, 231–38
Federal Bureau of Investigation (FBI), 39, 52
federal government, 225, 262
feminism, 20; feminist, 20, 111, 186, 189
Ferrall, Victor E., 120–21
Finland, 108, 112
Finn, Edward, 24, 31
Florida, Richard, 211; *Rise of the Creative Class*, 211
Forde, Timothy B., 123
Franklin, Benjamin, 268–69
Freire, Paolo, 137, 198–99, 203–4, 211. *See also Pedagogy of the Oppressed*
Frick Collection, 39, 75–76
future studies, 243–55; futuring, 245–49, 253–55; futurism, 243–48, 253–55

Gay, Geneva, 122–23
Gender Studies, 17, 19–20
Giroux, Henry, 191
Glisson, Susan, 229–38
global learners, 196, 202; global learning, 14
Google, 26, 142; Drive, 26; Earth, 19–20; Hangouts, 26
graduate education, 6, 28, 57, 83, 86, 118, 124, 140, 174, 177, 227, 248, 253, 255, 260. *See also* undergraduate education
grammar, 57, 71, 77, 96–101, 134–36, 140, 251, 260
Greene, Theodore, 72, 78n2, 79n7

Gregersen, Hal, 250
Grimm, Nancy, 135
Guerra, Juan C., 154, 158, 162, 164–65, 167n13

habits of mind, xvii, 107, 121, 136–40, 153
Haidt, Jonathan, 189–90
Hamilton College, 266–67
Hanley, Lawrence, 7
Hansberry, Lorraine, 183; *A Raisin in the Sun*, 183, 191–92
Harvard University, xii, 3–4, 63, 69n9, 78n1; *Harvard Business Review*, 250
Hawkins, Larycia, 185
Henninger, Ernest, 268
Herman, Amy, 39, 52, 53n10, 75–76. See also *Visual Intelligence*
higher education, ix, 5, 7, 13, 24, 40, 125, 137, 142–43, 152, 188, 191–93, 214–15, 231, 236, 243–47, 254, 265, 267–68
high-impact practices (HIPS), 13–21
Historically Black Colleges and Universities (HBCUs), 140–41, 214–15, 243–55
historians, xv, 73–74, 105, 174–75, 201, 211, 225–26, 238–39; history departments, 66. See also art history
Holdren, Tara Shoemaker, 113
Holly, Michael Ann, 73–74
hooks, bell, 83, 98, 189
Horner, Bruce, 141–42, 154, 162
Housen, Abigail, 58. See also Visual Thinking Strategies (VTS)
Hughes, John, 201
Hughes, Langston, 16, 19–20
humanism, 72–74, 77; humanistic education, 123
Huron Consulting Group, 265
Hutchins, Robert M., 114

identity, 4, 16, 81, 86–87, 90, 134, 160, 162, 175, 183, 208, 211, 213–16, 234, 247, 259
imagination, xi–xiv, 36–39, 104–5, 208–9, 254, 258, 267
immigrants, 72–73, 154, 201; immigration, xvi, 98

inclusion, xvi, 87, 96–98, 123, 188–89, 192, 210, 216, 226, 229, 234, 244, 249
inequality, 143, 197, 200, 202, 248, 264; inequity, 248
injustice, 85, 191, 248. See also social injustice
innovation, xiv, 8, 24, 26, 37, 51, 142, 184, 213, 216, 243, 246–48, 254, 266–68
Instagram, 25, 30–31
intellectualism, 99. See also anti-intellectualism
interdisciplinarity, xv, xvi, 3–8, 29, 40, 57–68, 102, 107, 162, 169–70, 173, 213, 244, 266; interdisciplinary studies, 102
iPads, 96, 119
Islam, xiii, 185
Italian Renaissance, 52n1, 72–74, 156–57, 161–65
Ivie, Robert, 184

Jackson, Mississippi, 122, 154, 211–14, 216
Jackson State University (JSU), ix, xiii, xv, 18, 53, 78n3, 95, 135, 140, 169, 173, 214, 264, 267
James, William, x, xii
Jefferson, Thomas, 200–201, 258
Jim Crow, 212, 214, 225–26, 238
jobs, 7–8, 95–96, 108, 112–13, 120, 124–25, 191, 261–63
Jobs, Steve, 142, 267
justice, 82, 85, 87, 231, 245, 248. See also social justice

Kalt, David, 209–10
Kant, Immanuel, 73, 78
Kartiganer, Lyn, 227, 230–32
Kaspar, Mike, 27
Kearns, David, 268
Keen, Andrew, 161–62
Kellum, Gloria, 230–31, 236
Khayat, Robert, 227–39
King, Martin Luther, Jr., 208
Knight, Lauren, 112
knowledge economy, 3–8. See also economy

Kogler, David, 262
Kojin, Haruka, 45–46; *Contact Lens*, 45–46
Konkle-Parker, Debbie, 122

Ladson-Billings, Gloria, 124
LaMothe, Kimerer, 82–84
languages, 50, 76, 136, 152, 156, 164, 259
learning management systems (LMS), 18–20, 26, 30, 36, 51, 53n16. *See also* Blackboard; Omeka
learning outcomes, 16, 24, 26, 51–52, 82, 96, 98, 137–39, 153, 245–46. *See also* educational outcomes; outcomes; student learning outcomes (SLOs)
Lee, Spike, 183; *Bamboozled*, 183, 191
Lemann, Nicolas, 152–53
liberal arts: disciplines, 4–8, 71, 75, 233, 247, 255; education, ix–xvii, 3, 8, 22, 24, 35, 62, 64, 68, 71, 75–78, 78n3, 81–90, 96, 106, 111–12, 120–21, 196–97, 202–6, 209, 213, 227, 243–44, 258–70
Liberal Education and America's Promise (LEAP), 13–21
liberal learning, ix–xii, xvii, 263
linguistics, 137, 140–41, 143, 154–65, 252
Lippmann, Stephen, 191–92
Lu, Min-Zhan, 154, 162
Lukianoff, Greg, 189–90

MacDowell, Kate, 48–50
Makker, Sumedha, 107
Margaret Walker Center, 18. *See also* Walker, Margaret
mathematics, x, 5, 36, 41–43, 45–46, 53n12, 77, 79n17, 111, 113, 126–27, 203, 250, 252, 259, 264, 267
McNay, Shannon, 125
Meaning of the Humanities, The, 72, 78n2, 79n7
meetings, 88, 122, 170–71, 173, 176, 227, 235–36; space, 170, 178
memory, 16, 90, 104, 106, 199, 225–39; memorization, 96, 106, 108, 113, 200
mentor, 16, 176–77, 247–48; mentoring, 7; mentorship, 171

Meredith, James, 225–39
Meredith Monument, 225–39
Middle East, xiii, 119
Miles College, 245, 253, 255
millennials, 98, 101, 216
Mills, C. Wright, 208–9
Millsaps College, 153–57, 200, 203, 212
Mississippi, 84, 122, 153–54, 164, 197, 209, 211–15, 216, 225–39, 238, 245; Mississippians, 164, 216, 225, 231
Mississippi State Sovereignty Commission, 214, 226
Mitchell, W. J. T., 58–59, 68n6
molders of consensus, 208–17
Mondale, Sarah, 200–201. *See also School: The Story of American Public Education*
Mondrian, Piet, 44–45
monolingual ideology, 134, 141–42
Mowry, Melissa, 4, 7
Mullins, Andrew, 235, 237
multilingual writers, 141–42
Museum of Modern Art, 58, 68n5
MyHistro, 19–20

National Council of Teachers of English (NCTE), 133, 139
National Endowment for the Arts (NEA), 78n3, 228–29
National Endowment for the Humanities (NEH), ix, 78n3
National Public Radio (NPR), xii, 211
Native Americans, 164, 251. *See also* American Indians
Nazi Germany, 72, 78n1, 212
Neatline, 51, 53n16
Neem, Johann, 263
Nelson, Jennie, 14, 16
neoliberalism, 3
New London Group, 133
New York City, 52n4, 58, 75, 230, 245
New York City Police Department, 39, 75
New York Times, 4, 39, 74–77, 142, 233
New York University (NYU), 72, 244
No Child Left Behind, 112
Northeast Mississippi Daily Journal, 231–32

Nuckles, Charles R., 123
Nussbaum, Martha, 267

Obama, Barack, 210, 261
Omeka, 18–20, 51, 53n16. *See also* learning management systems (LMS)
Oppenheimer, Daniel, 13
outcomes, 13–19, 24, 26, 51–52, 58, 61, 67, 82, 88, 96, 98, 102, 111, 126, 137–39, 141, 153, 175, 192, 239, 245–46, 250, 259, 261. *See also* educational outcomes; learning outcomes; student learning outcomes (SLOs)
outcomes-based education (OE), 137
Oxford, City of, 226, 229, 237
Oxford English Dictionary (OED), 159–60, 166n11, 167n16

Panofsky, Erwin, 71–78, 78n1, 78n2, 78n5, 78n6
partnerships, 6, 39, 58, 61, 67, 68n5, 77, 83, 86, 97, 106, 206
Patton, Sarah, 200–201. See also *School: The Story of American Public Education*
pedagogy, 13, 25, 27, 30, 36–37, 40, 50–51, 52, 83, 90, 95–102, 123–24, 134, 136–37, 153, 165, 198, 266; art history, 36–37, 40, 52; collaborative, 14, 18, 20, 26, 28–29, 113, 134, 176, 178, 196, 203, 215, 250, 252, 266; culturally relevant, 81, 124; culturally responsive, 122–23; dance activism, 90; nonhierarchical and nonregulatory, 137–41; STEM, 50–51; student sensitive, 118–27, 187–88, 249; writing, 134, 136, 141
Pedagogy of the Oppressed, 137, 198. *See also* Freire, Paolo
performing arts, 81–90
Persig, Robert, 211; *Zen and the Art of Motorcycle Maintenance*, 211
philosophy, x, xii, xiv, 4, 8, 79n7, 82, 84, 108–12, 122, 152, 210, 250, 252, 259; philosophers, xv, 73, 109–10, 142, 262, 268
photography, 65, 186; photographs, 28, 60–61, 65, 236
Pickard, Anna, 121–22

Pickering, Kristian, 124
platforms, 16, 17–20, 24–30, 51, 111, 120, 142, 162–63; blogging, 29–30; digital and technological, 16, 19–20, 25–26, 28, 51; integrated, 24; learning, 142; media, 162–63; pedagogical, 25, 27; publishing, 18; social media, 30
Plato, 109–10
political correctness, 183–93
political science, 29, 169, 173, 185, 252
polling, 244, 246, 249, 252
portfolios, 31, 155, 166n7; e-portfolios, 166n7; tenure, 176
PowerPoint, 19, 36
practical segregation, 226, 231–33, 239
precariat class, 5; precarity, 5
President's Committee on the Arts and the Humanities, 113
Presner, Todd, 5–6
Princeton University, 72, 78n2, 79n7
productivity, 137, 169–70, 173, 177–78
proficiency, 13, 51, 58, 98, 100, 269; communication, 100; visual, 51, 58; writing, 13, 98, 100
promotion and tenure, 169, 171, 177–78. *See also* tenure
publishing, 18, 169, 177
Pythagorean Theorem, 41–44, 53n12, 105; Pythagora, 42, 44

quadrivium, 245, 250–51, 260

racism, 188, 225, 238. *See also* white supremacy
Rausch, Sharla, 262–63
Rawlings, Hunter, 192
Ray, Paul, 210, 212–13
Redbook, The (*General Education in a Free Society*), 3–4
re-engineering, 243–55
reflection, 20–21, 60, 62, 64, 81, 88, 121, 134, 136, 138–39, 141–44, 238
remediation, 134–35, 153, 156
researchers, 7, 15, 28, 58, 107, 113, 122, 126, 134, 177, 190, 215, 254, 269; digital

humanities, 15; scientific, 254; urban policy, 28
Reverb.com, 209–10
rhetoric, 14–15, 71, 155, 215–16, 251, 260
rhetorical analysis, 18; authority, 139–43; awareness, 18, 21, 133–44; context, 136; encounters, 155–56; practices, 140; principles, 155, 157; problems, 134; skills, 141; strategies, 136–37. *See also* authority
Richards, Heraldo V., 123
Rietveld, Gerrit, 42–44
Roberts, Jennifer, 63–64
Roberts, Sara, 201–2
Rock, Chris, 190
Root-Bernstein, Michèle, 37, 52n5, 52n8
Root-Bernstein, Robert, 37, 39, 52n5, 52n8
Ross, Valeria, 235
Rossen, Rebecca, 86–87
Ruitenberg, Claudia, 137–38

Salaita, Steven, 185
Samuel, Twuan, 236–37
Sanders, Ashley, 169–70
Sankofa, 243, 254–55
Sarason, Seymour B., 204–5
Scheuer, Jeffrey, 112
Schneider, Carol, 263
School: The Story of American Public Education, 200–201. *See also* Mondale, Sarah; Patton, Sarah
schools of arts and sciences, 66, 96, 122, 124, 259, 265; grammar schools, 96; professional schools, 66, 75–76, 248, 261; public schools, 202; trade schools, 76
Shakespeare, William, 126, 152–65, 268; *Macbeth*, 163; *Richard III*, 156, 163; *Romeo and Juliet*, 156–59, 166n11; *The Taming of the Shrew*, 152, 158–59, 161, 163
short message service (SMS), 157–58, 163, 166n11
Silver, James, 225–26, 231–32, 239; *Mississippi: The Closed Society*, 225
Simone, Nina, 196–97, 206
Sizer, Theodore, 202, 205–6

skills-based education, 13, 66, 153, 197, 202–6
Skype, 26, 119
Slack Technologies, 121–22
Sly, Christopher, 159–61, 164
Smith, Adam, 263
Smith, Charles Saumarez, 76
Snider, Susannah, 125
social activism, 81, 90
social context, 7, 134, 137, 213
social injustice, 191, 248. *See also* injustice
social justice, 82, 85, 87, 245. *See also* justice
social media, 30–31, 36, 51–52, 119, 125, 249, 265
social sciences, xv, xvii, 125, 208, 214, 249, 263–64; social scientists, xv, 208, 213, 243
socio-behavioral sciences, 262, 265, 267
sociology, 7, 29, 112, 208–15, 217, 244, 250–51; sociologists, 142, 211, 262
Socratic method, 109, 247
Southeastern College Art Conference (SECAC), 37, 52n4
Southern Studies, 226–27, 229
standardized tests, 104–6, 108, 112–13, 134
standard written English (SWE), 134, 137–38, 157, 165
Science, Technology, Engineering, Art, Mathematics (STEAM), 5, 37, 40, 51–52
Science, Technology, Engineering, Mathematics (STEM), 36–52, 77, 101, 108, 119–20, 126, 260, 263
Strunk and White, 174; *The Elements of Style*, 174
student engagement, xvi, 14, 24–29, 86, 247
student learning outcomes (SLOs), 14–16, 18–19, 24, 26, 51–52, 82, 96, 98, 137–38, 153, 155, 245–46, 248, 251–54. *See also* educational outcomes; learning outcomes; outcomes
student success, 13–14, 19, 61, 123, 266
Sullivan, Margaret, 77
Surowiecki, James, 213–14; *The Wisdom of Crowds*, 213–14

surveys, 26, 41, 53n11, 53n12, 88, 155, 164, 186–87, 249, 251–53, 261, 268
Szent-Györgyi, Albert, 38–39

Teare, Chris, 126
tenure, 169, 171, 173–77, 225. *See also* promotion and tenure
testing, 96–101, 105, 108, 111, 113
textspeak, 157–58, 166n11
Thayer Junior High School, 205
tolerance, 62, 67, 121, 139
Tolerance of Ambiguity Scale, 62, 67
Tougaloo College, 212, 214, 245, 255
Trabasso, Tom, 100
transdisciplinary alliances and collaborations, 247, 270; competencies, 250–51; teaching and learning, 244, 247, 249
transformative-empathetic learning, 82, 84, 88, 90
translingual practices, 133–44, 153–54, 156, 158, 161–62, 164; translingualism, 152–65
Tree of Life, 41, 46–49, 53n15
trigger warnings, 184, 186–93
trivium, 245, 250–51, 260
Tsui, Lisa, 106–7
Turin, Mark, 20
Turkle, Sherry, 142
Twitter, 25, 31, 172

undergraduate education, 3, 13–16, 21, 28–29, 57–60, 67, 68n2, 122, 124, 163, 177, 208, 247–50, 253–54, 261–62. *See also* graduate education
University of Mississippi (Ole Miss), 225–39; University of Mississippi Medical Center, 122
University of Texas, 39, 53n10, 62, 75

Vasari, Giorgio, 36, 52n1
visual analysis, 39–40, 58, 60
Visual Intelligence, 53n10, 75. *See also* Herman, Amy
visual literacy, 37–38, 41, 57–68, 68n2, 68n6

Visual Thinking Strategies (VTS), 58, 60, 62, 64–65, 69n10. *See also* Housen, Abigail
vocabulary, 50, 64, 75, 87, 98–101, 137, 143, 161, 253
vocations, xvi–xvii, 253, 259, 262–63

Wade, Rahima C., 123–24
Walker, Margaret, 16, 18–19, 164; *For My People*, 18–19; *Jubilee*, 18. *See also* Margaret Walker Center
Walton, Gerald, 228–29
Wheaton College, 185
white supremacy, 226, 238. *See also* racism
Wilde, Oscar, 110
William the Conqueror, 160
William Winter Institute for Racial Reconciliation, 229–30. *See also* Winter, William
Wilson, Robin, 188
Winebrake, James J., 267
Winter, William, 216, 238. *See also* William Winter Institute for Racial Reconciliation
Women's Studies, 17, 19–20
workshops, 26, 60–61, 67, 176
World War II, 3, 206, 212
writing centers, 133–44; writing processes, 17, 135, 144, 174–77, 203

Yale University, 61, 68n5, 75, 79n7, 190
YouTube, 25, 27, 75, 157, 163

Zakaria, Fareed, 203, 268; *In Defense of a Liberal Education*, 203, 268

www.ingramcontent.com/pod-product-compliance
Lightning Source LLC
Chambersburg PA
CBHW030609230426
43661CB00053B/1909